"I found the book to be very informative, well researched and without a doubt the single most authoritative book I have read on the subject of building online communities. The coverage of already established online communities was vast and well documented. The real live examples were both informative and entertaining. I think I liked the about.com knitting chapter the best. I suppose it was because of the example of real life interaction with the community members and how they finished off the sentence as a group. Collaboration seemed to be the keyword."

—John Beal, CEO, FoxNet

"After a complete reading of the book I can tell: This book rules! It's the first to give a complete overview of online communities for both the beginner and experienced community-builder. Each option is explained clearly from the reader's point of view and from the creator/manager point of view. Both will learn great tips and tricks, and will obviously find THE solution for their communities needs. Aside from keeping and teaching the 'Internet spirit', this book explains you everything: from netiquette to technical difficulties... Now I understand how this 'news:' thing does work for example."

—Philippe Jadin, http://www.123piano.com/

"This book, the more I get into it, appears to fill a major void for explaining the nuts and bolts of the operation of the Online community."

—Bill Frederick, Frederick & Associates

"Another great book from the *Poor Richard's Series*. This book will help the novice or expert build a online community that will make the most out of the different components that turn a Web site into a community."

—Nathan Allan, Community Development Manager, Sausage Software

"I belong to 3 online communities and, now, I better understand them because I see the big picture. I learned more about online communities in the first chapter than I've ever read or heard."

—K.B. Scaife

"I highly recommend this book to anyone who is just beginning to learn about online communities and the important issues (privacy, spam, opt-in vs. opt-out) that you must understand in order to have a successful endeavor, whether you are just starting out or already managing a community online. More advanced readers who may already be aware of the issues will still want to buy the book for its reference value: the step by step instructions on how to set up your own email newsletters and IRC channels are great, and I especially liked the listing and explanation of those cryptic listserv commands."

—Kelly Haskins, Owner, Sitewinder Studios Web Design,
http://www.sitewinder.com/

"Can't think of anything you [Top Floor] could do better. Excellent work!"

—David Donhoff, Financial Evangelical Officer (F.E.O.),
Donhoff Development

"I have been in the electronics industry for the last 40 years the Internet and web design specifically for the last 15. I found the book very informative to a most enlightening degree, well written and easy to read."

—Dean Rainer, Director of Research and Development,
Intelligent Development Technology

"I know it's been said before but if you are new to the net or want to set up your own online community this is a must have book. It takes you by the hand and leads you through the ins and outs, good and bad of the magical world of communicating online. It's detailed, but easy to read and most importantly easy to understand. Buy the book, it will save you both time and money!"

—Warren Powers, Security Officer

Poor Richard's Building Online Communities

Create a Web Community for your Business, Club, Association, or Family

by
Margaret Levine Young and John Levine

TOP FLOOR PUBLISHING

Poor Richard's Building Online Communities:
Create a Web Community for Your Business, Club, Association, or Family

Copyright © 2000 Margaret Levine Young and John Levine

All rights reserved. Printed in the United States of America. No part of this book may be used or reproduced in any form or by any method, or stored in an electronic storage system, without prior written permission of the publisher except in the case of brief quotations in critical articles and reviews. Copying any part of this book for any purpose other than your own personal use is a violation of United States copyright law.

SAN#: 299-4550
Top Floor Publishing
8790 W. Colfax, Suite 107
Lakewood, CO 80215 USA

Feedback to the author: feedback@topfloor.com
Sales information: sales@topfloor.com
The Top Floor Publishing Web Site: http://TopFloor.com/
Cover illustration by Marty Petersen, http://artymarty.com/

Library of Congress Catalog Card Number: 00-105577

ISBN: 0-9661032-9-7

This book is sold as is, without warranty of any kind, either express or implied, respecting the contents of this book, including but not limited to implied warranties for the book's quality, performance, merchantability, or fitness for any purpose. Neither the author nor Top Floor Publishing and its dealers and distributors shall be liable to the purchaser or any other person or entity with respect to liability, loss, or damage caused or alleged to have been caused directly or indirectly by this book.

02   01   00   6 5 4 3 2 1

Trademark and service mark terms used in this book are the property of the trademark holders. Use of a term in this book should not be regarded as affecting the validity of any trademark or service mark.

Acknowledgments

The authors thank (in alphabetical order) Barbara Breiter, Lance Brown, Suzanne Bury, Lynn Calvin, Eric Dickerson, Howard Dobel, Gila Jones, Peter Kent, David "Tale" Lawrence, Doug Muder, Missy Ramey, David L. Rogelberg, Chuq von Rospach, Matt Wagner, Debbie Weiner, and Rebecca Whitney, for their help with this book.

About the Authors

Margaret Levine Young and **John Levine** have coauthored many computer books, including *Internet for Dummies*, *Windows 98: The Complete Reference*, *Internet: The Complete Reference*, and *E-mail for Dummies*.

Table of Contents at a Glance

Introduction

Part I: Introduction to Online Communities
   1. What Is Online Community? 3
   2. Online Community Options..19
   3. Participating Effectively 29

Part II: Mailing List Communities
   4. Finding, Joining, and Participating in Mailing Lists...........................37
   5. Creating and Managing Your Own Mailing List.................................67

Part III: Usenet Newsgroup Communities
   6. Finding, Joining, and Participating in Newsgroups........................117
   7. Creating and Managing Your Own Newsgroup...............................159

Part IV: Internet Relay Chat (IRC)
   8. Finding, Joining, and Participating in IRC...177
   9. Creating and Managing IRC Channels...195

Part V: Web-Based Communities
   10. Finding, Joining, and Participating in Web-based Communities.....211
   11. Creating and Managing Your Own Web-based Community 227

Part VI: Growing and Managing Your Community
   12. Publicizing Your Community...249
   13. Encouraging Sharing and Responding to Dissension......................263
   14. Making Money with Your Community...287
   15. Privacy, Spam, and Other Issues 295
   16. Managing Groups of Communities...307

Part VII: True-Life Stories
   17. The Computer Book Publishing List...323
   18. Knitting.About.com: Craftspeople 327
   19. The Comp.compilers Newsgroup..333
   20. The soc.religion.unitarian-univ newsgroup 339
   21. The UUA.ORG Mailing Lists: Running Hundreds of Communities...345
   Appendix: Resources for Community Managers......................................355

Table of Contents

Introduction

Part I: Introduction to Online Communities

  1. What Is Online Community? 3
    Why Participate in Online Communities 4
    Why Create Your Own Online Community 5
    How Online Communities Work 6
    Common Topics for Communities 12
    What Can Go Wrong 13
    The Six Stages of Online Communities 14
    Steps for Creating an Online Community 16

  2. Online Community Options 19
    Who Controls the Community 19
    Who May Join 20
    Who May Read the Content 22
    Who May Post Messages 22
    What You Can Post 23
    FAQS And Web Sites 27

  3. Participating Effectively 29
    Follow The Rules 29
    Netiquette 29
    Avoiding Flames 31
    Safety First 32
    Smileys And Abbreviations 33
    Other Ideas 34

Part II: Mailing List Communities

  4. Finding, Joining, and Participating in Mailing Lists 37
    Where Mailing Lists Live 38
    Mailing List Address 42
    What You Need to Join 44
    Finding Mailing Lists 44
    Steps for Participating in a Mailing List 45
    Setting Your Mailing List Options 49

Getting Help..50
Instructions For Web-Based Lists 51
Instructions for LISTSERV Lists 54
Instructions for ListProc Lists 57
Instructions for Majordomo Lists..59
Instructions for Lyris Lists 62
Mailing List Tricks 63

5. Creating and Managing Your Own Mailing List................................67
Choosing a Site for Your List...68
Choosing A Name For Your List 70
Creating a List 70
What to do After Your List Has Been Created............................73
Writing the Welcome Message tnd FAQ....................................75
Setting List Options 80
Managing List Subscriptions 83
Managing List Archives 85
Instructions for Managing Web-based Lists...............................87
Instructions for Managing Listserv Lists....................................88
Instructions for Managing Listproc Lists....................................95
Instructions for Managing Majordomo Lists.............................104
Instructions for Managing Lyris Lists 110
Getting More Information about List Management 111
Other Topics...112

Part III: Usenet Newsgroup Communities

6. Finding, Joining, and Participating in Newsgroups.......................117
How Usenet Newsgroups Work 117
Reading Newsgroup Messages 123
Finding Newsgroups of Interest 143
The Fine Points of Posting to Newsgroups..............................143
A Primer on How to Work with the Usenet Community.............148
For More Information about Usenet...156

7. Creating and Managing Your Own Newsgroup...............................159
Creating Newsgroups 159
Creating Alt Newsgroups 166
Running Your Own News Server and Private Newsgroups 167
Managing Public Newsgroups 171
Other Newsgroup-Management Issues....................................173

Part IV: Internet Relay Chat (IRC)

8. Finding, Joining, and Participating in IRC.....................................177
How IRC Works...177
Participating in IRC 180

Finding Channels of Interest 189
Other IRC Topics... 191
Getting More Information 193

9. Creating and Managing IRC Channels..**195**
Steps for Creating a Successful Private Channel 195
Choosing an IRC Network 196
Creating and Configuring Your Channel 197
Inviting, Removing, and Banning People 200
Reserving Nicknames and Channel Names 201
Administrative Commands.. 206
Rules for IRC Channels.. 207
Getting More Information 208

Part V: Web-Based Communities

10. Finding, Joining, and Participating in Web-based Communities.....**211**
How Web-based Communities Work... 212
Public Community Sites 217
Private Community Sites 222
Topic-Oriented Sites.. 222
Finding Web-based Communities 224

11. Creating and Managing Your Own Web-based Community............**227**
Designing Your Web-based Community 227
Setting Up Message Boards 232
Setting Up Web-based Real-time Chat 241
Writing Your Welcome Message and FAQ 248

Part VI: Growing and Managing Your Community

12. Publicizing Your Community..**249**
Creating a Home Page for Your Community................................... 250
Asking for Links... 251
Getting Listed in Directories... 252
Posting Announcements 253
Advertising Your Community 255
Maintaining Searchable Archives.. 259
Other Ideas.. 260

13. Encouraging Sharing and Responding to Dissension.....................**263**
Community Goals.. 263
Role of the Community Manager.. 264
Making Community Rules... 266
Areas in Which Communities Need Rules 267
Deliberate Disruptions 272
Encouraging Participation 280
Guiding And Encouraging Discussion 282

Running Moderated Communities 283

14. Making Money with Your Community **287**
Selling Banner Advertising 288
Selling Mailing List Ads 290
Selling Your Membership List 291
Selling Other Information 292
Selling Things via Affiliate Programs 292

15. Privacy, Spam, and Other Issues **295**
Preserving Privacy and Creating a Privacy Policy 295
Avoiding and Dealing with Spam 299
Copyright Issues 301
Libel, Harassment, and Responsibility for Online Material 304
Children's Issues 305

16. Managing Groups of Communities **307**
How Organizations Can Use Online Communities 307
Roles of the Site Manager 308
Creating and Maintaining Site-wide Information 310
Choosing, Training, and Supporting Community Managers 311
Making a Web Site for Your Organization's Communities 315
Policy Issues 316
Technical Issues 319

Part VII: True-Life Stories

17. The Computer Book Publishing List **323**
The Origins of the Computer Book Publishing List 323
Life on the List 324
Problems and Solutions 325
Value of the List to Its Sponsor 325
Summary 326

18. Knitting.About.com **327**
The About.com Web Site 328
Life in Knitting.About.com 329
Problems and Solutions 330
Summary 331

19. Comp.compilers **333**
The Origins of comp.compilers 334
Value of This Community to Its Members 335
Life in comp.compilers 335
Problems and Solutions 338
Summary 338

20. soc.religion.unitarian-univ **339**
The Origins of soc.religion.unitarian-univ 340

| Day-to-Day Management 341
       The s.r.u-u Modbot 341
       Summary 343
21. The uua.org Mailing Lists **345**
       The Origins of the UUA Mailing Lists 347
       Types of UUA Mailing Lists 348
       Life on the UUA Lists 349
       List Management 350
       Site Management 352
       Problems and Solutions 352
       Summary 354
Appendix: Resources for Online Community Managers **355**
       Resources for All Types of Online Community Managers 355
       Resources for Mailing List Managers 358
       Resources for Newsgroup Moderators and News Administrators 360
       Resources for IRC Channel Operators 365
       Resources for Web-based Community Managers 369

Introduction

Welcome to *Poor Richard's Building Online Communities*! Here are the two main points of this book:

- Finding and getting to know people who share your interests is one of the most interesting and useful things you can do on the Internet.
- You don't have to be a rocket scientist or spend thousands of dollars to create a community online. You probably already have the programs you'll need.

"Online community" and "virtual community" are two hot buzzwords in the Internet press these days. Many organizations (especially those with expensive Web sites) are interested in online communities as a way to get people to come to their Web sites and stick around. Unfortunately, these organizations seem to view their kind of online communities as a way of tricking you into viewing lots of Web pages so that you can see lots of banner ads and maybe buy something. Providing information that people can use, and fostering a sense of trust and belonging that underlies any successful community, is secondary.

This book takes a different approach. We'll show you how to find an online community with people discussing your interest, if such a community already exists. If you can't find one, or want to create a better one, we'll show you how to set up an online community of your own, using e-mail, the Web, or other Internet systems, including Usenet newsgroups and Internet Relay Chat (IRC). We'll show you how to create online communities that work, providing members with information and camaraderie. We'll help you promote your community so that prospective members can find it and join. If you need to make some money from the online community you create, we'll help you figure out how without ruining your community in the process.

Why did we choose to write this book in the *Poor Richard* series, which started with the best-selling *Poor Richard's Web Site*? The *Poor Richard's* books share an approach based on the no-nonsense, useful *Poor Richard's Almanack* that Benjamin Franklin published more than 200 years ago. This books tells you everything you need to know to build your own online community in a no-nonsense, hands-on way—just what you are looking for.

Other books about online community talk about how to spend lots of money and time creating large-scale community Web sites, which may be appropriate for big organizations but not too useful for the average Internet user. The most successful online communities aren't run by big organizations, though—they are run by people like you, people who have an area of expertise or a passion for their hobby and want to share it with others. You don't need to spend $10,000 on a community hosting company or design consultant when you can create a community for free using one of the free mailing-list services described in Chapter 5 or the free, Web-based community sites listed in Chapter 10. If you want to add message boards or real-time chat to a Web site you already run, we tell you how to do so for free in Chapter 11.

Of course, setting up an online community isn't all you need to do. You also need to know how to manage the programs involved, promote your community so that others can find it, protect the privacy of your members, and deal with the inevitable problems that happen whenever people get together. This book has down-to-earth advice about all those topics. Finally, you can learn from the experience of other online community managers by reading the case studies at the end of this book, which describe successful mailing lists, newsgroups, and Web-based communities. If you *do* work for an organization that needs to set up a group of online communities, we'll talk about that too, in Chapter 16.

Because the Internet is changing so fast, we have a Web site at http://net.gurus.com/prboc/ with updates to the information in this book. You can also write to the authors at prboc@gurus.com—we read all our reader mail, although we can't respond personally to every question.

We hope that you'll find useful communities on the Internet and consider creating one of your own. If you do set up an online community with help from *Poor Richard's Building Online Communities*, let us know about it by writing to prboc@gurus.com. We'll include a link to your community from our Web site at http://community.gurus.com.

—Margy Levine Young
and John Levine

Part I

Introduction to Online Communities

Chapter One
What Is Online Community?

Community is when people get together and get to know one another, and *online community* is when it happens over a computer network. The Internet plays host to hundreds of thousands of online communities—from church groups to business meetings to committees and interest groups of all types. Some online communities are run by businesses and nonprofits in order to communicate better within their organizations or with their suppliers or customers. Other communities are run by individuals for fun or profit, discussing hobbies, sports, religion, parenting, or almost any other topic you can think of. Online communities use several different mechanisms to communicate, including e-mail messages and the Web.

For example, we authors participate in these types of online communities:
- Several mailing lists for people who write books or articles about computers and the Internet. Since we work at home, chatting with the folks on these lists is like shooting the breeze with coworkers—these lists are where we can compare notes with other people who do what we do.
- A mailing list for members of our church. When something happens—an event is rescheduled or someone needs help—we can get the word out fast and cheaply.
- A Usenet newsgroup for users of Microsoft Access. We pick up valuable tips and tricks and can ask questions about Access databases we are working on.
- A mailing list for a committee that meets face-to-face only once a year. The rest of the year, we have an ongoing online meeting by e-mail—the meeting that never ends!
- A Web-based chat about the best-selling *Harry Potter* series of novels by J.K. Rowling. When will the next book be published? What do other

readers guess about the ongoing mysteries in the books? Inquiring minds want to know!

You can join a community that already exists, or you can start your own. (We think you'll want to do both!)

Why Participate in Online Communities

Here are some reasons to participate in an online community:

To learn or express your opinions about a topic, especially if you have specific questions. For example, if you are remodeling your house, a home renovation Web site is useful, but a place where you can ask questions can be even better.

To share experiences with people in similar circumstances. You can probably find communities of people who do the same job as you, play the same sports, belong to the same religion or club, suffer from the same ailment, or have the same special interest. You may be the only person who is building harpsichords in your town, but you can meet lots of harpsichord makers on the Internet!

To make friends who share your interests. If you want to meet people online, forget chat rooms and other places where lonely people hang out. Instead, join an online community on a topic that interests you. You'll have at least one thing in common with everyone there (an interest in that topic)!

To participate in a committee, club, or other group that meets via an online community. For example, some committees find that by communicating together over the Net, they can get more work done than by having face-to-face meetings.

To live a fantasy life without people knowing who you are in real life. Some online communities are designed to let people participate in a fantasy world—from dungeons-and-dragons-style medieval European castles to science-fiction starships, not to mention sexually oriented fantasy worlds.

To find a job. Why not? If you can demonstrate that you are knowledgeable in a community of people that includes prospective employers, you might end up with a job offer.

To sell something. But watch out—people in online communities are not there to be sold to. Read Chapter 14 before you try to post ads or come-ons online.

Why Create Your Own Online Community

You might choose to create your own online community for all the same reasons that you'd participate in an existing community, plus:

- **To discuss a topic that no one else is discussing.** If there's no online community discussion about your favorite topic, start one! Say you collect antique glass insulators and you'd like to talk about them, but there's no one else in town who shares your interest. You can bet that there are folks on the Internet who do!

- **To provide an online way for an existing community to get together.** An online community can be a great way for your extended family, your church, your club, or another existing group to communicate. Several Web sites are specifically designed to allow families (**My Family**, at http://www.MyFamily.com) or alumni groups (http://www.aya.yale.edu) to form communities.

- **To create a community with your own personal style.** As the creator and manager of an online community, you can make the rules and set the tone of your group.

- **To market a product or service.** A Web site is a good first step for marketing online (to find out why, see *Poor Richard's Internet Marketing and Promotions,* written by Peter Kent and Tara Calashain and published by Top Floor Publishing (visit http://www.poorrichard.com/promo/). But providing an online community can help, too. Your community can be directed at the types of people who might want to buy from you. If you demonstrate that you are knowledgeable, provide helpful information, and don't use a hard-sell approach, people will get a good impression of you and your products.

- **To provide support for customers of your product.** If you sell something or provide a service, you can let your customers support each other, and support them directly, via an online community.

- **To convince people of your way of thinking.** Got an opinion? You can create a community to discuss it and to try to convince people that you are right. However, if you are too strident or don't allow other people to express their opinions, no one will stick around to listen.

- **To share experiences with people.** If you've got a medical condition, family problem, or other life situation; you're fighting with a particularly stupid computer program; or you're dealing with some other situation, you can find other people who are in the same boat. You may have some useful advice for them—or they may have some for you.

To make money. The manager of an online community can make money by selling ads that are displayed to subscribers. See Chapter 14 to find out how this works. But remember—no one will come to see the ads unless you have useful and interesting material to offer!

Creating an online community takes some preparation and work, though—the rest of this book explains how to go about it.

How Online Communities Work

Online communities can communicate through several different systems. The most widely used types are mailing lists, Usenet newsgroups, and Web-based message boards. Other, less popular, venues include Internet Relay Chat (IRC), instant-messaging systems, virtual worlds, MUDs, and MOOs. The program you use to participate in a community depends on which system the community uses to communicate.

Online communities also fall into two categories, depending on how immediate the communication is among members. Communication on the Internet is one of these two types:

- **Asynchronous.** Happens when one person sends a message and other people read it sometime later. For example, e-mail is asynchronous because you don't know exactly when the recipient will read your message.

- **Real-time.** Occurs when the message is read almost immediately. Instant messaging is real-time because your message appears on the recipient's screen within seconds.

Online communities can use either asynchronous or real-time communication or both, depending on the preferences of the community members. Some people prefer asynchronous systems—like mailing lists, newsgroups, and message boards—because they can participate whenever they like and don't have to be online at a particular time. Other people like the immediacy of real-time systems—like IRC, Web-based chat rooms, and virtual worlds. If you are creating a community, you can choose the system that works best for your members or incorporate both types of communication.

The following sections describe each of the major ways that online communities communicate.

Table 1-1 summarizes the types of communities.

Community Type	Timing	Type of Program Members Use
Mailing lists	Asynchronous	E-mail program, like Outlook Express, Netscape Messenger, or Eudora
Newsgroups	Asynchronous	Newsreader, like Outlook Express, Netscape Newsgroups, Free Agent, or trn
Internet Relay Chat (IRC)	Real-time	IRC program, like mIRC, Microsoft Chat, Ircle, or iirc
Web-based message boards	Asynchronous	Web browser, like Netscape Navigator, Internet Explorer, or Opera
Web-based chat	Real-time	Web browser
Virtual worlds	Real-time	Virtual-world program, like The Palace
MUDs and MOOs	Real-time	Telnet program, like the telnet program built into Windows ME, Windows 98, or Windows 95, or a MUD or MOO client program (a telnet program adapted for use with MUDs and MOOs)

Table 1-1: Types of Online Communities.

Mailing Lists

Mailing lists allow community members to talk using e-mail messages. When you subscribe to a mailing list, you can send e-mail messages to a special address, and they are forwarded to all the other list subscribers. Some mailing lists allow only a few people to post messages, which all the subscribers can read; others permit any subscriber to post. Hundreds of thousands of public mailing lists are on the Internet, and who knows how many private ones.

To read and post messages to a mailing list, you use your e-mail program. Any e-mail program will do, although more powerful e-mail programs have features that can make mailing-list messages more convenient. For example, you can *filter* (presort) all the messages from the mailing list into a separate folder so that they aren't mixed in with your regular mail. Chapter 4 describes how to find, subscribe to, and participate in mailing lists, and Chapter 5 explains how to set up your own.

Mailing lists have the advantage that almost all Internet users have access to e-mail and know how to use an e-mail program. Also, messages arrive in each subscriber's mailbox, reminding the subscribers to participate. Setting up a new mailing list is a snap at one of the many free, Web-based mailing-list servers.

Disadvantages include the difficulty in going back to read past messages (unless you save all e-mail messages from the list in your own mailbox or unless the list has searchable Web-based archives, as many do). Also, e-mail programs aren't designed to display discussions: They don't easily group messages by topic, with the replies to each message.

Usenet Newsgroups

Usenet is a global system of bulletin boards (called *newsgroups*) on tens of thousands of topics. The newsgroups are arranged into *hierarchies* by topic, including computer, social, recreational, and other types of topics. For example, all newsgroups whose names start with rec are about recreational topics, all those that start with rec.games are about games, and rec.games.archery is about archery.

To read newsgroup messages or to post (send) your own, you need a *newsreader* program. You may already have a newsreader without knowing it: Netscape Communicator comes with Netscape Newsgroups, and Outlook Express has a built-in newsreader. Figure 1-1 shows the Netscape Newsgroups program displaying a message and the list of responses. Chapter 6 tells you how to find, read, and post to newsgroups, and Chapter 7 tells you how to create a newsgroup.

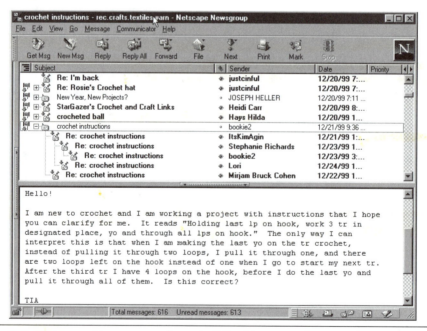

Figure 1-1: Netscape Newsgroups is part of the Netscape Communicator suite of programs.

One disadvantage of newsgroups is that many people don't know how to use them, even though most people have a newsreader built into their e-mail or browser program. Another disadvantage is that creating a newsgroup—especially in one of the popular "Big Eight" hierarchies, which are available throughout the Internet—is a long, drawn-out political process. Although you can create a newsgroup in an alternative hierarchy, not everyone has access to these less widely distributed newsgroups. One advantage of newsgroups is that newsreaders are good at displaying discussions and organizing messages by *thread* (a message and all its replies, including replies to replies). Another is that newsgroups can easily handle discussions with huge numbers of subscribers; popular newsgroups all have at least hundreds of thousands of subscribers.

Internet Relay Chat (IRC)

IRC lets groups of people talk in *real-time*: Messages are sent within seconds, and the people you are chatting with can respond right away. Mailing lists, newsgroups, and Web-based message boards aren't as immediate. The world of IRC is divided into networks and channels (like #hottub and #over40).

To participate in IRC, you need an IRC program like ircII, Microsoft Chat, or mIRC. Chapter 8 describes how to find and join an IRC channel, and Chapter 9 explains how to create and manage your own channels. Other types of real-time chat exist too, but are designed for use by small groups (for example, the Microsoft NetMeeting program and CU-SeeMe).

Our experience with IRC is that although many flourishing communities are out there, they tend to attract mainly people with lots of spare time (especially high school and college students) who don't mind waiting around for other people to type. It's also hard to find channels that are talking about specific subjects: Most people are just shooting the breeze or flirting with a mind to leaving with one other person for a private channel and a little cybersex. Interesting, maybe, but community, no, in our humble opinions. IRC channels exist only as long as someone is there chatting, and there's no concept of membership or subscription to a channel.

However, other types of communities can include IRC as one way for their members to communicate. For example, members of a mailing list might want to gather on an IRC channel on Tuesday evenings to discuss a specific subject.

Web-based Communities

Many Web sites include programming that allows people to post messages using their Web browsers. The messages appear on the Web page for

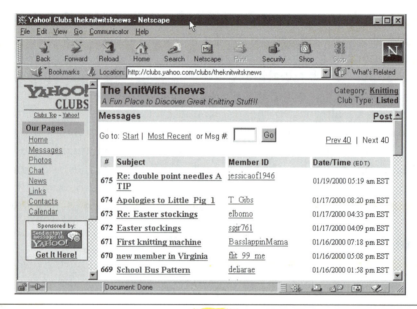

Figure 1-2: You use a Web browser to read and post messages on Web-based message boards.

other people to read. For example, the **About.com Knitting** Web site, at http://knitting.about.com, includes *forums* in which people interested in knitting can post messages. Figure 1-2 shows the list of messages in a forum: You just click a message to read it.

Web-based communities can also include Web-based chat, a system of real-time chat rooms that appear as part of a Web page. To participate in a Web-based message board (also called a *bulletin board*, *board*, or *BBS*) or chat, all you need is a Web browser, like Internet Explorer or Netscape Navigator. Chapter 10 explains how to find, read, and post to Web-based message boards and chat, and Chapter 11 tells how to set up your own.

Web-based communities have the advantage of being available to most Internet users because almost everyone knows how to use their Web browser. The message boards also display past messages so that you can look back through the earlier discussions to see whether your question was already answered or to get an idea of what the group is like. A disadvantage is that participants have to remember to go to the Web site to read new messages—they don't arrive in your mailbox to remind you. (Some Web-based message board systems include the option to send you new messages by e-mail.) Setting up a message board and chat room at one of the free community Web sites is easy, although you may not be able to keep the site from displaying its ads on your Web pages.

America Online Chat Rooms, CompuServe Forums, and Other Private-Label Systems

America Online (AOL, at http://www.aol.com/) and **CompuServe** (at http://www.compuserve.com/) are two online services that began as stand-alone services and then connected to the Internet. They provide community systems—AOL chat rooms and CompuServe forums—that are accessible to only their own members. If you use one of these services, it's worth participating in these systems; if you want to start your own community, though, we think that you should create one that can include participants from the entire Internet, not just from one service.

ICQ, AOL Instant Messenger, and Other Instant-Message Programs

Instant-message programs are designed primarily to let two people chat in real-time. Groups can also chat, but (like IRC channels) the group exists only as long as the people are chatting. We don't see these programs as a way to create online community (yet, anyway). For one-to-one chatting, check out these programs:

AOL Instant Messenger
   http://www.aol.com/aim/
ICQ
   http://web.icq.com/
MSN Messenger
   http://messenger.msn.com/
Yahoo Messenger
   http://messenger.yahoo.com/

Virtual Worlds, MUDs, and MOOs

Virtual worlds, like **The Palace**, at http://www.thepalace.com/, are programs that let you and other people communicate over the Internet, presenting a computer-generated world for you to move around in. *MUDs (Multi-User Dimensions)* and *MOOs (MUDs Object Oriented)* work the same way and are usually limited to text. Three Dimensional virtual worlds present (usually rather rough) pictures of the virtual world, which might be modeled on medieval England, a spaceship, or a ski slope. You use commands to create your own character, move around the world, say things to other people, and take other actions—the exact commands depend on the program. Some virtual worlds even allow you to create new parts of the world by issuing commands or by writing programs in a scripting language.

To participate in a MUD or MOO, you use a telnet program, which acts as a text-only terminal so that you can log on, type commands, and see messages from other participants. MUD-specific telnet programs have been adapted to send MUD commands and keep track of the MUD world. For more information on using a telnet program, see the **Internet Classics from the Internet Gurus** page, at http://net.gurus.com/telnet/. MUDs and MOOs, and more recently 3D virtual worlds, have hosted rich, ongoing online communities. For information about MUDs and MOOs, see the **MUD FAQ**, at http://www.mudconnector.org/mudfaq/, or the **MUD Resource Collection**, at http://www.godlike.com/muds/.

Most other virtual worlds require you to install a program on your computer in order to participate. The program communicates with the central server program for the virtual world and lets you see (and sometimes hear) what's going on. See **Get a World! Multi-User Virtual Worlds and Avatar Software**, at http://www.ccon.org/hotlinks/worlds.html, for links to the most popular Internet-based virtual worlds.

MUDs, MOOs, and other virtual worlds are great places to go to make friends, create a new persona for yourself, have fun, and (potentially) use up an incredible amount of time. (One of the questions in the MUD FAQ is "Is MUDding a game, or an extension of real life with gamelike qualities?" which might give you an idea of how dedicated some participants are.) However, it's hard to create your own world on any of these systems. You need to install and maintain MUD, MOO, or virtual world software.

Common Topics for Communities

Here are some of the most popular general topics for online communities:

Music, sports, politics, and other topics. Online discussion groups are talking at this moment about every conceivable topic, serious or fun, general or specific. Topics can range from aimless banter about the doings of your favorite band to formal, intellectual discussions about philosophy.

Families. Families can create their own online communities on several Web sites designed for the purpose (for example, **MyFamily.com**, at http://www.myfamily.com/). Family members can chat, make appointments, remind each other of their birthdays, and make group photo albums.

- **Committee business.** Committees, boards, task forces, and other groups meet to get some work done. In an online community, the committee can meet 24 hours a day, 7 days a week—or whenever a member decides to post a message.

- **Mutual support.** People who suffer from a physical or emotional ailment or face some other difficult situation may benefit from sharing with others in the same situation. There are online communities for every major disease, 12-step program, and other life trauma. Folks can bolster each others' confidence, share war stories, offer advice, and provide pointers to useful sources of information (usually in the form of links to useful Web pages).

- **Camaraderie.** It's fun to talk to other people who do the same thing you do for work or play or who have something else in common with you. This type of online community is especially rewarding for people who are isolated—people who work at home or who have an unusual career or hobby.

- **How-to.** Whether it's computer software, digital photography, knitting, or keeping chickens, you can get specific advice and answers to your pressing questions from an online community. There are groups for crafts, pets, musicmaking, and every possible way to use a computer.

- **Fantasy and role playing.** You don't have to be yourself in an online community. After all, you rarely run into anyone you know offline (in the Real World). So go ahead and pretend to be someone you're not, as long as you don't rip anyone else off or hurt anyone in the process! If you've always wanted to play in a band, what's to stop you from joining a group for saxophonists and talking about playing gigs? But watch out—if you cause trouble, it's not that hard for people to find out your real name and address. Stick to MUDs and MOOs (described earlier in this chapter) or harmless imagination.

What Can Go Wrong

At their best, online communities provide their participants with useful, timely information, friendly banter, and just the right number of jokes. In real life, however, communities can go sour. Here are some reasons *not* to participate!

- **Time.** We spend lots of time at our computers, and some people have suggested that it might be just a little *too much* time. We spend over an hour a day answering various types of messages that arrive over the Internet, and most of them are from the various online communities we belong to. The solution: Don't join too many communities at one time!

Aggravation. Online communication brings out the worst in many people. Some participants say things over the Internet that they would never say in person or over the phone! It's easy as you type at your computer to forget that real people are at the other end of the communication, with real lives and real feelings. If you've got enough stress in your life, choose your online communities carefully.

Looking like a fool. Be careful what you say in an online community. You never know who is listening! A good rule to follow is "Never post something that you would mind having posted on the wall next to the company water cooler or on the school bulletin board or sent to your mother." After messages on the Internet are written, they have the habit of escaping from their original audience into the wider world. This rule covers both personal attacks (saying mean or negative things about people) and leaking secrets (personal or those of your organization).

Liability. The legal implications of what is posted on the Internet, including messages exchanged within online communities, have yet to be thrashed out by the legal systems of the world. It's not yet clear what responsibility the managers of an online community have for what goes on there. For example, if a member posts copyrighted material, no one yet knows whether that member, or the community manager, or both, might be liable to be sued for damages by the copyright holder. Similar questions arise around libel and collusion (for professional discussions). If you plan to run an online community, you'll need to think about these questions up front. Be sure to read Chapter 13, which describes how to set the rules for online communities you create, and Chapter 15, which discusses some legal issues community managers face.

The Six Stages of Online Communities

Many online communities go through a series of stages (this series is based on *The Natural Life Cycle of Mailing Lists*, by Kat Nagel, this can be found at http://www.catalog.com/vivian/lifecycle.html):

1. **Enthusiasm abounds** as people find the group, get to know each other, and are excited about finally having people to talk to about their favorite topic (whatever it may be).

2. **New members are recruited** for the community so that as many people as possible can have the benefit of this terrific new resource. This stage can include complaints about *lurkers* (people who join, but never say anything) and an inability to imagine why *everyone* wouldn't want to join!

3. **The community prospers** as more and more people join and many topics are discussed.

4. **Real community develops** among the members. People help each other out, lots of good information is shared, leaders emerge, and the group develops a style and tone of its own. In-jokes appear, and some people display idiosyncratic characters—they may be especially funny or helpful or garrulous or always bring up the same subjects. Some people get to know each other well and have private conversations outside the community. Some people even arrange to meet in real life. At the same time, some members reveal themselves to be annoying, obnoxious, dreadful spellers, incapable of learning how to use the program that gives them access to the community, or people with way, way too much time on their hands. *Off-topic* threads develop (discussions off the topic of the community), along with some complaints about them.

5. **Dissension breaks out** among many community members because of off-topic discussions, problematic people, or the endless discussion about off-topic discussions and problematic people. There's lots of criticism (in the form of *flames*, or messages filled with personal attacks) and a few *flamewars* (extended bouts of flaming). Some people leave, and some people threaten to leave unless specific people are booted out, specific topics are banned, or rules are put into place to fix the situation. More messages are about the community and what to do about it than are about the original topic of the community.

Definitions of Some Terms

Archive—Collection of past messages shared over an online community, usually available over the Web.
Flame—Message filled with personal attacks.
Flamewar—Extended bout of flaming.
Lurking—Joining a community, but never saying anything. Most communities are composed of about 90 percent lurkers.
Member or **subscriber**—Someone who signs up to participate in an online community.
Online community—Group of people who participate in discussions over the Internet.
Post or **posting**—Message sent to the members of an online community, usually by one of its members.
Real life or **RL**—Life off the Internet.
Spam—Unsolicited commercial messages or ads.
Thread—Message and its replies (including replies to replies and so on).

6. a) **Everything falls apart**, and lots of people leave. Those who are left think that everything is great because only topics that interest them are discussed, in only the style they like. Few new people join, or, if they do, they don't feel welcome because of the tense mood of the group

b) **Or, the community learns** from its mistakes, and may make changes to fix the situation, but not in a way that stifles participation. Some people may leave, some topics may be banned, and some rules may be put into place. The group returns to Stage 4, although it slides into Stage 5 from time to time. New folks are still welcomed in and taught the ropes, old-timers don't get too smug or set in their ways, and the community continues happily on into the sunset. . . .

Steps for Creating an Online Community

Whatever the reason for starting your own online community, whichever system—mailing lists, newsgroups, IRC channels, or Web-based communities—you use to run it, and whatever the topic, here are the general steps to follow to create a new community:

1. **State your reason for creating the community**. Think about your personal goal for creating the community. For example, your goal in creating a mailing list about knitting might be to share tips and tricks with other knitters, or it might be to promote the sales of your self-published knitting pattern books.

2. **State the goals of the community—the problem that the community would solve for its members.** Community members' goals might be exactly the same as your goals in creating the community, or they might differ. For a knitting mailing list, participants might also be folks aspiring to make money by selling knitting pattern books, or they might be people looking for free patterns, or they might be new knitters looking for help. Your community can have more than one goal, as long as they don't conflict.

3. **Think about who would be interested in joining this community.** What kind of interactions would they want to have: a few formal, moderated, information-rich messages or more chatty, informal messages? Where would you find people like that? How much computer and Internet experience are they likely to have?

4. **Choose your venue.** Determine whether a mailing list, newsgroup, IRC channel, Web-based message board, chat room, or other venue would work the best for likely members of your community. You can make this choice

based on the likely Internet-savviness of your target group (for example, using Usenet newsgroups requires using a newsreader, which many newer Internet users have never tried) as well as on the services of the various venues (for example, some venues offer file-sharing or real-time chat). Chapters 4 through 11 describe mailing lists, newsgroups, IRC, and Web-based communities in detail, including how to start a community using each system.

5. **Decide who will manage your community.** Will you manage it yourself? If an organization is sponsoring a community, who within the organization will take responsibility for managing it?

6. **Think about the ground rules for the community.** Every community has some rules, to determine what types of messages are exchanged. Chapter 11 has ideas for how to make rules to further the goals of your community.

7. **Create the community.** Chapters 5, 7, 9, and 11 describe how to create a community using mailing lists, newsgroups, IRC, and the Web, respectively. Test the community with yourself and friends.

8. **Publicize your community**. Chapter 12 lists ideas for how to get the word out.

Then—have fun and watch the community grow! If you run into trouble, Chapter 13 includes ideas for dealing with common problems.

Chapter Two
Online Community Options

Online communities come in a wide variety of styles, from freewheeling communities where anything goes to tightly controlled communities with strict controls on who may join or post. If you want to participate in a community, it's important to know how the group works and what rules you will be expected to follow. If you want to create your own community, you'll have to decide how it should work (your options will depend on what type of community you create).

Who Controls the Community

Nearly every online community is controlled by one or more *community managers.* These managers may have different titles depending on the type of community: Mailing lists have list managers, list owners, or "list moms." No matter what the title, the community manager controls who may join, who may post (send messages that the community receives), and what rules guide what may be posted.

Here are some typical ways communities are managed:

A single manager can operate the group as his or her private party. For example, a mailing list to discuss a particular rock band might be run by the person who started it. What the manager says goes, and community members can follow the rules or leave.

A group of managers can be chosen by the community participants. When issues arise, the managers can confer and come up with a consistent policy for participants to follow. For example, the UUS-L mailing list (a discussion list for Unitarian Universalists) is run by a "junta" of longtime list subscribers. An IRC channel is run by its *channel operators* (*chanops*).

An organization can run the list, with employees or volunteers managing the community on the organization's behalf. In this case, rules can be particularly thorny since the actions of the managers reflect on the organization and complaints from the participants are usually reviewed by someone from the organization. For example, the Unitarian Universalist Association (UUA) hosts over 150 lists on its Internet host computer (uua.org), and a department of the UUA oversees the lists. Each list has one or more managers, and the managers must enforce the UUA's list policies.

Nobody is in charge of most Usenet groups—after a newsgroup is created, its operation is usually entirely automatic. In some cases this system works surprisingly well, as in the comp.arch newsgroup, where technically oriented people discuss computer architecture; in other cases it leads to never-ending flamewars. (Some newsgroups are *moderated;* see the section "Who May Post Messages," later in this chapter.)

Every well-run community provides a special e-mail address for contacting the community managers. See Chapters 5, 7, 9, and 11 for how to find out the manager address for a mailing list, newsgroup, IRC channel, or Web-based community.

Who May Join

Online communities can be *open* to anyone who wants to join, or *closed*, so that only the community managers can add people as participants.

If the purpose of a community is to allow anyone who is interested in a specific topic to discuss that topic, the community is usually open. For example, because discussions about art, music, politics, religion, sports, books, movies, or other topics might be of interest to anyone, most communities about these types of topics are open. On the other hand, if the discussion becomes divisive or if a small number of individuals sabotage the group, the community may decide to come up with a way to vet (screen) new members.

Some communities exist to allow specific groups of people to work together online. For example, a committee, board of directors, club, or other group can create a community. This type of community is usually closed, so that only the members of that committee, club, or whatever may join. In some cases, the community allows anyone to join and see what's going on, but only committee or club members may post messages: This approach is like a meeting that is open to the public for observation. Other communities let only committee or club members join, but anyone may post messages: This approach provides a way for anyone to contact that committee or club, but keeps the discussions private.

> **What If Everyone Isn't Online?**
>
> *If you are creating an online community for an existing group—a committee, club, scout troop, church, or other group—not everyone may be online. Those who don't have access to the Internet may feel excluded from the online community's information-sharing and decision-making activities. There are a couple of approaches, none of them perfect:*
>
> - *Get everyone online! Encourage people to get WebTV or other low-priced Internet appliances.*
>
> - *Suggest that non-Internet users go to the public library, which probably has an Internet-connected computer the public can use. Tell them to learn to use the Web browser on the library's computer and to sign up for a Web-based e-mail account like Hotmail (http://www.hotmail.com/) or Yahoo Mail (http://mail.yahoo.com/). For newsgroups, people can use the Deja.com (http://www.deja.com/usenet/) or RemarQ (http://www.remarq.com) Web sites if no newsreader program is available. Libraries may not let members of the public use their PCs for online chat and may not have IRC programs installed.*
>
> - *Suggest that non-Internet users visit a neighbor for access, using a Web-based mail account to receive e-mail. Internet-less members can visit Internet users when online chats are in session so that they can share a computer.*
>
> - *Print messages and get them to your Internet-less members. This method might work for mailing lists, newsgroups, and message boards, but it's no good for IRC and other real-time systems.*

Several problems may arise with a closed community:

Attracting new members may be hard because prospective members can't see what's going on within the community. If you start a community to discuss the works of science fiction author Ursula K. LeGuin, you may decide to limit the community to 100 members to keep the message traffic down. However, be sure to create a process that allows prospective members to get a sense of whether they'd like to join, and create a waiting list so that when people leave, you can fill their places.

Determining whether people are who they say they are can be time consuming. For example, if you were starting a community for church-based sexual education, you might want to limit participation to people who are actually teaching sex-ed classes at their churches. If someone e-mails you to request membership, how will you check that he or she is telling the truth? This issue arises in communities designed for people suffering from a specific physical or mental ailment. Ideally, the community should be only for patients and perhaps their families, but it can be hard to exclude people who will make fun of, give erroneous information to, or prey on the rest of the participants.

Who May Read the Content

A community creates *content*—that is, information (text, pictures, and in other forms). The content usually relates to the topic of the community, if any. Content can include an archive of the messages exchanged within the community, files uploaded by members (including pictures, sound clips, programs, or other types of files), Web pages of information written by community members, transcripts of chat sessions, and Web pages with links to resources of use to the community—whatever the community wants.

The community can choose whether some or all of its content can be read by outsiders. Here are some possibilities:

Anyone may read all the content. If a community is open and wants to attract new members, letting people see what the community has to offer is a good idea. For example, the rec.arts.bonsai Usenet newsgroup (about growing bonsai trees) allows anyone to read its postings.

Only members may read its content. Closed communities usually choose this option. Open communities may choose to restrict access to its content too, to prevent outsiders from harvesting the e-mail addresses of participants or to keep a sense of confidentiality and safety within the group. For example, a mailing list for cancer survivors might keep its message archives private.

Some content is public, some is private. A community may have some publicly accessible content, like a Web site with information and links, and some material that only members can see, like the exchange of messages among members. For example, a Web-based knitting community might maintain a publicly accessible library of knitting patterns on the Web but allow only members to read the messages posted to the community.

Who May Post Messages

One function of a community is to exchange messages with other community members, using e-mail (for mailing lists), newsgroup postings (for Usenet newsgroups), chat messages (for IRC and Web-based chat), or messages displayed on a Web site (for Web-based message boards). But who can post (send) these messages? Here are the most common options:

Anyone on the entire Internet. Some communities allow nonmembers to post messages, but this is usually a bad idea. Spammers and troublemakers can post messages, for example.

Any member of the community. Most communities use this option for discussions that involve the entire community. (Of course, in most communities, a small fraction of members do the lion's share of the posting, and many members prefer to "lurk" without posting.) If any member may post messages, the community may place a limit on the number of messages that each member may post per day, to prevent anyone from monopolizing the conversation.

Any community member, with the approval of the community managers. *Moderated discussions* include a mechanism whereby posts are routed to one or more *moderators* (usually the community managers) for approval before they are distributed or displayed to the community. The exact mechanism depends on the type of community (for example, moderated mailing lists and newsgroups route all posts to the moderators via e-mail, and the moderators approve or reject posts by sending another e-mail message to the list server or news server program that distributes messages to the subscribers). The moderators should establish what rules they will apply for approving postings, and the rules should be posted in a place that all members can read (a Web page or periodic posting on a mailing list or newsgroup). The moderators should handle all postings quickly, and when a posting is rejected, the author should receive a message with an explanation of why the posting wasn't acceptable.

Only community managers. For distributing announcements from the community managers, a community may have an *announcements area*, which may be a mailing list, newsgroup, or section of a Web site. For example, the community managers may post information about the community itself (rules, upcoming events), about the topic of the community (outside events in which members may be interested, news that relates to the topic of the community), or about the organization that runs the community (press releases from the organization, events the organization is holding, and staff changes within the organization).

What You Can Post

Most communities have guidelines for what kinds of messages can be posted to their discussions. Here are some common rules.

No Off-topic Messages

Many communities welcome messages on any topic, to help members get to know each other. Other communities focus on a specific topic and ban messages that are off-topic.

No Formatted Messages

Newer e-mail programs—like Outlook Express, Netscape Messenger, and Eudora—let users format messages using MIME or HTML formatting so that messages can include background images, bold, underlining, italics, and other niceties. However, if formatted messages are posted to a mailing list or newsgroup and other members of the community don't have programs that can display the formatting properly, the messages appear garbled, with formatting characters interspersed with the text. Many mailing lists and newsgroups forbid formatted messages.

No Attachments

Some communities exist to allow members to share files, usually graphics or sound files. These communities expect their members to have programs that can display or play these types of files (otherwise, why join?), and they allow members to attach files to their messages. Most other types of communities discourage attachments because many members don't have the programs to display them and attached files can be very large (sometimes filling up members' mailboxes). For example, if a member of a community posts an article she wrote as a WordPerfect document, few other members may be able to read it.

Instead of having members send attachments, most communities ask members to either post their files on a Web site and send its URL or post a message about the file and ask people to contact them privately if they want the file. Some communities (especially Web-based message boards) have libraries or archives where members can upload files for the use of other community members.

No Chain Letters or Virus Warnings

Chain letters are messages that ask you to pass them along to other people. Most communities ban them because most are fraudulent, most Internet users receive many copies of chain letters, and most are unrelated to the topic of the community.

Virus warnings are a type of chain letter because they usually ask you to pass them along to everyone you know. With rare exceptions, virus warnings are overinflated or fictional. (Some people refer to the virus warning itself as the virus!) Most communities frown on virus warnings and rely on their members to visit virus warning Web sites on their own (for example, the **McAfee.com Virus Information Library**, at http://vil.mcafee.com/, and the **Symantec AntiVirus Research Center**, at http://www.symantec.com/avcenter/).

No More Than One Language

Some communities require that messages be posted in one or two specific languages (usually English, or English and a language relevant to the content of the community). Other communities welcome messages in any language, but don't guarantee that they will be responded to (unless another member happens to speak that language). Some communities exist primarily for learning a language or culture, and all messages must be posted in that language.

No Copyrighted Material Without Permission

Posting someone else's work in its entirety is probably a violation of U.S. and international copyright law, unless you have permission from the copyright holder (usually the author or publisher of the work). Almost everything that has been written in the past 70 years is copyrighted, whether it is marked with a copyright notice or not. For example, if your mother sends you an e-mail to wish you a happy birthday, she owns the copyright on that message (unless she used a greeting card Web site, in which case the greeting card site probably retains the copyright on its image, background music, or design).

The U.S. copyright fair use clause (at the **U.S. Copyright Office's** Web site, at http://lcweb.loc.gov/copyright/, on page 5 of the file you download at http://lcweb.loc.gov/copyright/circs/circ21.pdf, taken from section 107 of the 1976 copyright law) says that "the fair use of a copyrighted work, . . .for purposes such as criticism, comment, news reporting, teaching (including multiple copies for classroom use), scholarship, or research is not an infringement of copyright." It goes on to say that factors to consider are the purpose, nature, amount, and effect on the market, including whether the use is for profit. The definition of fair use is deliberately fuzzy, and you'd have to get a ruling from a lawyer on any specific instance, but most communities make some kind of rule to avoid trouble with copyright violations.

No Ads

Some communities have a special place for commercial announcements that would be of interest to the community's members—for example, a Web-based message board about fantasy football might have a page on which people can place ads for products and services that relate to fantasy football. Most communities have a rule against people posting advertisements in discussions.

No Personal Attacks or Ethnic Slurs

For a community to feel like a safe place to participate, rules may be needed to protect its members from online verbal attack. These attacks can come in two forms: personal attacks on an individual and attacks on groups. Many communities have rules against both.

When discussions get spirited, people disagree, and disagreements are the mark of a healthy community in which honest, open debate happens. However, most communities encourage members to criticize the message, not the person making it. If someone says, "I knit almost everything using round needles" and you disagree, you're better off posting a reply that criticizes the idea ("Round needles are a lousy idea for knitting multicolor items, and here's why") rather than the person who expressed the idea ("People who use round needles are idiots who can't figure out how to use *real* needles").

No Disruptive Messages

Naturally, the definition of a disruptive message can be argued to death, but community managers have the responsibility for maintaining the community as a useful place for its members to exchange information. Here are some types of messages that community members may have to prevent because they disrupt the health of the community:

> **Endless posts on the same topic.** After a topic has been aired, community members may get tired of seeing the same discussion going around and around. The community manager may want to ask the participants to take the discussion offline (that is, have it by private e-mail, instant messaging, or some place other than in the community).
>
> **High volume.** If one person posts a lot of messages every day (where "a lot" depends on the norm for that community), the rest of the members may begin to feel that they are attending a lecture rather than participating in a discussion. Community managers may have the option of limiting members to a maximum number of messages per day (for example, three per day), or a maximum size of all the messages per day (for example, 100 lines of text per day). Posting a tremendous number of messages is called *flooding* and is banned in almost all communities.
>
> **Yelling and screaming.** A *flame* is a message that is insulting or provoking, a message that is designed to start or continue an argument (a *flamewar*).

Extended flamewars are annoying, upsetting, or just plain stupid enough that many community members leave rather than wade through the flames (or delete them all).

Are These Rules Censorship? Does the First Amendment Apply?

No, and no.

The First Amendment to the U.S. Constitution says, "Congress shall make no law respecting an establishment of religion, or prohibiting the free exercise thereof; or abridging the freedom of speech, or of the press; or the right of the people peaceably to assemble, and to petition the Government for a redress of grievances." (You can look it up yourself on the Constitution section of the **FindLaw Internet Legal Resources** Web site, at (http://www.findlaw.com/casecode/constitution/.) Nowhere in this amendment does it say that private individuals or organizations are required to allow anyone to say anything anywhere. It might be illegal for the U.S. government to prevent people from speaking their minds, but it's not illegal for groups that publish or otherwise disseminate information (like an online community distributing messages to its members) to make rules about what may and may not be posted. For example, it's not illegal for *The New York Times* to choose which letters will appear in its Letters to the Editor column.

When someone starts complaining that he or she is being deprived of First Amendment rights and that a community manager is practicing censorship, it's a sure sign that the complainer's grasp of free speech law is weak.

FAQS and Web Sites

Every online community needs a way for members and prospective members to find out how to join, how to quit, and how to behave in the community. The traditional document that contains this information is the *FAQ* (list of Frequently Asked Questions and their answers; rhymes with "quack"). Some FAQs are in the time-honored question-and-answer format, and others are organized by topic.

Where is the FAQ available? When you subscribe to a mailing list, the list server usually mails you the list FAQ as part of your subscription confirmation message. Many mailing lists and newsgroups post the FAQ on a regular basis, usually monthly. Most members don't actually read it monthly, but if someone has a question, they know that the answer will come around soon.

All Web-based message boards and many mailing lists, newsgroups, and IRC channels have Web sites that display the FAQ. Some include forms to fill out to

> ### Facts from FAQs
>
> *FAQs are a great source of information. By definition, information on a list of frequently asked questions is information that lots of people want to know. Some FAQs, especially those of mailing lists and newsgroups that have been around for years, are small treatises about the subject of the mailing list or newsgroup.*
>
> *You can read the FAQs of most Usenet newsgroups at the **FAQ** Web site, at http://www.faqs.org/. The FAQs of mailing lists aren't catalogued on the Web anywhere that we know of.*

join, quit, or change your community options. For example, the alt.support.stop-smoking newsgroup has its FAQ at http://www.swen.uwaterloo.ca/~as3/as3.html.

The problem with FAQs is that too few people read them. Most mailing list subscribers have had the experience of seeing messages on the list that ask how to unsubscribe. Even though all subscribers receive a welcome message with instructions for unsubscribing, and the FAQ (posted monthly) does too, there are always those who don't bother to read them.

One way to get information about comm-unity rules out to members is to append one rule at a time to the end of messages posted on the community, on a rotating basis (some list servers can be programmed to do this automatically). Every posting contains a little hint at the end about how to unsubscribe or what topics are acceptable or who to contact for help. It's a clever trick!

Chapter Three
Participating Effectively

No matter what the format of a community—e-mail mailing list, Usenet newsgroup, or Web-based message board—you need to think before you type. You are addressing dozens or hundreds of people you probably don't know, who don't know you, whose faces you can't see, and whose voices you can't hear (in most cases). In most online communities, the only thing that participants know about each other is what they read in community messages. So it pays to think about what kind of personality you want to present by your words.

Follow the Rules

As many people have pointed out, participating in an online community is a privilege, not a right. So follow the rules of the community. Read the welcome message you receive when you join, and refer to the section "What You Can Post" in Chapter 2—these rules apply to most communities.

Netiquette

Netiquette is Internet etiquette, the set of do's and don'ts that have evolved over the decades that the Internet has been in existence. Most rules of netiquette are the same as those that apply in other communication, but some are a little different. Here are ways to make friends and avoid offending people online:

Treat people like people. Since all you usually see when sending messages in an online community is your computer, it's easy to forget that you are conversing with real people. Treat people with the respect and humor you would use if you were speaking with them in person. If you disagree with something someone says, attack the idea, not the person.

Lurk first. In online communities, *lurking* is listening without saying anything. The word doesn't carry any threatening or negative overtones. Lurking is fine—in fact, when you join a new community, it's a good idea to lurk for a while (a few days or a week) before saying anything, to make sure that you know the ropes. Although they're rare, a small number of communities discourage lurkers, requiring active participation from all members. Generally, it's better to wait until you have something to say before chiming in.

Read the FAQ. Most communities have an *FAQ*, a list of frequently asked questions and their answers. It may be part of the welcome message you receive when you join the community, it may be posted on the community's Web site, or it may be distributed monthly. Before asking a question, make sure that it isn't answered in the FAQ. If you ask a question that is answered in the FAQ, other subscribers may sneer at you.

Send private remarks by private e-mail. If you have something to say that would be of interest to only one person, send it in private e-mail to that person (if possible) rather than post it to the community. If you are using IRC, "whisper," or send a private instant message, to the person.

Don't shout or make your messages hard to read. Shouting is achieved by typing in ALL CAPITAL LETTERS, so use all capitals only if you want to shout. Check your spelling and punctuation if you want other people to be able to read your message easily (rather than delete them after the first sentence), especially in a business-related community, where you want to show a professional face.

Quote the relevant part of the messages you refer to. If you are responding to a message from someone else, include a copy of enough of the other person's message to remind readers what the discussion is about. (This guideline doesn't apply to most Web-based message boards, where messages are usually shorter, and the previous messages are easily visible on the Web site.) Don't include the other person's entire message: Delete the headers and the parts of the message you aren't referring to.

Don't say anything if you don't have something new to add. Except in the most informal and chatty of communities, people usually hate postings that say only "Me too!" or "I don't know." Don't send a message if you don't have the answer to a question: Leave the airways free for those who do have the answer.

Don't post a private message from someone else. This guideline follows from the fact that when someone sends you a message (e-mail message, newsgroup posting, or other text) that he or she wrote, the author owns the copyright on that message. Legally, you don't have the right to distribute that message without his or her permission. Naturally, someone is unlikely to sue you over the copyright of one little message, but the principle is a good one: People own the words they write and should be consulted about what you plan to do with them. Following this guideline also prevents you from embarrassing someone by accidentally showing a message to the wrong people.

Avoiding Flames

If you don't want to get *flamed* (receive highly critical messages), here are some other tips:

Don't try to manage the conversation unless you are the community manager. Some duties of a community manager are to limit off-topic postings, prevent arguments from escalating into flamewars, and enforce other rules. If you aren't the community manager, don't post messages telling other people how to participate: That's the manager's job. It's bad enough when someone posts a problematical message, without a flood of messages complaining about the original message. If you must say something, send a private note to the person whose behavior you'd like to change.

Don't respond to trolls. A *troll* is a message that deliberately tries to provoke angry responses. If everyone would ignore deliberately obnoxious messages, they wouldn't disrupt the discussion. Instead, many community members feel the need to set the author straight, and a long round of arguing ensues—just what the person who posts the troll is trying to achieve. If people sound like they are unlikely to change their minds, don't bother trying. Of course, new community members may not recognize a troll, thinking that it's a sincere message: The community manager should respond

> **"Cat—The Other White Meat"**
>
> *A classic series of trolls occurred when someone joined the* rec.pets.cats *newsgroup, a discussion group for cat lovers, and posted recipes for roasted cat. If the message had been ignored, the newsgroup could have continued with its normal discussions. Instead, newsgroup members rose to the bait and posted outraged responses, and a flamewar of complaints and finger pointing resulted, making the group completely useless for its normal purposes for months.*

to newcomer responses to trolls privately, avoiding taking up the community's time and attention.

Safety First

The Internet is a big place, and you don't know who's out there. Participating in a business-related community, or in a closed community where you know the members personally, doesn't pose many dangers. But large, open communities in which people share information about their personal lives can pose problems. Here are some tips for avoiding them:

Don't assume that people don't know who you are. From your e-mail address, it's not hard to find out your name, address, and phone number. If you want to participate in a mailing list without using your regular address, get a Hotmail or Yahoo Mail account and send your messages from there. To participate in a newsgroup without using your regular address, post from a public, Web-based news service, such as **Deja.com** (at http://www.deja.com/usenet/). Web-based message boards don't usually gather much information about you, but watch out what data you supply when you register (for sites that require registration).

Don't provide irrelevant identifying information. Although a determined person can probably figure out who you are, there's no point making it easy.

Don't assume that messages will stay within the community. Assume that whatever you post on the Internet can be found by your employer, your school, and your mom. Many mailing lists maintain archives, and most newsgroups are archived on sites like **Deja.com** (http://www.deja.com/usenet/) and **RemarQ** (http://www.remarq.com/).

After you are connected to the Internet, never type your password. There is absolutely no reason to type your Internet password for any reason while participating in any online community.

Don't believe everything you hear. Specifically, people may not be who they say they are. Just because someone says that she is the purchasing manager at a large corporation doesn't mean she is in a position to place a large order with your company. And if someone says that she is a slender 19-year-old female college freshman, he might as easily be a curious 12-year-old boy or a lonely 52-year-old man.

Report problems to the authorities. If a participant contacts you privately with abusive, scary, or inappropriate messages, let the community manager know. If you know a person's e-mail address, you can also report the problem to his ISP (write to postmaster@*domain* or abuse@*domain* with the same domain as the person's e-mail address).

Don't let your kids participate without knowing some ground rules. If kids join online communities, they need to know not to reveal identifying information, not to believe everything they hear, not to type their password, and not to agree to meet people by phone or in person without your approval. They also need to know that if what they read online makes them uncomfortable, they should leave the conversation and talk to you.

Smileys and Abbreviations

To save typing (as well as to preserve that all-important in-group feeling), folks use lots of abbreviations in postings on online communities. Here are a few:

AFAIK.........as far as I know (but I may be wrong)

BTW ....by the way

FAQ ....frequently asked questions (and their answers)

FWIW.........for what it's worth

IANAL ....I am not a lawyer (but here's my opinion anyway)

IMHO.........in my humble opinion

IMNSHO....in my not so humble opinion

LOL ....laughing out loud

The Internet vs. The Real World

Even if you don't provide your real name in an online community, people may be able to figure out who you are. One woman participated in a sexually related community, thinking that she was anonymous. She didn't realize that the system allowed other members to find out her e-mail address. From her address, one community member figured out her name and city and looked her up in the phone book. She wasn't pleased to receive a call from a man she knew only from an online community, and who now knew where she lived. On the other hand, don't let your paranoia scare you off the Net altogether. One of the authors (John) has been active on Usenet for close to 20 years, each message has his address and phone number and mailing address in the signature, and he can count on the fingers of one hand the number of unwanted calls he's gotten as a result.

OTOH .... on the other hand

RL .... real life (as opposed to life on the Internet)

ROFL .... rolling on the floor, laughing (also ROFL and ROTFL)

RTFM .... read the manual

TIA .... thanks in advance

If you can't figure out an abbreviation, look it up in the Jargon File, at http://www.jargon.org/html/.

Smileys are little faces created by characters. To understand them, tip your head to the left. Here are a few examples:

| `:-)` | smiling | `;-)` | smiling and winking |
| `:-(` | frowning | `:-P` | sticking out tongue |

It's easy to overuse acronyms and smileys, but in informal discussions they can save lots of typing.

Other Ideas

Don't join too many communities at one time. It takes time to get to know the style of a community—online or in real life—as well as the people in the community. You'll spend many hours exchanging messages with community members before you truly feel a part of the group. Don't join another community until you are comfortable in the ones you already participate in (or have decided to leave one).

Use separate accounts or personalities for business and personal stuff. When you post messages to a mailing list or newsgroup, your message usually ends with your signature. If you program computers for a living and are participating in a model airplane newsgroup, you might want to use a different signature for your newsgroup messages, one with the URL of your model airplane Web site, for example. Some e-mail and newsreader programs allow you to create separate *personalities*, or at least separate signatures, for the different communities you post to. You can also consider using a Web-based e-mail address (like a Hotmail or Yahoo Mail address) for participating in mailing lists, although you then have to remember to check your mail at that Web site or, if the site permits, configure your mail program to pick up mail from the site.

Try to avoid posting messages when you are angry. If a message really ticks you off, go ahead and compose a really scathing reply. But don't send it. Instead, send it to yourself so that you can decide later whether it's really worth posting. Or read it on your screen, congratulate yourself for writing such a brilliant rebuttal, and delete the message. Another approach is to take a walk around the block before composing your response. Or use our mother's method: To remind yourself that the person you are angry at is a regular flesh-and-blood person with faults and foibles, tell yourself that her feet probably hurt while composing the original message.

Part II

Mailing List Communities

Chapter Four
Finding, Joining, and Participating in Mailing Lists

Mailing lists are the oldest type of Internet community since e-mail is one of the oldest Internet services. They are also one of the most popular forms of online community. A mailing list consists of a list of *subscribers* and a special address, called the *list address*, for reaching those subscribers. E-mail messages sent to the list address are forwarded to all the subscribers, as shown in Figure 4-1.

For example, if a mailing list named chickens@gurus.com is about domestic poultry (this is a theoretical list), messages sent to that address would be passed along to the list subscribers (people who had signed up to discuss chickens). If one person posted a question about whether chickens need extra light to lay in the winter, all subscribers would receive the question. When one or more

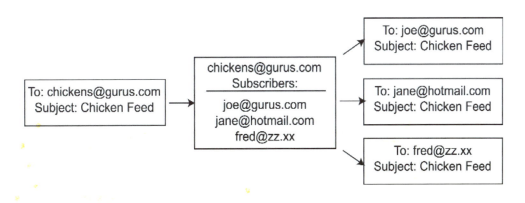

Figure 4-1: A mailing list distributes messages to all its subscribers.

subscribers posted answers to the question (yes, at least 15 hours a day), all subscribers would see the answer. An ongoing discussion results, with people chiming in with their theories and experience.

Where Mailing Lists Live

It's possible to run a mailing list by hand, and some lists are run that way. If you want to run a very small list, you can tell the subscribers to send messages to you, and you can forward messages to all the subscribers. (Chapter 5 has tips for automating this process if you have a smart e-mail program.) However, this process can be lots of work for the list manager, and messages don't get distributed until the manager downloads and reads his e-mail.

List Servers

Years ago (in 1986), an intelligent and creative programmer named Eric Thomas decided that distributing messages was a better task for a computer program than for a person. He wrote the first *list server*, a program that handles the distribution of mailing list managers automatically. A list server program has two parts:

Subscriber database. This program maintains the list of subscribers. Rather than require the list manager to handle subscriptions and unsubscriptions, the list server can accept e-mailed messages containing commands that add and delete people from the subscriber list. See the sections later in this chapter that have specific instructions for each list server program, to see which commands each list server understands.

Message distributor. This program receives messages sent to the list address and sends messages out to the subscribers of the list.

The first list server program, named **LISTSERV** (http://www.lsoft.com/), is still widely used and well maintained. Other popular list servers are **ListProc** (http://www.cren.net/), **Majordomo** (http://www.greatcircle.com/majordomo/), and **Lyris** (http://www.lyris.com). Other list servers are described at the **Mailing List Gurus Page: Mailing List Management Programs** page, at http://lists.gurus.com/mlms.html.

You communicate with list servers by (what else!) sending e-mail messages the program can understand. Each list server understands a slightly different set of commands. You send commands to subscribe to a list, unsubscribe from a list, and change your list subscription options. Some list servers have recently added Web interfaces so that you can subscribe, unsubscribe, set your subscription

Chapter 4: Finding, Joining, and Participating in Mailing Lists **39**

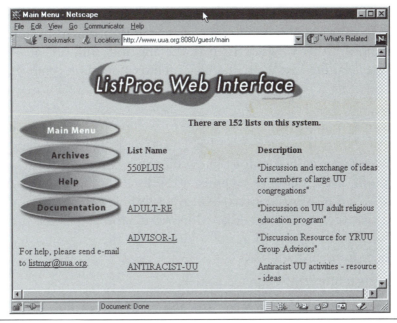

Figure 4-2: The ListProc list server also lets you subscribe to and read mailing lists over the Web.

options, and even read current and archived messages on the Web. Figure 4-2 shows the Web interface for the ListProc list server.

Mailing List Web Sites

Now that the Web has superceded e-mail in glitz, if not in usefulness, Web sites have emerged that act as list servers. You visit the Web site to subscribe to the list, to read the messages on the list, and to sign off if you don't want to continue to participate. You can have the list messages sent to you by e-mail if you'd prefer to read them using your e-mail program.

Some of these Web sites provide a "portal" to their mailing lists, letting you search for mailing lists by topic and read the messages on the Web site. One site, Topica, provides a searchable database of lists that includes both Topica-hosted lists and hundreds of thousands of other lists.

These Web sites support themselves by selling ad space in two places: on the Web pages that are displayed as you search for, subscribe to, and read lists, and in the messages themselves, adding advertisements at the end of each message posted to the list.

The most popular Web sites that host mailing lists are eGroups, ListBot, and Topica. (ONElist was also popular and was recently acquired by and combined with eGroups.) Other sites are listed in the appendix and on the **Mailing List Gurus Page: Mailing List Web Sites** page, at http://lists.gurus.com/webmlms.html.

eGroups (includes ONElist)

In addition to mailing lists, eGroups lets your group share files, have online voice chats, and share a group calendar. The eGroups home page lets you search for lists by topic, even if you don't know the exact name of the list you want to join. *Note:* In 1999, eGroups acquired ONElist, another popular mailing list Web site. When eGroups converted all the ONElist lists into eGroups lists, it promised that the original ONElist addresses for these lists would continue to work, while providing new eGroups addresses for the lists—just replace onelist with egroups in the list address.

Home page: http://www.egroups.com/

Registration: You can search for lists and read the postings on many public lists without registering, but you have to register to subscribe to lists.

Home page of a specific list: http://www.egroups.com/group/*listname*/info.html

Help: http://www.egroups.com/help/ or info@egroups.com

Help with a specific list: *listname*-owner@eGroups.com

Report unsolicited mail from eGroups or ONElist: abuse@egroups.com or http://www.egroups.com/info/nospam.html

ListBot

ListBot belongs to Microsoft and is labeled with its MSN brand. This well-designed mailing list site makes it easy to subscribe to a mailing list if you already know its name, although there's no way to search for lists by topic (yet):

Home page: http://www.listbot.com/

Registration: You don't have to register to subscribe to lists.

Home page of a specific list: http://*listname*.listbot.com

Help: http://www.listbot.com/faq.shtml

Help with a specific list: *listname*-owner@listbot.com

Trouble unsubscribing: http://www.listbot.com/cgi-bin/subscriber

Report unsolicited mail from ListBot: abuse@listbot.com

Chapter 4: Finding, Joining, and Participating in Mailing Lists **41**

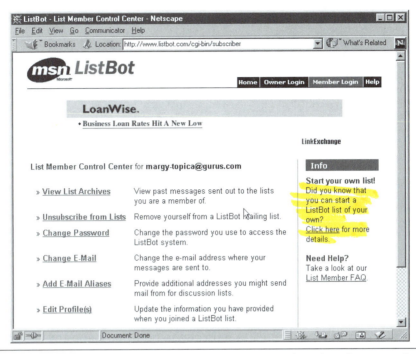

Figure 4-3: ListBot lets you browse, subscribe to, and read mailing lists over the Web as well as by e-mail.

Figure 4-3 shows the List Member Control Center page you see when you subscribe to a list.

Topica

Topica provides a *portal* (gateway) for mailing lists and includes the Liszt mailing list database for searching for a list by topic. It's easy to search for lists by topic, browse the messages (if the list is open for reading by nonsubscribers), and then subscribe if the list looks interesting. You have the option of receiving the messages by regular e-mail or reading them on the Topica Web site. Figure 4-4 shows the My Topica page you see when you register as a Topica user.

Home page: http://www.topica.com/

Registration: You can search for lists and read the postings on many public lists without registering, but you have to register to subscribe to lists.

Home page of a specific list: http://www.topica.com/lists/*listname*/

Help: Click the Help link at the bottom of the home page.

Report unsolicited mail from Topica: abuse@topica.com

Figure 4-4: Topica helps you find and subscribe to both Topica-hosted and other lists.

Mailing List Address

Each mailing list, whether run from a list server or Web site, has a number of addresses. Here are the most important ones.

List Address

Messages sent to this address are distributed to the subscribers of the list. (Not every message sent to the list address is distributed—some lists allow only subscribers to post messages, and some lists have moderators reviewing and approving each posting.) The list address is usually the name of the list followed by @ and the site hosting the list. For example, a list named jokes hosted at egroups.com would have the list address jokes@egroups.com.

Administrative Address

To subscribe to (*join*) or unsubscribe from (*leave*) most mailing lists managed by LISTSERV, ListProc, Majordomo, and other traditional list servers, you send commands to the *administrative address* of the list server. The administrative address is usually the name of the list server followed by @ and the host computer on which the list server runs. For example, the administrative address for the lists hosted by the Majordomo program running at gurus.com is majordomo@gurus.com. When you send commands to this address, they are read and executed by the Majordomo list server program.

Mailing list Web sites don't provide an administrative address for their lists. Instead, you can usually subscribe or unsubscribe by sending a blank message to a special address for the specific list: See "Subscribing to Web-based Lists by E-mail," later in this chapter.

> **Don't Send Commands to the List Address!**
>
> *To subscribe to or unsubscribe from a list, send a signoff or unsubscribe command to the administrative address, where the list server program will see it. Don't send the command to the list address, where all the subscribers will see it. This mistake usually earns you ridicule and criticism from the list subscribers because many people are sick of seeing misdirected signoff messages.*

Manager Address

Almost every mailing list has an address that reaches the list manager (or list owner). For most lists, the address is the list address with -request added just before the @. For example, the manager address for the chickens@gurus.com list would be chickens-request@gurus.com. If that doesn't work, try the list address with -owner added just before the @.

Subscription and Unsubscription Addresses

Some mailing lists have special addresses to which you can write to subscribe or unsubscribe to the list. For example, a list managed by the Lyris list server has the subscription address *listname*-subscribe@*hostname*. To subscribe to the list, you can just send a blank message to that address. Similarly, Lyris lists have an unsubscription address at *listname*-unsubscribe@*hostname* to which you can write to get off the list.

Home Page

Mailing lists hosted on mailing list Web sites automatically have a home page generated by the Web site. Here are the URLs for lists hosted by the most popular Web sites (replace *listname* with the exact name of the list):

eGroups: http://www.egroups.com/group/*listname*/info.html

ListBot: http://*listname*.listbot.com

Topica: http://www.topica.com/lists/*listname*/

For mailing lists with @onelist.com in the list address, go to the eGroups Web site and search for the list name.

Lists hosted on list servers may not have home pages because list servers don't automatically generate them. However, many list managers set up home pages for their lists, to provide subscription and unsubscription instructions, the FAQ for the list, and (sometimes) searchable list archives. Look in the welcome message for the list for the address of its home page, or search the Web for the name of the list.

What You Need to Join

All you need to join a mailing list is an e-mail address. Even if you don't have your own Internet account, you can sign up for an e-mail address at one of the many free Web-based e-mail services. Here are a few reputable ones:

MSN Hotmail
   http://www.hotmail.com/
MailCity
   http://www.mailcity.com/
Yahoo! Mail
   http://mail.yahoo.com/

Even if you do have an e-mail address, you might want to use a different address for your mailing list subscriptions. If you access the Internet from work and you want to participate in non-job-related mailing lists, you might not want your recreational list messages mixed in with your work messages (in fact, your employer may forbid it).

Finding Mailing Lists

Because hundreds of thousands of mailing lists are on the Internet, finding the one you want can be hard. Luckily, there are a number of searchable databases of mailing lists. Go to one of the following Web sites, type a word or phrase describing the topic you want to discuss, and see what turns up:

Do List.net: Lets you search by topic in either English or French.
   http://www.dolist.net/annuaire_en.asp
Liszt: Lets you search for mailing lists based on the list's names and descriptions or on words in messages in list archives. Liszt also categorizes hundreds of recommended lists.
   http://www.liszt.com/
PAML: Publicly Accessible Mailing Lists: One of the oldest lists of lists, maintained by Stephanie da Silva.
   http://www.neosoft.com/internet/paml/

Tile.net: Includes an alphabetical listing of lists by name and by domain (that is, the computer on which the list is hosted). You can also search lists by keyword.
http://tile.net/lists/

Topica: A newer list site, combining the Liszt searchable database with a free mailing-list hosting service: See the section "Mailing List Web Sites," earlier in this chapter. Topica sorts the results of a search by category, which makes it easier to find the list you are looking for.
http://www.topica.com/

These databases of mailing lists usually don't include mailing lists hosted at mailing list Web sites, unless the list owners have thought to submit their list information to the database. Some mailing list Web sites, including eGroups and Topica, provide the search box to find related lists at that site.

Steps for Participating in a Mailing List

Here is an overview of the task you are faced with if you want to participate in a mailing list. For specific instructions, skip down to the sections later in this chapter with instructions for Web-based lists, LISTSERV lists, ListProc lists, Majordomo lists, or Lyris lists.

If the list you are interested in is managed using another program, try sending the command `help` or `info listname` to the administrative address for the list, and read the instructions you receive.

Finding Out about the List

First off, get information about the list, to make sure that you want to join it. The informational message you receive should include a general description of the list, along with instructions for subscribing, rules for participating, and an address for writing to the list manager. For most list servers, send the command `info listname` to the administrative address for the list. For Web-based lists, the Web site contains information.

Subscribing

If the list looks interesting, you can go ahead and subscribe. How you subscribe and sign off from a mailing list depends on how it's managed. You have to contact the computer that hosts the list—either the list server program or the mailing list Web site—with the name of the list you want to join and your e-mail address. Many lists require that you confirm your subscription, to avoid *mailbombing* (when a malefactor subscribes someone else to lots of mailing lists so that the innocent victim's mailbox fills up with unwanted e-mail from all the lists). The confirmation usually involves the list server or mailing list Web site sending you a confirmation message to which you must reply.

Some lists require the list manager to approve the subscription (for example, lists that are open only to members of a club, committee, or class). The list manager may get back to you with questions about who you are and why you want to be on the list.

Saving Your Welcome Message

After you have subscribed to a list, you usually receive a *welcome message*, with information about the list. The welcome message usually includes how to unsubscribe, how to post messages to the list, how to contact the list manager, how to change your subscription options, and the rules for acceptable postings. Be sure to save this message! You will need it eventually, when you want to unsubscribe or you have a problem.

For Web-based lists, make a note of the mailing list's home page—the main page for the list. If you subscribed on the Web, you are probably looking at it; otherwise, see the section "Mailing List Web Sites," earlier in this chapter, to see how to find the list's home page. If you use Netscape Navigator, add the page to your bookmarks by pressing `Ctrl+D`. If you use Internet Explorer, add the page to your favorites by choosing Favorites|Add to Favorites from the menu bar.

Reading the Messages

List messages arrive in your e-mail inbox mixed in with the rest of your messages (see the section "Separating Your List Messages from the Rest of Your Mail," later in this chapter, for how to tell your e-mail program to display them separately). Once you are signed up and begin to receive messages from the mailing list, *lurk* (just listen, without posting) for a while—a week is good—to get an idea of the style of the list. Some lists are chatty, some are formal, and some are downright hostile, and you'll do better to match their style. See Chapter 3 for more pointers on list etiquette.

For Web-based lists (or any list that has a Web interface—check the welcome message you received), you can also read the list's messages on the Web site. If the list is configured so that only subscribers may read messages, you need to log in to the Web site before you can display the list's messages.

Posting Messages When You Have Something to Say

To post a message to a mailing list once you are subscribed, just send the message to the list address for the list (see "Mailing List Addresses," earlier in this chapter). List postings are regular e-mail messages, which you compose with your usual e-mail program (or on a Web site, if you use a Web-based mail service like Hotmail or MailCity). For Web-based lists, you can also go to the home page for the list and follow the links to compose and post a message.

Before you post to a list, be sure that you have done the following:

- **Read the welcome message** you received when you joined the list, especially the parts that explain what topics are appropriate, what topics are banned, and what other rules apply. Also refer to the section "What You Can Post," in Chapter 2, for rules that apply to most lists.
- **Follow the etiquette, privacy, and other guidelines** in Chapter 3.
- **Turn off formatting** in your e-mail program (see the section "Turning Off Message Formatting," later in this chapter, to find out how). Otherwise, many subscribers will see garbage characters mixed in with your text.

Check the Footers of Mailing List Messages to See How to Sign Off

If you want to sign off from a mailing list, take a careful look at a message you receive from the list. Frequently, instructions for unsubscribing appear at the end of the headers (just after the To, From, and Subject lines) or at the end of the message. Do not *post a message to the list asking to be taken off; instead, send a private message to the list manager if you can't figure out how to unsubscribe.*

Replying to Messages

If you click Reply to reply to a message from a list, be sure to check the address to which your new message is addressed. Some lists distribute their messages with the list address as the Reply-to address (the *Reply-to-address* is a line in the message headers that tells your e-mail program how to address replies to the message). Other lists use the original sender's address as the Reply-to address. You can change the address to which your message is addressed, and you should do so if it's wrong—just copy the list address or the address of the sender from the original message to the To line of your reply. Send a reply to the list if you think that lots of people on the list will be interested in your reply. Send a reply to the sender if your message is private or will be of interest only to her.

Seeing Who Else Is on the List

Most lists let subscribers see who else is on the list. The list manager may have turned off this feature, to provide subscribers with more privacy. Some list servers allow subscribers to *conceal* their names (to omit them from the list of subscribers that other subscribers can see).

If you send a command by e-mail to request the subscriber list, you receive it by return e-mail. Some names and addresses may be omitted for subscribers who asked to have their names concealed.

Reading the List Archives

Many lists save all past messages in files that are accessible by e-mail or over the Web by anyone, by only the subscribers, or by only the list manager. How you see the archives (if they are available to you) depends on where the list is based. Some lists don't have archives, to preserve the

---

Having Trouble Posting?

You subscribe to a list, try to post a message to the list, and get back an error message saying that you're not a list subscriber. What's up?

Some e-mail systems add a subdomain name to your e-mail address, just before the domain name and after the @. For example, several years ago MSN (Microsoft Network) users found their e-mail addresses (in the format xxx@msn.com) suddenly including the machine name "email" (xxx@email.msn.com) or "classic" (xxx@classic.msn.com). List servers didn't recognize these addresses and rejected postings from subscribers.

The same thing may happen to you. If a mailing list rejects a post from you as a nonsubscriber when you are a subscriber, take a look at the headers of your outgoing messages. Look for other forms that your e-mail address might take, including the addition of a subdomain to the right of the @. If your address appears in other forms, let the list manager know about it. The manager may be able to tell the list server that you have several addresses.

If you use eGroups, ListBot, or Topica, you can tell Topica that you post from several different addresses. In eGroups, click My Space and then User Info and then Add Alias. In ListBot, log in and click Add E-Mail Aliases. In Topica, click My Topica and then Email Addresses.

---

privacy of subscribers and to promote spontaneity (it can be embarrassing when someone dredges up a silly remark you made months ago). If the list has archives, you may be able to search it for messages by a specific person or that contain a specific word or phrase. It's a good idea to search the list archives before asking a question, to make sure that the question hasn't already been answered on this list.

If a list has a home page with archives, the easiest way to read back messages is on the Web. Otherwise, it's a two-step process via e-mail: First, you request a list of the files that contain the list archives (usually one file per month), and then you request a specific file.

Setting Your Mailing List Options

Once you are subscribed to and participating in a mailing list, you may want to change your *list options*, the configuration settings that control how and when you receive your messages. Your options, and how you change them, depend on which program manages the list. This section explains what the most often-used options do. For specific instructions for changing your list options, see the section later in this chapter that describes the type of list you are using: Web based, LISTSERV, ListProc, Majordomo, or Lyris.

Holding Your Mail

When you get back from a vacation, it's miserable to find thousands of messages waiting for you. You can turn off the mail from mailing lists temporarily and turn it back on when you return. Alternatively, you can unsubscribe from the list before you go and resubscribe when you return, but this method has several disadvantages. You lose your list settings (for example, whether you receive digests or individual messages), and, if the list is closed, you have to ask the list manager to let you back in.

The list server does not save up the messages you would have received while you were gone—you just miss them. For lists with archives, you can always read the missing messages from the archives.

Receiving Digests

For lists that generate many messages a day, you may prefer to receive each day's postings bunched together into one long message, called a *digest*. Some list servers and Web-based lists can do this, and some offer digests in two formats:

> Text digests. The messages appear one after the other in the body of the message. Some list servers provide a table of contents at the beginning of the message, listing the subjects of the messages.

MIME digests. Each message arrives as a separate attachment to the digest message. If your e-mail program can't handle MIME formatting, MIME digests look like a mess.

Most lists that offer digests send them out daily, or more often if the size of the digest reaches a set limit. As a subscriber, you can't control how often digests are sent.

Changing Your Address

When you change ISPs, your e-mail address changes, too. For every mailing list you are subscribed to, you've got to change your subscription address. Some lists let you change your address, and others require you to unsubscribe and resubscribe. Topica lets you have several addresses, and you can specify which list messages go to which address.

If you run into trouble changing your address, either unsubscribe and re-subscribe or write to the list manager and provide both your old and new addresses.

Concealing Your Participation

Some mailing list Web sites and list servers let you conceal your name and address so that they don't appear on listings of subscribers. The list managers can still see who you are, but other subscribers cannot. Of course, your e-mail address still appears on messages you post.

Getting Help

First, read the welcome message you received when you subscribed to the list. This message should contain instructions for unsubscribing, changing your subscription options, and other helpful advice.

AOL vs. Digests

If you have an AOL account and you receive mailing list digests, you may find them arriving in an unexpected format—as ZIP files. In an effort to save disk storage and download times, AOL converts long messages and attachments into ZIP files, or compressed files that need to be uncompressed using WinZip, ZipMagic, or another unzipping program. MIME format digests arrive ZIPped, too. Either switch your digests to text format, if your list server supports text digests, or learn to deal with ZIP files. You can download WinZip from **Nico Mak Software***, at* http://www.winzip.com/, *or ZipMagic, from* **Mijenix Software***, at* http://www.mijenix.com/. *Mac users can get unzipping programs from the* **Mac Orchard** *site, at* http://www.macorchard.com/.

For Web-based mailing lists, click the Help link on the Web site or write to support@*domain*, replacing *domain* with the domain name of the Web site (for example, listbot.com or egroups.com). See the section "Mailing List Web Sites," earlier in this chapter, for sources of help for the most popular mailing list Web sites.

For lists managed by a list server program, you can get a list of commands by sending the single word `help` in the text of a message to the administrative address for the list.

Another way to get help is to ask the list manager. Write to the manager at the manager address, which is usually the list address with -request inserted just before the @. The welcome message you received when you subscribed should also include the list manager's address.

Instructions For Web-Based Lists

To join, read, leave, or change the settings for a Web-based list, follow the steps in this section.

Web-based Lists - Getting Information

Go to the home page about the list. If the list address for the list ends in @egroups.com, @listbot.com, @onelist.com, @topica.com, or the domain of some other mailing list Web site, you can go to that site to get information. (For lists hosted at onelist.com, go to the eGroups Web site.) How can you tell whether the *domain* (the part after the @) is a mailing list Web site? Type www. into your Web browser followed by the domain name (for example, www.egroups.com) and see whether the Web page offers to help you subscribe to a list. The section "Mailing List Web Sites," earlier in this chapter, lists the most popular sites.

Web-based Lists - Subscribing

You can subscribe from the list's home page or by sending e-mail messages.

Subscribing to Web-based Lists on the Web

Follow these steps to subscribe to a Web-based mailing list (for example, to subscribe to a Topica-based list about a software program you are struggling with):

1. **Go to the Web site.** See "Mailing List Web Sites," earlier in this chapter, for the URLs of mailing list Web sites. Go to http://www.domainname/, where *domainname* is the part of the e-mail address of the list after the @. For example, if someone tells you about a list at knitting-

crochet@egroups.com, go to http://www.egroups.com/. For ListBot, you must already know the name of the list you want to subscribe to: Go to the Web page http://*listname*.listbot.com, replacing *listname* with the exact name of the list. Then skip to Step 6.

2. **Register**. If the Web site requests that you register before you can subscribe to a list, click the Register, Join, Log In, or similar link. Registration is free and quick—you fill out a Web form with your e-mail address, your name, and sometimes some demographic information (this information is usually optional, so try leaving the boxes blank). The Web site sends a confirmation message to your e-mail address to confirm that it's really you filling out the form. Once you've confirmed your registration by replying to that message (or clicking a Web link in the message), you're registered.

3. **Find the list you want to join**. If you know the name of the list, type it into the search box. Otherwise, try searching for words that relate to the topic you want to discuss. Some mailing list Web sites have a top-down topic arrangement of lists, so you can click a general topic (like Recreation) to see a page about lists of that type, with more links to more specific topics (like Crafts, Music, and Sports).

4. **Read about the list**. Read the description of the list and other information the Web site displays. Some lists let you read the current day's messages, or the archive of back messages, to see whether the messages are what you were hoping for.

5. **Click the Subscribe link**. The link may be named something else, like Join Community or Join This List.

6. **Fill out the form**. The Web site may ask how you'd like to read the messages on the mailing list—on the Web site, by e-mail, or not at all. Choose to read them on the Web site if you'd like to read the list messages only from time to time. If you'd like to see all messages as they appear, it's usually more convenient to read the messages by e-mail, so you don't have to remember to return to the Web site. ListBot, which doesn't require you to register before subscribing to a list, asks you to enter a password at this point.

7. **Confirm your subscription**. The Web site may send you an e-mail message to confirm that you really want to subscribe. Not all mailing list Web sites require a confirmation, since you may have confirmed your e-mail address when you registered (see Step 2).

You're subscribed! Wait for e-mail messages from the list to appear in your e-mail inbox (if you chose that option). At eGroups and Topica, you can read the messages at the Web site by clicking the Messages, Community, Discussion, or similar link.

Subscribing to Web-based Lists by E-mail

If you are already registered at the mailing list Web site that hosts the list, you may be able to subscribe by e-mail. Subscribe by sending a blank message to *listname*-subscribe@*hostname*. For example, to subscribe to the nprpuzzle@topica.com list (which discusses Will Shortz's puzzles on the National Public Radio show "Weekend Edition"), send a blank message to nprpuzzle-subscribe@topica.com.

eGroups and Topica provide an easy way to see the lists you are subscribed to. When you log in with your e-mail address and password, these sites display a page with the lists you have joined, with links for reading the list or changing your subscription options. Convenient!

Web-based Lists - Unsubscribing

To unsubscribe from a Web-based list, display the list's home page in your Web browser. Then click the Unsubscribe, Sign Off, Modify My Membership, Options, or Member Settings button (or a similar button).

Most mailing list Web sites also let you unsubscribe by e-mail. Write to the unsubscription address for the list, which is the list address with -unsubscribe inserted just before the @. For example, to unsubscribe from the venezuelans@listbot.com list, write to venezuelans-unsubscribe@listbot.com.

Web-based Lists - Seeing the List of Subscribers

Not all mailing list Web sites let you see the names and addresses of other subscribers. To protect subscribers from having their addresses "harvested" by e-mail junk mailers, these sites may omit or garble addresses. Go to the home page for the list and follow the links to view the members, if the list is configured for the subscriber list to be visible. Some Web-based lists also display other information about subscribers, like their names, locations, and other details.

Web-based Lists - Changing Your Subscription Options

You can change your subscription settings from the list's Web site. Start at the list's home page and follow the links to change your subscription settings.

Web-based Lists - Stopping Mail
Some mailing list Web sites don't provide a way to stop your mail. Some sites let you set your subscription to "Web only," which allows you to read the messages on the Web site without sending you the messages by e-mail.

Web-based Lists - Receiving Digests
Go to the list's home page and set your subscription option to receive digests. Most (but not all) mailing list Web sites provide daily digests.

Web-based Lists - Changing Your Address
Most mailing list Web sites let you update your e-mail address from a page on the Web site. Go to the home page for the list and follow the links to change your user information, which includes your mailing address. Some Web-based lists let you use several addresses, specifying which address to use for which list.

Web-based Lists - Concealing Your Name and Address
To make sure that your name doesn't appear on subscriber lists, go to the home page for the list and change your subscription settings. Some mailing list Web sites don't provide a way to conceal your address. Others conceal the real names and complete addresses of all subscribers when presenting messages to nonsubscribers, but display complete addresses to subscribers.

Web-based Lists - Reading the Archives
In addition to reading the archives of lists you subscribe to, you can read other lists on mailing list Web sites. Many Web-based lists are configured by the list manager as publicly accessible. From the list's home page, follow the Messages or Archives links.

Instructions for LISTSERV Lists
To join, read, leave, or change the settings for a LISTSERV list, you send e-mail messages to the administrative address for the list—the LISTSERV program that manages the list. The administrative address is in the form LISTSERV@*hostname*. For example, to subscribe to annerice@lists.psu.edu (a LISTSERV-managed list to discuss the popular novels of Anne Rice), you send a message to LISTSERV@lists.psu.edu.

In the commands that follow, replace *listname* with the name of the list (the part of the list address before the @). Send the commands in the text of an e-mail message to the admi-nistrative address (not the list address). See

Chapter 4: Finding, Joining, and Participating in Mailing Lists

the nearby sidebar, "Sending Commands to List Servers," for details about com-posing e-mail messages to send commands.

The LISTSERV program has an annoying habit of sending two confirmations for every command—one to tell you what happened and the other to tell you how many milliseconds of processing time the job took. Just delete these messages!

LISTSERV Lists - Getting Information

In the text of a message to the administrative address for the list, type this command:

`info listname`

In response, you receive the informational message about the list.

LISTSERV Lists - Subscribing

Send this command to subscribe to the list:

`subscribe listname yourname`

Replace *yourname* with your actual name (not your e-mail address, which the list server can glean from the headers of your message). You can abbreviate the subscribe command to sub. The names

Sending Commands to List Servers

When you send a command to the administrative address for a list (for example, to subscribe or unsubscribe), it doesn't matter what you type for the subject of the message—the list server ignores the subject line. Type the command(s) in the text of the message and send it as you would send any other e-mail message. Capitalization doesn't matter in most commands. If your e-mail program uses formatting (boldface, italics, etc.), turn formatting off. Type each command (if you are sending more than one) on a separate line, and don't leave any blank lines.

Omit the signature from your e-mail if you can so that the list server doesn't try to interpret your signature as commands. If you can't omit the signature, type end *on a line by itself after the subscribe command. Figure 4-5 shows a message to the ListProc program at* uua.org, *asking for information about the UUA-L list.*

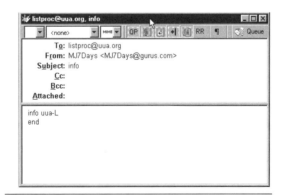

Figure 4-5: Sending commands to the administrative address for a list.

of many LISTSERV mailing lists end with -L—be sure to type the letter *L* rather than the number 1.

When the list server receives your `subscribe` command, it sends you a response. Most LISTSERV lists require that you confirm your subscription, by replying to the message you receive. Then you receive the welcome message for the list.

LISTSERV Lists - Unsubscribing
Send this command to sign off from the list:
> `signoff listname`
>
> or
>
> `unsubscribe listname`

LISTSERV Lists - Seeing the List of Subscribers
Send this command to receive a list of subscribers:
> `review listname`

LISTSERV Lists - Stopping Mail
Send this command to stop getting messages from the list:
> `set listname nomail`

Send this command to start receiving mail again:
> `set listname mail`

LISTSERV Lists - Receiving Digests
To receive digests rather than individual messages, send this command:
> `set listname digest`

To receive individual messages, send this command:
> `set listname nodigest`

LISTSERV Lists - Changing Your Address
LISTSERV doesn't have a command to change your e-mail address. Unsubscribe from your old address and resubscribe from your new address.

LISTSERV Lists - Concealing Your Name and Address
Send this command to prevent your name from appearing on subscriber lists:
> `set listname conceal`

LISTSERV Lists - Reading the Archives

Send this command to get a list of files that contain the archives:

`index listname`

You receive back a listing of the files. The archive filenames usually start with LOG followed by the two-digit year and two-digit month (for example, LOG0012 for the messages from December 2000). To see one of the files listed, send this command:

`get listname archivename`

Replace *archivename* with the name of the archive file. You receive back a message containing the messages for the month you requested.

Instructions for ListProc Lists

To join, read, leave, or change the settings for a ListProc list, you send e-mail messages to the administrative address for the list—the ListProc program that manages the list. The administrative address is in the form listproc@*hostname*.

Some ListProc installations provide the ListProc Web interface, a program that lets you use a Web site to subscribe, read messages, and other list-related tasks. Check the informational message (described in the next section) for the URL of the ListProc Web interface, if it exists for this list. If the ListProc Web interface is available, follow the instructions on the Web page. To use the interface, you must register using the same address with which you subscribed (or will subscribe) to mailing lists. Some lists are closed to nonsubscribers, and the Web interface needs to know who you are before it can decide which lists to give you access to. Figure 4-2, earlier in this chapter, shows one version of the ListProc Web interface.

The rest of this section about how to use ListProc describes sending commands to ListProc, but if your list is available via the ListProc Web interface, you can use the Web instead.

In the commands that follow, replace *listname* with the name of the list (the part of the list address before the @). Send the commands in the text of an e-mail message to the administrative address (not the list address). See the preceding sidebar, "Sending Commands to List Servers," for details about composing e-mail messages to send commands.

ListProc Lists - Getting Information

In the text of a message to the administrative address for the list, type this command:

`info listname`

In response, you receive the informational message about the list.

ListProc Lists - Subscribing
Send this command to subscribe to the list:
```
subscribe listname yourname
```
Replace *yourname* with your actual name (not your e-mail address, which the list server can glean from the headers of your message). You can abbreviate the subscribe command to sub. If the list name ends with -L—be sure to type the letter *L* rather than the number 1.

When the list server receives your `subscribe` command, it sends you a response. Most ListProc lists require that you confirm your subscription, by replying to the message you receive. Then you receive the welcome message for the list.

Be sure to save the welcome message because it includes your list password. Few commands require that you use your password, but you'll need to know it if you ever want to change the e-mail address by which you are subscribed. The welcome message recommends that you change your password, but almost no one ever does because the password is so rarely used. Don't bother!

ListProc Lists - Unsubscribing
Send this command to sign off from a list:
```
signoff listname
```
or
```
unsubscribe listname
```

ListProc Lists - Seeing the List of Subscribers
Send this command to receive a list of the subscribers to the list:
```
recipients listname
```
or
```
review listname
```

ListProc Lists - Stopping Mail
Send this command to stop getting messages from the list:
```
set listname mail postpone
```
Send this command to start receiving mail again as individual messages:
```
set listname mail ack
```

Or send one of these commands to start receiving mail again as digests (either MIME or text, as described in the next section):
```
set listname mail digest
set listname mail digest-nomime
```

ListProc Lists - Receiving Digests

To receive MIME digests rather than individual messages, send this command:
```
set listname mail digest
```

To receive text digests, send this command:
```
set listname mail digest-nomime
```

To receive individual messages, send this command:
```
set listname mail ack
```

ListProc Lists - Changing Your Address

Send this command to change the address to which ListProc sends you messages:
```
set listname address password new-address
```

Replace *password* with your list password and *new-address* with your new address. You can find your list password in the welcome message you received when you joined the list. It's usually a nine-digit number.

ListProc Lists - Concealing Your Name and Address

Send this command to prevent your name from appearing on subscriber lists:
```
set listname conceal yes
```

Send this command to allow your name to appear:
```
set listname conceal no
```

ListProc Lists - Reading the Archives

See the section "Reading the Archives of LISTSERV Lists," earlier in this chapter—the commands are exactly the same in ListProc. If your list is available using the ListProc Web interface, it's much more convenient than requesting archives by e-mail.

Instructions for Majordomo Lists

To join, read, leave, or change the settings for a Majordomo list, you send e-mail messages to the administrative address for the list—the Majordomo program that manages the list. The administrative address is in the form majordomo@*hostname*.

In the commands that follow, replace *listname* with the name of the list (the part of the list address before the @). Send the commands in the text of an e-mail message to the administrative address (not the list address). See the sidebar "Sending Commands to List Servers," earlier in this chapter, for details about composing e-mail messages to send commands.

The instructions below are for the widely used version 1.9x of Majordomo. A new version 2.0 was in development throughout 1999 and 2000 and may be available by the time you read this book. This version's commands will be similar, but with more options.

Majordomo Lists - Getting Information

In the text of a message to the administrative address for the list, type this command:

```
info listname
```

In response, you receive the informational message about the list.

Majordomo Lists - Subscribing

Send this command to subscribe to the list:

```
subscribe listname
```

You can abbreviate the `subscribe` command to `sub`. Majordomo lists let you subscribe from any e-mail account, by specifying your e-mail address on the command line, like this:

```
subscribe listname address
```

Replace *address* with the e-mail address you want to add to the mailing list.

When the list server receives your `subscribe` command, it sends you a response. Most Majordomo lists require that you confirm your subscription, by replying to the message you receive. Then you receive the welcome message for the list. The Majordomo confirmation message can be quite confusing. It requires that you copy a line out of the confirmation message and mail it back to the administrative address, something like this:

```
auth b78cb6a4 subscribe kideo yourname@yourisp.com
```

Reply with just that line, editing out everything else in the message.

Majordomo Lists - Unsubscribing

Send this command to sign off from the list:

```
unsubscribe listname
```

You can abbreviate the `unsubscribe` command to `unsub`. Majordomo lists let you unsubscribe from any e-mail account, by specifying your e-mail address on the command line, like this:

```
unsubscribe listname address
```

Replace *address* with the e-mail address you want to add to the mailing list.

Majordomo Lists - Seeing the List of Subscribers

Send this command to see a list of the list's subscribers:

```
who listname
```

Majordomo Lists - Stopping Mail

Majordomo doesn't have a way to hold your mail, so you have to unsubscribe and resubscribe.

Majordomo Lists - Receiving Digests

Majordomo handles digests differently from other list servers: a separate list distributes the messages as digests. The digested list always has the same name as the regular list, with `-digest` added just before the @. For example, to receive the chickens@gurus.com list as a daily digest, you'd unsubscribe from chickens@gurus.com and subscribe to chickens-digest@gurus.com.

To switch from receiving individual messages and begin receiving digests, sign off from the list and subscribe to the digested list. To switch back to individual messages, sign off from the digested list and subscribe to the regular list.

Majordomo Lists - Changing Your Address

Majordomo doesn't have a command to change your address; instead, unsubscribe and resubscribe. To remove your old address from the list, send this command:

```
unsubscribe listname old-address
```

Replace *old-address* with your old address. Then subscribe using your new address, by sending this command from your new account:

```
subscribe listname
```

Majordomo Lists - Concealing Your Name and Address

Majordomo doesn't have a command to conceal your name, although the list manager can disable the command to retrieve the list of subscribers.

Majordomo Lists - Reading the Archives

See the section "Reading the Archives of LISTSERV Lists," earlier in this chapter—the commands are exactly the same in Majordomo.

Instructions for Lyris Lists

To join, read, leave, or change the settings for a Lyris list, you can send e-mail messages to the administrative address for the list—the Lyris program that manages the list. The administrative address is in the form listproc@*hostname*. In the commands that follow, replace *listname* with the name of the list (the part of the list address before the @). See the sidebar "Sending Commands to List Servers," earlier in this chapter, for details about composing e-mail messages to send commands.

Lyris provides two other ways to give commands. You can use the Lyris Web interface, starting at the home page for the list and following the links. Or you can send blank messages to a special Lyris address, as described in the following sections.

Lyris Lists - Getting Information

In the text of a message to the administrative address for the list, type this command:

```
info listname
```

In response, you receive the informational message about the list.

Lyris Lists - Subscribing

Send this command to join the list:

```
subscribe listname yourname
```

Replace *yourname* with your actual name (not your e-mail address, which the list server can glean from the headers of your message). You can abbreviate the `subscribe` command to `sub`.

Alternatively, you can send a blank message to the address *listname-join@hostname* or *listname-subscribe@hostname*, where *listname* is the exact name of the list and *hostname* is the name of the computer where Lyris manages the list.

Lyris Lists - Unsubscribing

Send this command to leave the list:

```
unsubscribe listname
```

You can abbreviate the `unsubscribe` command to `unsub`. Alternatively, you can also send a blank message to the address *listname*-off@*hostname* or *listname-*unsubscribe@*hostname*, where *listname* is the exact name of the list and *hostname* is the name of the computer where Lyris manages the list.

Lyris Lists - Seeing the List of Subscribers

Send this command to receive a list of the list's subscribers:

```
review listname
```

Lyris Lists - Stopping Mail

Send this command to stop receiving messages from the list:

```
set listname nomail
```

Send this command to start receiving mail again:

```
set listname mail
```

Lyris Lists - Receiving Digests

To receive digests, send this command:

```
set listname digest
```

To receive individual messages, send this command:

```
set listname mail
```

Lyris Lists - Changing Your Address

If you can still send messages from your old account, send this command:

```
set listname email=[new-address]
```

Replaced *new-address* with your new address. Don't omit the square brackets.

Lyris Lists - Concealing Your Name and Address

Lyris doesn't have a command to conceal your name.

Lyris Lists - Reading the Archives

Use the Lyris Web interface to read messages in the list's archive.

Mailing List Tricks

If you plan to subscribe to many lists, you'll need to know how to edit the quoted text in replies to list messages, turn off message formatting (so that you can send plain-text messages), and separate your messages by list.

Deleting Extra Quoted Text

When you reply to a message, you might want to include part of the message to which you are replying. It's annoying to other subscribers if you include the entire message, especially if it's long and you are responding only to one part. It's *really* annoying if you include the text of any entire digest!

Most e-mail programs let you quote the message you are replying to—in fact, when you click Reply, the text of the original message appears, with > or | characters at the beginning of each line to show that it's a quote. Delete the boring parts and anything you don't refer to.

If you use AOL, you may not see the quoted text and you may not realize that the entire message will be included as a quote. Here's how to include just part of the original message in your reply: Select (with your mouse) the part of the original message you want to quote, and then click Reply. AOL quotes only the text you selected.

Turning Off Message Formatting

If you use an e-mail program that can send formatted messages, you need to know how to turn message formatting off. Most mailing lists require (or at least request) subscribers to post only plain-text messages rather than MIME-formatted or HTML-formatted messages. Here's how to turn formatting off in some popular e-mail programs:

Eudora Light and Eudora Pro. Choose Tools|Options from the menu bar. When you see the Options dialog box, choose Styled Text options from the category list. If you always want to send plain text, choose Send Plain Text Only. If you want to choose whether to send plain or formatted messages each time, choose Ask Me Each Time.

Netscape Messenger 4.7. When composing a message, click the Options button on the toolbar and set the Format box to Plain Text Only.

Outlook Express 5. While composing a message, choose Format|Plain Text from the menu.

Separating Your List Messages from the Rest of Your Mail

Messages from mailing lists usually aren't as urgent as other messages (with the exception of junk mail messages, which can be deleted without reading). You may find it handy to read your personal mail separately from your e-mail messages. It's also easier to follow a conversation on a list if you read all the list messages together rather than intermixed with personal messages and messages from other lists.

Not all e-mail programs can sort your mail for you, but some can, using filters or rules. A *filter* checks for particular text somewhere in the message, and for messages where the text appears, moves the message to a specified mailbox or

Chapter 4: Finding, Joining, and Participating in Mailing Lists **65**

otherwise treats it specially. For mailing lists, it's usually adequate to search for the name of the list in the To: line of messages to identify list messages.

Here's how to create filters or rules to sort your messages using several popular programs:

Eudora Light and Eudora Pro. Select a message from the mailing list and choose Special|Make Filter. When you see the Make Filter dialog box (as shown in Figure 4-6), adjust the entries so that they will match all messages from the mailing list. (Get rid of infor-mation about the specific message, like who sent it, and keep in-formation that describes all mailing list postings, like that they are addressed to the list address.) Specify that messages that match this filter get transferred to a mailbox, and give the mailbox a name. Click Create Filter. To see, edit, and delete filters later, choose Tools|Filters.

Netscape Messenger 4.7. Choose Edit|Message Filters to display the Message Filters dialog box. Click the New button to see the Filter Rules dialog box, as shown in Figure 4-7. Specify how to identify messages from a mailing list, and tell Netscape Messenger to move the messages into a folder (click New Folder to create one).

Outlook Express 5. Choose Tools|Message Rules|Mail to display the New Mail Rule dialog box (shown in Figure 4-8). In part 1 of the dialog box, choose whether to identify messages from the mailing list by the From address,

Figure 4-6: Eudora can sort your mailing-list messages into separate folders.

Figure 4-7: Tell Netscape Messenger how to identify a message from a mailing list.

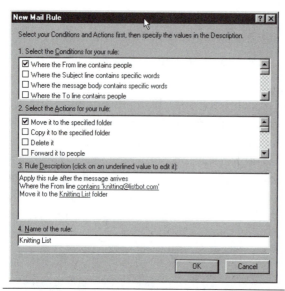

Subject line, message body (unlikely), or To address. In part 2 of the dialog box, choose Move It To The Specified Folder. In part 3, click the underlined text to specify the exact text that list messages contain (for example, the address that all list messages are from or to). In part 4, type a name for this rule.

Figure 4-8: You can describe a mailing list message to Outlook Express using the New Mail Rule dialog box so that Outlook Express can sort mailing list messages into a separate folder.

Chapter Five
Creating and Managing Your Own Mailing List

Unless you are the site manager for a list server program, you don't have to issue any long, complicated commands to create a mailing list. Creating a list is easy—using either a list server or mailing list Web site. What's harder is managing the list once it's up and running. Managing a list requires you (or someone you appoint) to help people subscribe and unsubscribe, answer subscribers' questions, guide the discussion on the list, create rules for behavior on the list, and enforce those rules.

If you are creating an open discussion list, make sure that there isn't already a list (or other type of online community) on the same topic. For instance, if you decide to start a discussion on the *Harry Potter* series of novels, you'll compete with several other lists on the same topic. Even if you do decide to start a list, it's a good idea to read the similar lists for a while to find out how you want to make yours different—perhaps the other Harry Potter lists are for kids, and you want yours to be for adults interested in serious literary analysis. Rather than plan to compete, you might want to contact the managers of existing similar lists to let them know about your list and how it will differ from theirs: You can plan to refer subscribers to their lists and ask them to refer subscribers to yours.

To find existing lists on a topic, see the section "Finding Mailing Lists" in Chapter 4. To find newsgroups by topic, see the section "Finding Newsgroups of Interest," in Chapter 6. To find IRC channels, see the section "Finding Channels of Interest," in Chapter 8. To find Web-based communities, see the section "Finding Web-based Communities," in Chapter 10.

Choosing a Site for Your List

If you belong to an organization (school, college, company, or other organization) or have a friend who runs a list server, ask her whether she will host a list for you. The person or organization who owns the host computer on which the list server runs may have a procedure for applying for a mailing list. For example, if you are connected with a college or university, you may be able to apply to a mailing list managed by the college's list server, but the list may have to be related to coursework or other college-related activity and the list may need the approval of a faculty member. The advantage of having your list managed by a list server is that subscribers won't have to see the ads that most mailing list Web sites display in mailing list messages, the list will be free, and you can probably get help from the hosting organization.

Your ISP (Internet service provider) may run a list server, and, as an account holder, you may be entitled to free or cheap list hosting. It's worth asking—call them or write to support@domain, where *domain* is your ISP's domain name.

If you can't get a free list-server-based list, you have three options: Use a mailing list Web site to host the list, pay a commercial list server to host your list, or install your own list server program on your PC.

Using Mailing List Web Sites

Mailing list Web sites host mailing lists, usually for free. Subscribers can use the Web site to read messages, post messages, and change their subscription options, or they can participate by sending and receiving e-mail messages. List managers also have a choice between using the Web site or e-mail messages to manage their lists. See the section "Mailing List Web Sites," in Chapter 4, for information about the most popular mailing list Web sites.

Subscribers will be subjected to ads, but signing up is easy via the Web interface, as is changing list options and reading list archives. Most mailing list Web sites charge nothing for you to create and manage. Be sure to read the advertising and privacy policies on the Web site, to find out where ads will appear as well as how the Web site can use your subscribers' e-mail addresses.

Mailing list Web sites are similar to Web-based community sites, like Talk City and Yahoo Clubs (described in Chapter 10). Although mailing list Web sites allow people to participate by using either the Web site or e-mail, Web-based community sites generally require people to participate via the Web site.

Using Commercial List Servers

Commercial list servers are companies that run list servers and host lists for a monthly or yearly fee. To find a commercial list server, start by asking your Internet service provider (ISP) whether it hosts lists for its account holders. Also check the following Web sites, which list commercial list servers:

List-Business.com's List-Hosting Service Providers
http://list-business.com/list-service-providers/

Vivian Neou's Internet Mailing List Providers List
http://www.catalog.com/vivian/mailing-list-providers.html

Brian Edmond's Internet Mailing List Providers List
http://www.gweep.bc.ca/~edmonds/usenet/ml-providers.html

The cost to host a list is usually modest, the list server company should provide you with support, and your list won't be cluttered with ads. On the other hand, some list servers don't provide Web-based subscriptions, subscriber settings, and list archives, so be sure to check whether they do if that's important to you.

Commercial list servers run a list server program, such as LISTSERV or ListProc: See the section "List Servers" in Chapter 4 for information about list servers. This chapter describes how to create lists using four list servers: LISTSERV, ListProc, Majordomo, and Lyris.

Installing Your Own List Server

Many list server programs are available for Windows, Mac, and Linux/UNIX computers. For example, the Lyris list server described in Chapter 4 and in this chapter runs under Windows. For information on list servers, see the **Mailing List Gurus Page: Mailing List Management Programs**, at http://lists.gurus.com/mlms.html, and follow the links to their Web sites.

If you want to run only a few lists, it's probably not worth installing and maintaining a list server on your own system. Here are a few tasks you'll be taking on:

Keeping your list server computer (the computer that runs the list server) online enough hours a day that list messages won't be delayed. For many large lists, with many messages, your server had better be online all the time.

Installing updates to the list server software.

Making backups of both the list server software and your list files.

Preventing spam and taking other security issues so that your lists can't be used by spammers to distribute messages to your subscribers, your mail server can't be used as a relay for junk e-mail back out to the Internet, and spammers can't "harvest" your subscribers' names for their own use.

In practice, if you have a UNIX or Linux box with a permanent connection via a network at school or work, you can run your own list server. The details of installing server software are beyond the scope of this chapter, but if you have some experience installing UNIX or Linux software or a friend who can help, it's an afternoon's project to install Majordomo. If your computer runs Windows NT or Windows 2000, LISTSERV Lite (a free version of LISTSERV for noncommercial use) isn't too hard to install (go to the **L-Soft International** Web site, at http://www.lsoft.com/, for more information).

Choosing a Name for Your List

The site that hosts your list may have some guidelines for list names, but here are our ideas:

- Keep the name short, but don't make it cryptic. Choose a longer name rather than a short name that no one can remember or spell. Early list servers limited list names to eight characters, but that limit rarely exists now.
- Some mailing list servers require that list names end with -L, but most don't. The -L reminds subscribers that messages come from a mailing list. One problem with using -L at the end of your list name is that small *L*s look like the number 1, and some people will get the list name wrong. We omit the *-L* when creating new lists.
- Avoid punctuation other than dashes. Most punctuation can confuse some e-mail programs and many people.

The list address for your list will be the list name followed by @ and the host name of the list server or mailing list Web site. For example, if you created a list named domestic-poultry at ListBot, the list address would be domestic-poultry@listbot.com.

Creating a List

Before you can create a list, you need to decide what the list will be called and how it will work. Read Chapter 2 for list-configuration options: For example, your list can have open or closed subscriptions, and messages can be readable by anyone or only by subscribers. Not every list server and mailing list Web site can support all the options listed in Chapter 2.

Creating a List-Server-based Mailing List

Only the list server site manager—the person in charge of installing and maintaining the list server program—can usually create a mailing list managed by that server. You provide the information about the list (name and configuration settings) to the site manager.

The site manager issues the actual command to create the list as well as the commands to create the archive files and e-mail addresses the list may require. When the site manager has created the list, make sure to find out:

The exact name of the list. The site manager may have changed the spelling, capital-ization, or punctuation to match the standards for lists managed by that server.

> **The list address.** It's usually *listname@hostname*, where *hostname* is the name of the computer on which the list server program runs.
>
> **The administrative address.** It's usually *listserver@hostname*, where *listserver* is the name of the list server program: See the section "Administrative Address" in Chapter 4 to find out why you'll need to know this.
>
> **The list password.** You will need the password when issuing commands that only the list manager can give.

The manager address. The list manager address that subscribers can use to contact you: Messages to this address are forwarded to your address automatically.

Also ask whether your list will be expected to follow site-wide policies, and find out who you can contact for help (usually the site manager).

Creating a Web-based Mailing List

You can create a list for free at a mailing list Web site: See the section "Mailing List Web Sites," in Chapter 4, for the most popular sites. Each site has links you can click to create a list. The general steps are shown in this list:

Getting Volunteers Together Online

The **Star Island Corporation** *(http://www.starisland.org) runs educational and religious conferences on a small island off New Hampshire, and each conference is run by a group of volunteers. Because the conferences run one at a time over the course of the summer, the volunteers who run the conferences rarely meet each other and get together for only one yearly meeting.*

Recently, the corporation started a private mailing list for the volunteer conference organizers. The corporation's sponsoring organization runs a list server and agreed to host the mailing list for free. Now the volunteers can communicate any time during the year for free, sharing problems and solutions.

You sign up as a list manager. This step is free. You provide your e-mail address and other information about yourself—feel free to leave boxes blank if the questions are too nosy.

You provide information about the list. You usually need to provide the list name, a one-line description of the list, a longer description of the list, and (optionally) the URL of the list's home page. You also specify whether the list is for announcements only (that is, only you can post messages), for moderated discussion (you must approve all postings), or for open discussion (all subscribers may post directly). The site may also ask whether to *archive* (keep) list postings.

You provide addresses of potential subscribers. You can provide a list of people who you think will want to subscribe to your new list. Some mailing list Web sites let you provide lists of opt-in and opt-out subscribers: Never use opt-out to add subscribers! (See the nearby sidebar "Do Not Add People without Their Confirmation!")

The site creates the list. You can go to the home page for the list, following the directions you receive. Your list is usually created within minutes. Figure 5-1 shows the Web page that ListBot displays when it has created a list—ListBot provides HTML that you can include in a Web page to help people join your new list. Figure 5-2 shows how the subscription link will look.

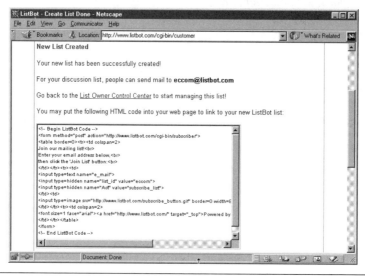

Figure 5-1: ListBot has created your list.

The site sends messages to the people you suggested as sub-scribers. You can send invitation messages asking people to reply if they want to subscribe to your list, assuming that you have a prior relationship with the people.

Be sure to make a note of the password you chose when you signed up as a list manager, the URL of the home page for your list, and other infor-mation the mailing list Web site gives you.

What to Do after Your List Has Been Created

Before you begin to publicize your list, whether it is run on a list server or a Web site, ensure that it works and make it presentable to the world.

Do Not Add People without Their Confirmation!

Using a list server or some mailing list Web sites, you can add people to your list without their having to confirm that they want to join. Don't do this! Go ahead and send people an invitation to join your list: This is called an opt-in *subscription because people have to take an action, like replying to your message, to subscribe. But don't add people and then notify them: This method is called* opt-out *because people have to take action to get off your list; it will greatly annoy your unwilling subscribers and brand you as a spammer.*

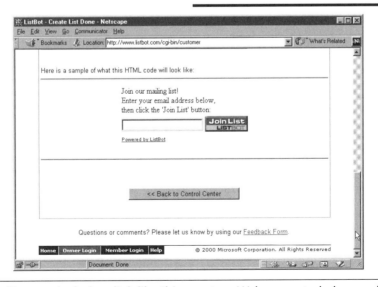

Figure 5-2: You can include a link like this one to a Web page, to help people subscribe to your list.

Checking the List Configuration and Learning How to Change It

Ensure that the list is configured with the options you specified and that your address appears as a manager. Check to make sure that the options set for the list are the ones you requested. Each Web site and list server has a different set of configuration options. For instructions on how to check and change your list's configuration, skip to sections later in this chapter that contain instructions for Web-based lists as well as those managed by LISTSERV, ListProc, and Majordomo, and Lyris.

Making Sure You Are Subscribed

Most mailing list Web sites subscribe you automatically if you are the list manager, but list servers usually don't (unless the site manager kindly subscribes you). Follow the instructions for adding a subscriber (yourself!) in the instruction sections later in this chapter. If you were already on the list, you receive an error message. If you weren't, you get a confirmation message. Either way, you're on!

You may want to subscribe to the list more than once. For example, AOL handles MIME digests strangely. If you have an AOL account, subscribe to your list from your AOL address and set your subscription to digests, so that you can see what digests look like to your AOL subscribers. Even if you don't have an AOL account, consider subscribing to your list from another address to receive digests.

Sending a Test Message

Send a message to the list address for the list. If you don't receive it within a few minutes, either you aren't subscribed to the list or the list isn't working. Try again later, or add a cooperative friend's address to the list and ask that person to try posting a message.

If messages don't get through, contact technical support for the Web site or list server that hosts the list. To check that the list server program (or mailing list Web site's e-mail server) is working, try sending the command `info listname` to the administrative address to see whether you receive the information file for your list (replace *listname* with the exact name of the list).

Checking the List's Description and Web Site

Each list-server-based list has a one-line description that appears in various places, like listings of lists hosted on the site or at the top of Web pages about the list. Make sure it's right!

For Web-based lists, each list has its own home page generated automatically by the site:

eGroups: http://www.egroups.com/group/listname/info.html

ListBot: http://listname.listbot.com

Topica: http://www.topica.com/lists/listname/

Take a look at this page to see that the information is correct and to add any other information the site lets you post.

Some list servers have a Web interface: If you have a list-server-based list, check with the site manager to find out whether yours does. Check the Web interface for your list to see that everything looks right.

Otherwise, consider creating a home page for your list, including the information from the welcome message and FAQ, described in the next section. Figure 5-3 shows the Web page for a list-server-based mailing list.

Writing the Welcome Message and FAQ

Most lists have a *welcome* message, an e-mail message that is automatically sent to each new subscriber. The welcome message should include how to unsubscribe, how to resubscribe, the rules for participating in the list, suggested topics, banned topics, the URL of the list's home page (if it has one), and how to contact the list manager. Some lists also have a farewell message that is sent to subscribers who sign off the list.

Lists usually also have an *FAQ*, a list of frequently asked questions and their answers. The FAQ can be the same as the welcome message (except for the "Welcome to the XXX List!" line at the beginning of the file) because new subscribers need to know the most frequently asked questions. Or the FAQ can be quite different—a distillation of the most popular topics that have come up on the list and the results of the discussions.

Looking at a Sample Welcome Message

Here's the text of a boilerplate welcome message you can use for your own list. This particular message includes instructions for a ListProc-based list, so be sure to replace the commands with instructions that work for your list (as well as replacing *listname* with the name of your list, *hostname* with the name of the host computer that manages your list, *listpageURL* with the URL of the home page for the list, and *adminaddress* with the administrative address for the list). The message suggests that people who want to test their e-mail not post to the list,

Figure 5-3: The Web site for a mailing list can include general information about the list, instructions for getting on and off, and searchable list archives.

and post instead to test@gurus.com, which is a mailbot run by the authors of this book.

```
***** The listname Mailing List *****

The listname mailing list is intended for discussing
subject. This file contains instructions and rules for
participating. This file is also available on the Web
at listpageURL.

HOW TO SUBSCRIBE

To subscribe to this list, send a message to
adminaddress with the following line in the text (not
the subject) of the message:

subscribe listname yourname

Replace "yourname" with your actual first and last
names (not your e-mail address, which the mailing list
system can find in your message headers). Don't include
any other text. If you can suppress including a
signature in the message, do so. If your name is long
```

or contains punctuation, enclose your whole name in quotes.

When our mailing list system receives your message, it will send a confusing confirmation message back to you. Click Reply to compose a reply, then click Send to send the reply without editing it. This reply confirms that you actually want to subscribe to the message, and that some malicious third-party isn't subscribing you against your will.

HOW TO SIGN OFF

To sign off of this list, send a message to *adminaddress* with the following line in the text (not the subject) of the message:

signoff *listname*

HOW TO RECEIVE DIGESTS OR INDIVIDUAL MESSAGES

To receive digests of messages (the entire day's message in one long message), send this command to *adminaddress*:

set *listname* mail digest

To receive individual messages, send this command:

set *listname* mail ack

HOW TO CONTACT THE LIST MANAGERS

If you have a problem or question about this list or about your subscription, write to the list managers at *listname*-request@*hostname*. Don't post a message to the list.

HOW TO POST

To post a message to the list, so all the subscribers see it, address your message to *listname@hostname*. Turn off formatting (HTML or MIME), and don't attach any files to your message. Messages should consist of plain text only.

WHAT TO POST

If you wrote it and it is of general interest to people who are interested in subject, post it. Here are some sample topics: ...

WHAT NOT TO POST

If your message doesn't clearly and directly relate to subject, don't post it.

Don't continue an irrelevant thread in any way (rebuttal, rebuke, rerun, revision, or remark). Don't post "me, too!" or "I don't know!" messages.

Don't post personal messages to a single subscriber. If mail to a person bounces, write to the list manager to get help contacting that person, but don't post to the list.

Don't post personal attacks. Make negative remarks about what people said (if you must), but not about people themselves. Do not point out grammatical, spelling, or usage errors.
If something cute, interesting, or funny is making the rounds, don't post it. We've already seen it.

If you are wondering whether your e-mail works, don't use the list to test it. Instead, send a message to test@gurus.com. A mailbot will reply, usually within a few minutes.

Here are some topics to avoid: ...

```
OTHER LIST RULES
Check your facts on anything you post. Do not under any
circumstances post virus warnings, chain letters, news
alerts, or anything else designed to be "forwarded to
everyone you know" to this list. Never post hearsay
without checking the fact yourself (searching the Web
to confirm the information usually takes only a few
minutes).

Direct all comments or suggestions about the list or
this message to the list manager at listname-
request@hostname. For more information about how to
participate in mailing lists, see The Mailing List
Gurus Page at http://lists.gurus.com/.

THE LIST'S HOME PAGE ON THE WEB

This mailing list has a Web site, too, that includes
the FAQ for the list as well as searchable archives.
The Web site is at listpageURL.
```

Viewing and Updating the Welcome Message, Farewell Message, and FAQ

It's a good idea to check the messages for your list every few months, to see whether they are still accurate (the messages don't change—your list does). For all list servers we know of, you can send the command `info listname` to see the FAQ for a list (anyone, not just the list manager, can send this command). Skip to the instruction sections later in this chapter for how to update the messages for Web-based lists and lists managed by LISTSERV, ListProc, Majordomo, and Lyris.

To change the welcome message or FAQ, get the existing message, edit it in a text editor, and install it as the replacement message. Since the welcome message and FAQ must be text, with no formatting characters, don't use a word processor to edit the files (or if you do, be sure to save the file as text). Keep the length of the lines to 65 characters or fewer so that they don't wrap around in e-mail. Be sure to check the spelling, grammar, and commands. Copy the finished message from your text editor or word processor into the e-mail message or Web page form you are using to install the new message.

Setting List Options

As list manager, you control how the list operates by choosing the configuration options described in this section. Options can control who may subscribe, who may post, and whether messages are saved in archives.

This section describes the types of options available for most lists and how to choose among them. For specific commands and instructions for setting the options for your list, skip ahead to the instruction sections for Web-based, LISTSERV, ListProc, Majordomo, and Lyris lists.

Subscription Options

You can set your list to be

Open (public) so that anyone can subscribe without your permission

Manager controlled so that anyone may apply for subscription and you can either approve or deny the request

Closed (private) so that you add subscribers directly, without a way for people to subscribe themselves

Some systems let you receive a notice when someone subscribes or signs off so that you can see who's coming and going. Some systems let you specify whether to require that a person provide a name or other information when subscribing. When someone subscribes, you can require that the person confirm the subscription (mailing list Web sites usually do this automatically). Because it's easy for someone to forge an e-mail message from someone else, receiving a message is a very insecure way to be notified that someone wants to be on a list. A practice known as *mailbombing* involves a malefactor forging subscription requests from a victim so that the victim begins receiving mailing list messages he didn't want—in some cases, to thousands of mailing lists.

To prevent your mailing list from being used for mailbombing, you should configure your list so that when someone subscribes, a confirmation message is sent to the person's e-mail address. The person must reply to the confirmation messages before she is subscribed to the list.

Digest Options

For high-volume lists, you may be able to give subscribers the option of receiving all the messages for each day (or other time period) in one long message rather than as individual messages. These combined messages are called *digests*. Most mailing list Web sites provide daily digests for all their lists, so there's usually nothing for you to configure.

Most digests consist of a series of messages separated by a blank line or other separator: The digest may start with a table of contents, listing the subjects and authors of the messages in the digest. This digest format is known as *text digests* or (more obscurely) as *RFC 1153 digests*. Other digests are in MIME format, with each message attached to the digest message as a MIME attachment. The format of your digests—text or MIME—depends on the system that manages your list: Some list servers let you specify the format of the digest. Web-based lists generally don't let you specify digest formats.

Privacy Options

Most list servers (and some mailing list Web sites) let you control who may see subscriber lists, who may read messages posted to the list, who may post messages, and who may read the list archives. (Archives are described later in this chapter.)

How Replies Are Addressed

Some list servers let you determine how replies to messages are addressed, which are controlled by the Reply-to line in headers of messages distributed by the list server. If the Reply-to line of outgoing messages contains the list address, then when a subscriber clicks Reply, the resulting message will be addressed back to the whole list. If the Reply-to line contains the address of the person who sent the message, clicking Reply creates a private message back to that person, not to the list. How you want this option set depends on whether you'd like to encourage or discourage on-list discussion.

Web-based mailing lists don't usually let you control this option—replies are addressed to the list.

Posting Options

You can control whether nonsubscribers may post messages to your list. Some systems also let you set a limit for the number of messages each subscriber may post per day, or a limit on the total number of messages posted to the list. Setting a limit for all messages is a good idea because it may prevent a *mail loop* (two programs sending mail to each other endlessly) from inundating your subscribers with messages. If you want to approve each message before it is posted, see the next section.

Moderation Options

Most lists are unmoderated, so that subscribers can post messages without anyone reviewing them before they are distributed to subscribers. Some lists are moderated, so that the list manager, or other moderators, review each message. And some lists allow only the managers to post—these lists operate more like newsletters than like online discussions. When a list is moderated, the moderator(s) may be the list managers or may be another person or group. Here's how moderation usually works (the details depend on the list server or Web site):

1. The list server sends the message to the moderator(s).

2. The list server may also send a message back to the poster to let her know that the message has been sent to a moderator for review.

3. The moderator(s) reviews the message. He may accept the message, reject the message, or accept an edited version of the message by sending commands to the list server. It is good list-management policy for moderators to write directly to the poster if they reject a message, indicating why the message was rejected and what the poster could do about it.

4. When the list server receives an approval message, it distributes the original message to the list. When it receives a rejection message, it discards the original message.

Some list servers let moderators edit messages before approving them for distribution. As long as subscribers trust moderators not to change the content of their messages, the ability to edit messages can be useful: The moderators can remove unwanted formatting characters or unnecessarily long quotes from other messages.

Some lists can be configured so that you can choose which subscribers need to be moderated—that is, whose messages need to be approved by the moderators. For example, you might set new subscribers to have their messages moderated for a few weeks and then allow them to post to the list directly. Or you might need to review the messages of specific hotheads who tend to start flamewars. But don't try to do this secretly, thinking that subscribers won't notice—you'll look like a tyrant and a sneak if you try to control people's posts without letting them know up front what the rules are.

Changing or Adding Managers

A list can have more than one manager, and having more than one is a good idea for large or active lists. Co-managers can help each other when they go on vacation or get busy, help each other make policy for the list, and back each other up if things become contentious on the list. Remember that when you add someone as a manager of your list, this person has the same powers you do—including removing you as manager.

If the list is moderated, see the preceding section, "Moderation Options," to find out how to specify who approves messages; the moderators don't have to be the same people as the list managers.

Managing List Subscriptions

Once your list is up and running, your list-management duties include helping people get on and off your list. Here are general pointers about adding and deleting subscribers, changing subscribers' subscription options, and other management tasks. For specific instructions, skip down to the instructions section for the type of list you manage: Web-based lists, LISTSERV, ListProc, Majordomo, or Lyris.

Adding Subscribers

It's a bad idea to add subscribers who have not requested you to do so—this particularly nasty type of spamming is called *mailbombing*. Instead, add only people who have asked to be on your list. For open lists, you may want to tell the person how to subscribe by herself so that she learns about how lists work, rather than do the job yourself. See Chapter 12 for how to publicize your list so that people will ask to subscribe!

Deleting Subscribers

Some people have an amazingly hard time getting off mailing lists, even when the instructions are staring them in the face. You may want to explain to the subscriber how he can get off the list himself so that he won't have trouble the next time, or you may give up and delete the subscriber yourself. Other list subscribers get annoyed when they see "get me off this list!" messages posted to the list, so it's a good idea to help these clueless folks off your list quickly and quietly.

Occasionally, you may get a note from someone who wants to get off your list, but the person's address doesn't appear on your list, as far as you can tell. Get a list of subscribers (see the preceding section) and look for the person who wants off.

If you can't find the mysterious subscriber, you have several possibilities:
- The subscriber's mail is forwarded from one address to another, and you need to know at which other addresses your subscriber receives mail.

- The subscriber's address changed since she subscribed, because of one ISP's being bought by another or other reasons.
- The subscriber's mail system allows addresses in more than one format. For example, an MSN subscriber may use the address
username@msn.com,
username@email.msn.com, or
username@classic.msn.com.
Look for variations on the person's address, especially the first part of the host name part (after the @).

Handling Bounced Messages

When messages to a subscriber bounce, you receive the error messages that result. If the error looks like a permanent one—no such user at that address, for example—you should delete the person from your list to avoid more error messages. Before you do so, though, read the bounce message to see why it bounced.

The message may say that the problem is temporary—for example, the host computer is not responding, the person's mailbox is full, or the error message says something about a "transient error." In this case, you may want to leave the person on the list. To avoid getting lots of bounced messages until the problem is resolved, you might want to switch the person to receive the daily digest of messages rather than individual messages, if your list server or Web site offers digests.

Many list servers forward to the list managers any messages addressed to owner-listname@hostname, assuming that these messages are error messages about bounces—as they usually are. Occasionally, though, someone writes to the *owner-* address by mistake.

LISTSERV allows list managers to set the list header option `Auto-Delete= Yes,Semi-Auto` to automatically delete subscribers for whom LISTSERV receives bounces with errors that are usually permanent, like user `not found` and `No such userID`. ListProc has a similar system, called "auto-delete-subscribers."

The problem with automatic-deletion systems is that if a person's mail bounces for a day or two and then fixes itself, LISTSERV and ListProc may already have deleted the person from your list. Forthcoming versions of these programs will have more sophisticated systems that will keep track of how many days a person's mail has bounced and delete him after a specific number of days or after receiving a specific number of bounced messages.

Changing Subscribers' Options

Subscribers may have trouble setting their own list options, such as whether they receive individual messages or digests. You can either explain to each subscriber how to change settings or make the changes yourself. Like teaching people how to sign off a list, sometimes it's just easier to do it yourself. For Web-based and Majordomo-based lists, subscribers don't have many settings, so there's usually no way for the list manager to change them for the subscriber.

Banning Users

All list servers and mailing list Web sites let you unsubscribe people from your list, and some allow you to prevent people from trying to return. Some let you prevent subscribers from posting, which can be useful when a subscriber needs a cooling-off period during a flamewar. Of course, it's harder to prevent a banned subscriber from opening up a free mailbox at a Web site like Yahoo Mail or Hotmail and returning. (In one case we know, after being banned, a subscriber resubscribed to the list using two new accounts and proceeded to carry on conversations with himself on the list. These pseudo-accounts are often called *sock puppets*.) If necessary, you may need to set your list so that you must approve all new subscriptions—at least until the problem subscriber gives up and goes away. See Chapter 13 for more information dealing with trouble on your list.

Managing List Archives

Archives are files that contain the messages that have been posted to your list. If list messages contain information that people might want to refer to later, archives are a good idea. But if list messages are primarily conversational or contain personal or sensitive information that subscribers might not want read later, especially by a wider audience, archives can be a waste of disk space or downright dangerous. You may be able to control who has access to list archives: only the list managers, all list subscribers, or the general public.

Some list archives (those of some list-server-based lists) are available by sending commands to the list server, but list archives are increasingly available over the Web. The Web sites for these archives may show messages by date, by sender, or in response to a search. See the section "Reading List Archives," in Chapter 4, to find out how people can access your list's archives.

Configuring Your List's Archives

For a list-server-based list, you can ask the list server site manager to set up archiving for your list. Some list servers let the list manager control who can access the archives, and others require the list server site manager to set access permissions.

There's no easy way to edit the archives later; for instance, to remove factual errors, copyright material posted illegally, or attached files that contain viruses. If necessary, ask the site manager to edit the file for you.

Commercial Archiving Services

Several Web sites archive mailing lists—that is, the systems that run the Web sites subscribe to lists, store the messages, and display messages in response to people's searches. Some list managers appreciate the services of these archiving services because they provide easy-to-use, Web-based, keyword-searchable archives for their lists. Other list managers feel ripped off by archiving services because they make money by displaying ads while displaying content generated by hard-working and generally unpaid list managers. The keys to a good list archive site, in our opinion, are that the site archive lists only when requested to by the list manager; that public archives not include the e-mail addresses of posters; and that the site not pretend to own the messages. A few sites have displayed messages from mailing lists as though they were posted in the site's own discussion groups—a clear no-no.

Here are some Web-based archiving services that look good:

eScribe (also provides Web page hosting and chat rooms for mailing lists)
 http://www.escribe.com/
Geocrawler
 http://www.geocrawler.com/
ListQuest
 http://www.listquest.com/

Here are archiving sites that aren't perfect:

The Mail Archive (anyone can add a list, without permission of the list manager, and they display subscribers' e-mail addresses)
 http://www.mail-archive.com/
RemarQ (adds lists without permission from the list owners and makes lists look like they are run by RemarQ itself)
 http://www.remarq.com/

Instructions for Managing Web-based Lists

For Web-based lists, you use the Web site to perform all list-management tasks. Start at the home page for the list, log in as manager, and follow the links to see the settings for your list. Figure 5-4 shows part of the page that the list manager of a ListBot-hosted list sees. We can't give you step-by-step instructions for mailing list Web sites because the design of the sites changes every few months, but here is some general information. Some mailing list Web sites let you send commands by e-mail, if you prefer working by e-mail to using the Web.

Most mailing list Web sites let you update the description of the list, the welcome message, the farewell message (if any), the FAQ, whether the list is open or closed, digest options, privacy options, posting options, moderation options, and who the list managers are. You can also see the current list of subscribers, add and delete subscribers, and read the messages that have been posted to the list. Some mailing list Web sites also let you change the subscription settings for your subscribers.

Web-based lists usually don't have all the commands available on list servers. For example, there's usually no way to control the format or frequency of digests, or allow a subscriber to read the list but not post, or to prevent someone from subscribing (short of making all new subscriptions require your approval). Topica lets you set someone to Auto Reject so that the list rejects all posts from that person.

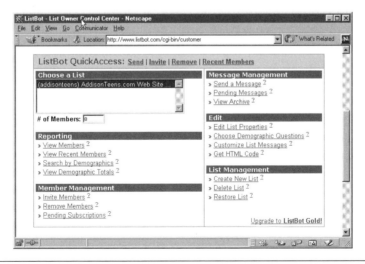

Figure 5-4: ListBot lets the list manager change list settings, see who's subscribed, and change the list configuration from a Web page.

Web-based lists almost always have archives available on the Web site, and you can usually control whether they are readable by anyone or only by list subscribers. Follow the links from the list's home page to the archive (or past messages) configuration pages. Some mailing list Web sites make list archives public unless you specify otherwise, but hide the mailing addresses of the message authors so that posters don't get lots of private e-mail (or spam) from nonsubscribers.

Instructions for Managing Listserv Lists

You communicate with LISTSERV by sending it commands in e-mail. See the section "Instructions for LISTSERV Lists," in Chapter 4, to find out how to send commands to the administrative address for your new list. In the instructions that follow, replace *listname* with the exact name of the list, and *password* with the password you establish for the list. (You, as list manager, use this password for giving management commands. Don't share this password with subscribers!)

Setting Your LISTSERV List Password

First, set up a password for the list. To tell LISTSERV what password you want to use from here on out, send this command to the administrative address for the list:

```
PW ADD password
```

Replace *password* with the password you want to use (keep it short, with no spaces). You'll need this password when you send other list manager commands to LISTSERV. When you receive a confirmation message from LISTSERV (to make sure that it's really you), reply to the message with the single word *OK* in the body of your message.

Getting the List Header for LISTSERV Lists

To see how your list is configured (or to prepare to change the configuration), send this command:

```
GET listname (HEADER PW=password NOLOCK
```

Note the single open parenthesis in the command. You receive a copy of the list header, preceded by a `PUT listname LIST PW=xxxxxxxx` command. The list header contains the configuration options for the list, one per line, with the option name and equal sign and the settings (for example, `Subscription=`

Chapter 5: Creating and Managing Your Own Mailing List **89**

`Open,Confirm`). Each line begins with an asterisk. Here is a sample response to the `GET` command:

```
PUT POULTRY-L LIST PW=XXXXXXXX
*
* Discussion of domestic chickens, ducks, and geese
*
* Ack= No
* Confidential= No
* Daily-Threshold= 100
* Files= No
* Mail-Via= Distribute
* Notebook= No
* Notify= Yes
* Reply-To= List,Respect
* Review= Public
* Send= Public
* Stats= None,Owner
* Subscription= Open,Confirm
* Validate= Store only
*
* Owner= test@gurus.com (Virginia A. Snodgrass)
*
* Errors-To= Owner
*
* This list discusses domestic poultry: chickens, ducks
and geese.
* For more information, send "INFO POULTRY-L" to
LISTSERV@gurus.com.
```

Changing LISTSERV List Options

To change the configuration settings for your list, follow these steps:

1. Send this command (without the `NOLOCK` option) to get the list header and "lock" your list for editing: `GET ` *`listname`* ` (HEADER PW=`*`password`*

2. You receive the list header, preceded by a `PUT ` *`listname`* ` LIST PW=xxxxxxxx` command, in an e-mail message.

3. Copy the list header, including the `PUT` command, to a new message addressed to the administrative address for the list.

4. Edit the values of the configuration options in the list headers. Don't disturb the asterisk at the beginning of each line or the settings that you don't want to change. Leave the setting name (the part before the equal sign on each line).

5. Replace the xxxxxxxx in the PUT command with the list password.

6. Turn off your signature, if you use one, so that it isn't added to the end of this message.

7. Send the message. LISTSERV replaces the old list headers with your new version. You can send the command GET *listname* (HEADER PW=*password* NOLOCK again to see how your new settings look.

Be careful: If you foul up the headers, your list may work strangely or not at all! If this happens, ask the LISTSERV site manager for help.

Changing a LISTSERV List's Description

To fix the one-line description of the list, get your list header as described in the section "Getting the List Header for LISTSERV Lists," earlier in this chapter. The description appears as the first line of the list headers, just after the PUT command. Leave the asterisk and the space at the beginning of the line, and replace the rest of the line with your new description line. When you are done, install the updated list headers as described in that section.

Viewing and Updating the Welcome Message and Farewell Message

To see the welcome message, send this command:
GET *listname* WELCOME PW=*password*

To see the farewell message, send this command:
GET *listname* FAREWELL PW=*password*

To see the info file (FAQ), send this command:
INFO *listname*

To install a new welcome or farewell message, compose a message to the administrative address for the list. On the first line of the message, type a command, replacing *listname* with the exact list name, and *password* with the list password. For the welcome message, use this command:
PUT *listname* WELCOME PW=*password*

For the farewell message, type this command:
PUT *listname* FAREWELL PW=*password*

After the command, which appears on the first line of the message, copy the text of the message from your text editor or word processor so that it starts on the second line of the e-mail message. Edit the message as needed to eliminate line endings that appear in the wrong place. Make sure that your e-mail program doesn't add a signature to the message, or else your signature will appear at the end of the welcome message or FAQ. Then send off your message.

To update the info file, e-mail the file to the site administrator and ask that it be installed as your list's info file.

Setting Subscription Options for LISTSERV Lists

Get your list header as described in the section "Changing LISTSERV List Options," earlier in this chapter. Edit the Subscription line of the headers like this:

To make the list closed so that the only way people can get onto the list is for you to use the `ADD` command, change the Subscription line to `Subscription= Closed`.

To make the list manager-controlled, use `Subscription= By Owner`.

To make the list open, use `Subscription= Open`.

To require that people reply to a confirmation message when subscribing (recommended), use `Subscription= Open,Confirm`.

To delete subscribers automatically when their e-mail messages bounce, use `Auto-Delete= Yes,Semi-Auto`.

Install the updated list headers as described in the section "Changing LISTSERV List Options," earlier in this chapter.

Setting Digest Options for LISTSERV Lists

Get your list header as described in the section "Changing LISTSERV List Options," earlier in this chapter. Edit the Digests line to read `Digest= Yes,Same,Daily` for daily digests (the `Same` indicates that the digest information is stored in the same place as the regular information on the list server). For other digest options, check with your LISTSERV site administrator. Install the updated list headers as described in the "Changing LISTSERV List Options" section, earlier in this chapter.

Setting Privacy Options for LISTSERV Lists

Get your list header as described in the section "Changing LISTSERV List Options," earlier in this chapter. Edit the Review line to determine who can see the list of subscribers:

`Review= Private` allows only subscribers

`Review= Owners` allows only the list managers

`Review= Public` lets anyone get a subscriber list

Install the updated list headers as described in the "Changing LISTSERV List Options" section, earlier in this chapter.

Controlling How LISTSERV Replies Are Addressed

Get your list header as described in the section "Changing LISTSERV List Options," earlier in this chapter. Set the Reply-to line to `Reply-to= List,Respect` for replies to be addressed to the list or to `Reply-to= Sender,Respect` for replies to be addressed to the original poster. The optional `Respect` keyword means to keep (respect) any Reply-to lines already present in mail sent to the list. Install the updated list headers as described in the "Changing LISTSERV List Options" section, earlier in this chapter.

Setting Posting Options for LISTSERV Lists

Get your list header as described in the section "Changing LISTSERV List Options," earlier in this chapter, make the following changes, and install the updated list headers as described in that section. You can control who may post and how many messages can be distributed by the list each day.

Controlling Who May Post

The Send settings control who can post messages. Use the `Send= Private` setting to allow only subscribers to post or use `Send= Private,Confirm` to require subscribers to confirm (with a message saying "OK") that the post really came from them. Use `Send= Public` to allow anyone to post to the list.

You can configure the list so that subscribers can post directly, and posts from nonsubscribers are sent to an editor (usually the list manager) for approval: Use the `Send= Editor` and `Editor= address,(listname)` settings (replace address with the *address* to which nonsubscriber postings should be sent, and don't forget the parentheses around the list name).

Limiting the Number of Messages

To set a maximum number of postings per subscriber per day, you can modify the Daily-Threshold setting for your list. The Daily-Threshold setting controls how many total messages from all subscribers can be distributed, but you can add a second number that sets a limit per subscriber. For example, `Daily-Threshold= 50,3` sets the limit for the whole list to 50 messages a day, and the limit for each subscriber to 3 messages a day.

Setting Moderation Options for LISTSERV Lists

Get your list header as described in the section "Changing LISTSERV List Options," earlier in this chapter, make the following changes, and install the updated list headers as described in that section.

Use the line `Send= Editor,Confirm` to tell LISTSERV to send messages to the moderator, and use the line `Editor= address` to specify the moderator's address. The moderator resends the message to the list if he approves of it or lets the poster know that he is rejecting it. The moderator can edit the message before posting it to the list. For example, these lines tell LISTSERV that prboc@gurus.com is the moderator for the list:

```
Send= Editor,Confirm
Editor= prboc@gurus.com
```

If the moderator doesn't need to be able to edit the messages before posting them, use the setting `Send= Editor,Hold`. When the moderator receives a message for approval, she can just reply to LISTSERV with the message `OK`.

You can list several addresses on the Editor line, but only the first one will receive postings for approval. The rest of the editors will be allowed to post without moderation, though. To set LISTSERV to send messages for approval to each of a group of moderators in turn, list the moderators on `Moderator=` lines, like this:

```
Send= Editor,Confirm
Editor= 1stguy@gurus.com
Moderator=
1stguy@gurus.com,2ndguy@gurus.com,3rdguy@gurus.com
```

If you want all the moderators to receive all messages, add `All,` to the beginning of the list of moderators, like this:

```
Moderator=
All,1stguy@gurus.com,2ndguy@gurus.com,3rdguy@gurus.com
```

You can configure your list so that messages from only specified subscribers are moderated and messages from other subscribers are posted directly. Send the following command to the administrative address for the list, replacing *address* with the address of the subscriber whose posts you want to moderate:

`SET listname REVIEW FOR address`

Changing LISTSERV List Managers

Get your list header as described in the section "Changing LISTSERV List Options," earlier in this chapter, make the following changes, and install the updated list headers as described in that section. Edit the Owner line to include the addresses of the list managers, separated by commas. For example, this Owner line creates three list managers:

`Owner= georgew@wh.gov,jadams@wh.gov,tomj@wh.gov`

LISTSERV lets you specify another set of addresses to which to send error messages. If only some of the list managers want to deal with error messages or if you've roped someone else into reading them, use the `Errors-To` line, with a list of the addresses that will receive error messages (separate the addresses by commas).

Adding and Deleting Subscribers

To add a subscriber, send this command, replacing *address* with the person's e-mail address and *name* with the person's name:

`ADD listname address name`

If you don't want the person to receive confirmation and welcome messages (for example, if you are complying with a request to delete a person's old address and add the new address), add `QUIET` to the beginning of the command, like this:

`QUIET ADD chickens-L cal@whitehouse.gov Calvin Coolidge`

To delete a subscriber, send this command:

`DEL listname address`

To avoid the person's getting a confirmation message (for example, if his mail is bouncing anyway), add `QUIET` to the beginning of the command.

Getting a List of Subscribers

Send this command:

`REVIEW listname`

Changing Subscribers' Options for LISTSERV Lists

Send this command to find out what the subscriber's current subscription settings are, replacing *address* with the subscriber's address:

   QUERY *listname* FOR *address*

To change a setting, send the following command, replacing *option* with a subscription setting, like MAIL (receive mail), NOMAIL (don't receive mail), DIGEST (receive digests), NODIGEST (receive individual postings), CONCEAL (omit from subscriber lists), NOCONCEAL (include on subscriber lists), POST (allowed to post), or NOPOST (not allowed to post):

   SET *listname option* FOR *address*

Preventing People from Subscribing or Posting

To prevent a subscriber from posting, send this command, replacing *address* with the person's address:

   SET *listname* NOPOST FOR *address*

To allow the subscriber to post again, send this command:

   SET *listname* POST FOR *address*

Configuring the Archives of LISTSERV Lists

You have to ask the LISTSERV site manager to set up archiving for your list, if it's not already archived. List archives are stored in the notebook for the list, and only the LISTSERV site manager can change some of the settings on the Notebook line of the list headers. Ask your LISTSERV site manager to set the Notebook line to include Public (for anyone to be able to see the archives), Private (for only subscribers to see the archives), or Owner (for only the list manager to see the archives).

Instructions for Managing Listproc Lists

You communicate with ListProc by sending e-mail commands. See the section "Instructions for ListProc Lists," in Chapter 4, to find out how to send commands to the administrative address for your new list. In the instructions that follow, replace *listname* with the exact name of the list, and *password* with the list password you get from your ListProc site administrator when he creates the list.

Checking Your ListProc List Options

Send this command to the administrative address for the list:

   config *listname password*

You receive a listing of the list settings that are in effect. The command `review listname` does the same thing and includes the subscriber list.

The ListProc list settings look like this (in part):

```
Configuration of ListProcessor(tm) list one-piece-
knitting@uua.org
VISIBLE-LIST
OPEN-SUBSCRIPTIONS
SUBSCRIPTION-MANAGERS [owners] (inactive)
SEND-BY-SUBSCRIBERS
STATISTICS-TO-OWNERS
REVIEW-BY-SUBSCRIBERS
ARCHIVES-TO-ALL
NO-ARCHIVE
UNMODERATED
DELIVERY-ERRORS-TO [owners]
DIGEST daily 00:01 0 0
MESSAGE-LIMIT 50
COMMENT "Knitting without seams: one-piece knitting techniques"
NO-AUTO-DELETE-SUBSCRIBERS
REPLY-TO-LIST
CONFIRM-ALL-SUBSCRIPTIONS
DONT-CONFIRM-ALL-UNSUBSCRIPTIONS
NO-ALTERNATE-ADDRESS-COMMANDS
DONT-ALLOW-EMPTY-SUBSCRIBER-NAMES
OWNERS test@gurus.com
PASSWORD circular
OWNER-CONTROLLED
```

Changing ListProc List Options

To change the configuration settings for your list, you send commands that start with `config listname password` followed by the setting you want to change. You can then send the command `config listname password` again to see what your new settings look like.

Changing Your ListProc List Password

If you want to change the list password, which you'll need when changing list settings, adding or deleting people, or approving messages, send this command:

`config listname password password newpassword`

Replace *password* (the one in italics) with the existing password and *newpassword* with the new password you want to use. For example, to change your password from bluesuede to elvispresley, you'd send this command:
```
config rocknroll-L bluesuede password elvispresley
```

Changing a ListProc List's Description

To replace the existing one-line description with a new one, send this command:
```
config listname password comment description
```

Replace *description* with a one-line description (no more than about 75 characters). If the line wraps to a second line, you need to separate your command into two lines, using the & continuation character at the end of the first line, like this:
```
config listname password comment &
description
```

For example, this command sets the description of the Windows Millenium Edition list:
```
config winme newoslist comment &
Discussion of the Windows ME operating system
```

Viewing and Updating the Welcome Message and FAQ

To see the welcome message, send this command:
```
edit listname password welcome -nolock
```

To see the FAQ (info file), send this command:
```
info listname
```

To install new welcome or info messages, compose a message to the administrative address for the list. On the first line of the message, type a command, replacing *listname* with the exact list name, and *password* with the list password. For the welcome message, use this command:
```
put listname password welcome
```

For the info message, use this command:
```
put listname password info
```

After the command, which appears on the first line of the message, copy the text of the message from your text editor or word processor so that the message starts on the second line of the e-mail message. Edit the message as needed to eliminate line endings that appear in the wrong place. Make sure that your e-mail program doesn't add a signature to the message, or else your signature will appear at the end of the welcome message or FAQ. Then send off your message.

Setting Subscription Options for ListProc Lists

In addition to choosing whether your list is open or closed, you can require confirmations or appoint people as *subscription managers* (people who assist the list managers by handling subscription and unsubscription tasks).

Setting ListProc Lists Open, Closed, or Manager Controlled

To make your list closed so that the only way to subscribe is for the list manager to send an ADD command, send this command:

```
config listname password closed-subscriptions
```

To make the list manager controlled, send this command (it also automatically changes the list configuration to allow only subscribers to post or access the subscription list or archives):

```
config listname password owner-subscriptions
```

To make the list open, send this command:

```
config listname password open-subscriptions
```

Requiring Confirmations and Names

It's a good idea to require that people reply to a confirmation message when subscribing, so also send this command:

```
config listname password confirm-all-subscriptions
```

To require that people provide a name when subscribing (the default for ListProc), send this command:

```
config listname password dont-allow-empty-subscriber-names
```

To let people subscribe without providing a name (that is, they can just send `subscribe listname`), send this command:

```
config listname password allow-empty-subscriber-names
```

Creating Subscription Managers

ListProc lets you create subscription managers, who are like list managers but receive only the list management messages about people who want to subscribe or unsubscribe. To add subscription managers, send this command:

```
config listname password subscription-managers addresses
```

Replace *addresses* with a list of the addresses of the subscription managers, separated by commas. To remove subscription managers, send this command:

```
config listname password remove-subscription-managers addresses
```

Automatically Deleting Subscribers

To tell ListProc to delete people whose messages bounce, send this command:

   `config `*`listname password`*` auto-delete-subscribers`

To turn this system off, send:

   `config `*`listname password`*` no-auto-delete-subscribers`

Getting Notified about Subscriptions and Unsubscriptions

You can ask ListProc to notify you when people subscribe or unsubscribe. Send these commands:

   `set `*`listname`*` preference ccsubscribe`
   `set `*`listname`*` preference ccunsubscribe`

Setting Digest Options for ListProc Lists

If you don't want to provide digests of your list, send this command:

   `config `*`listname password`*` no-digests`

For daily digests, send this command:

   `config `*`listname password`*` daily `*`hh:mm`*

Replace *hh:mm* with the time each day when you want ListProc to send out the digest, or omit this part to get digests sent at midnight. For weekly digests, send this command:

   `config `*`listname password`*` weekly `*`day`*

Replace *day* with the name of the day of the week when you want digests sent.

For monthly digests, send this command:

   `config `*`listname password`*` monthly`

If you want people to receive digests when they subscribe, unless they send a command to switch to individual messages, send this command if you want people to receive MIME digests:

   `config `*`listname password`*` default mail digest`

Send this command if you want people to receive text digests:

   `config `*`listname password`*` default mail digest-nomime`

Setting Privacy Options for ListProc Lists

ListProc enables you to control who can see the list of subscribers, whether your list appears on the ListProc list of lists, and who can read the list archives.

Controlling Who Can See the Subscriber List

To control who can see the list of subscribers, send one of these commands:

`config `*`listname password `*`review-by-all` for anyone to be able to see the list—a bad idea

`config `*`listname password `*`review-by-subscribers` for subscribers only

`config `*`listname password `*`review-by-owners` for list managers only

You can set a default for new subscribers to specify whether their addresses are concealed (omitted from subscriber lists), by sending this command:

`config `*`listname password `*`default conceal yes`

The list managers can see all addresses, whether they're concealed or not.

Concealing the Existence of Your List

You can omit your list's name from ListProc's response to the `lists` command (which generates a list of all lists managed by that ListProc program) by sending this command:

`config `*`listname password `*`hidden-list`

This command also changes the list settings so that only subscribers can see the subscriber list, see list archives, and post messages.

Controlling Who Can See the List Archives

To specify who may read the list archives, send one of these commands:

`config `*`listname password `*`archives-to-owners` for list managers only

`config `*`listname password `*`archives-to-subscribers` for all list subscribers

`config `*`listname password `*`archives-to-all` for anyone to be able to read the list archives

Controlling How ListProc Replies Are Addressed

Send this command if you want replies to be addressed back to the list address:

`config `*`listname password `*`reply-to-list`

Send this command if you want replies to be addressed to the sender of the original message:

`config `*`listname password `*`reply-to-sender`

Setting Posting Options for ListProc Lists
To control who may post, send one of these commands:

To allow only subscribers to post, send `config listname password send-by-subscribers`.

To allow anyone to post (usually a bad idea), send the command `config listname password send-by-all`.

To allow only the list managers to post, send `config listname password send-by-owners`.

To set a limit to the number of all messages to be processed per day, send this command:

`config listname password message-limit number`

Replace *number* with a number: 50 is a good limit, except for high-volume lists. There isn't a way to set limits for individual subscribers.

Setting Moderation Options for ListProc Lists
ListProc lets moderators approve messages in one of two ways:

Moderated-no-edit. ListProc sends you a copy of the message, with a message number. To approve the message for distribution, you send the message `approve listname password number` (replacing *number* with the message number). To reject the message, send `discard listname password number`. You can't edit the message: You just give it thumbs-up or thumbs-down.

Moderated-edit. ListProc sends you a copy of the message. If you want the message distributed to the list, you post it to the list yourself, editing as appropriate. If you don't, you don't post the message.

To make your list moderated-no-edit, send this command:

`config listname password moderated-no-edit addresses`

To make it moderated-edit, send this command:

`config listname password moderated-edit addresses`

Replace *addresses* with the addresses of the moderators, separated by spaces. To add a moderator, send the command again, adding the new moderator's address to the command. To remove a moderator but keep the list moderated, send this command:

`config listname password remove-moderators address`

If you don't want the list to be moderated, send this command:

`config `*`listname password`*` unmoderated`

ListProc doesn't have a system for rotating among moderators. If you want to share the work without all the moderators getting all the messages, set up a mailbox (at a free e-mail Web site or other location) and tell all the moderators how to retrieve mail from that mailbox. Whoever reads an approval message is responsible for approving or discarding it and then deleting the message from the shared moderators' mailbox.

Changing ListProc List Managers

To add a list manager, send this command (replacing *address* with the address of the new list manager):

`config `*`listname password`*` owners `*`address`*

To remove a manager, send this command:

`config `*`listname password`*` remove-owners `*`address`*

You can specify a separate set of addresses to receive error messages, if only some of the list managers want to deal with them. These error messages include bounced messages from subscribers. Send this command (replacing *address* with one or more addresses that will receive error messages):

`config `*`listname password`*` delivery-errors-to `*`address`*

To tell ListProc not to send error messages to someone, send this command:

`config `*`listname password`*` remove-errors-to `*`address`*

Adding and Deleting Subscribers

To add a subscriber, send this command, replacing *address* with the person's e-mail address and *name* with the person's name:

`add `*`listname password address name`*

If you don't want the person to receive confirmation and welcome messages, send this command:

`quiet add `*`listname password address name`*

To delete a subscriber, send this command:

`del `*`listname password address`*

To avoid the person's getting a confirmation message, add `quiet` to the beginning of the command.

Getting a List of Subscribers

Send this command:

`review `*`listname`*

or
```
recipients listname
```

Changing Subscribers' Options for ListProc Lists

To see the settings for a subscriber, send this command, replacing *address* with the subscriber's address:

```
set listname for address
```

You get a message with settings listed like this:

```
ADDRESS = prboc@gurus.com
MAIL = ACK
PASSWORD = 917904113
CONCEAL = NO
```

To change a setting for a subscriber, send this command:

```
set listname option for address
```

Replace *option* with one of the following subscription settings:

`mail ack`, to receive individual postings

`mail digest`, to receive MIME digests

`mail digest-nomime`, to receive text digests

`mail postpone`, to hold mail

`conceal yes`, to omit the person's address from subscriber lists

`conceal no`, to include the person's address on subscriber lists

If you don't want the subscriber to get a confirmation message about the change, add `quiet` to the beginning of the command.

To change someone's address, send this command:

```
set listname address password newaddress for oldaddress
```

Replace *password* with the list password, *newaddress* with the person's new address, and *oldaddress* with the address that is currently subscribed to the list. This is the only `set` command that requires you to include the list password. ListProc sends a confirmation message to both the new and old addresses.

Preventing People from Subscribing or Posting

To prevent a person from posting, send this command, replacing *address* with the person's address:

```
ignore listname password address
```

This command tells ListProc to ignore all commands or postings from that address. Be sure to unsubscribe the person first if you don't want her to continue to receive list postings.

Configuring the Archives of ListProc Lists

Ask your ListProc site manager to set up archiving for your list. The archives are usually stored in a separate file for each month's postings. To control who can see the archives, send one of these commands:

For public archives send;
`config listname password archives-to-all`.

For access by subscribers only, send;
`config listname password archives-to-subscribers`.

For access by list managers only, send;
`config listname password archives-to-owners`.

If your ListProc installation includes the ListProc Web interface, ask your ListProc site manager to make your archives available on the Web interface. The `archives-to-all`, `archives-to-subscribers`, and `archives-to-owners` settings apply to the Web interface, too.

Instructions for Managing Majordomo Lists

You communicate with Majordomo by sending commands. See the section "Instructions for Majordomo Lists," in Chapter 4, to see how to send commands to the administrative address for your new list. In the instructions that follow, replace *listname* with the exact name of the list, and *password* with the list password. (These instructions are for Majordomo 1.9x; if Majordomo 2 is ever released, its operation will be slightly different.)

Checking Your Majordomo List Options

Send this command to the administrative address for the list:
`config listname password`

You receive a listing of the list settings that are in effect. Majordomo has far fewer settings than LISTSERV and ListProc:
```
subscribe_policy = closed
restrict_post = knitters-anon: knitters-anon-extra
reply_to = knitters-anon@gurus.com
admin_passwd = tangledup
which_access = list
get_access = list
```

```
who_access = closed
subject_prefix = [knitters-anon]
```

If there is a digest version of your list (with the name *listname*-digest), send the command `config listname-digest password` to get the settings for the digest version, too.

Changing Majordomo List Options

To change the settings for your list, follow these steps:

1. Send the command `config listname password`. You receive a message containing the list settings.

2. Copy the settings into a new e-mail message addressed to the administrative address for the list.

3. Edit the settings, leaving the part to the left of each equal sign unchanged.

4. Turn off your signature, if you use one, so that it isn't added to the end of this message. Add the line `newconfig listname password` as the first line of the message, and send the message. Majordomo installs your new settings to replace the old ones. You can send the command `config listname password` again to confirm your new settings.

Changing Your Majordomo List Password

If you want to change the list password, send this command:

`passwd listname password newpassword`

Replace *password* with the existing password for the list and *newpassword* with the new password you want to use. Don't include a # in your password.

Changing a Majordomo List's Description

Get your list header as described in the section "Changing Majordomo List Options," earlier in this chapter. Change the text after the equal sign on the `description =` line to contain the description line you want to use. Install the updated list headers as described in that section.

Viewing and Updating the Welcome Message and FAQ

To see the welcome message, send this command:

`intro listname`

To see the FAQ (info file), send this command:

`info listname`

To install new messages, compose a message to the administrative address for the list. On the first line of the message, type a command that tells Majordomo that you are updating a list message. For the welcome message, use this command:

`newintro listname password`

To install a new FAQ, use this command:

`newinfo listname password`

After the command, which appears on the first line of the message, copy the text of the message from your text editor or word processor so that it starts on the second line of the e-mail message. Edit the message as needed to eliminate line endings that appear in the wrong place. Make sure that your e-mail program doesn't add a signature to the message, or else your signature will appear at the end of the welcome message or FAQ. Then send off your message.

Setting Subscription Options for Majordomo Lists

Get your list settings as described in the section "Changing Majordomo List Options," earlier in this chapter, make the following changes, and install the updated list settings as described in that section. To make your list closed, change the `subscribe_policy` line to `subscribe_policy = closed+confirm`. To make it open, change the `subscribe_policy` line to `subscribe_policy = open+confirm`. Majordomo also allows the setting `subscribe_policy = auto+confirm`, which means that anyone can subscribe his own address, but only list managers can subscribe someone else's address. The `+confirm` tells Majordomo to confirm each subscription request by sending a message to the subscriber to which he or she must respond.

When someone tries to subscribe to a closed list, the list managers receive a message asking for approval. To approve the subscription, send this command to Majordomo:

`approve password subscribe listname address`

Replace *address* with the subscriber's address. (This is the same command you use to add people to the list even if they didn't send in a subscription request.)

Setting Digest Options for Majordomo Lists

Ask the Majordomo site manager to create a digested version of your list, and specify the time period (usually daily). The new list will have the name *listname*-digest. Subscribers who want the digest format must unsubscribe from the regular list and subscribe to the digest list. When you change the settings for the main list, be sure to consider whether you also need to change them for the digest list: Majordomo doesn't automatically update the digest settings.

Majordomo sends out a digest every time the size of the digest reaches a certain size—the default size is 40K. You can set the maximum size (make it smaller to distribute the digest more often, or larger for less often.) Get your list settings as described in the section "Changing Majordomo List Options" earlier in this chapter, change the `max_length` line to a different number (in kilobytes), and install the updated list settings as described in that section. Most Majordomo installations automatically send a digest every night if any messages are waiting to be sent.

You can tell Majordomo to send out a digest right away (with whatever messages are waiting to be sent) by sending this command:

```
mkdigest listname-digest password
```

Setting Privacy Options for Majordomo Lists

Get your list settings as described in the section "Changing Majordomo List Options," earlier in this chapter; edit the `who_access`, `get_access`, `index_access`, and `which_access` lines; and install the updated list settings as described in that section. Each of these access options controls who can use one of Majordomo's commands:

- `who_access`. Controls who can use the `who` command to see the addresses of subscribers to the list

- `get_access`. Controls who can use the `get` command to retrieve list archives and related files

- `index_access`. Controls who can use the `index` command, which returns an index of files available via the `get` command

- `which_access`. Controls who can use the `which` command to find out which lists you're subscribed to

For each of these, if only subscribers should be able to use the command, set the corresponding option to `list`. For example, this command specifies that only list subscribers may use the `who` command:

```
who_access = list
```

To allow no one to use the `who`, `get`, `index`, or `which` command, set the corresponding option to `closed`. To permit anyone to use them, set the option to `open`. For example, this command lets anyone see the index of files for the list:

```
index_access = open
```

Controlling How Majordomo Replies Are Addressed

Get your list settings as described in the section "Changing Majordomo List Options," earlier in this chapter, edit the `reply_to` setting, and install the updated list settings as described in that section. You can set the `reply_to` setting to the list address if you want replies to go to the list. For example, if the list is named model-train-buffs and it's hosted at gurus.com, the `reply_to` setting would look like this:

```
reply_to = model-train-buffs@gurus.com
```

To send replies to the author of each message, use the keyword `$SENDER`:

```
reply_to = $SENDER
```

Setting Posting Options for Majordomo Lists

Get your list settings as described in the section "Changing Majordomo List Options," earlier in this chapter. To allow only subscribers to post, change the `restrict_post` line to `restrict_post = listname`. Install the updated list settings as described in that section.

Setting Moderation Options for Majordomo Lists

Get your list settings as described in the section "Changing Majordomo List Options," earlier in this chapter, edit the moderate setting, and install the updated list settings as described in that section. To make your list moderated, set the moderate setting to `moderate = yes`. If you don't want the list moderated, set `moderate = no` or remove the moderate line.

Once the list is moderated, messages are bounced (rejected) to the list managers, with the addition of the word *BOUNCE* and the list name to the subject line. To approve a message, follow these steps:

1. Compose the message addressed to the list address (not the administrative address).

2. On the first line of this new message, type `Approved: ` *password* (replacing *password* with the list password).

3. Copy the text from the original message to your new message. Leave out the headers and text in which Majordomo bounces the message. Start with the headers of the original message (when the subscriber sends the message to the list address). Don't leave a blank link between the `Approved:` line and the headers of the original message.

4. Make sure that your e-mail program doesn't add your signature or other text to the message. Don't format the message or use attachments.

5. Send the message.

When Majordomo receives the message, if the password is correct, it removes the `Approved:` line and posts the rest of the message.

Changing Majordomo List Managers

The list manager is kept as part of the list host's mail setup, not as part of Majordomo, so you have to ask the site manager to change the address of a list manager.

Adding and Deleting Subscribers

To add a subscriber, send this command, replacing *address* with the person's e-mail address:

```
approve password subscribe listname address
```

To delete a subscriber, send this command:

```
approve password unsubscribe listname address
```

Getting a List of Subscribers

Send this command:

```
who listname
```

Preventing People from Subscribing or Posting

Majordomo provides the `taboo_header` and `tabbo_body` options to flag problematic posts. These options let you specify strings or patterns that, if they appear in the header or body of the message, cause Majordomo to bounce the message to the moderator rather than post it. You can use these features to catch e-mail from persistently unruly people, to ban contentious or worn-out topics, or otherwise to intercept possibly unwanted messages.

The `taboo_header` and `taboo_body` options are multiline options, in this form:

```
Taboo_headers   << END
/Subject:.*your mother /i
/From:.*flamer@annoying.com/i
END
```

The first line tells Majordomo that you are starting a list of items to look for in the headers of messages, and that the list will end on the next following END line. There follow as many lines as you like, identifying taboo items, followed by a line with the word END. The `taboo_body` option works the same way.

Each line within the `taboo_header` and `taboo_body` option is a Perl language "regular expression" pattern enclosed in slashes (/). The full details of regular expressions are too complex to list here, but the most useful expression is .* (which matches any arbitrary string). In the preceding example, the taboo headers are any Subject line that contains `your mother` or any From line that contains flamer@annoying.com. The letter i at the end of each pattern makes the pattern case insensitive so that it will match upper- and lowercase.

You can put as many patterns as you want into the `taboo_headers` and `taboo_body` lines. Once you've edited them into the configuration file, install the updated list settings as described earlier.

Configuring the Archives of Majordomo Lists

Ask the Majordomo site manager to set up archives for the list. To control who can see the archives, change the `get_access` setting. To limit access to subscribers, use the setting `get_access = listname`.

Instructions for Managing Lyris Lists

You can communicate with Lyris by sending commands (see the section "Instructions for Lyris Lists," in Chapter 4, to find out how to send commands to the administrative address for your new list). But it's easier to use the Web site for your Lyris program. Using the Web interface, display the List Admin Menu page and choose the List Info link. Figure 5-5 shows part of the long Web page that includes all the options you can set.

You can see and change the list's description, whether the list is open or closed, digest options, moderation options, privacy options, posting options, how replies are addressed, and who the list managers are. You can also add and delete subscribers, change subscribers' settings, ban users from posting or subscribing, configure your list's archives, and look at a log of list activity. You can specify headers and footers to be added to messages or digests. If the list is moderated, you can approve or reject messages, and you can set individual subscribers as `approved` so that their posts are distributed without having to pass by the moderators. To change the welcome message and FAQ, click the List Documents link.

Chapter 5: Creating and Managing Your Own Mailing List **111**

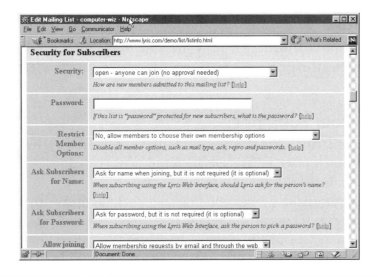

Figure 5-5: Setting list options with the Lyris Web interface.

Getting More Information about List Management

Here are the URLs of Web pages with more information about how to manage lists:

LISTSERV List Owner Manual
   http://www.lsoft.com/manuals/1.8d/owner/owner.html
ListProc List Owner Manual
   http://www.cren.net/listproc/docs/

Majordomo List Owner Manual
   http://www.greatcircle.com/majordomo
   http://www.visi.com/~barr/majordomo-faq.html (an FAQ)
   http://www-uclink.berkeley.edu/major/major.admin.html (an excellent manual)
Lyris List Owner Manual
   http://www.lyris.com/help/ListAdministrator.html
The Mailing List Gurus Page
   http://lists.gurus.com/

List server programs have lots of capabilities that we didn't have the space to cover here—it's a good idea to read the list manager's manual for your list server. For Majordomo list managers, ask your Majordomo site manager to provide the list owner file that comes with the program.

Other Topics

As you settle into list management, you'll develop your own style for dealing with your subscribers. Here are some list management ideas you might find useful.

Educating Your Subscribers

Some lists make sure that the list feels like a community by making new members earn their place in it. Here are some steps you can take to help ensure that new subscribers learn the ropes:

- In the confirmation or welcome message, include the instructions for the list so that there's no excuse for subscribers not to know the rules. (Of course, most won't read them, but there's no way to force them to!) Make the point that it is subscribers' responsibility to keep the list a good place to be.
- Configure the list so that new subscribers are set to "review" or "moderate" (not all list managers or mailing list Web sites have this option). Their posts will be reviewed by you (or the list moderators) for a fixed period (days or weeks) or until you feel that they are following the guidelines for posting. When new subscribers earn "unmoderated" status, tell them so, with a reminder about the rules and that violations can lose them that right.
- If subscribers violate the rules for posting, set them to `nopost` or `ignore` so that they can't post to the list for a short period. Let the list know that the person won't be allowed to respond to messages (otherwise, people may wonder why the person is ignoring them!).
- If your list configuration lets you add a standard footer to list messages, add a footer that includes the URL of the FAQ (info message) for the list, which should include instructions for unsubscribing and rules for participation.
- Create form letters (e-mail stationery) with the answers to the most common posting problems ("Don't post list server commands to the list; send them to the administrative address" or "Don't post copyrighted material without permission"). See the next section for some examples.

Standard Responses to Problems

Here are frequently asked questions and frequently perpetrated gaffes by list subscribers and how you can respond:

Posting copyrighted material. Tell subscribers that if they didn't write it, they can't post it unless they have permission from the copyright holder. This rule includes private e-mail from other people. Many people think it's cute to post quotes from Bill Gates, stories from *Even More Chicken Soup for the Soul*, and other generally heartwarming material to mailing lists, regardless of the actual topic of the list. That is not only boring, it's also illegal. Tell them to stop.

Excessive quoting. Tell subscribers to include only the relevant part of the message to which they are responding. Delete the headers, the signature, and unrelated points. If they receive messages in digests, delete all the other messages, too, and change the subject line from `Re: Digest 490` to `Re:` followed by the subject of the original message.

Personal attacks. Tell subscribers to criticize ideas and statements, but not to criticize people. It's great when people feel that they know each other well enough from your online community that they can imagine what others are like, but attacking other lists members is not okay.

Formatted mail. Tell subscribers to send plain-text messages, without MIME or HTML formatting. See the section "Turning Off Message Formatting," near the end of Chapter 4, to find out how people can send unformatted messages.

Attachments. Unless your list allows attachments (for example, your list is for swapping graphics or sound files), tell subscribers to send files to people privately, not on the list. A subscriber can announce on the list that she has a file of interest and ask people to contact her privately if they'd like the file sent to them. Or a subscriber can post a file on the Web and post a message containing the URL.

Advertisements. Most lists have a no-ads policy. Tell subscribers that they can mention products that they have personally used and that relate to the topic of the list.

Chain letters. Tell your subscribers not to pass along chain letter, virus warnings, or any other "send this to everyone you know!" messages, no matter how urgent the messages purport to be.

Exit Polls

If your list lets you know when someone leaves (this is an option with some mailing list Web sites and list servers), consider asking departing subscribers why they are leaving. Send an e-mail message telling them that you're sorry to see them go and asking what caused them to decide to unsubscribe. You might want to offer a list of possible reasons, like these:

Too many messages. You might want to suggest digests to people who choose this reason.

Subscribed by accident and never meant to join the list.

Unsubscribed by accident and will resubscribe.

Leaving temporarily and will come back. For example, she's going on vacation or entering a busy period of her life.

Switching to another e-mail address.

Too many off-topic messages.

List is too contentious or messages are too offensive. If you get many of these, you might want to ask the most contentious subscribers to tone down their rhetoric.

No longer interested in the topic of the list.

Based on the reasons that people leave, you might choose to handle on-list arguments differently, make more of an effort to keep the list on-topic, or make other changes to make the list more useful to your subscribers.

Moving Your List to a Different Server

Moving your list is a pain, but sometimes you have to do it. Your old list server may be closing down, or you may be losing your access to it (for example, by graduating from college, leaving a job, or switching ISPs). If you choose to move your list to another host, don't forget to do the following:

1. Create a new list at the new site (mailing list Web site or other list server installation) with settings to match the old list. Follow the instructions earlier in this chapter to get a list of the current settings of your old list, and create a new list to match. You might want to take the opportunity to review the settings you have been using and then change those you've been unhappy with.

2. Test the new list. Make sure you are subscribed to it and post a message to the list.

3. Update your FAQ, welcome message, mailing list Web site, and any other documentation about the list to include the new list address, new administrative address, new manager address, and new commands. Install the new FAQ and welcome message for the new list.

4. Search Liszt, Topica, and other list databases for mentions of your list, and notify them of the new address of the list.

5. Search the Web for mentions of your list, and contact the webmasters of the pages you find, letting them know the updated name and address of the list.

6. Get a list of the current subscribers of the old list (following the instructions earlier in this chapter) to refer to later.

7. When you feel that the new list is ready for use, post a message on the old list, announcing that the list is moving. Include instructions for subscribing to the new list. Tell people that the conversation will begin on the new list right away, and that the old list will be terminated as of a specific date. Also include an address at which people can write to you with questions. You might also want to post the new FAQ to the old list.

8. Wait for people to arrive on the new list!

9. Post the announcement of the new list on the old list at least one more time. Not all the subscribers will join the new list—some have lost interest, some never check their e-mail, and some have gotten too busy to participate.

10. On the date you promised to close down the old list, post a message saying that the list is officially terminated. If you can close the list down yourself, do so; if not, request the site administrator to close it down.

11. If you find that lots of people don't move from the old list to the new list, you might want to send private messages to your former subscribers, explaining the move once again and offering to add them to the new list.

Another method of getting subscribers to move over to the new list is to subscribe them yourself. That is, you can get a list of the current subscribers of the old list and send commands to the new list to add everyone to the new list. But there is a problem with this method: Inevitably, some people won't figure out that the new list is the same list they were subscribed to and will complain vociferously that you are mailbombing them by signing them up for a list they didn't request. Also, you can use the move as a way to weed out the deadwood from your list—the people who didn't care if they were on it and the people whose messages disappeared into dead accounts or broken mail servers. Don't worry if your subscriber list is smaller—it's also cleaner!

Part III

Usenet Newsgroup Communities

Chapter Six
Finding, Joining, and Participating in Newsgroups

Usenet is like a distributed bulletin board system, with messages distributed over the Internet. A Usenet *newsgroup* is roughly analogous to a mailing list, but on a vastly larger scale. A busy newsgroup can have several hundred messages a day read by hundreds of thousands of people. It's one of the oldest systems on the Internet, dating back to 1979, and was for many years the primary way that Internet users had online discussions. (Until a few years ago, no mailing list server could have handled the number of people that read a typical newsgroup.)

In recent years, the volume of traffic and increasing amounts of spam have made it challenging for people to get started with Usenet, but many newsgroups remain useful and interesting. Moreover, as we discuss in the next chapter, it's quite possible to use the same Usenet software for private discussions, often an excellent alternative to large mailing lists.

How Usenet Newsgroups Work

To impose a little order on the chaos, Usenet newsgroups are named using a hierarchical naming system so that newsgroups on related topics have related names. Newsgroup messages are distributed around the Internet by news server programs; to read newsgroup messages, you use a newsreading program. Here's how newsgroup names and programs work.

The Newsgroup Hierarchies

Each group has a name composed of words separated by a dot; for example, soc.religion.unitarian-univ. The top level of the newsgroup name is the first part of the name, up to the first dot—in this case, soc for socially oriented newsgroups. The second part of the name is the part up to the next dot (or to the end, if the name has only two levels)—religion for discussions about religion. The third part of this newsgroup name is unitarian-univ, for Unitarian Universalists. (Each level of the newsgroup name is limited to 14 characters because of limits in older Usenet software.) Newsgroup names can have two, three, four, or more parts, depending on how specific the newsgroup topic gets. The first (leftmost) part of the name is the *hierarchy*.

In Usenet's early years, the relatively few newsgroups that existed were all lumped into a few hierarchies, notably net, which included nearly all publicly distributed groups. In 1987, the number of newsgroups had become large enough that leaders of the Usenet community rearranged the newsgroups into seven hierarchies—the Big Seven, as described in the following list. Usenet administrators are not professional librarians, and the assignment of groups to hierarchies can be a bit quirky. One more hierarchy was added later, to create the Big Eight. Since then, each Big Eight hierarchy has had many more subgroups added, and a huge number of organizational, regional, and special-purpose hierarchies have sprung up.

The Big Eight hierarchies and their topics are shown in this list:

- **comp.** Computers, hardware and software, programming, communications, and computer-related organizations. It is the largest and most vigorous hierarchy because of Usenet's origin in the computer science community. It includes about 950 groups. (The exact number increases month by month as new groups are created.)
- **humanities.** The humanities. This top-level category was created only a few years ago to be added to the Big Seven and is still nearly unused. The only group with any traffic in it is humanities.lit.authors.shakespeare.
- **news.** Usenet itself, and the management thereof. It includes news.announce.newusers, which contains frequently posted copies of new user introductory material, and news.newusers.questions, where new users can ask and sometimes get answers to questions. It also includes technically oriented groups about news administration and running discussions about proposed new newsgroups. About 30 groups.
- **rec.** Recreation of all sorts, including antiques, movies, writing, boating, cooking, gambling, arts and crafts, jokes, jokes that are funny, and recreational drugs. About 750 groups.
- **sci.** Science, construed rather broadly. These groups range from aeronautical engineering to agriculture to astronomy to medicine to mathematics and cryptography. About 200 groups.

soc. Social topics, including regional and national culture, genealogy, history, and a large number of religious groups ranging from Biblical literalism to Sikhs. About 250 groups.

talk. Topics that engender long arguments, especially politics. About 30 groups.

misc. Everything else—a grab bag including business, education, exercise and fitness, children, transportation, and very-high-volume for-sale and help-wanted groups.

There is one more widely distributed hierarchy

alt. "Alternative" groups. The alt hierarchy was originally created in protest against the rather tedious procedure required to create a Big Eight newsgroup. Literally anyone can create a newsgroup in the alt hierarchy, and many thousands of alt newsgroups exist, most completely unused or containing only spam. A few alt groups, such as alt.folklore.computers, are actively used. The largest amount of alt traffic is in the alt.binaries groups, which contain text-encoded binary files, including an awful lot of pictures of naked people. The volume in alt.binaries newsgroups is so high that some ISPs don't carry them, not for moral reasons, but because they don't want to dedicate enough disk space to store the newsgroup messages.

Many other hierarchies exist, including hierarchies for specific countries (the hierarchy name is usually the same two-letter country name abbreviation that is used at the end of domains for that country, like br for Brazil) and for regions (like ba for the San Francisco Bay area and ne for the Northeastern section of the United States). Hierarchies are frequently referred to with a dot and an asterisk following the hierarchy name (for example, comp.*), indicating all newsgroups whose names begin with comp.

News Servers

Usenet newsgroup messages are distributed by *news servers*, or Internet host computers running programs that store and send newsgroup messages to people who want to read them. Each news server keeps a set of newsgroups—usually not the entire set of existing newsgroups—and *articles* or *postings* (messages) that have been sent to each newsgroup. Each news server is run by a person, the *news manager* or *news administrator*, who chooses the groups her server will carry. Almost every server connected to the public Internet carries the Big Eight hierarchies as well as some local and regional groups.

There are also private news servers with newsgroups unique to each server and not distributed to the rest of the Internet. For access to those groups, you need to connect directly to the server that carries them, with a username and password. For example, Microsoft runs a news server with newsgroups about new versions of software under development.

To read and post messages to Usenet newsgroups, you need to be able to connect to a news server. When you sign up for an Internet account, your ISP should tell you the name of the news server it runs so that you can connect to it. The news server is usually named news followed by a dot and the ISP's domain name (for example, news.mindspring.net).

Traditionally, every ISP ran its own news server. As the volume of news has increased and the fraction of ISP customers who look at Usenet has dropped, many ISPs now contract out news service to specialized *news providers*, like Supernews. From the user's point of view, there's not much difference: You connect to the news provider's news server rather than to one at your local ISP. News providers generally try to carry every newsgroup distributed anywhere on the planet, including hierarchies in languages other than English. (Some interesting discussions are in fj., but only if you have a news program that can display Japanese characters and you can read Japanese.)

News Distribution

News servers handle both news *reading* by individual people and news *transfer* from one server to another. Unlike e-mail messages, which are addressed to an individual person or set of people (or mailing list address), newsgroup messages are tagged with a newsgroup name and sent out to the world. Anyone with access to a news server can read any messages available on that news server. In practice, people generally choose a small set of newsgroups and read those. Each person's newsreading software keeps track of which messages the person has seen so that the news server doesn't have to remember who's seen what.

Newsgroup messages are passed from server to server by *flooding*, where each news server sends all the messages it has to all the servers with which it exchanges newsgroup messages (*adjacent* servers). (This good type of flooding is different from flooding on chat venues, in which the term refers to posting too many messages too quickly.) To make the flooding reasonably efficient, each message stored on a news server contains a *path*, a header line with the list of news servers through which it has already passed. When one server is sending newsgroup messages to another, the sending server doesn't send messages for which the receiving server already appears in the path. Even with this optimization, a server may receive several copies of the same message, in which case it just discards the duplicates, using the message's message ID (a unique message identifier) as the key.

Because the volume of newsgroup postings is so large, news server managers limit the number of newsgroup messages on their servers in two ways: by selecting hierarchies and by *expiring* old articles (deleting the oldest articles to make room on the disk for new ones). Each manager chooses which hierarchies his server will carry, based on the interests of the users and the disk and network capacity of the news server. A typical news server might carry the Big Eight, some local or regional newsgroups, and perhaps alt.* if the demand warrants. Articles arriving for newsgroups the server doesn't carry are discarded, and in most cases the adjacent news servers are configured to send only the hierarchies the server accepts.

Every news server expires newsgroup messages on a regular basis, typically once a day. The news server manager sets the expiration periods, which can vary by newsgroup as well as by the size of the article and other criteria. Individual articles can contain a suggested expiration date, which the server may or may not honor. Typical expiration times range from a few days to a week or two.

The result of this complex distribution and storage scheme is that newsgroup distribution is less than perfect. After a message is posted, it can take anywhere from a few seconds to a few days to percolate out to the rest of the Internet. Some messages don't make it to some parts of the Internet, particularly in newsgroups that aren't carried on every news server. If you're coming into the middle of a thread of messages, it's quite possible that the earlier ones will already have expired. In practice it isn't usually a big problem, and you can look in public archives, notably Deja.com (described later in this chapter), for missing messages; if a conversation seems to have a missing link, however, it probably does.

Newsreading Programs

Unlike incoming e-mail, which most people download to their own computers, newsgroup messages are usually read online (while connected to the Internet) with the messages fetched from the news server you ask for them. The reason is that you usually want to read most if not all of the messages in your mailbox, but you rarely want to read all messages in a newsgroup—there are just too many.

The traditional way to read newsgroups is using a specialized *newsreading* program, such as trn or slrn in UNIX and Linux or Free Agent in Windows. More recently, newsreaders have become integrated with mail programs and browsers, so Outlook Express, Netscape Communicator, and Pine all contain adequate newsreaders (although not as flexible as the specialized ones). Also, several Web sites now let you participate in newsgroups over the Web, making them resemble Web-based message boards.

All newsreaders provide the same basic functions:

Selecting which newsgroups to read. Newsreaders let you subscribe to newsgroups, which means only that the newsreader remembers that you want to read this newsgroup and keeps track of which messages you've already read. Unlike subscribing to a mailing list, subscribing to a newsgroup doesn't involve signing up with any central authority. Your newsreader can display a list of all newsgroups your news server carries (usually tens of thousands), new newsgroups that have been formed since the last time you checked), or only newsgroups to which you have subscribed.

Selecting articles within a newsgroup. Newsreaders usually display messages in a newsgroup by *thread*; that is, with an original message followed by all the responses to that message, along with the responses to those responses (ad infinitum). Replies to a message are usually indented below the original message. Most newsreaders can also sort messages by date or author.

Reading articles. All newsreaders can display the text of articles, and some can also display attached graphics files (described in the next section).

Posting messages to newsgroups. You can post new messages to start a new thread, or you can post follow-up messages in reply to existing articles.

Sending e-mail responses to message authors. If your reply won't be of interest to most readers of the newsgroup, e-mail your reply directly to the author rather than post it to the newsgroup. Most newsreaders let you do this easily.

The better newsreaders also provide ways to set filters to control which articles you see. The reason is that many newsgroups have a great deal of chitchat, and it's helpful to skip topics that you know you're not interested in and authors who never have anything interesting to say.

Uuencoded Files

Along with text, newsgroup messages can include files, usually graphics files. The files are encoded as text so that they can pass through the Usenet distribution system using a method called *uuencoding*. Most newsreader programs can decode and display uuencoded files contained in newsgroup messages.

Reading Newsgroup Messages

This section describes how to participate in Usenet newsgroups by using the most popular newsreading programs.

Configuring Your Newsreader

Unless your ISP preconfigured your newsreading program, you have to enter a little configuration information the first time you start it. The information you're likely to need includes

News server name. The name of the computer that handles news service for you. Although usually it will be at your ISP with a name like news.yourisp.com, sometimes it may be a server at a news provider company. Your ISP can tell you this information.

News login and password (optional). If you use a news server at a news provider or a private news server, you have to log in. You usually use the same login and password as you use to connect to your ISP. If your ISP runs its own news server, you generally don't have to log in.

If you want access to the newsgroups on private news servers, you have to configure them in your newsreader. It requires the same information: the name of the server and a username and password combination. Most newsreaders can be configured to connect to several different news servers—for example, your ISP's server and your company's private news server. Your newsreader keeps track of which server you use to read each newsgroup to which you subscribe.

The first time your newsreader connects to a news server, it has to download the complete list of newsgroups available on that server. Because news servers can have 10,000 or more groups, the download can take a couple of minutes. Your newsreader needs to do this only once—the next time you connect, it retrieves only updates to the newsgroup list.

Reading Newsgroups with Netscape Newsgroups

Netscape Communicator has included an adequate if not fabulous newsreader since version 3.0. In this section, we describe the news features of version 4.7, which are in the part of the program named Netscape Newsgroups. (Earlier versions named the newsreader Netscape Collabra.) You can download the latest version of Netscape Navigator from **Netscape NetCenter**, at http://home.netscape.com/computing/download/.

Configuring Netscape Newsgroups

1. In Netscape Communicator, choose Edit|Preferences to display the Preferences dialog box.
2. On the Category list down the left side, if the Mail & Newsgroups category isn't expanded (if it doesn't display subcategories below it), click the little + box to its left.
3. Click the Newsgroup Servers category. The Preferences dialog box displays a list of news servers that Netscape already knows about.
4. If the news server you plan to use already appears on the list, you're done. If not, click Add to display the Newsgroup Server Properties dialog box.
5. In the Server box, type the name of the news server. You can use the default settings for everything else.
6. Click OK to add the news server, and click OK to dismiss the Preferences dialog box.

The Netscape Communicator Services Window

After you have configured the news server, open the Netscape Messenger window by either clicking the icon with two word balloons on the Netscape status bar or choosing Communicator|Messenger from the menu. (You can also choose Communicator|Newsgroups, although you get more or less the same

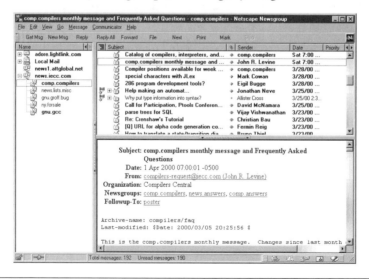

Figure 6-1: The Netscape Communicator Services window displays both e-mail and newsgroups.

window.) You see a Netscape Communicator Services or Netscape Newsgroup window like the one shown in Figure 6-1. The window has three sections: a list to the left showing your mailboxes and news servers (ignore the mailboxes, which are for reading e-mail), a list in the upper right corner listing the messages in the selected newsgroup, and a box in the lower right corner displaying the selected newsgroup message.

Subscribing to Newsgroups

To see the list of newsgroups to which you can subscribe, right-click the news server's name and select Subscribe to Newsgroups. You see the Subscribe to Newsgroups window (as shown in Figure 6-2), where you can browse the set of newsgroups available and subscribe or unsubscribe as desired.

Netscape lists the hierarchies because a list of all newsgroup names would be thousands of names long. To see the newsgroups a hierarchy contains, click the + box to the left of the hierarchy name or double-click the hierarchy name. When you see a newsgroup that looks interesting, select it and click the Subscribe button.

You can also search for newsgroup names that contain a word or part of a word. Click the Search tab in the Subscribe to Newsgroups dialog box, type a word in the Search For box, and click Search Now. The Newsgroup Name box lists newsgroups whose names contain that word.

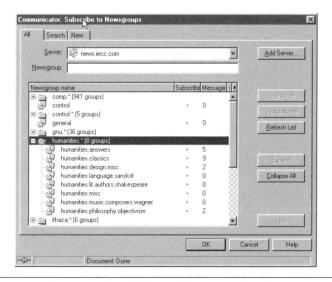

Figure 6-2: Netscape displays a list of hierarchies—double-click a hierarchy to see the newsgroups it contains.

When you have subscribed to some newsgroups, click OK. The newsgroups to which you have subscribed appear in the mailbox and newsgroup list on the left side of the Netscape Communicator Services window.

Reading Newsgroup Messages

To read a newsgroup, click in the newsgroup list. The first time you click a newsgroup name, Netscape may ask how many message headers you want to download to get started: the headers of all newsgroup messages stored on the news server or just the first 500. Make your choice and click Download. Netscape displays the message headers—date, author, and subject—in the upper right part of the window.

Subscribed newsgroups appear roughly like mailboxes in the Netscape Communicator Services window, except with messages sorted by topic. Only the first message in each thread appears (or the first unexpired message, if the original message has been deleted from the news server). If more messages are in the *thread* (the replies to that message), a + box appears to the left of the subject—click it to see a list of the messages.

Click a message to see it in the lower right part of the window, or double-click the message to display it in a separate window. To display the next message, you can choose Go|Next|Unread Message or press its keyboard shortcut: N (just plain N, with no Alt or Ctrl). If you decide to skip the rest of the messages in this thread, choose Message|Ignore Thread or press K (for kill).

Posting Messages

To post a message to start a new thread (a message unrelated to an existing message), click the New Msg button on the toolbar or press Ctrl+M. To reply to the current message, click the Reply button or press Ctrl+R. Either way, you see a Composition window like the one shown in Figure 6-3. In the address area at the top of the window, you can choose Group to post the message to a newsgroup, To or Cc to e-mail the message to someone, or both. By default, Netscape posts responses to the newsgroup you are now reading.

Replying to the Author of a Message

To reply by e-mail to the sender of a message, right-click the message and choose Reply to Sender Only or Reply to Sender and Newsgroup. Compose the message and click Send to mail it.

Chapter 6: *Finding, Joining, And Participating in Newsgroups*

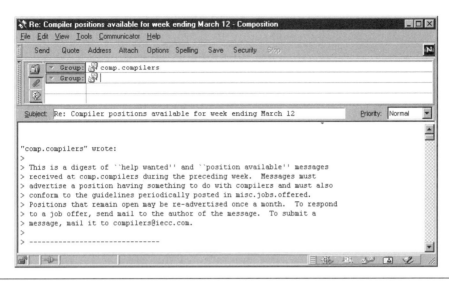

Figure 6-3: Composing a message with Netscape Messenger.

Unsubscribing from a Newsgroup
Click the newsgroup name on the left side of the Netscape window and press the Del key. You don't delete the newsgroup from the news server; you just tell your newsreader to delete it from your list of subscribed newsgroups.

Getting New Messages from the News Server
To get any new messages that have arrived at the news server, choose a newsgroup from your list of subscribed newsgroups. If Netscape doesn't automatically fetch the new messages, click the Get Msg button on the toolbar.

Reading Newsgroups with Outlook Express
Outlook Express provides newsreading features similar to Netscape's. This section describes Outlook Express 5.0. Although the features don't change much between versions, some menu items move from one menu to another. You can download the latest version of Outlook Express from the **Internet Explorer** home page, at http://www.microsoft.com/windows/ie/.

Configuring Outlook Express
When Outlook Express starts, it shows a default window with a variety of options; near the middle of the window is Set Up a Newsgroups Account. Alternatively, choose Tools|Accounts to display the Internet Accounts window,

and then click the Add button and choose News from the menu that appears. Either way, an Internet Connection Wizard walks you through the process of setting up a news account, entering the e-mail address to use (usually the same one you use everywhere else), the name of the news server, and a few other options. When you are done, Outlook Express offers to download the set of newsgroups from the news server. Choose Yes—even though the download may take a few minutes, you need to get the list of newsgroups from which you can choose.

Subscribing to Newsgroups

When Outlook Express is done downloading the list of newsgroups your new server carries, you see the Newsgroup Subscriptions window (as shown in Figure 6-4), where you can subscribe to newsgroups of interest. You can also display this window later by right-clicking the name of the news server on the Folders list and choosing Newsgroups from the menu that appears.

Outlook Express displays all newsgroups the new server carries, arranged alphabetically. To subscribe to a newsgroup, double-click the newsgroup name. To search for newsgroups whose names contain a word or part of a word, type the word in the Display Newsgroups Which Contain box, near the top of the Newsgroup Subscriptions window.

When you have subscribed to the newsgroups that interest you, click OK. You see the Outlook Express window.

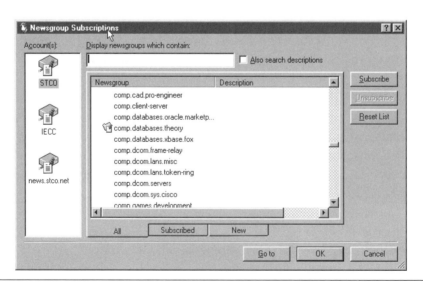

Figure 6-4: Outlook Express doesn't display newsgroups by hierarchy—you see a long, alphabetical list.

Chapter 6: Finding, Joining, And Participating in Newsgroups **129**

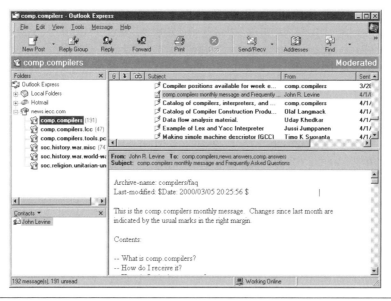

Figure 6-5: Reading news with Outlook Express.

The Outlook Express Window

The Outlook Express window (as shown in Figure 6-5) usually includes a Folder list down the left side that displays both your e-mail mailboxes and the news servers Outlook Express knows about. The newsgroups to which you have subscribed appear indented below the news server name that carries that newsgroup.

Reading Newsgroup Messages

To read a newsgroup, double-click the newsgroup name on the Folders list to see the list of articles in the newsgroup. If the newsgroup includes lots of messages, a delay may occur while Outlook Express fetches the headers for the new messages from the newsgroup. The list of messages appears in the upper right part of the window.

Messages are usually grouped by threads, which Microsoft calls *conversations*. A thread with more than one message has a + box to its left: click it to see the list of messages in the thread. Click a message to display the message in the preview panel in the main window, in the lower right part of the window. Or double-click the message to display it in its own window. You can press Ctrl+U to display unread messages one at a time.

To help sift through large numbers of messages, Outlook Express lets you *watch* (select) or ignore threads (conversations). On the list of message headers, note that the space to the left of the subjects has three column headers: a paper clip (showing which messages have attachments), an arrow (showing which messages you've marked to download later), and a pair of glasses (showing which messages you've told Outlook Express to watch or ignore). To watch a thread, click in the glasses column to the left of the message subject so that a pair of glasses appears. To ignore a thread, click again so that a red slashed circle appears. Henceforth, new messages in watched or ignored threads will also be marked as watched or ignored. Usually, you want to make ignored messages completely invisible; to do so, select View|Current View from the menu and choose Hide Read or Ignored Messages. You can also define filtering rules to do more complex marking or deleting: Choose Tools|Message Rules|News.

Posting Messages

To reply to a message, click the Reply Group icon to post a follow-up to the newsgroup. To post a new message, click New Post. All these icons display a window (as shown in Figure 6-6) in which you can compose your new message.

Don't use stationery in messages you post to newsgroups because it uses HTML formatting, which most newsgroups do not welcome. Click the Spelling icon on the toolbar before you click Send—thousands of people may read your message.

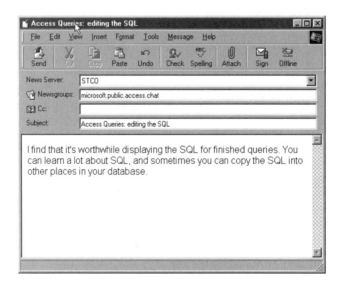

Figure 6-6: Composing a message with Outlook Express.

Replying to the Author of a Message

When you are displaying a message, click the Reply icon to e-mail a response to the message's author. Compose your message and click Send.

Unsubscribing from a Newsgroup

If you don't want to read the messages from a newsgroup any more, right-click the newsgroup name on the Folders list and choose Unsubscribe from the menu that appears.

Reading Newsgroups with Free Agent

Free Agent (from Forté, Inc.) is a popular freeware news program for Windows. Free Agent is a limited version of Agent, a powerful commercial news program. This section describes Free Agent version 1.21, which you can download from the **Forté** Web site, at http://www.forteinc.com/. If you like Free Agent, consult the Web site for a list of additional Agent features and consider buying Agent.

Configuring Free Agent

The first time you run Free Agent, it displays a setup window in which you have to type the name of your news server, outgoing (SMTP) mail server, e-mail address, and name. If you have already configured another newsreader on your computer, you can try clicking the Use Information from Another Program button. Then Free Agent connects to your news server and downloads the complete list of available newsgroups, which can take several minutes.

The Free Agent Window

Free Agent lets you configure the layout of its main window, but normally it contains three parts, as shown in Figure 6-7:

The newsgroup list in the upper left part of the window. This list can display all available newsgroups or only the newsgroups to which you have subscribed.

The message list in the upper right part of the window, displaying messages in the selected newsgroup.

The text of the current message.

If you want to change the layout of the Free Agent window, choose Options|Window Layout from the menu. You can also adjust the sizes of the three window sections by clicking and dragging the divider lines.

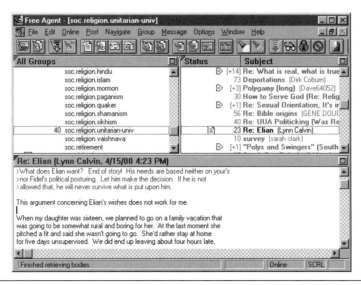

Figure 6-7: The Free Agent newsreader window.

Subscribing to Newsgroups

Free Agent displays the list of newsgroups in the upper left part of its window. Click the window header to switch among all groups (all available newsgroups on the news server), subscribed groups (newsgroups to which you have subscribed), and new groups (groups that have recently been added to your news server). To subscribe to a newsgroup, display all groups or new groups and scroll down the alphabetical list of newsgroups. Right-click on a newsgroup and choose Subscribe from the menu that appears. An icon appears to the left of the newsgroup to show that you have subscribed to it.

Alternatively, you can double-click a newsgroup name to display a window that offers to download some newsgroup messages so that you decide whether to subscribe. To set the properties that control when newsgroup messages are downloaded and how long Free Agent keeps them, right-click the newsgroup name and choose Properties from the menu that appears.

Reading Newsgroup Messages

Display the list of subscribed groups in the upper left part of the window, and click the Get New Messages in Subscribed Groups button (the leftmost button on the toolbar). Click the newsgroup you want to read. The message headers for that newsgroup appear in the upper right part of the window. To the left of each message header is a number (the number of lines in the message). Some messages are the first message in a thread and have a + box to their left: Click the + box to see the list of messages in the thread.

To read a message, click the message header and press Enter or double-click the message header. Free Agent downloads the text of the message and displays it in the lower part of the window. To display the next unread message in the newsgroup, press Ctrl+N.

Posting Messages

To reply to the current message by posting a follow-up article in the same newsgroup, click the Post Follow Up Message button on the toolbar or press F. To send a message on a new topic, click the Post New Usenet Message button or press P. Free Agent switches from the normal window layout to display a window in which you can compose a message, as shown in Figure 6-8.

Free Agent includes the text of the original message—delete the parts you don't reply to. To post your message, click Send Now. To skip posting the message and return to the normal Free Agent window, click Cancel.

Replying to the Author of a Message

To send an e-mail message to the author of the current message, click the Post Reply Via Email button on the toolbar or press R. Compose your message and click Send Now.

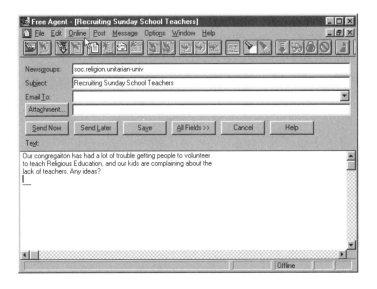

Figure 6-8: Posting a message with Free Agent.

Unsubscribing from a Newsgroup

If you don't want to continue to read the messages in a newsgroup, right-click the newsgroup name on the Subscribed Groups list. Choose Subscribe from the menu that appears (even though you are unsubscribing). Free Agent asks whether to keep the messages you downloaded for that newsgroup.

Getting More Messages

To download the new messages in all the newsgroups to which you are subscribed, click the leftmost icon on the toolbar, the Get New Messages in Subscribed Groups button.

Reading Newsgroups with Pine

Pine is a widely used, text-only, mail and news program for UNIX and Windows. Although its newsreading features aren't very strong, if you use Pine for your mail anyway, it can be handy to read a little news.

Configuring and Running Pine

Pine treats all mail and news as collections of folders. Each news server is a single collection of folders, and most copies of Pine are set up with the local server as one of its configured collections. (If not, ask your local Pine expert for configuration help.)

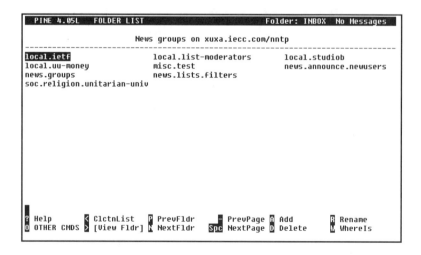

Figure 6-9: Choosing newsgroups with Pine.

Chapter 6: Finding, Joining, And Participating in Newsgroups

Nearly all Pine commands are single characters. Run Pine, and then press M to get to the main Pine menu if it's not already displayed. Then press L to see the folder list. You see a list of mail and news folders, like this:

```
Mail
    Local folders in mail/

    News on xuxa.iecc.com/nntp
        News groups on xuxa.iecc.com/nntp
```

Use the arrow keys (or the mouse, if you use Windows) to move to the News collection, and press Enter to expand it if the list of newsgroups isn't displayed. You see the list of newsgroups you have subscribed to, as shown in Figure 6-9.

Subscribing to Newsgroups

To subscribe to a newsgroup, go to the Main menu and then to the folder list, and then select the news collection; you can use Add and Delete to change the list of your subscribed newsgroups.

Reading Newsgroup Messages

After you see the list of newsgroups, move through the list with the arrow keys and press Enter to open a newsgroup folder, as shown in Figure 6-10. Pine

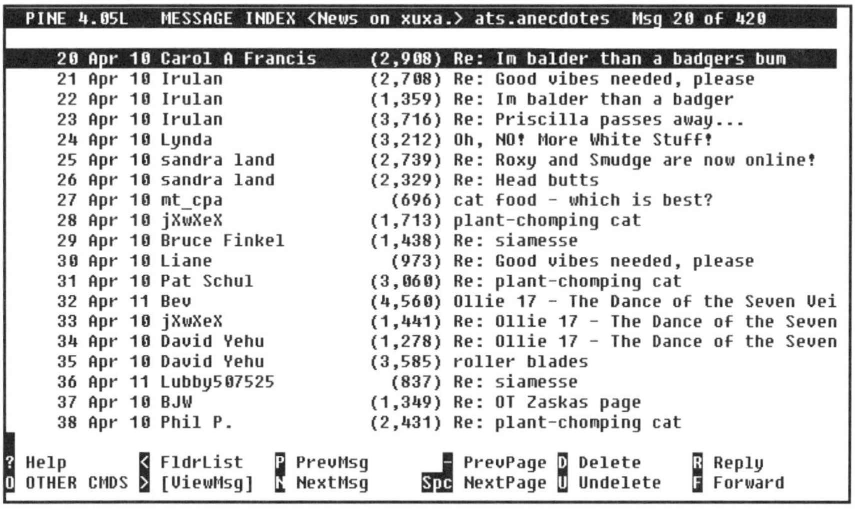

Figure 6-10: Choosing messages with Pine.

treats a newsgroup folder nearly identically to a mail folder, displaying all unread messages.

To read a message, move the cursor to it and press Enter. You can press the Tab key to move from message to message. Press D to delete a message and remove it from your message list (but not from the news server.)

Posting Messages

Posting a news item is also similar to writing a mail message. To reply to a news item, press R for reply. Pine asks whether to post the reply to the newsgroup; the alternative is to reply to the sender. To post a new article, press C for create—Pine asks whether to create a newsgroup article or an e-mail message.

Because Pine is primarily an e-mail program, it doesn't have the powerful threading and filtering features that other newsreading programs do; if you read lots of newsgroups, the investment of learning about another program will be well spent.

Reading Newsgroups with Trn

Trn (for *t*hreaded *r*ead *n*ews) is probably the most widely used newsreader on UNIX systems. If you use UNIX, trn is as good a program to start with as any because it works and it's free. If your system doesn't have trn, it may well have rn, an older, less powerful newsreader.

Configuring Trn

Your UNIX system administrator should already have configured your system to connect to the news server. The first time you run trn (by typing trn and pressing Enter), it wants to know which newsgroups you plan to subscribe to. You can also subscribe to newsgroups later. Trn displays something like this:

```
Can't open /usr/home/margy/.rninit
(Revising soft pointers -- be patient.)
Unread news in news.announce.newusers         5 articles
Unread news in soc.religion.unitarian-univ509 articles

Checking for new newsgroups...
```

Trn creates a file named .newsrc (yes, it starts with a dot) to keep track of which newsgroups you subscribe to and which articles you've already seen. If you've never run trn, it guesses that you want to subscribe to every single newsgroup available on your system—usually a huge list! If you have already run trn, it wants to know whether you want to subscribe to the newsgroups that have been created since the last time you ran it.

Trn displays each newsgroup and asks whether you want to subscribe:
```
Newsgroup misc.business.product-dev not in .newsrc --
subscribe? [ynYN]
```
For each newsgroup, you can press one of these keys:

Y to subscribe (when trn asks where to put the newsgroup, press Enter)

N not to subscribe

Shift+Y to subscribe to all the newsgroups (a bad idea because there may be thousands)

Shift+N not to subscribe to any newsgroups

Because most news servers carry tens of thousands of newsgroups, you probably don't want to answer this question for each available newsgroup. Press Shift+N to tell it to stop asking.

Trn commands consist of a single letter, without pressing Enter afterward. Capitalization counts—lowercase and uppercase letters can do different things.

Quitting Trn

When you're tired of reading newsgroup messages, you leave trn by pressing q (for quit). Depending on where you are, you may have to press it two or three times.

Subscribing to Newsgroups

To subscribe to a newsgroup, type the following line (and replace *newsgroupname* with the exact name of the newsgroup):
```
G newsgroupname
```
When you press Enter, trn asks where to put the newsgroup on your list (in your .newsrc file). Press Enter to tell trn to put the new newsgroup at the end of the file. After you've subscribed to a newsgroup, each time you run trn it asks whether you want to read the messages in those groups. To see the newsgroups you are subscribed to, press Shift+L.

Reading Newsgroup Messages

When you run trn, it goes through each newsgroup to which you are subscribed and asks whether you want to read the messages:
```
====== 509 unread articles in soc.religion.unitarian-
univ -- read now? [+ynq]
```

For each newsgroup, you can choose one of these keys to press:

Y ....To read the articles now

+ (Shift+=) ....To enter the article selector for this newsgroup, which lets you mark the headers of the messages you want to read

N ....To skip the newsgroup for now

U ....To unsubscribe from the newsgroup

If you press Y, trn displays the first part of the first unread article in the newsgroup. The screen looks something like this:

```
rec.pets.chickens #6281
From: fred@glooble.net (Fred) [1]
[1] Getting rid of older chickens
Organization: Glooble Net Global Access
Date: Sat Aug 7 06:48:03 2001
+
We need to get rid of our chickens, because the hen
house has to go. Any ideas of what we should do with 14
hens that are no longer laying? Meatballs?

End of article 6281 (of 6281) -- what next? [npq]
```

If the message is too long to fit on the screen, a MORE prompt appears at the bottom—press the Spacebar to see the next screenful. If you don't want to see the rest of the article, press N to go on to the next article or Q to leave the newsgroup and go on to the next newsgroup.

When you get to the end of the article, trn asks what to do next:

```
End of article 143515 (of 143520) -- what next? [npq]
```

Here are the most commonly used commands you can use when you have just read an article:

K (for kill) ....If you find an article to be totally uninteresting. Trn skips (marks as already read) both the rest of that article and any other articles in the newsgroup that have the same title.

Shift+J (for junk) .To skip the entire rest of the thread.

B ....To back up one page.

N or the Spacebar ...To read the next unread article.

Q ....To quit reading this newsgroup.

Posting Messages

To post a follow-up article to the current article, press F (or Shift+F, if you want to include a quoted copy of the article to which you are replying). Trn runs the Pnews program, which asks you a few questions. The first, if you ran it directly rather than from inside trn, is the name of the newsgroup or newsgroups. (You can post a single article to several newsgroups at a time if it's appropriate.) Type the name of the newsgroup or newsgroups (separate them with commas). Trn asks for the subject of the message and then for the distribution (press Enter to use the default setting). Then trn asks once more whether you're absolutely, positively certain that you want to post an article, and, if you choose Yes, runs your text editor. When you have written your message and exited the text editor, you can press one of these keys:

S . . . . To send the message

E . . . . To edit it again

A . . . . To abandon it

Replying to the Author of a Message

To e-mail the author of the current message, press R (or Shift+R, if you want to quote the article you are replying to). Trn runs your text editor, where you can compose your message. The file you're given to edit contains header lines for the e-mail message, notably Subject and To, which you can edit if you want. When you leave the editor, you can press S, E, or A, as explained in the preceding section.

Choosing the Threads to Read

Rather than read the messages one at a time in the order in which they appear, you can ask trn to show you a list of the threads that have new messages and choose which messages to read. (This ability to select threads is what the t in trn is all about.) When trn asks whether you want to read messages, press + rather than Y to select the thread selector. You see a list that looks like Figure 6-11, showing the threads that contain unread messages.

The list of threads rarely fits on one screen. The letters in the left column are key letters you press to choose articles to read. Figure 6-9, for example, contains six threads, with the letters *a, b, d, e, f,* and *g* (trn skips letters sometimes). You press B, for example, to see the article about Thomas Paine. Then press the Spacebar or > to see the next screenful of threads. The prompt line tells you how far you are through the list. You can press any of these keys:

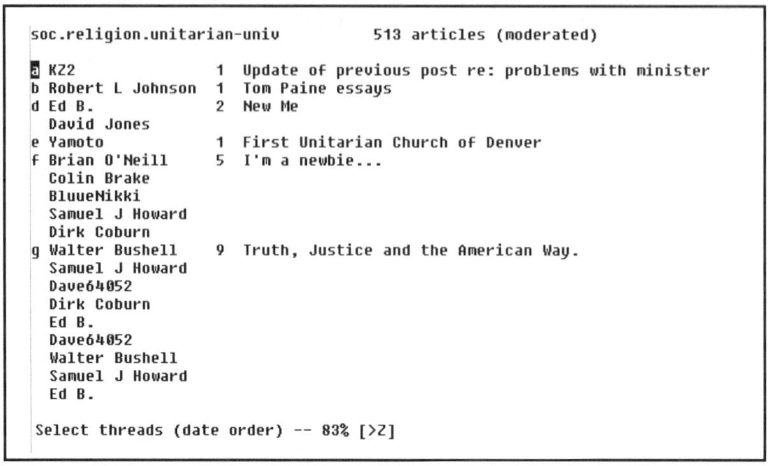

```
soc.religion.unitarian-univ         513 articles (moderated)
a KZ2                    1  Update of previous post re: problems with minister
b Robert L Johnson       1  Tom Paine essays
d Ed B.                  2  New Me
  David Jones
e Yamoto                 1  First Unitarian Church of Denver
f Brian O'Neill          5  I'm a newbie...
  Colin Brake
  BluueNikki
  Samuel J Howard
  Dirk Coburn
g Walter Bushell         9  Truth, Justice and the American Way.
  Samuel J Howard
  Dave64052
  Dirk Coburn
  Ed B.
  Dave64052
  Walter Bushell
  Samuel J Howard
  Ed B.

Select threads (date order) -- 83% [>Z]
```

Figure 6-11: Choosing which threads to read with trn.

< (Shift+,) to display the preceding page of the thread list.

> (Shift+.) to display the next page of the thread list.

Spacebar to display the next page of the list of threads—if you're at the end of the list, trn starts showing you the articles you selected.

Shift+D to start displaying the selected articles while killing (marking as read) any unselected articles on the screen.

Shift+Z to start displaying the selected articles but not kill the unselected ones.

When you press Shift+D or Shift+Z to start reading the messages in your selected threads, you see the first message of the threads you selected.

Unsubscribing from Newsgroups

When you are reading a newsgroup, if you decide that you don't want to read it any more, press U to unsubscribe.

Creating a Kill File

In most newsgroups, a bunch of running discussions go on, and some discussions are much more interesting than others. You can permanently ignore the uninteresting ones by using a *kill file*. When you encounter an uninteresting article, press Shift+K to kill all current articles with the same title and to put the title in your kill file for the current newsgroup. In the future, whenever you start reading that newsgroup, trn checks for any new articles with titles in the kill file and automatically kills them so that you never see any of them.

Using kill files can save a great deal of time and lets you concentrate on discussions that are actually interesting. You can edit kill files to remove entries for discussions that have died down or to add other kinds of article-killing commands. If you press Ctrl+K while you're reading a newsgroup, it starts the text editor (usually vi or emacs on UNIX machines) on the group's kill file. Kill files look like this:

```
THRU 4765
/One more point about gun control/j
/Let's keep talking about abortion/j
```

The first line notes how many articles have been scanned for killable topics (so that trn can save time by not rescanning all newsgroup messages each time). Subsequent lines are topics you don't want to read (the J at the end means that articles with that topic will be "junked," or marked as read). You remove a topic by deleting its line in the kill file. After you're finished, save the file and leave the editor: You return to what you were doing in trn.

Sometimes you may also find that certain people write articles you never want to read. You can arrange to kill all the articles they write. Press Ctrl+K to edit the newsgroup's kill file, and at the end add a line like this:

```
/Elvis Presley/h:j
```

Between the slashes, type the author's name as it appears on the From line at the beginning of his articles. You don't have to type the entire contents of the From line—just enough of it to uniquely identify the person. At the end of the line, after the second slash, type h:j (which means to junk articles with that text on the From line). Then save the kill file and exit the editor.

Decoding Binary Files

When a newsgroup article contains a binary file (usually a graphics file), trn doesn't decode it automatically, unlike the Windows programs described earlier in this chapter. The binary files are converted to text by uuencoding them, which makes the message look like this:

```
section 1/1 file zarkon.gif
begin 644 zarkon.gif
M1&\@&5O&QE(&&%C='5A;&QY(')Y&4@:6X@=&AE(&AEV4@97AA;7!L97,L(&=&\@
:V5E('=H870@=&AE(&AE2!D;VE0&4@&\_#0H_
'
end
sum -r/size 15557/71
```

To decode the file, press E and then Enter to decode it. The decoded file is stored in your News directory on the UNIX system. Some uuencoded files are sent in several parts; press E in turn when viewing each of them to reconstruct the original file.

Reading Newsgroups on the Web

Several Web sites let you read and post newsgroup articles through the Web. If your ISP doesn't have a news server, these Web sites are a good alternative:

Deja.com's Usenet Discussion Service
http://www.deja.com/usenet/

HotBot Usenet
http://hotbot.lycos.com/usenet/

Newsguy
http://www.newsguy.com/

RemarQ
http://www.remarq.com/

Deja.com is particularly good because it also provides a huge searchable archive, going back to 1995, of most of the articles posted to Usenet newsgroups. Figure 6-12 shows the list of threads in the misc.education newsgroup. RemarQ is more confusing because it mixes together mailing lists, newsgroups, and Web-based message boards and tries to make them all look as though they are run by RemarQ.

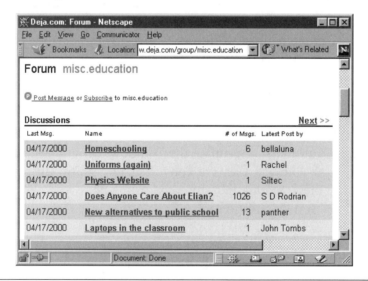

Figure 6-12: Reading newsgroups on the Deja.com Web site.

Finding Newsgroups of Interest

To get started with Usenet newsgroups, be sure to read these newsgroups:

news.announce.newusers (announcements for new Usenet users).

news.newusers.questions (question-and-answer newsgroup for folks who are new to Usenet).

news.answers (a collection of FAQs from many other newsgroups—you can't ask questions, but if you browse the FAQs, you'll find lots of answers).

After you are comfortable reading newsgroups, with the tens of thousands of newsgroups that exist, how do you find the ones you want to read? Most Usenet users settle down to a small list of groups they read regularly, maybe a dozen or two. Here are some suggestions on how to find groups of interest:

- Even if you usually read news with a newsreading program, it can be useful to search for groups and articles at Deja.com. After you've found a group of interest, you can subscribe to it in your regular newsreading program.
- Always read the messages in a newsgroup before posting. The group might not be about what you think it is. For example, the group comp.arch is about computer architecture, but every few weeks someone who clearly has never looked at the group sends a question about archiving software.
- See whether the newsgroup has FAQ messages. The FAQ may present a recent article in the group, or you can look for it in the **Internet FAQ Consortium** collection, at http://www.faqs.org/.
- Remember that you can subscribe and unsubscribe to Usenet groups as often as you want. If a group looks interesting, subscribe for a few days; then, if you don't find it as interesting as it initially appeared, just unsubscribe. Nobody but you will know.

Some people who believe that they have an extremely urgent question blast it to a dozen possibly relevant newsgroups, ending with "Please respond to me since I don't read this newsgroup." Don't do that because newsgroup members tend not to appreciate this kind of hit-and-run posting.

The Fine Points of Posting to Newsgroups

Usenet is a very large and very fractious set of communities that has grown up over the past 20 years. Because both the technology and the history are somewhat different from those of e-mail, Usenet has its own set of management issues that people should understand in order to use it effectively.

Posting Your First Message

Before you post any messages to other newsgroups, post your first message to either misc.test or alt.test, two newsgroups that exist only to provide a place to post as many test messages as you list without annoying people. Posting test messages to other newsgroups is a sure way to get criticized.

First subscribe to misc.test or alt.test so that you will see your test message when it appears. Then post your test message. Within a day or two (perhaps hours), you should see your posting. Some news servers monitor these newsgroups and automatically send e-mail responses to you to confirm that your posting was received at other sites, too.

Asking Questions about Usenet

If you have a question about how to read newsgroup messages, find newsgroups of interest, post messages, or do anything else that has to do with Usenet newsgroups and newsreading programs, post your question to the news.newusers.questions newsgroup—that's what it's there for. Before you post, though, read the FAQs listed at the end of this chapter, and read the articles in the news.newusers.questions newsgroup. If you don't find your answer, then post. Don't post test messages to news.newusers.questions!

Cross-posting Messages

Usenet has always permitted *cross-posting*, or posting a single article to two or more newsgroups. Unlike sending e-mail to multiple recipients, cross-posting doesn't create multiple copies but instead tags a single message with multiple newsgroup names. This method both saves space and lets news programs handle cross-posted messages sensibly, not showing you a message when it appears in one group if you've already seen it in another group.

Used carefully, cross-posting is the right way to send a message that's appropriate for more than one group. For example, if you have a question about whether pet ferrets get along with cats, it would be appropriate to cross-post it to both rec.pets.ferrets and to rec.pets.cats.health+behav. On the other hand, occasionally people cross-post articles to vast numbers of marginally relevant or irrelevant groups, which is a terrible idea. It brands the poster as a fool and is likely to get the article canceled as spam (see the section "Cancels and Spam," later in this chapter).

Posting to Moderated Newsgroups

Some newsgroups are *moderated*. Rather than post messages directly to moderated groups, newsreading software e-mails them to the moderator, who reads them and then posts articles that meet the guidelines for the group, possibly after some editing.

Originally, newsgroup moderators were individuals, and many moderators still are. (See Chapter 19 about comp.compilers, a newsgroup that one of the authors of this book has moderated for 15 years.) In recent years, many newsgroups have used multiple moderators, to spread out the load and keep the newsgroup from being totally dependent on one person. (For example, the moderator of rec.radio.broadcasting died unexpectedly in 1999, and it took months to find a new moderator and get the group going again.)

Since 1994, some newsgroups have been entirely or partially *robomoderated*, using a program that handles the approval process. Some groups, such as soc.religion.unitarian-univ (see Chapter 20) are completely robomoderated, with the program accepting or rejecting all incoming messages. Others are partially automated, with messages from some people approved automatically and others passed to one or more human moderators. Robomoderator programs usually check for spam, duplicate messages, and messages from people who have been banned from the newsgroup.

Most moderators, human and otherwise, send an automated acknowledgment message when your message is received, often including information about the charter of the newsgroup, the moderation policy, and the location of the group's FAQ. After your message is processed and either posted or rejected, you often get another note.

Moderation policies vary as much as moderation mechanics do. Some newsgroups moderate very loosely and permit anything vaguely relevant to the newsgroup's nominal topic. Others insist on hewing closely to the topics listed in the charter and reject most articles sent to the newsgroup. Most moderated newsgroups enforce technical requirements as well: Messages usually must be plain text (no HTML, rich text, or encoded binary files), the message must have a valid return address, and other basic requirements.

If your message doesn't appear on a moderated newsgroup within a reasonable period (two or three days), you can write politely to the moderator and ask whether there's a problem. The system that forwards e-mailed messages to moderators occasionally breaks, and it's possible that your message (or the approval message) was lost. Complaining that it's taking too long is counterproductive: Moderators are all volunteers and do their moderation work when they have time. If your message is rejected, there's no appeal because Usenet has no central management. Complaining about rejected messages is equally counterproductive and just annoys the moderator. Usenet is not a democracy, even though some people, rarely the ones who actually spend the time and money to make it work, wish it were.

Cross-posted messages to moderated newsgroups have always presented a problem because there's no clearly correct way to handle them. In practice, a message cross-posted to one or more moderated newsgroups is sent to the moderator of one of the moderated newsgroups. (Which newsgroup it's sent to is unpredictable and depends on details of the news setup at the author's news server.) When a message is posted to one moderated newsgroup and a small number of unmoderated newsgroups, the moderator usually posts it as is, except in some newsgroups with explicit "no cross-post" rules. If a message is posted to two or more moderated newsgroups, the result is quite unpredictable. Although some moderators have informal agreements permitting cross-posts to each other's newsgroups, most don't, and your message is likely to be posted to only one of the newsgroups or returned. Our advice is to avoid the problem altogether and not to cross-post messages to moderated newsgroups.

Forging Your Return Addresses

Spammers frequently harvest addresses from Usenet messages to send their junk e-mail to. An unfortunate result of this practice is that some people use a forged address in messages they post to newsgroups. Then, if you reply to those messages by e-mail, your message never gets to the author.

In some cases, the address is forged in a way that's supposed to be easy for people to fix. For example, AOL lets its subscribers add a string to the end of the address, so an address might appear as fred29478@aol.comINVALID. Other people stick extra letters in the middle of the address, such as joenospam@mindnospamspring.net—you take out the `nospam` to get the actual address. Other people put completely fake addresses on the From line (like see.address@below) with a hint in the text from which you're supposed to be able to guess the real address. Spammer harvesting programs are supposed to be fooled by these fake addresses, although real people can figure out the real address of the poster. (Of course, spammers are no fools and keep improving their harvesting programs to detect the most common methods of disguising addresses.)

Altering your return address so that it can't be harvested by a program but can still be understood by a human being is frequently called *munging* (short for Munge Until No Good). A *munged address* is one that has been altered so that a human being can theoretically fix it again.

Some newsreading programs, including Outlook Express, don't display the sender's e-mail address in a message, so munged addresses may not even be visible when you're sending a response. In Outlook Express, to check whether an address looks forged, you need to right-click the address on the To or Cc line, select Properties, and then look at the e-mail address. If the address is forged, there's no good way to fix it in the message; the best you can do is to click Add to Address Book, edit the e-mail address in the address book, save the address, delete the forged address from the To line of your message, and add the corrected address. Needless to say, few Outlook Express users go to this effort, so the effect of forged addresses is to make it nearly impossible to reply to Usenet posts by e-mail, which forces many Outlook Express users to post messages to newsgroups that ought to have been sent by private e-mail.

For more about forging and munging your return address, see the **Address Munging FAQ**, at http://members.aol.com/emailfaq/mungfaq.html.

Cancels and Spam

Usenet has always had a provision for canceling messages so that you can get rid of messages you later regret having sent. Canceling a message sends a second *control* message that advises news servers to delete the original message. Every newsreading program has a command to let you cancel the message you're reading, as long as it's one you wrote yourself. You're not supposed to be able to cancel other people's messages.

The original intent of cancel messages was to allow people to cancel their own messages, but in recent years their use has expanded considerably. It's easy for Usenet experts to create cancel messages to cancel anyone's messages, not just their own. Canceling other people's messages is considered unethical except in two cases: newsgroup moderators and spam.

Newsgroup moderators can cancel any message in the groups they moderate. Occasionally they do this to retract a message approval; more commonly they cancel messages with forged approval information that didn't properly pass through the moderator. In a few groups, notably news.admin.net-abuse.* and a few of the sexually oriented alt.* groups, *cancel wars* break out, in which vandals send out many forged cancellations of messages in a group. In the news.admin.net-abuse groups, a program called Dave the Resurrector identifies the forgeries and reposts most illegitimately canceled messages. If you see a message with REPOST on its subject line, that's probably why.

By far the largest use of cancel messages is to get rid of *spam*, messages posted many times to vast numbers of newsgroups. A handful of well-known system managers around the world run spam-canceling programs that look for multiply-posted messages and automatically cancel messages that are posted too many times. Although the definition of "too many" has evolved over time, the current convention uses a metric, invented by Seth Breidbart, known as the Breidbart Index, or BI. To get the BI of a message, find all copies of the message and add up the square roots of the number of newsgroups each copy was posted to. For example, if three copies are posted to 1, 9, and 16 newsgroups, the square roots are 1, 3, and 4, so the BI is 8. Any message with a BI of 20 or greater for copies posted within 45 days is cancelable. (See the **Breidbart Index Definition** page, at http://www.stopspam.org/usenet/mmf/breidbart.html, for more details.)

In the Big Eight hierarchies of newsgroups, spam canceling is quite effective, and most people see relatively little spam in those newsgroups, even though the amount of spam sent and canceled usually exceeds the number of legitimate messages. What this means for regular users is twofold:

- Messages you post might accidentally be canceled as spam if they resemble existing spam closely enough. The usual case is that someone posts a follow-up to spam saying "This looks like spam," quoting the entire original. So don't do that. The appropriate response to spam is to look at the message headers and send a polite e-mail to the ISP where the spam originated.
- If you were even thinking of Usenet spamming, don't.

A Primer on How to Work with the Usenet Community

The following guide to participating in Usenet newsgroups is on the Web at http://www.deja.com/info/primer3.shtml. Originally written more than a decade ago by Gene Spafford ("Spaf," one of Usenet's elder statesmen) and maintained by Mark Moraes and Chuq von Rospach, it is one of the best distillations of Usenet advice.

The easiest way to learn how to use Usenet is to watch how others use it. Start reading the news and try to figure out what people are doing and why. After a couple of weeks, you will start understanding why certain things are done and what things shouldn't be done. Documents are available describing the technical details of how to use the software. These are different depending on which programs you use to access the news. You can get copies of the documents from your system administrator. If you do not know who that person is, he or she can be contacted on most systems by mailing to the account news, usenet, or postmaster.

Never Forget That the Person on the Other Side Is Human

Because your interaction with the network is through a computer, it is easy to forget that there are people "out there." Situations arise where emotions erupt into a verbal free-for-all that can lead to hurt feelings.

Please remember that people all over the world are reading your words. Do not attack people if you cannot persuade them with your presentation of the facts. Screaming, cursing, and abusing others only serves to make people think less of you and be less willing to help you when you need it.

If you are upset at something or someone, wait until you have had a chance to calm down and think about it. A cup of (decaf!) coffee or a good night's sleep works wonders on your perspective. Hasty words create more problems than they solve. Try not to say anything to others you would not say to them in person in a room full of people.

Don't Blame System Administrators for Their Users' Behavior

Sometimes, you may find it necessary to write to a system administrator about something concerning his or her site. Maybe it is a case of the software not working or a control message escaping, or maybe one of the users at that site has done something that you feel requires comment. No matter how steamed you may be, be polite to the system administrator—she may not have any idea of what you are going to say and may not have any part in the incidents involved. By being civil and temperate, you are more likely to obtain that person's courteous attention and assistance.

Never Assume That a Person Is Speaking for the Whole Organization

Many people who post to Usenet do so from machines at their office or school. Despite that, never assume that a person is speaking for the organization from which he is posting articles (unless the person explicitly says so). Some people put explicit disclaimers to this effect in their messages, but this is a good general rule. If you find an article offensive, consider taking it up with the person directly or ignoring it. Learn about kill files in your newsreader and other techniques for ignoring people whose postings you find offensive.

Be Careful What You Say about Others
Remember: You read Usenet; so do as many as 3 million other people. This group quite possibly includes your boss, your friend's boss, your girlfriend's brother's best friend, and one of your father's beer buddies. Information posted on the Internet can come back to haunt you or the person you are talking about.

Think twice before you post personal information about yourself or others. Although this advice applies especially strongly to groups like soc.singles and alt.sex, even postings in groups like talk.politics.misc have included information about the personal life of third parties that could get them into serious trouble if it got into the wrong hands.

Be Brief
Never say in ten words what you can say in fewer. Say it succinctly, and it will have a greater impact. Remember that the longer you make your article, the fewer people will bother to read it.

Your Postings Reflect on You—Be Proud of Them
Most people on Usenet will know you only by what you say and how well you say it. They may someday be your coworkers or friends. Take some time to make sure that each posting is something that will not embarrass you later.

Minimize your spelling errors and make sure that the article is easy to read and understand. Writing is an art, and to do it well requires practice. Because much of how people judge you on the Internet is based on your writing, such time is well spent.

Use Descriptive Titles
The subject line of an article is there to enable a person with a limited amount of time to decide whether to read your article. Tell people what the article is about before they read it. A title like "Car for Sale" in rec.autos does not help as much as "66 MG Midget for sale: Beaverton, OR." Don't expect people to read your article to find out what it is about because many of them won't bother. Some sites truncate the length of the subject line to 40 characters, so keep your subjects short and to the point.

Think about Your Audience
When you post an article, think about the people you are trying to reach. Asking UNIX questions on rec.autos will not reach as many of the people you want to

reach as if you asked them on comp.unix.questions or comp.unix.internals. Try to get the most appropriate audience for your message, not the widest.

It is considered bad form to post to both misc.misc, soc.net-people, or misc.wanted and to some other newsgroup. If it belongs in that other newsgroup, it does not belong in misc.misc, soc.net-people, or misc.wanted.

If your message is of interest to a limited geographic area (apartments, car sales, meetings, or concerts, for example), restrict the distribution of the message to your local area. Some areas have special newsgroups with geographical limitations, and the recent versions of the news software allow you to limit the distribution of material sent to worldwide newsgroups. Check with your system administrator to see what newsgroups are available and how to use them.

If you want to try a test of something, do not use a worldwide newsgroup! Messages in misc.misc that say "This is a test" are likely to cause large numbers of caustic messages to flow into your mailbox. Newsgroups that are local to your computer or area should be used. Your system administrator can tell you what they are.

Be familiar with the group you are posting to before you post! You shouldn't post to groups you do not read or post to groups you've read only a few articles from—you may not be familiar with the ongoing conventions and themes of the group. One normally does not join a conversation by just walking up and talking. Instead, you listen first and then join in if you have something pertinent to contribute.

Remember that the Usenet newsgroup system is designed to allow readers to choose which messages they see, not to allow posters to choose sets of readers to target. When you're choosing which newsgroups to post in, ask yourself, "Which newsgroups contain readers who would want to read my message" rather than "Which newsgroups have readers to whom I want to send my message?"

Be Careful with Humor and Sarcasm

Without the voice inflections and body language of personal communications, a remark meant to be funny can easily be misinterpreted. Subtle humor tends to get lost, so take steps to make sure that people realize you are trying to be funny. The Internet has developed a symbol called the smiley face. It looks like :-) and points out sections of articles with humorous intent. No matter how broad the humor or satire, it is safer to remind people that you are being funny.

Also be aware that satire quite frequently is posted without any explicit indications. If an article outrages you strongly, you should ask yourself whether it just may have been unmarked satire. Several self-proclaimed connoisseurs refuse to use smiley faces, so take heed or else you may make a temporary fool of yourself.

Post a Message Only Once

Avoid posting messages to more than one newsgroup unless you are sure that it is appropriate. If you do post to multiple newsgroups, do not post to each group separately. Instead, specify all the groups on a single copy of the message. This technique reduces network overhead and lets people who subscribe to more than one of those groups see the message once rather than have to wade through each copy.

Please Rotate Messages with Questionable Content

Certain newsgroups (such as rec.humor) have messages in them that may be offensive to some people. To make sure that these messages are not read unless they are explicitly requested, they should be encrypted. The standard encryption method is to rotate each letter by 13 characters so that an *a* becomes an *n*. This method is known on the network as *rot13*; when you rotate a message, the word *rot13* should be on the Subject line. Most software used to read Usenet articles has some way of encrypting and decrypting messages. Your system administrator can tell you how the software on your system works, or you can use this UNIX command (don't forget the single quotes!):

```
tr '[a-m][n-z][A-M][N-Z]' '[n-z][a-m][N-Z][A-M]'
```

Summarize What You Are Following Up

When you are following up someone's article, be sure to summarize the parts of the article to which you are responding. This allows readers to appreciate your comments rather than try to remember what the original article said. It is also possible for your response to get to some sites before the original article.

Summarization is best done by including appropriate quotes from the original article. Do not include the entire article because it will irritate the people who have already seen it. Even if you are responding to the entire article, summarize only the major points you are discussing.

When Summarizing, Summarize!

When you request information from the network, it is common courtesy to report your findings so that others can benefit. The best way of doing this is to take all responses you received and edit them into a single article that is posted to the places where you originally posted your question. Take the time to strip headers, combine duplicate information, and write a short summary. Try wherever possible to credit the information to the people who sent it to you.

Use Mail— Don't Post a Follow-up

One of the biggest problems on the network is that when someone asks a question, many people send out identical answers. When this happens, dozens of identical answers pour through the Net. Mail your answer to the person and suggest that she summarize to the network. This way, the Internet will see only a single copy of the answers, no matter how many people answer the question.

If you post a question, please remind people to send you the answers by mail and at least offer to summarize them to the network.

Read All Follow-ups and Don't Repeat What Has Already Been Said

Before you submit a follow-up to a message, read the rest of the messages in the newsgroup to see whether someone has already said what you want to say. If someone has, don't repeat it.

Check the Headers When Following Up

The news software has provisions to specify that follow-ups to an article should go to a specific set of newsgroups—possibly different from the newsgroups to which the original article was posted. Sometimes the groups chosen for follow-ups are totally inappropriate, especially as a thread of discussion changes with repeated postings. You should carefully check the groups and distributions given in the header and edit them as appropriate. If you change the groups named in the header or if you direct follow-ups to a particular group, say so in the body of the message—not everyone reads the headers of postings.

Be Careful about Copyrights and Licenses

After something is posted on the network, it is *probably* in the public domain unless you own the appropriate rights (most notably, if you wrote the thing yourself) and you post it with a valid copyright notice; a court would have to decide the specifics and there are arguments for both sides of the issue. Now that the United States has ratified the Berne convention, the issue is even murkier (if you are a poster in the United States). For all practical purposes, though, assume that you effectively give up the copyright if you don't put in a notice. Of course, the *information* becomes public, so you mustn't post trade secrets that way.

Cite Appropriate References

If you are using facts to support a cause, state where they came from. Don't take someone else's ideas and use them as your own. You don't want someone pretending that your ideas are theirs; show them the same respect.

Mark or Rotate Answers and Spoilers

When you post something (like a movie review that discusses a detail of the plot) that might spoil a surprise for other people, please mark your message with a warning so that they can skip the message. Another alternative would be to use the rot13 protocol to encrypt the message so that it cannot be read accidentally. When you post a message with a spoiler in it, make sure that the word *spoiler* is part of the Subject line.

Remember That Spelling Flames Are Harmful

Every few months, a plague called the *spelling flame* descends on Usenet. It starts out when someone posts an article correcting the spelling or grammar in some article. The immediate result seems to be for everyone on the Internet to turn into a sixth-grade English teacher and pick apart each other's postings for a few weeks. This process is not productive and tends to cause people who used to be friends to get angry with each other.

It is important to remember that we all make mistakes and that many users on the Internet use English as a second language. A number of people also suffer from dyslexia and have difficulty noticing their spelling mistakes. If you feel that you must make a comment on the quality of a posting, please do so by mail, not on the network.

Don't Overdo Signatures

Signatures are nice, and many people (who use UNIX) can have a signature added to their postings automatically by placing it in a file named `$HOME/.signature`. Don't overdo it. Signatures can tell the world something about you, but keep them short. A signature that is longer than the message itself is considered to be in bad taste. The main purpose of a signature is to help people locate you, not to tell your life story. Every signature should include at least your return address relative to a major, known site on the network and a proper domain-format address. Your system administrator can give this information to you. Some news posters attempt to enforce a four-line limit on signature files—an amount that should be more than sufficient to provide a return address and attribution.

Limit Line Length and Avoid Control Characters

Try to keep your text in a generic format. Many (if not most) of the people reading Usenet do so from 80-column terminals or from workstations with 80-column terminal windows. Try to keep your lines of text to fewer than 80 characters for optimal readability. If people quote part of your article in a follow-up, short lines will probably show up better, too.

Also realize that many, many different forms of terminals are in use. If you enter special control characters in your message, your message may become unreadable on some terminal types; a character sequence that causes reverse video on your screen may result in a keyboard lock and graphics mode on someone else's terminal. You should also try to avoid the use of tabs because they may be interpreted differently on terminals other than your own.

Do Not Use Usenet as a Resource for Homework Assignments

Usenet is not a resource for homework or class assignments. A common new user reaction to learning of all these people out there holding discussions is to view them as a great resource for gathering information for reports and papers. Trouble is, after seeing a few hundred such requests, most people get tired of them and won't reply anyway—certainly not in the expected or hoped-for numbers. Posting student questionnaires automatically brands you a newbie and does not usually garner much more than a tiny number of replies. Furthermore, some of those replies are likely to be incorrect.

Instead, read the group of interest for a while, and find out what the main threads are. What are people discussing? Are there any themes you can discover? Are there different schools of thought?

Post something only after you've followed the group for a few weeks, after you have read the Frequently Asked Questions posting if the group has one, and if you still have a question or opinion that others will probably find interesting. If you have something interesting to contribute, you'll find that you gain almost instant acceptance and your posting will generate a large number of follow-up postings. Use these in your research; it is a far more efficient (and accepted) way to learn about the group than to follow that first instinct and post a simple questionnaire.

Do Not Use Usenet as an Advertising Medium
Advertisements on Usenet are rarely appreciated. In general, the louder or more inappropriate the ad is, the more antagonism it will stir up. The news.announce.newusers posting "Rules for posting to Usenet" has more on this in the section "Announcement of professional products or services." Try the biz.* hierarchies instead.

Avoid Posting to Multiple Newsgroups
Few things annoy Usenet readers as much as multiple copies of a posting appearing in multiple newsgroups (called *spamming*, for historical reasons). A posting that is cross-posted (it lists multiple newsgroups on the Newsgroups header line) to a few appropriate newsgroups is fine, but, even with cross-posts, restraint is advised. For a cross-post, you may want to set the Followup-To header line to the most suitable group for the rest of the discussion.

For More Information about Usenet
The news.announce.newusers newsgroup is a moderated newsgroup to which a small number of very informative articles are posted semi-weekly or weekly. Your news server should always have the most recent version of these articles, but in case it doesn't, you can also read them on the Web:

> Welcome to Usenet
> http://www.faqs.org/faqs/usenet/welcome/part1/
> What Is Usenet?
> http://www.faqs.org/faqs/usenet/what-is/part1/
> What Is Usenet? A Second Opinion
> http://www.faqs.org/faqs/usenet/what-is/part2/
> FAQs for New Usenet Users
> http://www.faqs.org/faqs/by-newsgroup/news/news.announce.newusers.html
> Emily Postnews Answers Your Questions on Netiquette (be sure to read before posting!)
> http://www.faqs.org/faqs/usenet/emily-postnews/part1/
> How to Find the Right Place to Post (FAQ)
> http://www.faqs.org/faqs/finding-groups/general/
> Rules for Posting to Usenet
> http://www.faqs.org/faqs/usenet/posting-rules/part1/
> Hints on Writing Style for Usenet
> http://www.faqs.org/faqs/usenet/writing-style/part1/
> Advertising on Usenet: How to Do It, How Not to Do It
> http://www.faqs.org/faqs/usenet/advertising/how-to/part1/

Here are some other Web sites to read for more information about Usenet newsgroups:

The Official Usenet Primer
   http://www.deja.com/info/primer1.shtml
Usenet Info Center
   http://metalab.unc.edu/usenet-i/home.html
news.newusers.questions Official Home Page
   http://www.geocities.com/nnqweb/
Deja.com's Usenet FAQ
   http://www.deja.com/info/usenet_faq.shtml
Moderated Newsgroups FAQ
   http://www.swcp.com/~dmckeon/mod-faq.html

Chapter Seven
Creating and Managing Your Own Newsgroup

The Usenet system of newsgroups is maintained by a decentralized group of system managers who run news servers on the Internet. Over the years, clear rules have arisen to govern how newsgroups are created in the Big Eight hierarchy (comp, humanities, misc, news, rec, sci, soc, and talk, as described in Chapter 6). Creating a newsgroup in the alt hierarchy or in local or regional hierarchies is usually easier. You also have the option of running your own news server and starting your own newsgroup hierarchy. This chapter describes the various ways you can create a newsgroup and how to manage a newsgroup (either unmoderated or moderated) after it's created.

Creating Newsgroups

When you create a newsgroup, you have to decide whether to create it in the widely distributed Big Eight hierarchy or in the less widely carried `alt` or other hierarchies. Although Big Eight newsgroups are hard to create, requiring proposals, waiting periods, and public votes, they are also the most widely available and arguably the most prestigious.

Creating Big Eight Usenet Newsgroups

The complete directions for creating a Big Eight newsgroup are posted periodically in news.groups and are quoted in this section. Two newsgroups are devoted to discussing the creation of new newsgroups: news.announce.newgroups, which contains announcements about proposed groups, and news.groups, which contains discussion about the proposals.

Although the operator of each news server decides which groups to carry, for the Big Eight almost everyone accepts the advice of David "Tale" Lawrence, an administrator at the Internet Software Consortium who informally oversees the creation process. Although the process is informal, it has a series of well-defined steps, described in more detail in the next section, "Guidelines for Usenet Group Creation," David Lawrence's document.

The standard steps for creating a Big Eight newsgroup are shown in this list:

1. An initial Request For Discussion (RFD) that proposes the group and its charter is made.

2. Discussion occurs—usually lots of discussion. Frequently, the RFD is rewritten in response to the discussion, possibly changing the proposed name, charter, and moderation policy.

3. If the proposal survives the discussion (many don't), a Call For Votes (CFV) is made to start the straw poll.

4. A voting period of about a month begins, during which anyone who is so inclined can vote for or against. As you might imagine, electioneering is frequent and ballot box stuffing not unknown.

5. Vote tabulation takes place after the voting period is over, with an opportunity to examine the votes so that people can challenge forged or miscounted ones.

6. If the vote passes by a sufficient margin, the group is created.

Creating a Big Eight newsgroup is a lengthy process that intentionally requires lots of effort by the newsgroup's proponents. Before you try to create one, read the news.groups newsgroup for a few weeks to see what's involved and whether you're willing to volunteer for that much punishment. In many cases, it makes more sense to start a mailing list and try to make a newsgroup only if the traffic on the mailing list grows to the point where it's unwieldy. Also read *The Big Eight Newsgroup Creation Process*, at http://www.eyrie.org/~eagle/faqs/big-eight.html.

Guidelines for Usenet Group Creation (for Big Eight Newsgroups)

This section contains an article that is posted periodically to the news.groups newsgroup by David Lawrence: it is reprinted here with his permission. We have added our own explanations in square brackets. This article is also available on the Web, at http://www.faqs.org/faqs/usenet/creating-newsgroups/part1/.

Requirements for Group Creation

These are guidelines that have been generally agreed upon across Usenet as appropriate for following in the creating of new newsgroups in the "standard"

Usenet newsgroup hierarchy. They are *not* intended as guidelines for setting Usenet policy other than group creations, and they are not intended to apply to "alternate" or local news hierarchies. The part of the namespace affected is comp, humanities, misc, news, rec, sci, soc, or talk, which are the most widely distributed areas of the Usenet hierarchy [the Big Eight hierarchies].

Any group creation request which follows these guidelines to a successful result should be honored [by news server administrators], and any request which fails to follow these procedures or to obtain a successful result from doing so should be dropped, except under extraordinary circumstances. The reason these are called guidelines and not absolute rules is that it is not possible to predict in advance what "extraordinary circumstances" are or how they might arise.

It should be pointed out here that, as always, the decision whether or not to create a newsgroup on a given machine rests with the administrator of that machine. These guidelines are intended merely as an aid in making those decisions.

The Discussion

group-mentors@acpub.duke.edu [the group of subscribers of a closed mailing list] is a body of volunteers experienced with the newsgroup creation process. They assist people who want to propose new groups with the formation and submission of a good proposal. It is strongly encouraged, though not required, that they be contacted with an outline of the basic idea for a proposal, and a mentor will work with the proponents to submit a formal proposal. People who have experience with the [following] process and wish to help others should contact group-mentors-request@acpub.duke.edu to join:

1. A request for discussion on creation of a new newsgroup should be posted to news.announce.newgroups, news.groups, and any other groups or mailing lists at all related to the proposed topic if desired. news.announce.newgroups is moderated, and the Followup-to header will be set so that the actual discussion takes place only in news.groups. Users on sites which have difficulty posting to moderated groups may mail submissions intended for news.announce.newgroups to newgroups@isc.org. The proposal must be in the format defined in ***How to Format and Submit a New Group Proposal*** [which is posted periodically to the news.groups newsgroup and is on the Web at http://web.presby.edu/~jtbell/usenet/newgroup/how-submit.faq]. [Also read the article ***Guidelines on Usenet Newsgroup Names***, which is on the Web at http://www.faqs.org/faqs/usenet/creating-newsgroups/naming/part1/.]

    The article should be cross-posted among the newsgroups, including news.announce.newgroups, rather than posted as separate articles. Note that standard behavior for posting software is to not present the articles in any groups when cross-posted to a moderated group; the moderator will handle that for you. [The idea is for all discussion about creation of the newsgroup to occur in news.groups so that everyone involved can see all sides of the arguments.]

2. The name and charter of the proposed group and whether it will be moderated or unmoderated (and if the former, who the moderator[s] will be) should be determined during the discussion period. If there is no general agreement on these points among the proponents of a new group at the end of 30 days of discussion, the discussion should be taken offline (into mail instead of news.groups) and the proponents should iron out the details among themselves. Once that is done, a new, more specific proposal may be made, going back to Step 1 above. [After a newsgroup is created, you can't change it from moderated to unmoderated or vice versa without taking it up in news.groups again, so it's better to get the moderation right in the first place.]

3. Group advocates seeking help in choosing a name to suit the proposed charter or looking for any other guidance in the creation procedure can send a message to group-advice@isc.org; a few seasoned news administrators are available through this address.

The Vote

The Usenet Volunteer Votetakers (UVV) are a group of neutral third-party votetakers who currently handle vote gathering and counting for all newsgroup proposals. The coordinators of the group can be reached at contact@uvv.org; contact them to arrange the handling of the vote. The mechanics of the vote will be handled in accord with the paragraphs below:

1. *After* the discussion period, if it has been determined that a new group is really desired, a name and charter are agreed upon, and it has been determined whether the group will be moderated and if so who will moderate it, a call for votes [CFV] may be posted to news.announce.newgroups and any other groups or mailing lists that the original request for discussion [RFD] might have been posted to. There should be minimal delay between the end of the discussion period and the issuing of a call for votes. The call for votes should include clear instructions for how to cast a vote. It must be as clearly explained and as easy to do to cast a vote for creation as against it and vice versa. It is explicitly permitted to set up two separate addresses to mail yes and no votes to provided that they are on the same machine, to set up an address

different than that the article was posted from to mail votes to, or to just accept replies to the call for votes article, as long as it is clearly and explicitly stated in the call for votes article how to cast a vote. If two addresses are used for a vote, the reply address must process and accept both yes and no votes *or* reject them both.

2. The voting period should last for at least 21 days and no more than 31 days, no matter what the preliminary results of the vote are. The exact date that the voting period will end should be stated in the call for votes. Only votes that arrive on the vote-taker's machine prior to this date will be counted.

3. A couple of repeats of the call for votes may be posted during the vote, provided that they contain similar clear, unbiased instructions for casting a vote as the original, and provided that it is really a repeat of the call for votes on the *same* proposal (see #5 below). Partial vote results should *not* be included—only a statement of the specific new group proposal, that a vote is in progress on it, and how to cast a vote. It is permitted to post a *mass acknowledgment*, in which all the names of those from whom votes have been received are posted, as long as no indication is made of which way anybody voted until the voting period is officially over.

4. *Only* votes *mailed* to the vote-taker will count. Votes posted to Usenet for any reason (including inability to get mail to the vote-taker) and proxy votes (such as having a mailing list maintainer claim a vote for each member of the list) will not be counted.

5. Votes may not be transferred to other, similar proposals. A vote shall count only for the *exact* proposal that it is a response to. In particular, a vote for or against a newsgroup under one name shall *not* be counted as a vote for or against a newsgroup with a different name or charter, a different moderated/unmoderated status, or (if moderated) a different moderator or set of moderators.

6. Votes *must* be explicit; they should be of the form "I vote for the group foo.bar as proposed" or "I vote against the group foo.bar as proposed." The wording doesn't have to be exact—it just needs to be unambiguous. In particular, statements of the form "I would vote for this group if . . ." should be considered comments only and not counted as votes.

7. A vote should be run only for a single group proposal. Attempts to create multiple groups should be handled by running multiple parallel votes rather than one vote to create all of the groups.

The Result

1. At the completion of the voting period, the vote-taker must post the vote tally and the e-mail addresses and (if available) names of the voters received to news.announce.newgroups and any other groups or mailing lists to which the original call for votes was posted. The tally should include a statement of which way each voter voted so that the results can be verified.

2. *After* the vote result is posted, there will be a five-day waiting period, beginning when the voting results actually appear in news.announce.newgroups, during which the Net will have a chance to correct any errors in the voter list or the voting procedure.

3. After the waiting period, and if there were no serious objections that might invalidate the vote, and if 100 more valid YES/create votes are received than NO/don't create votes *and* at least two-thirds of the total number of valid votes received are in favor of creation, a *newgroup control message* [a special Usenet message that only news server administrators can usually create] may be sent out. If the 100 vote margin or two-thirds percentage is not met, the group should not be created.

4. The newgroup message will be sent by the news.announce.newgroups moderator at the end of the waiting period of a successful vote. [Don't try to send it out yourself!]

5. A proposal which has failed under point 3 above should not again be brought up for discussion until at least six months have passed from the close of the vote. This limitation does not apply to proposals which never went to vote or polls that were canceled or invalidated.

Additional References

If you want to create a new group, the following additional documents should be read before you begin the process:

How to Format and Submit a New Group Proposal
http://web.presby.edu/~jtbell/usenet/newgroup/how-submit.faq

How to Write a Good Newsgroup Proposal
http://web.presby.edu/~jtbell/usenet/newgroup/good-proposal.faq

Usenet Newsgroup Creation Companion (may be outdated)
http://web.presby.edu/~jtbell/usenet/newgroup/creation-companion.faq

What Is Usenet?
http://www.faqs.org/faqs/usenet/what-is/part1/

Creating soc.religion.unitarian-univ

The creation process for soc.religion.unitarian-univ *was fairly typical of the process for a potentially controversial group. Some participants in a very active mailing list named* UUS-L *noted the lack of a Unitarian Universalism (UU) newsgroup and started discussing the possibility of one in* news.groups.

It quickly became apparent that the news.groups *regulars would not be likely to vote for an unmoderated religion group because of a long history of arguments in the existing ones. Since UUs have a long tradition of largely unfettered discourse, the proponents suggested using robomoderation for the first time in a Big Eight (then Big Seven) group. This strategy was practical because one of the proponents (one of the authors of this book) was already running a regional robomoderated group and had the facilities and experience to do so. There was also considerable discussion about what to call the group. It clearly was* soc.religion.something, *but the exact something was elusive. The obvious name,* soc.religion.unitarian-universalist, *wasn't possible because many news systems limit group names to 14 characters per segment. People tried to come up with 14 character names that used equal amounts of both names, like* unitrn-unvslst, *but none was satisfactory. Others suggested going to the other extreme,* soc.religion.uu, *but that was no good because of possible confusion that the group was a joke about the well-known uucp network package. The best compromise was just to hack the long part of the name off at 14 characters.*

Shortly after the CFV went out, the operator of a religious bulletin-board system in suburban New York started sending out messages urging people to vote against soc.religion.unitarian-univ *because most Unitarian Universalists aren't Christian. Nothing could have been better calculated to stir up the free-speech and Libertarian sympathies of Usenet users; as a result, when the voting ended,* soc.religion.unitarian-univ *was approved by a vast margin, far more than any newsgroup ever.*

After the vote was over, the new moderators set up the necessary software to run the group, David Lawrence sent out a newgroup message, and the group went live. The newsgroup's Web site is at http://sruu.iecc.com/. *Chapter 20 talks more about this newsgroup.*

Creating Alt Newsgroups

The alt hierarchy was originally created to circumvent the arduous newsgroup creation procedure described in the preceding section. However, by now there are traditions that sort of govern how alt newsgroups are created, too. You can create an alt newsgroup without going through this (shorter) set of steps, although some news servers won't carry it unless you do. So many silly, useless, and unused alt newsgroups have been created over the years by people showing off to their friends that some news server administrators choose not to create alt newsgroups that have not been created using this process. If you create an alt newsgroup without following the process, many people won't have access to your newsgroup because their news servers won't carry it.

Steps for Creating an Alt Newsgroup

The recommended procedure for creating an alt newsgroup is discussed in the article "So You Want to Create an Alt Newsgroup," written by David Barr and posted regularly in the alt.config newsgroup, where the creation of new alt newsgroups is discussed. It's also on the Web, at http://www.visi.com/~barr/alt-creation-guide.html and http://www.faqs.org/faqs/alt-creation-guide/.

In short, here's what you do:

1. **Figure out what to call your newsgroup.** The alt hierarchy has lots of sub- and sub-subhierarchies. People will find your newsgroup more easily if it has a logical name that follows the conventions set up by existing newsgroups. Look for similar alt newsgroups groups and put yours close to them: Start your newsgroup name with alt.binaries (for distributing pictures or programs), alt.books (for discussions about books), alt.comp (about computers and computing), alt.culture (about popular or classical culture other than music), alt.current-events (for short-lived world events), alt.fan (for fan clubs), alt.games (for games other than sports), alt.lang (about language, or a particular language), alt.music (about music), alt.politics (about politics), alt.religion (about religion or a particular religion), alt.sex (about sex), alt.society (about social issues), alt.sport (about a sport), alt.sports (about a particular sports team), and alt.tv (about TV shows). Each part of a newsgroup name (from one dot to the next) is limited to 14 letters and numbers with no other punctuation. Stay away from acronyms, which may not be understood outside your local country: Instead, spell out the subject of the acronym (for example, law-enforce rather than fbi).

2. **Post a proposal to alt.config.** It doesn't have to be anywhere near as formal as a Big Eight RFD because, despite some occasional wishful thinking to

Chapter 7: Creating and Managing Your Own Newsgroup **167**

the contrary, alt groups don't have charters and there's no voting process. Include the proposed newsgroup name in the subject of your posting. Many news server administrators refuse to create alt groups that haven't been discussed in alt.config, and you want them to be able to find your message.

3. **Wait a week and read the comments on alt.config.** Some comments will probably be good ones. Folks may respond with ideas about improvements to your newsgroup name or charter or point out an existing newsgroup or mailing list that covers your topic.

4. **At the end of the week, if you still want to create the group, do so.** Creating an alt group or any other group involves sending a specially formatted newgroup message. See *How to Write a Good Newgroup Message*, at http://www.gweep.bc.ca/~edmonds/usenet/good-newgroup.html, for details on sending it out. Keep in mind that most Windows newsreading programs cannot create newgroup messages (of the popular ones, only Agent can) and that many news server managers reject any newgroup messages from their users to prevent mischief. If you want to create a group, it's best to get your news server administrator on board so that she can help with the details.

Additional References

For more information on creating alt newsgroups, read these articles, which are posted regularly to the alt.config newsgroup:

The Beginners Guide to Creating New alt.* Groups
http://usenet.cjb.net/

Guide for Writing an alt. Newsgroup Proposal
http://homepages.go.com/~eacalame/proposal.html

How to Create an ALT Newsgroup
http://nylon.net/alt/newgroup.htm

Index of FAQs about Starting an "alt" Newsgroup
http://www.faqs.org/usenet/alt/

Running Your Own News Server and Private Newsgroups

If you want to run private newsgroups, you can run your own *news server*, the program that stores and delivers newsgroup messages. Your news server can be *public* so that anyone can read the newsgroups the news server hosts, or it can be *private* so that people need a username and password to connect.

Running a News Server

News servers communicate with each other and with newsreaders using a protocol named *NNTP* (Network News Transport Protocol). Nearly every UNIX or Linux system is shipped with the popular freeware INN news server (read the **INN FAQ**, at http://blank.org/innfaq/, for details). Windows NT systems can run the freeware Tortoise system; the **Tortoise** home page is at http://tortoise.maxwell.syr.edu/. Several commercial, high-performance news servers are available, such as Dnews and Typhoon, although they're overkill for private news servers unless you anticipate thousands of users posting gigabytes of news.

If you want people to be able to use your news server, you also need a full-time Internet connection and, preferably, a domain name. A cable modem or DSL line might be adequate, although most Internet service providers discourage or forbid customers from running their own news servers. The most likely place to be able to run a public news server is on either the campus network of a college or university (if you are student, staff, or faculty member) or a company's network (if you are an employee).

Note: If you install a news server on a computer that is on an organization's internal network and the organization has a firewall system that connects the network to the Internet, either your news server has to be "outside" the firewall or the firewall must be configured to permit outsiders to connect to the NNTP port on the news server.

NNTP and Server Security

Because Usenet dates from an era when security was much less of an issue than it is now, the security features on news servers are relatively primitive. *NNTP*, the network protocol used by news servers, runs in two slightly different modes: newsfeed and reader. When two news servers exchange articles as peers, they use *newsfeed* mode to transfer articles in bulk. When a newsreader program connects to a news server to read news and perhaps post articles, it uses *reader* mode. Most private news servers are *standalone*: They don't communicate as peers with any other news servers, so we won't describe newsfeed in more detail here.

In reader mode, the news server can use the newsreader's IP address to control access to newsgroups. You can also set account names and passwords for the news server. (The account name and password need have no relation to either the account name used to connect to the ISP nor the address used on any messages the user posts.) Users can be granted access to read, post, or

Chapter 7: Creating and Managing Your Own Newsgroup 169

both, based on either IP address, username, or both, and they can be limited to certain newsgroups.

Consider this extract from the `nnrp.access` file used by the INN news server. Each line consists of five fields: the network address, username, password, access, and newsgroups:

```
*:RP:john1:topsecret:*
*.furble.net:R:fred:dref:*,!local.*
10.1.2.*:RP:::*
```

The first line says that user `john1` can connect from anywhere with a password and can read and post to all groups. (An asterisk is the usual UNIX wildcard.) The second line says that user `fred` can connect with a password from any host at furble.net and can read all newsgroups except local.*. This could be useful for a casual user who connects through a dial-up ISP. The third line grants full access without logging in to anyone on network `10.1.2`, granting access to all users on the local network in this example. Although other news servers use different syntax, the facilities are similar.

It's up to you to decide how to set up your news server security, but do not under any circumstances grant Post access to outside users without a password. Spammers are constantly scanning for "open" news servers, and if they can post to your server, you can expect to find it filled with spam every morning. Grant Post access only to known users using passwords or restricted to the local network. For users elsewhere, either you can create a small number of shared accounts that your users can all use, changing the password from time to time so that it doesn't get spread around too much, or you can give each user a separate account, depending on your security goals. Separate accounts are certainly more secure, but they're also more work. In a business environment, it may well be adequate to have one account per department, changing the department's password either every few months or when someone leaves.

The procedure for creating these entries is simplicity itself: Edit the file that contains them, typically /var/news/etc/nnrp.access. You'll have to be the news user or UNIX or Linux superuser to do so.

Creating and Managing Private Newsgroups

On a private news server, the server's manager is responsible for maintaining all the groups. It's possible and usually desirable to delegate the work of writing and posting the FAQ for each local newsgroup and maintaining order (where possible) on the newsgroup. See Chapter 16 for more ideas about delegating the management of individual newsgroups.

Naming Your Newsgroups

You can assign any newsgroup names you want, although it's a good idea to use names that are unlikely to conflict with names used anywhere else (especially the Big Eight hierarchies in use within Usenet), in case you later want to make your groups available on other servers. The most straightforward way to make them unique is to pick a fairly long prefix (hierarchy name) for the group that reflects your server or organization's name. For example, for our Internet Gurus Central site, we might use a prefix of netgurucent so that groups could be named netgurucent.announce, netgurucent.search, and so forth. Users rarely have to type the names of newsgroups, so there's no reason to make the names short, but do keep in mind the limit of 14 characters per component that some news servers impose. A short prefix like ng is not a good idea because there are an awful lot of possible organizations with those initials.

Creating Newsgroups on Your Server

Although the details of newsgroup creation vary from one news server program to another, the procedure for INN is typical. For each group, you need the newsgroup's name, whether it's moderated, and, if so, the address to which to e-mail new messages for approval.

In INN, the `ctlinnd` command handles newsgroup creation. The command looks like this:

```
ctlinnd newgroup group.name type comment
```

Replace *group.name* with the complete name of the new newsgroups. Replace *type* with a code: Use `y` if users can post to the group, `m` if the group is moderated, and `n` if the group is read-only (useful for newsgroups sent from another new server). The *comment* is usually the e-mail address of the person who created the group on the local server. If the group is moderated, you need to add a line to your system's /var/news/etc/moderators file listing the name of the newsgroup and the moderator's address.

After a newsgroup is created, it's immediately available for use on your new server, and the next time any user starts a newsreader that connects to your news server, the newsreader should report the new newsgroup and offer to subscribe to it. The newsgroup is invisible to the rest of the Usenet world because the newsgroup exists only on your news server.

Managing Local Newsgroups

Unless you have an unusually ill-behaved set of local users, managing local newsgroups is not much work.

Each of your newsgroups needs an *expiration time* that determines how long messages for that newsgroup are stored. If your spool disk is large and the traffic in your groups is not huge, you can set an expiration time in weeks or even months so that the news server can archive messages to the group. On the other hand, if the group has lots of traffic without great historical value, such as status reports generated every 20 minutes by a software subsystem, it would make sense to expire articles in a few days.

Each newsgroup should have a formal or informal manager that looks at the newsgroup's contents every once in a while and takes action if the newsgroup is straying off topic or the tone is becoming unpleasant. (If it's straying off topic, the best action might be to make a new newsgroup for the strayed-to topic.)

For moderated groups, you'll need a human or software moderator to approve articles, as described in the section "Managing Moderated Newsgroups," later in this chapter. After articles are approved, they're treated like articles in any other newsgroups.

Managing Public Newsgroups

Unmoderated public newsgroups are considerably harder to manage than private ones because literally anyone in the world can post to them. The management tools are limited to jawboning (or, more likely, e-mail-boning) people who post inappropriate messages and posting a periodic FAQ message to remind people what the group is about and to squelch boring or contentious topics. Moderated newsgroups are easier to manage because the moderators control which postings get distributed.

FAQ Facts

Most Usenet newsgroups have *FAQs*, Frequently Asked (or Answered) Questions, posted regularly to the group. A good FAQ can be a treasure trove of useful information. Although the exact contents of FAQs vary a great deal, typical contents include:

The charter of the newsgroup or a summary of it (the charter of Big Eight newsgroups is determined when the newsgroup is created)

Answers to questions that new visitors always ask (the original meaning of FAQ)

Pointers to related resources on the Web

Books, magazines, and other resources relevant to the newsgroup's topic

Unlike mailing list FAQs, newsgroup FAQs don't need to discuss how to subscribe, unsubscribe, or set subscription options because those details depend on which newsreader a user is using and do not vary from group to group.

The main thing that makes an FAQ posting a newsgroup's FAQ is that it's posted regularly to the group. If a newsgroup is moderated, the moderator is the logical person to post the FAQ; in an unmoderated group, however, anyone can do so. Most FAQs are posted automatically by software that runs once a week or once a month, although there's no reason—at least at first—that the FAQ's author can't post it manually. On a UNIX or Linux system, you can use the crontab program to post the FAQ automatically.

After an FAQ has gotten to the point where it's reasonably stable, it's a good idea to arrange to cross-post it to the moderated news.answers newsgroup, which is a collection of the FAQs of all (or many) newsgroups. Anything posted to news.answers is automatically archived at the **Usenet Newsgroup FAQs by Hierarchy** FTP site, at ftp://rtfm.mit.edu/pub/usenet-by-hierarchy/ (which is accessible by using a Web browser), and many other places around the Internet. The people who run news.answers don't much care about the contents of the FAQs that are posted, although they have some firmly enforced mechanical rules about header formats that make it possible to archive and catalog all the FAQs in news.answers. The *.Answers Submission Guidelines* are described in ftp://rtfm.mit.edu:/pub/faqs/news-answers/guidelines. Many hierarchies have their own *.answers newsgroups, too. When you post your FAQ to news.answers, assuming that it meets the guidelines, the moderators will tell you that it's okay to cross-post to news.answers and the *.answers group in the hierarchy where your newsgroup lives. (For example, if your FAQ is for the comp.os.ctss newsgroup, it would be cross-posted to news.answers and comp.answers.)

For more information on FAQs, see the Infinite Ink *Finding and Writing FAQs* page, at http://www.ii.com/internet/faqs/.

Managing Moderated Newsgroups

The moderator or moderators of a newsgroup have almost complete control over the contents of the group. For the first decade-and-a-half of Usenet's existence, each moderated newsgroup was manually moderated by a single individual. Since the advent of robomoderation in 1994, moderation policies have become lots more varied. Moderation policies in use now include

> **Traditional manual moderation.** Each article is examined by the human moderator and posted or rejected.

Moderation panels. Several individuals share moderation duties. In some newsgroups, each individual moderates articles that come to her, and others do group moderation with the approval or disapproval of a given number of moderators needed to make the decision about an article.

Partial robomoderation. Messages from people known to be responsible or that pass keyword filters are approved automatically, and others are subjected to human scrutiny.

Primary robomoderation. All articles are handled automatically, except perhaps for a few users who are hand-moderated. Robomoderated groups usually require registration, with each author having to respond to a one-time challenge message to verify that the author's e-mail address is valid.

The simplest case, a single moderator hand-approving articles, can be handled with a POP mailbox for the newsgroup's e-mail and the Agent newsreader in Windows or a simple shell script in UNIX or Linux. For more complex schemes, a technically sophisticated moderator can write his own robomoderation programs or use one of the moderation packages available on the Internet. The most popular package is the freeware **STUMP**, at http://www.algebra.com/~ichudov/stump/, which handles most varieties of manual or semi-manual group moderation. It's free for use on UNIX and Linux systems, or its author offers a commercial hosting service for moderators who'd rather pay someone else to deal with software hassles.

A moderator may want to create a Web site and article archive for the group. Group archives have become less important now that **Deja.com** (at http://www.deja.com/), **RemarQ** (at http://www.remarq.com/), and other sites archive messages automatically for free. There's no particular trick to creating a newsgroup Web site—it's no different technically from any other Web site. For newsgroup archives, a variety of free archiving programs are available on the Internet, including **Hypermail** (at http://www.hypermail.org/), a program that turns mailboxes full of messages into Web pages, and **Glimpse** (at http://webglimpse.org/), a full-text search system.

Other Newsgroup-Management Issues

This section talks about a few other newsgroup-management issues you should know about.

Cross-posting to Moderated Newsgroups

Cross-posted articles to moderated newsgroups (that is, articles posted to several newsgroups at one time, including one or more moderated newsgroups) rarely work the way that people expect them to. If you post an article to several newsgroups, one of which is moderated, the article will be sent to the newsgroup's moderator and not posted to the other newsgroups at all. (If it were posted separately to moderated and unmoderated groups, multiple copies of the article would be floating around, a situation that Usenet software tries to prevent.) If the moderator decides to approve the posting, she can edit the Newsgroups line before posting the article to control to which unmoderated newsgroups the article is posted. Some moderators post articles as is, some trim down the list of newsgroups, and some permit no cross-posting—they either strip off all other newsgroups before posting or return cross-posted articles unposted.

Cross-posting an article to more than one moderated newsgroup is even more problematical. News server software will pick one of the newsgroups arbitrarily and e-mail it to that newsgroup's moderator. There is no consensus on what moderators should do with such messages. Some moderators e-mail the messages to the moderators of the other newsgroups so that all the moderators can approve them. A few newsgroups have informal agreements permitting cross-posting between moderated newsgroups. As often as not, the first moderator won't notice that another moderated group is on the Newsgroup line and will post the message without consulting the other moderators. The article then appears in all newsgroups! (Usenet software provides no technical protection against moderators approving articles in newsgroups other than their own.) Probably the best strategy (if you moderate a newsgroup) is not to allow cross-posting to other moderated newsgroups.

Forgeries

The situation where one moderator cross-posts an article into another newsgroup is an example of a more general problem: approval forgery. It's technically easy for anyone to forge an approved moderated article merely by adding an Approved header line to the article before posting it. (The theory, which works pretty well in practice, is that because there's no technical challenge to forging approvals, there's little incentive for people to do so just to prove that they can.) Most groups have no problem with forged posts. The few that do can use a service named the **PGP Moose** (described at http://people.qualcomm.com/ggr/pgpmoose.html). The moderator can sign each approved article using a published PGP (Pretty Good Encryption) key. PGP Moose software runs on several news servers around the Internet; whenever the software sees in a PGP-Moose–nprotected newsgroup a message that doesn't have the right PGP signature, the PGP Moose automatically sends out a cancel message to delete the offending message.

The PGP Moose is an example of what's been called *retromoderation*, moderating a newsgroup by letting people post anything and then having the moderator cancel messages that don't meet the moderation standards. No newsgroups use retromoderation because it doesn't work very well. Cancel messages don't always catch up with the messages they're supposed to cancel, meaning that different news servers will have different sets of canceled and uncanceled articles. The impetus for retromoderation was the delay in posting caused by traditional hand moderation in moderated groups. Robomoderation solved that problem because robomoderated messages are usually posted within a minute or two of arriving at the moderator's system.

Spam Canceling

Usenet has a horrendous but largely invisible spam problem. As mentioned in the section "Cancels and Spam" in Chapter 6, vast amounts of spam are detected and canceled every day. For the most part, this system of automatic cancellations is invisible to users and even to newsgroup moderators, but now and then a cancel message from a spam-canceling program will land in the moderator's mailbox. Remember that spam-canceling programs are your friends, and even though spam-cancel messages technically may be forged messages in a moderated newsgroup, the good they do far outweighs any technical violation of moderation rules.

Part IV

Internet Relay Chat (IRC)

Chapter Eight
Finding, Joining, and Participating in IRC

Internet Relay Chat, or *IRC*, is a worldwide system of real-time chats, predating the World Wide Web by many years. In theory, IRC is a way for individuals around the world to have stimulating, fascinating, online discussions. In reality, IRC is more often a way for bored undergraduates to waste time. However, some ongoing communities exist on IRC, and IRC can be a useful way for mailing lists, newsgroups, or Web-based communities to get together for real-time chat.

How IRC Works

To participate in IRC, you need an IRC program like mIRC, Ircle, Microsoft Chat, or ircii. You use this program to connect to an *IRC server*, an Internet host computer running a program that serves as a switchboard for IRC messages. IRC servers are organized into *networks*, groups of IRC servers that exchange messages with each other—when you connect to any IRC server in a network, you can communicate with people who are connected to any other IRC server on that network. Because each IRC network can have thousands of people connected to its servers at the same time, discussions are divided into *channels*; when you connect to an IRC server and join a channel, you see the messages sent to that channel and you can send messages to that channel. (Channels are the IRC equivalent of AOL chat rooms.) When you type a message and press Enter, your message appears on the screens of other participants in the channel within seconds (or, if the system is running slow, minutes).

IRC Networks

IRC servers are organized into networks of servers that talk to each other. Many IRC networks have Web sites that describe the rules of the network and provide a list of the servers to which you can connect to use the network. Here are the three biggest networks and their Web sites:

EFnet (the original IRC network, Eris Free Network)
http://www.efnet.net/
Undernet (the first spin off network)
http://www.undernet.org/
http://servers.undernet.org/ (list of IRC servers)
DALnet (another large IRC network)
http://www.dal.net/

All EFnet IRC servers are connected to each other, all Undernet servers are connected, and all DALnet servers are connected. All the folks on EFnet can talk to each other regardless of which EFnet server they connect to. Servers on one IRC network don't connect to servers on other networks. Someone on EFnet can't talk to someone on Undernet, for example. When you choose a network, you choose the universe of people you'll be hanging out with on IRC. After you have spent some time on IRC, you probably will develop a preference for one network—the one where your friends hang out.

Lots of smaller IRC networks exist: See the section "Web Sites of IRC Networks," in the Appendix, for the Web sites of many more. Some IRC network Web sites include Web-based Java applets that enable you to join IRC channels from the Web site, without using a separate IRC program.

IRC Servers

After you've chosen which IRC network you want to connect to (try one of the big three if you are starting out), connect to the IRC server nearest you (the section "Connecting to an IRC Server," later in this chapter, describes how to use your IRC program to connect). Check the network's Web site, or see whether your IRC program includes a list of IRC servers that includes servers on your chosen network. Use a nearby server, if available, because using a local server is the polite thing to do and because it probably will respond faster than a server farther away. Because servers come and go frequently, be sure to consult the Usenet newsgroup alt.irc for more complete and up-to-date lists.

When you connect to an IRC server, you specify the name of the server (for example, irc.acestar.org) and the port on that server, which is a number. Lists of IRC servers usually include the port numbers you can use to connect to that server. Unless it's specified otherwise, use port 6667 on any IRC servers.

IRC servers are run by *IRC operators*, or *IRCops*.

Channels

IRC conversations are organized into channels, with each channel dedicated to a single topic, at least in theory. Because any user can create a channel, you get some funky channel names and lots of channels with just one participant, waiting for other people to show up. Channel names are single words (no spaces) that start with a pound sign (#), or sometimes an ampersand (&)—for example, #daytraders is a channel dedicated to professional stock traders. Some channels exist all the time, and others are around only at particular times. The big three IRC networks (EFnet, DALnet, and Undernet) have thousands of channels at any given moment.

Some channels have friendly conversations, some are specifically for new IRCers to ask questions, some are about sex (big surprise), and some contain one bored, lonely person waiting for someone to take pity on him (yes, it's usually a him). Choosing the right channel is the key to your IRC experience.

> **What If You Can't Get In?**
>
> *Frequently, when you try to connect to a server, you can't. Instead, you see an error message, such as "No Authorization" or "You have been K-lined." These messages mean that the IRC server is full or that too many people from your particular Internet service provider are connected now or have been connecting frequently in the past. When this happens, just try another IRC server.*

When you connect to an IRC server, you can display a list of the channels carried by that server. Each of the major IRC networks has thousands of active channels. The section "Joining a Channel," later in this chapter, describes how to select a channel to join.

Channels are run by *channel operators* (or *chanops* or *ops*), who can kick people out, ban people (prevent them from rejoining), and set channel options. Each channel has a one-line topic, which can be changed by the channel operators at any time; the topic appears on channel listings, to help people decide which channel to join. Channel operators can usually be identified by nicknames that start with an at sign (@).

Nicknames

When you connect to an IRC server, you choose a nickname by which you will be identified. You can't use a nickname that is already in use by anyone connected to any of the servers on the same network. When you connect, if the nickname you chose is already in use, you see an error message. You can use an

IRC command (described in the section "Changing Your Nickname," later in this chapter) to switch to a different nickname.

IRC Programs

To participate in IRC, you need an IRC program (also called an *IRC client program*). For Windows users, we recommend **mIRC** (http://www.mirc.com/); for Mac users, we suggest **Ircle** (http://www.ircle.com/). These and many other IRC programs are available from the **TUCOWS** Web site (http://www.tucows.com/). Windows 98 and Windows Millennium Edition (Me) come with Microsoft Chat, another IRC program. Although America Online and CompuServe don't provide IRC access directly, you can run mIRC or Ircle to connect to IRC servers via an AOL or CompuServe connection. UNIX and Linux users can use the classic text-only irc or ircii programs after which all the others are modeled.

In the rest of this chapter, we describe how to use IRC with the mIRC program; Ircle and Microsoft Chat work similarly.

IRC Commands

In the early days of IRC, IRC programs required users to type commands rather than click buttons and choose commands from menus. (The UNIX and Linux irc and ircii programs still do.) These IRC commands still work in mIRC and most other IRC programs. IRC commands all start with a /, and you can use some commands only by typing them.

To give a command, type it in the same box where you type messages for the channel. For example, you can join a channel by using the `/join` command, like this:

```
/join #hottub
```

Table 8-1 shows some commonly used IRC commands.

Participating in IRC

Regardless of which IRC program you use, the steps for participating in IRC are practically identical:

1. Install and configure your IRC program if you haven't ever used it.
2. Establish contact with an IRC server.
3. Tell the server your nickname.
4. Join a channel. (Some IRC programs let you join several channels at one time.)
5. Listen until you have an idea what is going on.
6. Chime in!

Configuring Your IRC Program

When you start mIRC or another IRC program, you have to tell it a few things about you. Figure 8-1 shows the mIRC Options dialog box (you display it by choosing File|Options or pressing `Alt+O`). This dialog box also lets you choose to which IRC server you want to connect as well as configure lots of program options.

If your IRC program asks for your real name, you can type a pseudonym. If it asks for your e-mail address, leave it blank if you want to remain anonymous. Some IRC programs let you type a preferred nickname and an alternative nickname to try if the first one is already in use when you connect. All nicknames on an entire IRC network must be different from each other, so try a peculiar variation on your name or a fanciful name.

Command	Description
/away message	Leave an explanation when you are away from the keyboard
/dcc chat nickname	Start a DCC chat with nickname
/dcc send nickname filename	Send file to nickname via DCC
/ignore nickname	Suppress the display of messages from nickname
/ignore -l	List people you are ignoring
/ignore -r nickname	Remove nickname from your ignore list
/ignore -r	Remove everyone from your ignore list
/invite nickname channel	Invite nickname to join channel
/join channel	Join channel, or create it if it doesn't already exist
/list -min x -max y	List channels with at least x and no more than y people
/list *text*	List channels that contain text in the name
/me action	Displays your nickname and action as a message in the current channel
/mode nickname +i	Become invisible so that your nickname doesn't appear on user listings
/mode nickname -i	Stop being invisible
/msg nickname message	Sends a private message to nickname
/nick nickname	Change your nickname to nickname
/notify nickname	Add nickname to your notify list
/part	Leave the current channel
/quit reason	Disconnects from the IRC server, displaying reason in all the channels you were in
/who channel	List the participants in the channel
/whois nickname	Find out more about nickname

Table 8-1: IRC Commands.

Don't use your username (the first part of your e-mail address) as your nickname if you want to remain anonymous. Experienced IRCers can tell which Internet service provider you're using, and, if your nickname is the same as your username, they can figure out your e-mail address.

Connecting to an IRC Server

In mIRC, you use the mIRC Options dialog box to choose which server to connect to. Choose File|Options, and then choose Connect from the list of categories. Choose a server from the drop-down list at the right. Choose a server on the network you want to try, and select one that's geographically near you. Then click OK.

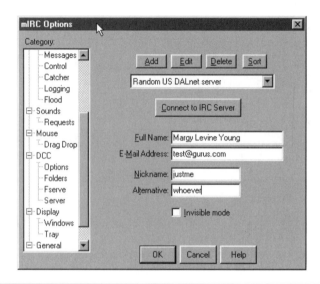

Figure 8-1: Configuring the mIRC program.

You're ready to try connecting to a server. Click the Connect button (the leftmost button on the toolbar). A Status window appears, showing messages from the IRC server. If everything works, welcoming messages from your server appear in the Status window, usually including the *MOTD* (message of the day) with rules that apply to IRC participants. If you get an error message, go back to the first step and try another server.

Don't worry if you see "Ping? Pong!" in the Status window. This message just means that your IRC server checked that you were still there ("Ping?") and mIRC responded ("Pong!").

If the server you want to connect to doesn't appear on the mIRC Options window's server list, you can click the Add button and fill in information about the server: Type a description or name in the Description box, the address of the server in the IRC Server box, and the port (usually 6667) in the Port box.

Changing Your Nickname

On some IRC servers, frequent participants can reserve their favorite nickname so that no one else can use it (see the section "Reserving Your Nickname with NickServ," in Chapter 9). The NickServ program, which runs on some IRC servers, keeps track of the reserved nicknames and the password for each nickname. If the nickname you chose is either in use by or reserved by someone else, you see these messages in the Status window when you connect to an IRC server:

```
-NickServ- This nick is owned by someone else. Please
choose another.
-
-NickServ- If this is your nick, type: /msg NickServ
IDENTIFY <password>
-
NickServ- Your nick will be changed in 60 seconds if
you do not comply.
```

If you do nothing, the NickServ program changes your nickname automatically, usually to a nickname consisting of Guest and a number.

You can change your nickname in response to these messages from NickServ or whenever you want to start using a different nickname. Type this IRC command in the message box in the Status window or in any channel window:

/nick *nickname*

Replace *nickname* with the nickname you want to use—for example, type /nick freddyboy

IRC confirms your new nickname.

Joining a Channel

After you are connected to an IRC server, you can join a channel. To see a list of channel names in mIRC, click the Channels Folder button (the third button from the left on the toolbar). Figure 8-2 shows a typical list. This is not the list of all available channels, which is really long. Instead, it's the list of the channels that mIRC's author recommends for new IRC users.

If the channel you want to join appears on the list, click it and click Join. Otherwise, type the channel name in the box at the top of the mIRC Channels Folder window. If you have never done this, try the #irchelp channel or the designated help channel for the IRC network you are using (check the network's Web page for channel names).

When you join, a window for the channel appears. If you join more than one channel, each channel appears in its own window. The window has three parts: a list of people in the channel (the rightmost column), the box in which you type what you want to say (the bottommost line), and the conversation occurring in that channel (the rest of the window). The title bar of the window includes the

Figure 8-2: mIRC lists some recommended channels.

name and description of the channel: Figure 8-3 shows two channel windows: one for #CyberAngels and one for #Family_Chat.

After you have joined a channel, everything that people on the channel type appears in the window. Whenever someone joins or leaves a channel, a message is sent to all remaining participants; when you join a channel, everyone else immediately knows that you're a participant. Messages that people type are preceded by their nickname, as shown in this example:

`<JoeBlow> But what do you do with the woodchucks after you catch them?`

mIRC displays a list of people in the channel on the right side of the channel's window.

You can type an IRC command to join a channel if you know the exact channel name. Type this command in the box at the bottom of the Status window or any channel window:

`/join channel`

Replace *channel* with the exact channel name, including the # at the beginning.

When you join a channel, you join a conversation in progress—usually, several conversations whose remarks are intermixed. Following the conversation can be hard because it's not always obvious who is replying to whom. People sometimes

Chapter 8: Finding, Joining, and Participating in IRC   185

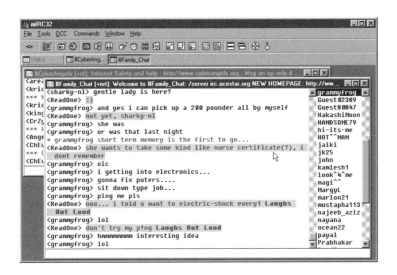

Figure 8-3: mIRC enables you to join several channels at the same time.

precede their remarks with the name of the person they are talking to, which helps. Start by reading one person's remarks and the replies to that person.

If you join a channel that doesn't exist, the IRC server creates it for you—you just created your own channel! See Chapter 9 to learn how to run an IRC channel.

Displaying a List of Channels

To see a complete list of channels the IRC server carries, click the List Channels button (the fourth one from the left end of the toolbar). In the List Channels dialog box that appears, you tell mIRC what kind of channels you are looking for, to avoid downloading and wading through a huge list of thousands of channels. You can specify text that must appear in the channel name or topic or the minimum and maximum number of people in the channel.

If you enter 3 for the minimum number of users, you reduce the size of your channel list enormously and are unlikely to miss many interesting conversations. When you have set your criteria, click the Get List! button. A window appears, and the list of channels begins to appear. On a busy day, the list can take several minutes to arrive. mIRC sorts the channels alphabetically and shows the name, number of people in it, and description. After you have displayed the list of channels, you can scroll up and down the list. To join a channel, double-click it.

You can also use the `/list` command to see a list of channels. The list appears in a new window. To limit the length of the list, you can specify the minimum and maximum number of participants, like this:

`/list -min x -max y`

Replace *x* with the minimum number of people (at least 3), and *y* with the maximum. You can also see a list of channels whose names or topics contain text you specify, like this:

`/list *text*`

Replace *text* with the letters you want to match. For example, type this command to see channels with names that include `help`:

`/list *help*`

Leaving a Channel

You can leave a channel you tire of by closing the channel's window or typing the `/part` command. Then you can join another channel or exit your IRC program. If you want to leave all the channels you are in and disconnect from the IRC server, you can use the `/quit` command, like this:

`/quit reason`

Replace *reason* with a parting message, which will be displayed in all the channels you are leaving.

When you exit the mIRC program, you leave all your channels and disconnect from the IRC server.

Sending Messages to a Channel

When you want to say something in a channel you have joined, make sure that your cursor is blinking in the box at the bottom of the channel window (click in the box if it's not). Then type your message and press `Enter`.

As is so often the case on the Internet, naive users can easily make fools of themselves. When you join a channel, lurk for a while. Don't immediately begin typing—wait to see the tenor of the conversation. Then type away.

Finding Out about Participants

To get more information about the people in a channel, use the `/who` command, like this:

`/who channel`

Replace *channel* with the channel name, including the # at the beginning. The Status window (not the channel window) shows the result of the `/who` command, with one line per person. The line for you includes the name and e-mail address you typed when you set up mIRC.

To find out more about someone, press Alt+B to display the mIRC Address Book window. In the Nick box, type a nickname and then click the Who Is button. Information about the person appears in the rest of the boxes in the window, including his name and e-mail address (that is, the name and e-mail address the person configured his IRC program to display, which may not be correct) and the channel (or channels) the person is on. Then click the Finger button to see whether the person's ISP has any other information (finger is a UNIX command that displays information about a user).

Alternatively, you can type the /whois command, like this:

```
/whois nickname
```

Be sure to use this method to see what other IRCers can find out about you. Some Internet service providers include your home phone number and other personal information in their finger information. Work or school accounts may include your department, dorm, or other personal information. If you meet some creep on IRC, you may not want him to be able to call you!

You can tell your IRC program to let you know when friends connect to the IRC server you are using. Your *notify list* is a list of the nicknames of people you want to keep track of. Click the Address Book button on the mIRC toolbar to see the mIRC Address Book in which you can enter the nicknames of friends. Make sure that the Enable Notify check box is selected.

Another way to add someone to your notify list is by typing this command:

```
/notify nickname
```

When anyone on your notify list connects to the same IRC server you are on, mIRC displays a message.

Displaying Actions

You can send messages that describe what you're doing or what you want the folks in your channel to think that you are doing. You use the /me command, like this:

```
/me smiles slyly
```

Type the command in the box at the bottom of the channel window. The line appears like this (assuming that your nickname is ZacsMom):

```
* ZacsMom smiles slyly
```

Sending Private Messages

IRC lets you send messages directly to individuals. To send a message to an individual, double-click the person's nickname. A window appears in which you can type a message, as shown in Figure 8-4. When you press Enter, the message is sent to that person.

You can also send a private message by using the /msg command, like this:

`/msg nickname message`

Replace *nickname* with the person's nickname and *message* with the message you want to send.

If someone sends a private message to you, that message appears in a new window, containing only messages between that person and you. You can respond by typing a message in the box at the bottom of the window and pressing Enter. If you don't want to respond or you're done with the conversation, close the window.

Your private conversation can be routed through a dozen IRC servers, and the operators of any of these servers can log all your messages. Don't say anything that has to be really private.

If you'd like someone to join a channel you are in, you can use the /invite command, like this:

`/invite nickname channel`

For example, this command invites newbie3 to join the #irchelp channel:

`/invite newbie3 #irchelp`

The person you are inviting gets a message inviting him to join the channel you suggest.

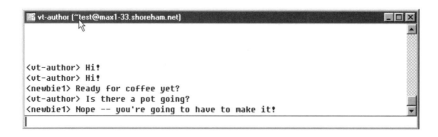

Figure 8-4: You can exchange private messages with another IRC participant.

A more private way to converse is via *DCC*, Direct Client Connections. You don't have to be on the same channel as the person you want to talk to; you just have to know the person's nickname. Click the DCC Chat button on the mIRC toolbar, type the person's nickname, and click OK. A window opens while mIRC waits for the other person to respond. When someone tries to start a DCC chat with you, mIRC asks whether you want to chat with the other person. If you click Chat, mIRC opens a window for the discussion. Your DCC chat window is just like a minichannel with only two people in it.

The IRC command to start a DCC chat is

```
/dcc chat nickname
```

You can also use DCC commands to send files to other people. For example, you could send a picture of yourself to a person you have just met. When someone tries to send you a file, mIRC displays a dialog box that lets you choose whether to accept it. If someone offers to send you a file, however, we suggest declining unless you know the person. Unsolicited files tend to be unbelievably rude and disgusting or can include viruses. To send a file via DCC, click the DCC Send button on the toolbar or type this command:

```
/dcc send nickname filename
```

Letting People Know You Are Away

If you go away from the keyboard, you can leave a message for others on IRC who may send you a message. Type this command:

```
/away message
```

Replace *message* with the reason you are away or whatever you'd like people to know, like this:

```
/away Getting coffee again - be right back!
```

This message appears when other people send you a private message or use the /whois command to find out about you.

Finding Channels of Interest

The vast majority of IRC channels contain only idle chatter. Here are some ways to find a channel on a specific topic:

EFnet Channel List, at http://www.irchelp.org/irchelp/chanlist/, provides a searchable list of the channels available on EFnet.

IRCnet Channel Search, at http://www.ludd.luth.se/irc/list.html, lets you search for channels on the IRCnet network.

Liszt's IRC Chat Directory, at http://www.liszt.com/chat/, is part of the Liszt Web site, which provides searchable databases of mailing lists and newsgroups. You type a specific channel name, or a word that might appear in the description of a channel, and Liszt tells you when channels meet your description and what IRC networks the channels are on. Clicking the name of a channel is supposed to run your IRC program, although this technique works only if you have configured your browser to do so.

Talk City Web site, at http://www.talkcity.com/, lets you search for channels on the Talk City IRC servers, which you can access via its Web site or by using special IRC programs (see the sidebar "Talk City Combines IRC and the Web").

Undernet Channel Search, at http://www.cservice.undernet.org/ (click Search), is another way to find a channel.

Many channels have their own Web sites. To find them, start at **Yahoo** (at http://www.yahoo.com/), and choose Computers and Internet, Internet, Chats and Forums, IRC, and Channels. Also check the section "Web Sites of IRC Networks," in this book's appendix.

Choosing the right channel can make the difference between a boring or offensive IRC experience and a good one. Which channels are good depends on which network of servers you use (EFnet, DALnet, Undernet, or another network). On all networks, try these channels:

- **#helpdesk**, **#irchelp**, **#ircnewbies**, **#newbies**, **#new2irc**, or similar channels for getting started
- **#hottub** and **#chat** for general hanging around
- **#mirc**, **#new2mirc**, or **#mirchelp** for getting help with mIRC
- **#ircle** for help with the Mac Ircle IRC program

You can also take a look for channels designed for folks in your age range, with names such as #teen, #21+, and #34_to_45. If you speak (type) a

---

Talk City Combines IRC and the Web

Talk City (http://www.talkcity.com) is a Web "front end" for its IRC server at chat.talkcity.com. You can chat using the Talk City Web site or by using Talk City-specific chat programs (which display lots of ads, leaving a small amount of screen space for your chat). The Talk City version of the popular Pirch chat program for Windows 95, Windows 98, and Windows NT is TC Pirch, and Mac users can run TC Ircle. You can download TC Pirch and TC Ircle for free from http://www.talkcity.com/download/.

language other than English, try one of the many non-English channels out there—#espagnol, #francais, #brasil, #polska, or #42 (Finnish), for a start. Channels that contain the word *warez* concentrate on illegally exchanging copyrighted software programs, which is illegal and explicitly forbidden on most IRC servers.

Other IRC Topics

Lags and Netsplits

When an IRC network gets busy, *lags* (delays) can develop. Worse, groups of IRC servers can get disconnected from each other so that the IRC network is split into two or more sections—a *netsplit*. When a netsplit occurs, it appears that lots of people quit an IRC server at the same time and then all reappear when the IRC server's connection is fixed.

You can't do anything about lags and netsplits. If they get bad, consider switching to a different IRC network or coming back at a less busy time.

IRC Etiquette

Here are some rules of IRC netiquette:

1. When you join a channel, listen for a few minutes until you pick up the thread of the conversation (or conversations). Don't immediately start saying "Hello!" to everyone.

2. Don't use all capital letters; it's similar to shouting.

3. Speak (type) the language that's appropriate for the channel and on the topic the channel is about (if any).

4. Don't send inane messages, such as "Does anyone want to talk?" If you want people to talk to you, say something interesting. It doesn't have to be exactly erudite—"What about those Mets!" or "Cold enough for you?" should do. "I'd like to talk about movies" or "Anybody like cooking?" are good, too.

5. If you have something to say to someone that isn't of general interest to the group, send it privately (see the section "Sending Private Messages," earlier in this chapter).

6. Don't flood (send lots of messages real fast so that no one else can get a word in edgewise). Flooding gets you banned on many IRC channels.

Getting Banned

If you break the rules of a channel, you can get banned from that channel, which means that you can't rejoin it. Channel operators ban people (see the next chapter to find out how). If you think that you were banned from a channel in error, send a private message to one of the channel operators explaining the situation.

If you break the rules of an IRC server, you can be banned from connecting to that server. Sometimes entire domains are banned (or *K-lined*) from connecting to a server because of bad behavior on the part of users from that domain.

Becoming Invisible

You can block people from finding out about you with the `/who` and `/whois` commands. Type this command to set your mode to invisible:

`/mode nickname +i`

To turn off invisibility, type this command:

`/mode nickname -I`

Even when you are invisible, other participants in the same channels you are in can see your nickname.

Blocking Messages

If a participant in an IRC channel sends annoying, abusive, or just boring messages, you can tell your IRC program to ignore them—not to display messages from this person on your screen. Type the `/ignore` command, like this:

`/ignore nickname`

This command adds the person's nickname to your list of people to ignore. If the person keeps sending messages from another nickname, you can type her e-mail address instead (at least the username from which she is connected to IRC). Use the `/whois` command to find out the person's e-mail address. If you have lots of trouble, become invisible (as described in the preceding section) and change your nickname. Only other people on your channel see your new nickname.

To see who's on your ignore list, type

`/ignore -l`

(That's a lowercase *L*). To remove someone from your list, type this command:

`/ignore -r nickname`

To erase everyone from your list, type

`/ignore -r`

The Dangers of IRC

The Internet is pretty anarchic, and IRC is one of the more extreme parts of the anarchy. In particular, all you really know about the people you're chatting with is their nicknames and who they purport to be. Unfortunately, some IRC users have a sick sense of humor and delight in offering other chatters "helpful speed-up files" that in fact delete their files instead or let these folks crack into others' accounts. Also, many users have a completely different persona in IRC than they do in real life: These users alter details of their age, interests, lifestyle, gender—you name it. In some cases, the makebelieve is fun; in others, it's just strange. Chat all you want; just keep in mind that not all your IRC friends may be who or what they claim to be.

If someone on IRC tells you to type a command, don't do it. Nefarious people may suggest that you type commands that can make it possible for other people to use your Internet account, scramble your disk, or otherwise diminish your quality of online life.

Also, IRC is no place for kids, unless you're right there looking over their shoulders. In our experience, IRC has the highest porn-to-nonporn ratio on the entire Internet.

Bots

Some people in IRC channels aren't actually people—they are programs, called bots. A *bot* is a program that reads the messages on an IRC channel and responds in preset ways. For example, a simple (but very annoying bot) could respond to messages about people entering the channel by sending a "Hello!" message. (This type of bot, an *auto-greeting bot*, is frowned on.)

Some bots have useful purposes, like automatically kicking out people who flood the channel (by sending many lines of text quickly—many channels have a limit of about five lines of text in five seconds) or people who use dirty words. A few channels even have bots that run word games with the human participants. Chapter 9 describes bots that are useful for running IRC channels.

Some IRC servers ban all bots because of the trouble they can cause. Others use bots to enforce the rules in channels.

Getting More Information

For more information about Internet Relay Chat, see these Web sites:

IRChelp.org Internet Relay Chat (IRC) Help Archive

http://www.irchelp.org/

NewIRCusers.com (helpful information about IRC and other types of real-time chat)
http://www.newircusers.com/

A Short IRC Primer (long)
http://www.irchelp.org/irchelp/ircprimer.htm

Chapter Nine
Creating and Managing IRC Channels

We don't recommend choosing IRC (Internet Relay Chat, described in the preceding chapter) as the sole location for an online community—it has no central storage place for archives and shared files, and the only type of communication is real-time. Many Internet users don't have IRC programs installed, and it's hard to keep an IRC channel running uninterrupted under your control. However, if you run another type of online community, you may want to create IRC channels as a way for your community members to have real-time chats.

Steps for Creating a Successful Private Channel

If you want to set up one or more IRC channels for the use of your community members, follow these steps:

1. **Decide which IRC network you want your channels to be on.** (See the next section, "Choosing an IRC Network.")

2. **Choose a channel name that is not likely to be taken.** Ideally, make sure that only community members know the channel name, to avoid other people trying to crash your channel.

3. **Create the channel** (see the section "Creating and Configuring Your Channel," later in this chapter).

4. **Register your channel** so that you can maintain control of it (see the section "Reserving a Channel Name with ChanServ," later in this chapter, if your IRC network uses ChanServ, or refer to the instructions on your IRC network's Web site). If you are using the channel for one time and don't plan to use it again, skip this step.

5. **Configure your channel**, using both IRC `/mode` commands (described in the section "Creating and Configuring Your Channel") and ChanServ or

other channel-registration system commands (see the later section "Reserving a Channel Name with ChanServ").

6. **Test your channel** with a few friends.

7. **Add instructions to your community Web site about how members can participate** in IRC channels in general and your channels in specific. (You can include a link to the *Internet Gurus IRC* article, at http://net.gurus.com/irc/). Include dates and times when people should show up. If you make the real-time chats a regular event, community members can get used to coming at the same time each week or month, making it much more likely that enough members will show up at the appointed time to have an interesting chat. Also include the rules for real-time chats (see the section "Rules for IRC Channels," later in this chapter, for ideas).

8. **Connect to your IRC channel during your scheduled IRC chats** (show up a bit early so that you have time to test things out).

9. **Refine the dates, times, and rules as you go along, based on how your chats go**. Consider inviting special guests, choosing topics for chats, or creating other special events to attract community members to chats.

Choosing an IRC Network

Before you create an IRC channel, choose on which IRC network to create it. (See the section "How IRC Works," in Chapter 8, for a description of IRC networks and servers.) Different networks provide different services to communities that want to maintain channels. Choose a community with these two facilities:

Channel registration, a system that lets you register and maintain your channel name so that other people can't create a channel by the same name while your channel is not in use. Channel-registration programs include ChanServ, Channel Service (on Undernet), and ASIRC (on AnotherNet).

Nickname registration, a system that lets people reserve nicknames so that your community members can use the same nickname each time you chat. (Keeping track of changing nicknames can be confusing.) The original system was named NickServ, but there are other systems, like AnotherNet's ASIRC.

Here are some IRC networks to consider (read the Web pages and FAQs for each IRC network before making your choice because network facilities may change):

AnotherNet (http://www.another.net/chat/) runs a special IRC server named ASIRC (AnotherNet Secure IRC), which requires users to register before chatting. ASIRC provides channel registration, nickname registration, and other services.

DALnet (http://www.dal.net/) provides NickServ (for reserving nicknames), ChanServ (for registering channels), and MemoServ (for sending messages and files to other people even when they are offline). DALnet doesn't require people to register before connecting to their IRC servers, but the security isn't as tight as AnotherNet's. For instructions on using NickServ and ChanServ, see the section "Reserving Nicknames and Channel Names," later in this chapter.

Undernet (http://www.undernet.org/) runs a channel-registration program named CService, which runs bots named X and W on registered channels. Each registered channel has one channel manager (the person who registered the channel) and as many channel operators as needed, with a complete set of security levels. For details, see the **Undernet Channel Service** page, at http://www.cservice.undernet.org/, and **Undernet's Channel Operator's FAQ**, at http://www.undernet.org/documents/chanops.html.

EFnet, the original IRC network, doesn't provide nickname or channel registration. Many smaller IRC networks run NickServ, ChanServ, or both. To check whether an IRC network runs NickServ, connect to a server on the network and type these commands:

```
/msg nickserv help
/nickserv help
```

To check whether ChanServ is running, send these commands:

```
/msg chanserv help
/chanserv help
```

Creating and Configuring Your Channel

When you create a channel, you are its channel operator. As channel operator, you can set the topic and mode of your channel and decide who is allowed to join the channel.

Creating an IRC Channel

To start your own IRC channel, just make up a name and issue a `/join` command. In mIRC, click the Channels Folder button on the toolbar, type the name of the new channel in the box, and click Join. IRC creates the channel automatically when you try to join it. A window appears for the new channel. Initially, you are the only participant in the channel.

You are your new channel's operator (*chanop*). An at sign (@) appears before your name on the list of channel participants. Before you leave the channel, be sure to designate at least one other person as chanop so that someone can remain in charge (see the section "Appointing Additional Channel Operators," later in this chapter).

Setting the Topic

On the list of available channels on an IRC server, most channels have a one-line description, or topic. Any channel participant can use the /topic command to set the topic line, like this:

/topic *channel topic*

Replace *channel* with the exact channel name (including the #) and *topic* with the new topic. For example:

/topic #cephalopods Squid, cuttlefish, and their cousins

The chanop can configure the channel so that only chanops can set the channel's topic, by typing this command:

/mode *channel* +t

If other channel participants try to change the topic, they receive an error message. The chanop can remove this restriction by sending this command:

/mode *channel* -t

Seeing Who's on the Channel

mIRC displays a list of channel participants down the right side of the channel window, but you can get more information about the participants by typing this command:

/who *channel*

You see a listing like this (for a channel named #poorrichard):

```
#poorrichard margyly H@ ~test@max1-30.shoreham.net :1
Margy Levine Young
#poorrichard john H@ xuxa@iecc.com :0 nobody in
particular
#poorrichard peterk H framistan-23@evergreen.edu :0
Peter the Great
#poorrichard missy H xyz@abc.com :1 Missy D
#poorrichard becky H dartangnan@indy.net :0 Becky
Whitney
```

Making a Channel Private

When a channel is created, it is public, so it appears on lists of channels that other users display. You can make the channel private or secret:

Private channels appear on lists of channel names, but other people can't tell which participants are in it.

Secret channels don't appear on lists of channel names.

Private and secret channels are useful if you want only selected people (like the members of your online community) to participate.

To make a channel private or secret, you use the `/mode` command, which has many options. The command to make your channel private looks like this:

`/mode channel +p`

To make the channel secret, type this command:

`/mode channel +s`

To remove the private and secret designations, type these commands:

`/mode channel -p`
`/mode channel -s`

You can also prevent people outside the channel from sending messages to the channel (via the `/msg` command). For example, people use the `/msg` command to invite the participants of your channel to join their channels. To prevent outside messages, send this command:

`/mode channel +n`

To allow messages from outsiders, send this command:

`/mode channel -n`

Making a Channel Moderated

A *moderated* channel is one in which only the channel operators and participants with *voices* can send messages. The chanop can send this command to make a channel moderated:

`/mode channel +m`

To allow all participants to send messages (remove moderation), send this command:

`/mode channel +m`

To give a participant a voice so that he can send messages, type this command:

`/mode channel +v nickname`

Participants who have been granted voices have a plus sign (+) next to their nicknames. To remove someone's IRC voice, send this command:

`/mode channel -v nickname`

Setting a Maximum Number of Participants

You can limit the number of people who can join your channel by typing this command:

`/mode channel +l number`

(The character after the plus sign is a lowercase letter *L*.) To remove the limitation, type

`/mode channel -l`

Appointing Additional Channel Operators

A channel should have an operator at all times—if a channel has no operator, no one can issue chanop-only commands. Before you disconnect from IRC, be sure to appoint someone else as a chanop, by using this command:

`/mode channel +o nickname`

After you've made someone else a chanop, that person has all the same powers that you do, so be sure that you trust someone before giving her chanop status. She can revoke your chanop status, kick everyone off the channel, or both.

You can strip a person of chanop status by using this command:

`/mode channel -o nickname`

Inviting, Removing, and Banning People

As channel operator, you are responsible for maintaining order on the channel. Your main tools are control of who is on the channel and the ability to kick out those who don't follow the rules.

Inviting People to Join the Channel

The chanop can configure the channel as *invite-only*, which means that people can't join the channel unless they are invited by a channel operator. Type this command:

`/mode channel +i`

To let people join the channel without an invitation, type this command:

`/mode channel -i`

When you want to invite someone to join your channel, send this command:

`/invite nickname channel`

Removing People from the Channel

If someone is causing trouble on your channel, you can kick the person out by typing this command:

`/kick channel nickname`

To prevent a person from returning, ban her from the channel:
`/mode channel +b nickname`

It's a good idea to ban a person first, before kicking her off, so that she can't sneak back into the channel while you are typing the `ban` command.

To remove a ban, type
`/mode channel -b nickname`

To see a list of the people who are banned from your channel, type
`/mode channel +b`

When you ban someone, she can come back using another nickname. To attempt to ban someone no matter what nickname she is using, you can type her e-mail address rather than her nickname in the `/mode +b` command. To find out a person's e-mail address (or at least the address from which the person is connected to the IRC server), use the `/whois` command, described in Chapter 8.

Reserving Nicknames and Channel Names

Some IRC networks use systems that let people reserve nicknames and channel names (see "Choosing an IRC Network," earlier in this chapter, to see which IRC networks provide these services). This section describes how to use NickServ, a widely used nickname-reservation system, and ChanServ, a popular channel-registration system, along with AnotherNet's ASIRC system.

When you issue commands to NickServ, ChanServ, and other registration systems from a windowing program like mIRC, look in the Status window for the results of your commands—they don't appear in channel windows.

Reserving Your Nickname with NickServ

If you use an IRC network that has NickServ running, you can send commands to NickServ to reserve your nickname so that no one else can use it when you aren't connected to the IRC server. Some NickServ installations respond to the `/nickserv` commands listed in this section, and others require you to type `/msg nickserv` to control NickServ. If the commands listed in this section don't work for you, try adding *msg* as the first word of the command, before *nickserv*.

Registering and Using Your Nickname

First, check whether someone else has already registered the nickname you want to use by typing this command:
`/nickserv info nickname`

Connect using the nickname you want to register, and type this command to send to NickServ a message reserving your nickname:

`/nickserv register `*`password`*

Replace *password* with a password (which is case sensitive) by which you will identify yourself each time you connect to the IRC network and want to use your reserved nickname. NickServ registers the nickname you are now using. If the nickname is already in use or registered, NickServ doesn't let you reserve it.

After you have registered a nickname, you must identify yourself whenever you want to use it. You type this command, using the same password (and the same capitalization) that you typed when you registered the nickname:

`/nickserv identify `*`password`*

You can change your password later. First, identify yourself to NickServ so that you are using your nickname. Then type this command:

`/nickserv set passwd `*`newpassword`*

Replace *newpassword* with the new password. (NickServ changes the password for the nickname you are now using.)

Protecting Your Nickname from Use

If you don't want anyone else to be able to use your registered nickname, type this command:

`/nickserv set kill on`

When someone connects to the IRC network using your nickname, NickServ asks for the password. If the person doesn't supply it, NickServ changes the nickname. You can turn off this protection by typing this command, although it's not recommended:

`/nickserv set kill off`

If you didn't use the `kill on` option and someone else is using your nickname, you can ask NickServ to tell the person to switch to a different nickname. Type this command:

`/nickserv recover `*`nickname password`*

NickServ asks the other person to type your password (which presumably she doesn't know) and changes her nickname so that you can use yours.

Unregistering a Nickname

NickServ unregisters your name after a specified time if you haven't used the nickname—usually 25 days. After identifying yourself to NickServ as the owner of the nickname (using the `/nickserv identify` command), you can delete the registration of your nickname by typing

`/nickserv drop `*`nickname`*

Other NickServ Information

Occasionally, when you disconnect from the IRC server (especially if the disconnection is the result of a netsplit or other communications problem), the server doesn't log out your nickname. This situation prevents you from reconnecting with your nickname because the IRC server thinks that the nickname is already in use. To end the "ghost" session and free up your nickname, type this command:

`/nickserv ghost `*`nickname password`*

For more information about NickServ, read **DALnet's NickServ page**, at http://www.dal.net/services/nickserv/.

Reserving a Channel Name with ChanServ

IRC servers that run the ChanServ program enable you to reserve a channel name so that only you can create and operate the channel. You must have a registered nickname to register a channel. Some ChanServ installations respond to the `/chanserv` commands listed in this section, and others require you to type `/msg chanserv` to control ChanServ. If the commands listed in this section don't work for you, try adding *msg* as the first word of the command, before *chanserv*.

Registering a Channel Name

To find out whether someone else is using the channel name, type this command:

`/chanserv info `*`channel`*

After connecting to the IRC server using a registered nickname, create the channel (or join the existing channel)—you must be an operator in the channel when you register it. Then send this command:

`/chanserv register `*`channel password description`*

Replace *channel* with the channel name you want to register (including the preceding #), *password* with the password you will use to identify yourself when giving commands about this channel, and *description* with a one-line description of the channel. ChanServ replies with a confirmation message. If the channel name is already registered to someone else, ChanServ rejects your registration.

If you don't want to run the channel any more, you can drop ChanServ's registration of the channel by typing this command:

`/chanserv drop `*`channel`*

Many commands require that you identify yourself to the ChanServ programs so that it knows that you have authorization to give the commands. To identify yourself to ChanServ, type this command:

`/chanserv identify` *`channel password`*

Replace *password* with the password you specified when you created the channel.

Creating SuperOps and AutoOps

After you have registered a channel name, people may try to join this channel at any time, day or night. As founder of the channel, you can't be around as channel operator all the time! Instead, you can designate other people to manage the channel when you can't be there. You can create two types of operators:

AutoOps (or AutoOperators) are automatically set to be channel operators (chanops) when they join the channel.

SuperOps (or SuperOperators) are automatically set to be chanops when they join the channel and can create AutoOps.

SuperOps and AutoOps must have registered nicknames. (Otherwise, you can type their e-mail addresses rather than their nicknames when you type the following commands, although it's not recommended.)

To make someone a SuperOp or AutoOp, type one of these commands:

`/chanserv aop` *`channel`* `add` *`nickname`*
`/chanserv sop` *`channel`* `add` *`nickname`*

To remove someone from the list of SuperOps or AutoOps, type one of these commands:

`/chanserv aop` *`channel`* `del` *`nickname`*
`/chanserv sop` *`channel`* `del` *`nickname`*

To see a list of the SuperOps or AutoOps for your channel, type one of these commands:

`/chanserv aop` *`channel`* `list`
`/chanserv sop` *`channel`* `list`

You see a listing like this:

```
-ChanServ- AutoOp search results for channel #PoorRichard
-ChanServ- 4 Peter  (peter@iecc.com)
-ChanServ- 3 Missy  (md@gurus.com)
-ChanServ- 2 Becky  (test@gurus.com)
-ChanServ- 1 JohnL  (info@abuse.net)
-ChanServ- [4 match(es) found]
```

You may want to make sure that no one other than the SuperOps and AutoOps whom you have designated can be operators on the channel (that is, you may want to prevent your SuperOps and AutoOps from granting other people operator status). You can turn on the Opguard facility with this command:

```
/chanserv set channel opguard on
```

To turn Opguard off, type this command:

```
/chanserv set channel opguard off
```

Setting the Topic, Description, and URL

After you have registered your channel, configure it using the `/chanserv set` commands. You can control who can set the topic of the channel by using the TopicLock feature. To allow only the founder (you) to change the topic, type this command:

```
/chanserv set channel topiclock founder
```

To allow SuperOps to change the topic, type

```
/chanserv set channel topiclock sop
```

To allow anyone to change the topic, type

```
/chanserv set channel topiclock off
```

To change the one-line description of the channel that ChanServ displays, type this command:

```
/chanserv set channel desc description
```

ChanServ can display the URL of your channel's Web page whenever people join the channel. Type this command:

```
/chanserv set channel url yoururl
```

Replace *yoururl* with the complete URL (starting with http://) of your channel.

Locking the Channel's Modes

Each channel has various modes that control how it works (see the section "Creating and Configuring Your Channel," earlier in this chapter, for many of the `/mode` commands that channel operators can use). You can tell ChanServ not to let anyone change the channel's modes by typing this command:

```
/chanserv set channel mlock modelocks
```

Replace *modelocks* with a plus sign (+) followed by the modes to be locked on, and then a minus sign (-) followed by the modes to be locked off. For example, this command locks the `n` (accept outside messages) and `t` (only chanops can set the topic) modes on, and the `i` (invitation-only), `s` (secret), and `p` (private) modes off:

```
/chanserv set #poorrichard mlock +nt-isp
```

Setting ChanServ Privacy

To tell ChanServ to make your channel private so that it doesn't appear on ChanServ's channel lists, type this command:

`/chanserv set `*`channel`*` private on`

You can turn ChanServ privacy off by typing

`/chanserv set `*`channel`*` private off`

Other ChanServ Information

You can change the password for the channel by typing this command:

`/chanserv set `*`channel`*` passwd `*`password`*

Replace *password* with the new password you want to use.

ChanServ has many other commands you can use to control how your channel works. For more information, read **DALnet's ChanServ page**, at http://www.dal.net/services/chanserv/.

Reserving Nicknames and Channel Names on AnotherNet

AnotherNet's ASIRC server handles the reserving of nicknames. To use AnotherNet, you sign up for a free membership using the **AnotherNet Chat Standard Membership Sign-up**, at http://www.another.net/chat/signup.shtml. As part of the registration, you choose a username. After your registration is processed and you are connected to an AnotherNet IRC server, you can type this command to reserve a nickname:

`/nreg `*`nickname`*

Each AnotherNet user can register as many as three nicknames.

AnotherNet uses this command to reserve a channel name:

`/creg `*`channelname`*

Administrative Commands

Several commands can tell you about the IRC network and server you are using. To see a link of the servers in the network, type

`/links`

To see the name of the server and of the IRC administrator who runs it, type

`/admin`

If your IRC server seems slow, you can switch to another server on the same IRC network by typing this command:

`/server `*`servername portnumber`*

Replace *servername* with the name of another server on the network (use the /links command to see the names of other servers). Replace *portnumber* with the port number to use when connecting to that server, or leave it out to connect on the default port, 6667.

Each IRC server has a message of the day (MOTD), which may include useful information about how to contact the IRC administrator or about schedule maintenance that could slow communication. If you miss the MOTD when it scrolls by in your Status window when you first connect, you can display it again by typing this command:

/motd

To get an idea of how busy your IRC server is, you can use the /lusers command to see a listing of the number of users who are connected, the number of servers on the network, the number of IRC operators who are online, the number of channels, and other information. The user count includes the total number of people connected along with the number who are "invisible" (blocked from view by other IRC users).

Rules for IRC Channels

Most IRC channels have at least a few rules, to keep troublemakers from making conversation impossible. Here are some rules to consider for your channel:

No flooding. Most IRC channels have a limit on how many messages you can post how quickly. For example, some channels limit messages to no more than five in any five-second period—more than that number is considered flooding.

No repetition. Many channels prohibit users from posting the same message more than once, at least within a minute or so.

No warez. *Warez* are illegally distributed programs, usually copies of commercial programs. Because distributing copyrighted material without the permission of the copyright holder is illegal in most countries, most IRC networks prohibit doing so.

No child pornography. The distribution of sexually explicit material that involves children is illegal in many countries and is prohibited on most IRC networks.

No illegal activities. To protect the administrators of the network, most IRC networks prohibit illegal activities, like planning crimes.

No swearing. On family-oriented channels, you can institute acceptable-language rules.

You may want to add rules which are specific to the community that is gathering on the channel—for example, rules about sticking to the topic or about attacking people.

Getting More Information

Table 9-1 lists the most useful commands for channel operators.

Here are some Web sites with information about running IRC channels:

DALnet's ChanServ page
http://www.dal.net/services/chanserv/

DALnet's NickServ page
http://www.dal.net/services/nickserv/

IRC Operators Guide (for the people who run IRC servers)
http://www.irchelp.org/irchelp/ircd/ircopguide.html

Command	Description
/admin	Display IRC server information
/chanserv aop channel add nickname	Add nickname as AutoOp for registered channel
/chanserv aop channel del nickname	Delete nickname as AutoOp for registered channel
/chanserv aop channel list	List AutoOps for registered channel
/chanserv drop channel	Cancel registration of a registered channel
/chanserv help	Get information about ChanServ, if it is running
/chanserv identify channel password	Identify yourself to ChanServ as an operator of a registered channel
/chanserv info channel	Get information about a registered channel
/chanserv register channel password desc	Register channel with one-line description
/chanserv set channel desc description	Set description for a registered channel
/chanserv set channel mlock modelocks	Lock channel mode
/chanserv set channel opguard off	Turn off Opguard
/chanserv set channel opguard on	Run Opguard to control who can be a channel operator
/chanserv set channel passwd password	Set password for registered channel
/chanserv set channel private off	Remove ChanServ privacy
/chanserv set channel private on	Make registered channel private on ChanServ
/chanserv set channel topiclock founder	Allow only the channel founder to change the topic
/chanserv set channel topiclock off	Allow anyone to change the topic
/chanserv set channel topiclock sop	Allow only SuperOps to change the topic
/chanserv set channel url yoururl	Set URL for registered channel
/chanserv sop channel add nickname	Add nickname as SuperOp for registered channel
/chanserv sop channel del nickname	Delete nickname as SuperOp for registered channel
/chanserv sop channel list	List SuperOps for registered channel
/creg nickname	Register channel (AnotherNet only)
/invite nickname channel	Invite nickname to join channel

Command	Description
/join channel	Create channel, if channel doesn't exist
/kick channel nickname	Kick nickname off the channel
/link	Display list of connected IRC servers
/mode channel +b nickname	Ban nickname from joining the channel
/mode channel -b nickname	Remove the ban on nickname
/mode channel +i	Allow people to join by invitation only
/mode channel -i	Allow people to join without an invitation
/mode channel +l number	Limit channel to number participants
/mode channel -l	Allow unlimited participants
/mode channel +m	Make channel moderated (only chanops can send messages)
/mode channel -m	Remove moderation (allow any participant to send messages)
/mode channel +n	Prevent outside messages to the channel
/mode channel +o nickname	Make nickname a chanop on channel
/mode channel -o nickname	Remove chanop status from nickname on channel
/mode channel -n	Allow outside messages to the channel
/mode channel +p	Make channel private
/mode channel -p	Remove private mode from channel
/mode channel +s	Make channel secret
/mode channel 0-s	Remove secret mode from channel
/mode channel -t	Allow any channel participant to set the topic
/mode channel +v nickname	Let nickname send messages in a moderated channel
/mode channel -v nickname	Prevent nickname from sending messages in a moderated channel
/motd	Display the IRC server's message of the day
/nickserv drop nickname	Delete your registration of nickname
/nickserv ghost nickname password	Terminate ghost session using your registered nickname
/nickserv help	Get information about NickServ, if it is running
/nickserv identify password	Identify yourself to NickServ with your current nickname
/nickserv info nickname	Get information about who has reserved nickname
/nickserv recover nickname password	Kick off someone who is using your registered nickname
/nickserv register password	Register your current nickname with password
/nickserv set kill off	Let others use your registered nickname
/nickserv set kill on	Prevent anyone else from using your registered nickname
/nreg nickname	Register nickname (AnotherNet only)
/server servername portnumber	Switch connection to another IRC server
/topic channel topic	Set the topic for the channel
/who channel	Display listing of channel participants
/join channel	Create channel, if channel doesn't exist
/kick channel nickname	Kick nickname off the channel

Command	Description
/link	Display list of connected IRC servers
/mode channel +b nickname	Ban nickname from joining the channel
/mode channel -b nickname	Remove the ban on nickname
/mode channel +i	Allow people to join by invitation only
/mode channel -i	Allow people to join without an invitation
/mode channel +l number	Limit channel to number participants
/mode channel -l	Allow unlimited participants
/mode channel +m	Make channel moderated (only chanops can send messages)
/mode channel -m	Remove moderation (allow any participant to sendmessages)
/mode channel +n	Prevent outside messages to the channel
/mode channel +o nickname	Make nickname a chanop on channel
/mode channel -o nickname	Removes chanop status from nickname on channel
/mode channel -n	Allow outside messages to the channel
/mode channel +p	Make channel private
/mode channel -p	Remove private mode from channel
/mode channel +s	Make channel secret
/mode channel 0-s	Remove secret mode from channel
/mode channel +t	Allow only chanops to set the topic

Part V

Web-Based Communities

Chapter Ten
Finding, Joining, and Participating in Web-based Communities

The Web is not particularly well suited for creating community. With mailing lists and newsgroups, people subscribe to the communities in which they want to participate, and new messages appear in people's e-mail and newsreader programs. With Web-based communities, people have to remember to come back to the Web site to read new messages, and casual visitors are more common—it's harder to build up a sense of closeness and trust in a Web-based community. Also, unlike most mailing lists and Usenet newsgroups, Web-based communities are almost always paid for by advertising, so they frequently lack a sense of grass-roots organization. It's always obvious (from the ubiquitous ads) that someone is making money off the community.

On the other hand, Web-based communities are easy for people to find because they are included in the big Web search engines and directories, like Yahoo and AltaVista. Finding mailing lists and newsgroups is harder since the directories that list them aren't as well maintained, and the information isn't as well organized. Some Web sites keep track of which communities you have joined and alert you when new messages appear.

To encourage community members to return and participate, community Web sites offer all kinds of services, including e-mail accounts and customized start pages for your Web browser. If you don't mind reminding yourself to return to a Web site to participate in a community (instead of getting reminded by messages arriving in your mailbox or newsreader), try Web-based communities! This chapter describes how to find and participate in them, and the next chapter explains how to start your own.

How Web-based Communities Work

Two mechanisms allow community members to communicate on Web pages: message boards and real-time chats. Clubs combine the two, as well as offer other community services. Unfortunately, Web sites use the terms "chat," "message boards," "conferences," "clubs," and "forums" almost interchangeably. But they aren't all the same!

Message Boards

Most Web-based communities occur on *message boards,* programs that allow people to post messages on a Web page. A message board (also called *bulletin board, discussion board, board,* or *forum*) is run by a program connected to the Web page. Figure 10-1 shows a message board on the Yahoo Clubs site.

A message board appears as a Web page with a list of messages that have been posted on the board. To read a message, you click its subject line on the list. Previous and Next buttons let you move from message to message. Some message boards list messages chronologically, some list them by *thread* (topic), and some give you a choice.

If you have something to say, you click a link (usually labeled Post) that displays a form to fill out. You type a message into a box on the Web page and click a Post or Submit button. The message board program processes the message you typed, adds it to the message board's list of messages, and displays

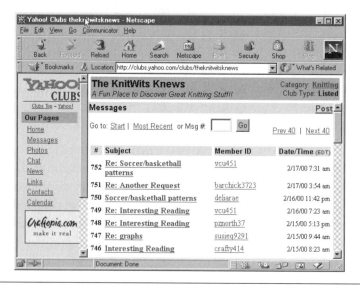

Figure 10-1: Yahoo clubs include message boards, real-time chat, photo pages, and a calendar of events.

the message on the Web page. Message-board messages remain on the Web page for days, weeks, months, or years (depending on the Web site) for other people to see.

Community Web sites that offer lots of message boards usually organize them by topic (sometimes called a *folder*), and some allow you to start a message board on a new topic. Message boards are great for asking questions because lots of other people will see your question and can post responses. We find that postings on message boards usually stay on topic, perhaps because most message board programs provide a way for the message board manager to delete off-topic messages.

Some message boards let you search past postings by topic. Some boards also let you choose between seeing the messages in chronological order and grouped by thread (topic).

Real-time Chats

Some Web-based discussions (we call them *real-time chats*) happen in *real-time*—that is, when you type a message and press Enter, the message appears within a few seconds on the screens of the other participants. If you're not connected when the chat occurs, you don't get the messages.

Many Web-based chats work by downloading a Java program to your computer and running it in conjunction with your Web browser to display chat messages. A new browser window may appear, or the chat messages may appear in your regular browser window. Figure 10-2 shows a typical chat session, with messages scrolling down a window within the browser window. There is usually a list of the names (or *handles*) of the people in the chat room, and some sites let you send and receive private messages with others in the chat room or see additional information about them.

To participate, click in a one-line box (usually at the bottom of the window), type a message, and press Enter or click the Send button. Your message appears in the list of chat messages within a few seconds.

Real-time chat discussions are usually confusing and stray off-topic since participants are typing as fast as they can to respond to other people's messages. We find that even if a chat has a topical name—FoodTalk or Movie Reviews, for example—the discussion rarely has much to do with that topic. Most of it is idle chatter at best!

Sometimes a celebrity or expert (even a computer book author, on occasion) is invited to attend a chat, and the other chat participants can ask questions. Because these chats are more likely to contain information rather than random banter, transcripts are sometimes kept so that folks who couldn't make the chats can read them later. Other real-time chats are run by a computer program, usually one that acts as the master of ceremonies for a game. For example, several chats are for people who like anagrams: The program that runs the chat room poses word-scramble problems that the human participants compete to solve.

Clubs

A *club* is a Web-based community that includes a message board, real-time chat, and other services. A few club sites (including eGroups, which is described in Chapter 5) offer mailing lists as well (that is, the site can e-mail you copies of messages posted on the message board). A Web-based club may also offer the following services:

Home page, with an introduction, frequently asked questions, and other information of interest to club members.

Web pages for each member, where members can post information about themselves.

Links page, with links to Web pages that have been suggested by members.

Photo page, where members can post graphics files (usually photos) of club-related items. For example, members of a knitting club might post pictures of their completed knitting projects.

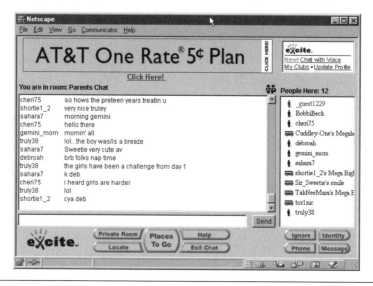

Figure 10-2: Real-time chat lets you exchange messages right away, but the discussions are rarely focused on a topic.

Schedule of events, including upcoming, live online chats and events in the real world.

Clubs can be public (or *listed*) so that anyone may join, or private (*unlisted*) so that participants are limited to people whom the founder or owner of the club invites.

A few Web-based club sites also provide e-mail mailboxes for each member so that you can send and receive e-mail from the Web site. This doesn't have much to do with the club, but it encourages you to return often to the Web site. Most major Web portal sites (Yahoo, AltaVista, Excite, and Lycos, for example) host clubs, along with message boards and real-time chat, as a way to get people to use their sites.

A few sites offer specialized clubs for families, alumni groups, and other groups that want to meet online.

Web Sites That Display Mailing Lists and Newsgroups

Some Web sites that *look* like they run lots of interesting Web message boards actually display mailing lists or newsgroups run by other people. For example, the **RemarQ** site, at http://www.remarq.com, offers thousands of discussions that appear to be run by RemarQ itself. In reality, RemarQ displays a combination of Usenet newsgroups, mailing lists that it hosts, and mailing lists run by other people, often without the consent (or even the knowledge) of the people who run the mailing lists. Many mailing list managers resent that RemarQ earns advertising revenue from displaying messages from communities it does nothing to help run. Similarly, **Deja.com** (at http://www.deja.com) displays Usenet newsgroups on its Web site, although it doesn't try to conceal the source of these communities. **HotBot**, now owned by Lycos, presents Usenet newsgroups when you click the Discussion Groups link or start at http://hotbot.lycos.com/usenet/.

If you like a Web interface to Usenet, Deja.com and HotBot are reasonable ways to read and post Usenet messages, although for other than the most casual reading, we find that we greatly prefer specialized news programs like Agent (for Windows) and trn (for UNIX and Linux) to sift through the often vast numbers of messages (see Chapter 6).

Voice Chat

Several Web sites let people talk over the Internet, assuming that their computers have microphones and speakers:

HearMe
http://www.hearme.com/lobbies/

Roger Wilco
  http://www.resounding.com/

However, because large groups of people (more than about three) have trouble using voice communication (try a conference call by phone!), these systems are better suited to private conversations among community members than by the community at large.

Graphics and 3D Chat

Many community Web sites use graphics to give participants a visual world in which to move around and interact with other people. The best-known of these is **The Palace Visual Chat**, at http://www.thepalace.com/. Tutorials for using The Palace have been written (try http://www.itsnet.com/home/lminer/palace/), Web sites distribute props and music you can use as part of your Palace character (http://www.dnaco.net/~beavis/Kaitlyn.html), and you can even visit a Palacaholics page (http://www.lag.com/palacaholic/).

To participate in a Palace Web site, you have to download and install the Palace software, available for free from The Palace Web site, at http://www.thepalace.com/. Then you can choose a community from the Palace Web site or start at **Cybertown Palace** (http://www.cybertown.com/palace.html).

Another system of 3D chats requires Blaxxun Contact, a browser plug-in you can download from the **Blaxxun** home page, at http://www.blaxxun.com/. The Blaxxun site also provides links to worlds that use Blaxxun, like **Cybertown**, at http://www.cybertown.com.

Where Web-based Community Sites Live

Several types of Web sites include message boards, clubs, and real-time chats:

- **Public community sites** contain many clubs, message boards, and real-time chat on a variety of topics. For example, **Yahoo Clubs** (at http://clubs.yahoo.com/) hosts discussions on thousands of subjects, including both public (listed) and private (unlisted) clubs. These sites usually offer lots of the other services listed in the preceding section.

- **Private community sites** host private clubs for existing groups—families, committees, and other groups—that need a Web-based place to meet.

- **Topic-oriented sites** host a few message boards or real-time chats. For example, the **Unitarian Universalist Association** (at http://www.uua.org/) has a large site with pages of interest to Unitarians and Unitarian ministers, including one page with a message board for newcomers.

Public Community Sites

Here are some of the biggest and most popular community Web sites—sites that offer public Web-based community in the form of clubs, message boards, real-time chat, and other services. Many also offer private (unlisted) clubs.

About.com   http://www.about.com/

About.com (formerly The Mining Company) not only hosts clubs with message boards and real-time chats but also pays experts to run each topic-related club. Each About.com club is considered a separate site, with the URL http://*clubname*.about.com. Each site has a guide who runs the site, selecting information to appear on its home page, answering questions, and suggesting topics for message boards, chats, and polls. Each site also includes an event calendar, pages of links, an e-mail newsletter, articles collected by the guide, and topic-related shopping links. When you join About.com, you get a start page at http://members.about.com/*username* (replace *username* with the username you choose when you register), listing links to the About.com sites you've joined.

AltaVista Communities
http://live.altavista.com/socialize/

AltaVista is a Web portal, search engine, Web mail service, free ISP, and more. You might think that clicking Message Boards on the AltaVista home page (at http://www.altavista.com) would take you to a general message board site, but you'd be wrong—you jump to Raging Bull (at http://www.ragingbull.com/community/), a financial message board site. Instead, click the Chat or Live! link and then the Community link, or start at the URL just listed.

Like Yahoo Clubs, AltaVista provides clubs, with a full range of community services. Unfortunately, the clubs are mixed in with the

---

Knitting.about.com

An example of a successful Web-based club is the knitting club at About.com (at http://knitting.about.com). The message board is full of questions from new folks and answers from more experienced knitters. The file-sharing pages include information about knitting books, classes, teachers, and a large collection of knitting patterns contributed by club members. The guide for knitting.about.com, Barbara Breiter, sends out an e-mail newsletter once or twice a week to announce new patterns and other files that have been posted to the site and serves as a reminder for members to check the site's message board. Chapter 18 describes how Knitting.about.com works.

home pages of AltaVista members—clubs are distinguished by a little blue icon showing people (home pages, usually of companies trying to sell something, have a green house icon).

Delphi Forums http://www.delphi.com/

Delphi, one of the first Internet service providers (ISPs), has hosted online communities since before the Web existed. Now, Delphi offers Web-based *forums,* which include message boards and real-time chat (using text, a comic-book format, or—if your computer has microphone and speakers—voice), as shown in Figure 10-3. Once you've registered as a member, you can create forums, too. (Delphi Forums recently merged with another company to form a new company, Prospero Technologies.)

eGroups http://www.egroups.com/

eGroups (also known as ONElist) hosts mailing lists that are described in Chapter 4. An eGroup *group* is like a club and includes message boards, real-time chat, voice chat, an event calendar, and a links page. If you want your group membership to work like a mailing list, tell eGroups to mail you new messages as they are posted on the group's message board.

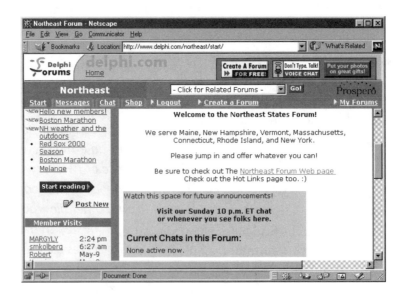

Figure 10-3: Delphi was one of the first Internet community sites.

Excite Chat http://www.excite.com/communities/chat/

For real-time chat, click the links in the Chats section of the Excite home page or start at http://www.excite.com/communities/chat/. The Excite Avatar Chat formats the chat messages to look like a Pokémon-style comic book.

Excite Communities http://www.excite.com/communities/directory/

Excite, another Web portal, Web directory, and search engine, supports message boards, clubs, and real-time chats. Excite Clubs include message boards, real-time chat, photo pages, calendars, and links pages. Click Clubs from the Excite home page or start at http://www.excite.com/communities/directory/, which displays a directory of the topics of existing public clubs. Join Excite (which also gives you an Excite mailbox and personalized Excite start page) to participate in clubs. You can also start your own public or private club.

Excite People & Chat Message Boards http://boards.excite.com/boards/

Click Message Boards from the Excite home page, at http://www.excite.com, to see the message boards, or start at http://boards.excite.com/boards/. The message boards don't work as well as the clubs at building community—most are people selling something or topics with one message waiting for a response.

FriendFactory http://www.friendfactory.com/ or http://www.friendfactory.co.uk/

FriendFactory is owned by Sony UK, so it's got a British flavor. It hosts communities that include discussions (message boards) and chats. It also has a German-language site, at http://www.friendfactory.de. When you register, you have to download the ConnectionCenter program in order to participate.

GO Network Communicate http://www.go.com/Community/

Start at this URL, or click the Community tab on the GO.com home page (at http://www.go.com). GO Network includes the former Infoseek site and hosts message boards and real-time chat by topic.

Lycos Chat http:// chat.lycos.com/

Lycos Chat provides real-time chats, including scheduled chats with celebrities, on hundreds of topics. Even if you registered with Lycos Clubs, you have to register again with Lycos Chat. You can use *HTML chat* (that is, your browser displays chat messages with no help from another program) or *Java chat* (a Java program, or applet, runs to help your browser display chat messages more quickly and attractively).

Lycos Clubs http://clubs.lycos.com/

The Lycos Network is another major Web portal. Lycos Clubs includes message boards, photo pages, links pages, calendars, and real-time chat. (To start, click Clubs from the Lycos home page at http://www.lycos.com or start at the listed URL.) Lycos Clubs also provides Web pages where club members can share files, respond to polls, and see the results of polls. You can download a Java program called NetClubs Neighborhoods to allow real-time and private chats with club members.

Lycos Message Boards http://boards.lycos.com/

From the Lycos home page, click Message Boards or start at this URL. Strangely, last time we checked, posting to the message boards requires a separate registration, even if you've already registered at Lycos Clubs.

The Mote http://www.themote.com/

The Mote hosts a small number of interesting message boards.

MSN Web Communities http://communities.msn.com/home

MSN hosts communities, which may include message boards and real-time chats, on many subjects. Some communities are run by MSN itself, and others are managed by Internet users.

Network54 http://network54.com/

Network54 includes *forums* (message boards), real-time chat, and closed *groups* (private message boards and chats).

Snap Clubs http://clubdirectory.snap.com/

Snap is General Electric's competitor to Yahoo. Snap clubs include the usual message boards, real-time chat, and photo pages.

Talk City http://www.talkcity.com/

Talk City, as shown in Figure 10-4, offers a full range of club-like communities for a wide variety of topics. Click the Discussion Boards link for message boards. You can bookmark discussions you want to monitor so that Talk City can let you know when new messages appear. Talk City chats are also accessible via Internet Relay Chat; for details, see the Chapter 8 sidebar "Talk City Combines IRC and the Web."

Chapter 10: Finding, Joining, and Participating in Web-based Communities   221

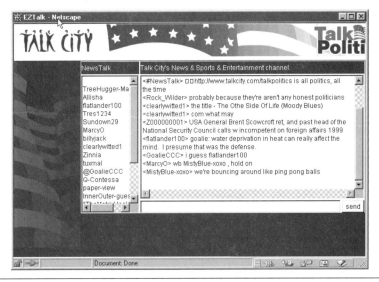

Figure 10-4: Talk City downloads its EZ Talk program into your browser to display real-time chat messages.

Theglobe.com   http://www.theglobe.com/

Theglobe.com hosts clubs that include message boards and shared files. You can also have the messages e-mailed to you (as a mailing list; see Chapter 4).

USA TODAY The Nation Talks   http://usatoday.com/community/mb/index.htm

The *USA TODAY* Web site hosts message boards on news, current events, and many other topics.

The WELL   http://www.thewell.com/

The WELL (originally the Whole Earth 'Lectronic Link) was one of the first places where online community developed, way before the Web. It hosts more than 260 conferences (message boards).

Yahoo Clubs   http://clubs.yahoo.com/

Yahoo is a major Web portal, Web directory, and search site. Yahoo Clubs (at the listed URL or click the Clubs link from the Yahoo home page, at http://www.yahoo.com) hosts hundreds of clubs on specific topics, arranged in a directory that uses the same structure as the Yahoo Web directory. You have to join Yahoo to participate in clubs, but if you've ever registered for any Yahoo service (like Yahoo Mail), you are already registered. Each club includes every possible community service and is very easy to use. Figure 10-1 shows the list of messages in the KnitWits News knitting club.

Private Community Sites

Some community sites are designed for existing groups to meet rather than as places for new communities to form. These sites customize their clubs for use by families, committees, or other types of groups.

eCircles.com http://www.ecircles.com/

eCircles helps you meet with your family, friends, teammates, or schoolmates online and is also designed to help you organize big events or trips that include lots of people. *Circles* (clubs) include message boards, photo pages, calendars, file sharing, text chat, and voice chat.

JointPlanning.com http://www.jointplanning.com/

Groups of all types can use JointPlanning.com to share Web-based calendars, to-do lists, address books, voting, message boards, and other files.

MyFamily.com http://www.myfamily.com/

MyFamily.com is designed specifically for communicating with friends and family (see Figure 10-5). When you set up a site for your family, members can share a calendar, family news pages, photo album pages, real-time chat, family tree pages, recipes, stories, book reviews, and other information.

Topic-Oriented Sites

Here are some sites that include interesting message boards (many also host real-time chats):

AAII (American Association of Individual Investors)
http://www.aaii.com/msgboard/

AnswerPoint (ask a question, provide an answer)
http://answerpoint.ask.com/

BootsnAll.com (travel)
http://www.bootsnall.com

CBS MarketWatch Wealth Club (investing)
http://messages.marketwatch.com/

CBS Sportsline (sports)
http://cbs.sportsline.com/u/community/

Chapter 10: Finding, Joining, and Participating in Web-based Communities **223**

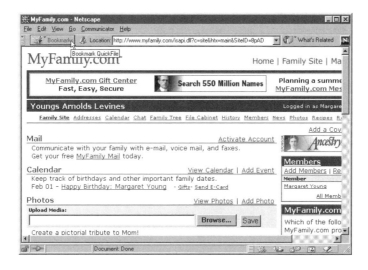

Figure 10-5: MyFamily.com hosts private sites for extended families.

CNN/Sports Illustrated: Your Turn (sports)
http://boards.cnnsi.com/

E! Online (entertainment)
http://www.eonline.com/Community/

EdGateway: Communities, Resources, and Discussions for Educators
http://edgateway.net/

ESPN.com Community
http://community.espn.go.com/

Family Education Network (education and parenting)
http://familyeducation.com/

Gamespot Forums (games)
http://www.gamespot.com/forums/

IMDB (The Internet Movie Database) Message Boards
http://us.imdb.com/Boards/

iVillage: The Women's Network
http://www.ivillage.com/

The Motley Fool (investing)
http://www.fool.com/

MSN MoneyCentral Community (investing)
http://moneycentral.msn.com/community/

ParentsPlace.com (pregnancy and parenting)
http://parentsplace.com/

SeniorNet RoundTables (senior citizens)
   http://www.seniornet.org/ (click Discussions)
Senior-site.com (senior citizens)
   http://seniors-site.com/
SheClicks.com ("A woman's way to work the Web")
   http://www.sheclicks.com/
Slashdot ("News for Nerds"–each article has a message board for comments)
   http://www.slashdot.org
The Student Center Teen Forums (teens)
   http://www.teenforums.com/
   http://studentcenter.org/
TIME.com Boards & Chat (news and views)
   http://www.time.com/time/community/
UltimateTV.com (television)
   http://www.ultimatetv.com/interact/
VirtualTourist.com (travel)
   http://www.virtualtourist.com/
ZDNet Community (computers and the Internet)
   http://www.zdnet.com/filters/community/

Finding Web-based Communities

The most interesting communities (of all types) are those on specific topics because their members have something to say other than "Hi!" and "Where are you from?" Here are three strategies for finding Web-based communities on a topic you want to discuss.

Try the Forum One Directory

Alternatively, you can try **Forum One**, at http://www.forumone.com/, a searchable index of over 300,000 Web message boards and Web-based chats. Forum One, as shown in Figure 10-6, doesn't include every Web-based community by any means, although it has lots and includes recommendations by category.

When you search on a word or phrase, Forum One displays a listing of message boards, clubs, and Web-based chats that include that word or phrase in the title or in individual messages. You can click the link to go to that message board, club, or chat, although if the site requires registration, you have to complete the registration before you can proceed. When you click a link from Forum One to the Web site, the link doesn't always lead directly to the chat page; instead, you may arrive at another location on the Web site, so you'll have to look around.

Chapter 10: Finding, Joining, and Participating in Web-based Communities   225

Figure 10-6: Forum One enables you to search for Web-based message boards by topic.

Forum One includes communities from Yahoo Clubs, Delphi Forums, and many other sites, but it doesn't have up-to-date listings for all the major community sites (searches for topics on which we knew there were eGroups, Excite Clubs, or other communities didn't always turn them up).

Search Each of the Major Community Sites
The communities in the major Web-based community sites aren't all included in the Forum One directory. If Forum One doesn't turn up a community on your topic, go to the Web sites listed in the "Public Community Sites" section, earlier in this chapter. Search each site for your topic, or use the site's directory links to find it.

Find the Web Site That Might Host a Community
If the first two methods don't provide results, search for a Web site on the topic. Then see whether the site has a community section, message board, or real-time chat page. Many Web sites include one or two message boards for discussing the content of that Web site, as a guest book or for asking questions that pertain to the Web site.

Chapter Eleven
Creating and Managing Your Own Web-based Community

If you run a Web site and you want to let visitors communicate with each other and with you, create a Web-based community. You can use message boards, real-time chat rooms, or both in your community. (Message boards and real-time chat rooms are described in Chapter 8.) Before you can set up your community, you have to decide what message board or chat software you will use, how your Web site will be designed, and what community policies you will put in place. This chapter describes how to design and create your own Web-based community.

Designing Your Web-based Community

Your Web site can include many components to support one or more communities. It may include many Web pages with one or more types of message boards and real-time chat pages.

Organizing Your Community Web Site

Your Web-based community probably won't fit on one Web page: Instead, think about how you want the information to be organized as a suite of Web pages. The community section of your Web site might have these pages:

Community home page, with news, upcoming events, one feature article, and links to the other pages

Message board page(s), where members can read and post messages

Real-time chat page(s), where members can sign on for a chat

Member profile page, where members can read each other's profiles and post or update their own profiles so that community members can learn more about each other (this page might also let members upload pictures of themselves or of their community-related work)

News and articles page about the topic of the community, with links to archives of past articles

Links page, with links to other Web sites that relate to the topic of your community

Calendar page, listing community events, including real-time chat events, events on the Internet, and events in the offline world

Files page, with links to files that have been uploaded by community members (graphics files or other files to be shared among members)

Help page, with instructions

Rules or terms-of-use page, with the rules for who may read messages, who may post messages, what may and may not be posted, and what the consequences will be (see Chapter 13)

Privacy policy page (see the section "Preserving Privacy and Creating a Privacy Policy," in Chapter 15)

History page, with the story of how the community came into existence and information about who's behind it, to give prospective members insight into your point of view

Shopping page, with a way to order community-related merchandise (which might include anything from T-shirts with the community logo to books that have been discussed on the message board)

Your community doesn't need to have all these pages right from the start, and you can redesign the community Web site as you go along, in response to suggestions from community members.

The community you are creating might also divide into several communities or be one community with several subgroups. For example, if you are creating a community of parents, you might want to have separate areas—with separate message boards, real-time chat, news, and links—for the parents of children of different ages or special needs. You might want to start your community with one message board and plan to branch out as the community grows.

Types of Message Boards

Most message boards work basically the same way: You see a list of messages posted to the message board, you can view a message by clicking its link, and

Chapter 11: Creating and Managing Your Own Web-based Community

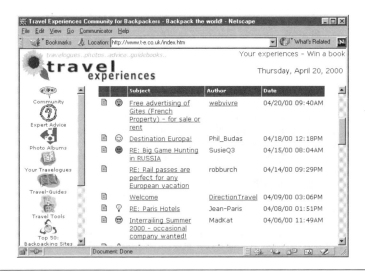

Figure 11-1: The **Travel Experiences Community for Backpackers** (http://www.t-e.co.uk/) can display messages chronologically.

you can click a link to post a new message or a reply to an existing one. Some message boards require you to sign in before you can see the messages or before you can post messages. Some message boards display messages in a chronological list (called an *unthreaded*, or *linear*, message board), as shown in Figure 11-1. Other message boards arrange the messages into threads (a message with all its replies), with replies to each message indented below the original message (see Figure 11-2). Threaded message boards may also display a list of topics with the number of replies to each question: Click the topic to see the list of messages (as shown in Figure 11-3). Some message boards let you choose whether to see messages by date or by thread.

Types of Real-time Chat

There are many Web-based, real-time chat systems. Some operate independently of any other chat system, and others (like TalkCity) provide a Web interface to Internet Relay Chat (IRC), the Internet-based chat system that predates the Web (see the section "Internet Relay Chat [IRC]," in Chapter 1). Most chat systems have a standard look and feel: You sign in with a username that will precede your remarks, you see a scrolling window of messages with a smaller window listing the current participants in the chat, and you send a message by typing it in a box

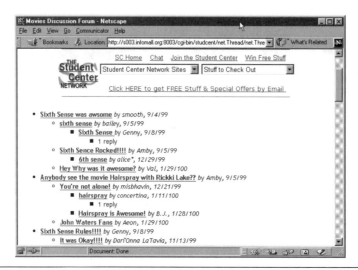

Figure 11-2: TeenMovies.org (http://www.teenmovies.org) has threaded linear message boards.

and pressing Enter or clicking Send (as shown in Figure 11-4). Some chat systems give you other capabilities:

- Send private messages to people who are in the same chat room as you.
- Send files to people in the same chat room.
- Format your messages with colors and fonts.
- View information about people in your chat room.

Figure 11-3: Homeforums.com (http://www.homeforums.com/) messages are displayed by topic, with the number of messages in each topic.

Chapter 11: Creating and Managing Your Own Web-based Community

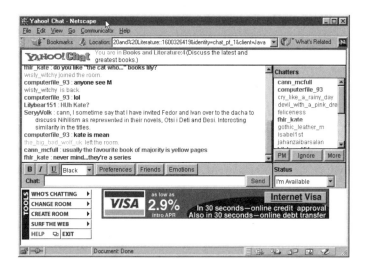

Figure 11-4: Yahoo Chat lets you choose the color and formatting of your messages.

The way most Web sites include chat rooms on their Web pages is by using *Java applets*, small programs written in the Java programming language. These applets can be called by the HTML code on a Web page. Some Web sites display chat rooms by using CGI (a method that Web pages use to call programs) to call Perl scripts on the Web server. CGI-based chat can be a little slower than Java-based chat because CGI runs the chat scripts on the Web server rather than on the participant's computer.

Because chat occurs in real-time, people who show up at your Web site can chat only with the other people who are at your site at the same time. Consider planning regularly scheduled events so that community members know that if they appear at your site, they can find a lively group of people to chat with. Announce these events on the community Web site. Events may be general get-togethers or may have specific topics, depending on the style of your community.

Other Design Decisions

Read Chapter 2 for community configuration options: For example, your Web-based community can be public or private, and message boards can be readable by anyone or only by members. Not every message board and Web-based real-time chat system can support all the options listed in Chapter 2.

Setting Up Message Boards

Your Web community can include one or more message boards, depending on the message volume and whether your community wants to discuss different types of topics in different conversation spaces.

Options for Setting Up Message Boards

If you want to add message boards to your Web site, you have three options: Link to a site that hosts messages boards, contract with a site to run a custom message board for you, or install your own message board software.

Linking to a Message Board Web Site

Several Web sites let you set up your own message board—many of them also let you create your own mailing lists. You can include links from your Web site to your message board at the message board Web site. The sites support themselves by displaying ads on your message boards. Some offer an ad-free version if you are willing to pay a fee for the message board.

Here are some Web sites that let you create message boards to which you can link, along with a message board manager Web site that lets you customize the appearance of the message board, control who can access the board, and delete unwanted messages:

BeSeen
   http://www.beseen.com/board/
Boardhost
   http://www.boardhost.com/
Casual Forums
   http://www.casualforums.com/
Delphi Forums (users must register with Delphi to participate; also supports voice chats)
   http://www.delphi.com/
EZBoard (as shown in Figure 11-5)
   http://www.ezboard.com
Novogate (formerly ForumsGalore)
   http://forumsgalore.com/
Talk City's eFriends (hosts clubs that include message boards and real-time chat for as many as 50 people)
   http://www.talkcity.com/

Chapter 11: Creating and Managing Your Own Web-based Community

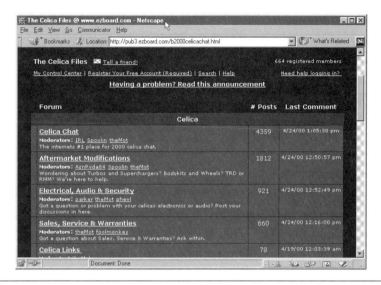

Figure 11-5: You can create an EZBoard message board for free.

For other message boards you can create and link to, see the **CGI Resources Index** (http://cgi.resourceindex.com/) and choose Programs and Scripts, Remotely Hosted, and Bulletin Board Message Systems.

Advantages of linking to a message board at a message board Web site include the ones in this list:

- Creating the message board is quick, easy, and free.
- These sites make it easy for people to sign up for your message board.
- You don't have to install or support any software.

Disadvantages include the issues shown in this list:

- Because you don't have control over the software that runs the message boards, you can't customize it to make it perfectly match the design of the rest of your Web site—although most message board Web sites let you customize the layout, background color, font, and graphics on the message board pages.
- People may be confused about when they are on your site and when they are on the message board Web site. (With good design, people may never notice that they are on another site.)
- People will see the ads the message board Web site displays.
- People may have to sign up on the host site rather than on your site, so the message board Web site controls the information they collect about

your community's participants.
- The message board Web site may maintain ownership of the communities' member profiles and messages.

Linking to a message board Web site can be a great way to get your community off the ground: Later, if you choose, you can move your community to your own site (if the message board Web site lets you).

Contracting with a Message Board Service

Several companies offer customized message board hosting so that the message boards appear to be part of your own site. You can choose how the message boards look and work, without having to create the software. Some services include real-time chat and other online community elements—like calendars, file pages, and link pages—and can design and create your whole community Web site. These services include

Caucus Systems
http://www.caucus.com/

CyberSites (see Figure 11-6)
http://www.cybersites.com/

EShare Expressions
http://www.eshare.com/products/internet/expressions/

Ichat (part of KOZ.com)
http://www.ichat.com/

Participate.com
http://www.participate.com/

PeopleLink
http://www.peoplelink.com/

Prospero Technologies (formerly WellEngaged, used by The WELL)
http://www.prosperotechnologies.com/

RemarQ
http://www.remarq.com/corporate/partners.html

VCIX Community Management Service (CMS)
http://www.vcix.com/solutions/cms.htm

Here are some advantages of contracting with a company to provide customized message boards (and other online community elements):

- You don't have to develop and maintain message board software.
- The message boards can match the rest of your Web site in design and user interface.

Chapter 11: Creating and Managing Your Own Web-based Community **235**

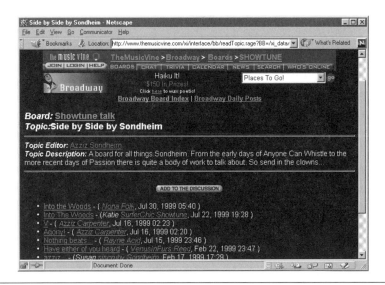

Figure 11-6: CyberSites operates a group of Vines Networks, including TheMusicVine.

- You can control whether ads are displayed and, if so, which ones (and you collect the ad revenue).
- You control the management policies of the community, and you own the messages and other information.
- People sign in with your site rather than with another site, so you control member profile information.

The main disadvantage is cost.

If you are planning a Web site that includes many communities and have the budget for it, contracting with an existing message board Web site to provide custom message boards can be a good way to get your communities started without losing control of the look and feel of the communities and the data in them.

Installing Your Own Message Board Software

If you decide to run your own message board software, you don't have to start from scratch. Many public domain, freeware, shareware, and commercial message programs are available. Many are written in Perl, a language that is supported on most Web servers. Some also support real-time chat or allow message boards to be used as mailing lists or newsgroups. Here are a few:

ArsDigita Community System (toolkit for creating intelligent message

boards, based on the Oracle 8i RDBMS)
http://www.photo.net/wtr/thebook/community.html
http://software.arsdigita.com/

bCandid's Twister Discussion Server (commercial software)
http://www.bcandid.com/products/

DCForum99 (Perl based)
http://www.dcscripts.com/dcforum99.shtml

Discus (for Windows 98, Windows NT, and UNIX)
http://www.discusware.com/discus/

The Ultimate Bulletin Board ("UBB," Perl based)
http://www.ultimatebb.com/

UltraBoard 2000 (Perl based)
http://www.ub2k.com/

WebBBS (shareware)
http://www.awsd.com/scripts/webbbs/

WebBoard (message boards can also be accessed as mailing lists or Usenet newsgroups)
http://webboard.oreilly.com/

WebCrossing (Windows 95, Windows 98, Windows NT, MacOS, UNIX, and Linux; freeware version is limited to 1,000 page views per day; message boards available as mailing lists and newsgroups; supports real-time chat)
http://www.webcrossing.com/

WWWBoard (Perl based; freeware)
http://worldwidemart.com/scripts/wwwboard.shtml

WWWThreads (Perl and SQL based)
http://www.wwwthreads.com/

Figure 11-7 shows a demo WWWThreads message board at the WWWThreads Web site.

Many other message board programs are available; for other software, check these Web sites:

CGI Resource Index
http://cgi.resourceindex.com/ (choose Programs and Scripts, Perl, and then Bulletin Board Message Systems)

Conferencing Software for the Web
http://thinkofit.com/webconf/

Here are a couple of advantages of installing your own message board software:

Chapter 11: Creating and Managing Your Own Web-based Community 237

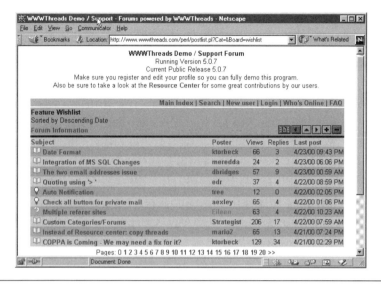

Figure 11-7: WWWThreads can run on almost any Web server that has Perl and an SQL database.

- You can customize the software any way you want, including appearance, permissions, and registration.
- You control the information that people provide when they register.
- You control whether ads are shown, and, if they are, you get the revenue.

Even if you use existing programs without modifying them, some disadvantages exist:

- You need an Internet host computer on which to run the programs, probably a UNIX, Linux, Windows NT, or Windows 2000 system with Perl. If you host your Web site at a Web hosting company or ISP, check with someone about the type of system it uses and whether you can get permission to install and run message board programs.
- You need expertise in installing software on UNIX, Linux, Windows NT, or Windows 2000 systems.
- You need ongoing expertise in maintaining the software, including troubleshooting, restarting the programs when trouble arises, and installing upgrades.
- You need to consider backup systems for your Internet host computer and Internet connection if it's important for your Web community to be available without interruption.

Creating Message Boards

The steps for setting up a message board depend on the type of message board software you or your message board Web site are running, although some general steps are necessary no matter what the system:

1. **Choose a name and one-line description for your message board.** Make sure that the name is easy to spell and remember. Keep the name short, but don't make it cryptic. Choose a longer name rather than a short name that no one can remember or spell. Avoid punctuation other than dashes. Most punctuation can confuse some programs and many people.

2. **Create the message board.** If you are creating a message board at a message board Web site like eGroups, you can set it up yourself, by following the links at the Web site and filling out forms. Figure 11-8 shows a Web page in the process of creating a message board at Boardhost. If you contract with a company for custom message boards, the company will create the message boards to your specifications. If you are using your own message board software, refer to the documentation that comes with the programs: Usually, after you install the message board software, you add instructions (in the form of CGI code) to your Web page to call the message board program to display a message board on that page. You will end up with a Web page that displays a message board. The message board system will

Figure 11-8: Boardhost.com creates a message board you can link to from your site.

Chapter 11: Creating and Managing Your Own Web-based Community **239**

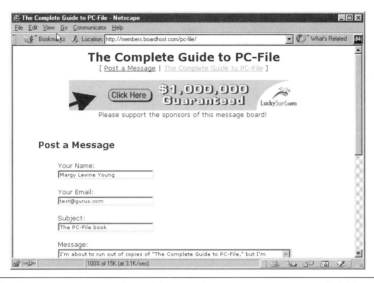

Figure 11-9: Test your message board by posting a message yourself (this message board was created by Boardhost).

also provide you with a manager password that allows you (or the community manager) to manage the message board.

3. **Test the message board.** Before linking to the message board page from anywhere else, or publicizing its existence, test it out (as shown in Figure 11-9). Test both how the message board works for a user and how the manager functions work. Post some test messages—long ones, short ones, and empty ones—and make sure that you can delete them. If the message board requires that people register before reading or before posting, test to make sure that these functions work. Check that the Web page which contains the message board looks right, with the correct instructions and graphics.

4. **Write a welcome message and an FAQ.** See the section "Writing Your Welcome Message and FAQ," later in this chapter, for details.

5. **Create links to the message board page from other pages on your Web site.** Add links throughout your Web site—you might want to add a Community or Discussion Group button to the standard set of navigation buttons that appear on the pages of your site. Some message board systems provide prewritten HTML to use in your Web pages (as shown in Figure 11-10).

6. **Publicize your new message board.** See Chapter 12 for ideas. You might want to e-mail invitations to people who have visited your Web site and signed a guest book, for example.

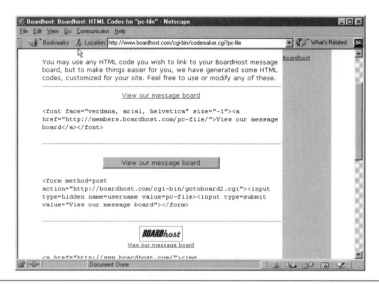

Figure 11-10: Boardhost provides several prewritten HTML snippets you can use to link to your message board page.

Managing Message Boards

As the manager of a message board, your duties depend on the features of the message board software you are using. For example, Figure 11-11 shows the Web page that the Boardhost system shows the message board manager.

Here are some of the jobs many message boards let managers perform:

Delete messages that don't belong. If a message is off-topic or breaks the rules of the community, you can (and should) delete it.

Post administrative messages. Some message boards allow the manager to post specially formatted messages.

Format the message board Web pages. Many message board systems let you control how the Web pages look so that you can make them match the rest of your Web site. You can usually also choose how messages are displayed: by date, by thread, or either, allowing the user to choose.

Control who can post. You may be able to control whether people can post pictures or links within their messages as well as who is allowed to read and post messages. If your message board requires people to register before posting, you can usually also ban people from posting. Some message boards can be configured to require a username and password before they can view messages.

Chapter 11: Creating and Managing Your Own Web-based Community 241

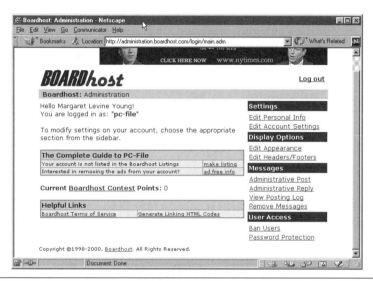

Figure 11-11: Boardhost lets the message board manager delete messages that have been posted to the board and control who can read and post.

View the logs. You can see who has visited the message board, who has posted, and other information about message board activity and visitors.

Also see Chapter 13 for ideas for guiding the discussion and dealing with trouble.

Setting Up Web-based Real-time Chat

If you want your community members to be able to chat together in real-time—that is, send and receive typed messages within seconds of sending them, to have a typed on-the-spot conversation—you can include one or more chat rooms as part of your Web community.

If you do use chat rooms, it's a good idea to post times during which people should congregate. No one wants to sit watching a screen and waiting for other people to show up—and few people will. If you want other people to be there when participants arrive, post regular dates and times on your Web site. Be sure to consider time zones when setting times—for example, if your audience is likely to include people from across the United States, set times that work for people on both coasts. If your community has members from around the world, no time will work for everyone, so you might want to stick with message boards rather than chat or schedule chats at several times for people on different continents.

Options for Setting Up Web-based Real-time Chat

Your real-time options are similar to those for adding a message board: Link to a chat page on a chat Web site, contract for custom chat rooms, or install and run your own Web-based chat software. Many message board systems described in the preceding sections also support chat. Most Web-based chat systems create their own, separate chat spaces, but a few (mainly Talk City) provide a Web entryway into Internet Relay Chat, described in Chapters 8 and 9.

Linking to a Chat Web Site

Several Web sites let you create a real-time chat for free. They provide a chunk of HTML code that you copy into your Web page to display the chat room on that page. The HTML calls a Java *applet* (a small application written in the Java programming language) that is stored on the chat Web site's Web server. When a visitor views your Web page, the chat Web site's chat applet runs on that person's computer and displays a sign-on window for your chat room. When the person signs in, the applet displays the chat room messages, using the other Web site's server to exchange messages among the people in the chat room. Figure 11-12 shows a Web page running a chat applet.

Here are a few Web sites where you can sign up to get the HTML code to display a chat room on your own Web pages:

BeSeen
   http://www.beseen.com/chat/
MultiChat
   http://www.tectonicdesigns.com/chat/
QuickChat (highly rated; uses a private IRC server)
   http://www.planetz.net/quickchat/
Talk City's eFriends (hosts clubs that include message boards and real-time chat for as many as 50 people)
   http://www.talkcity.com/
XOOM (shown in Figure 11-12; uses the ParaChat software mentioned in the next section)
   http://xoom.com/chat/

See Figure 11-15 "Embedding Chat Room HTML," later in this chapter, for an example of how you can display a chat room on your Web site using a program provided by a chat Web site. For other chat services, see the **CGI Resource Index** (start at http://cgi.resourceindex.com/ and choose Programs and Scripts, Remotely Hosted, and Chat).

This list shows some advantages of using embedded HTML to display a chat room hosted on a chat server:

- It's free, easy, and quick.

Chapter 11: Creating and Managing Your Own Web-based Community **243**

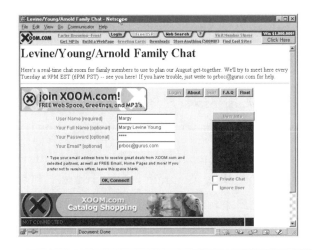

Figure 11-12: XOOM provided the chat applet for this Web-based chat page.

- You can create temporary chat rooms for a specific purpose and then delete them when the purpose is over.

Disadvantages are shown in this list:

- The chat service displays its ads on your Web page.
- You don't have much control over the format of the chat room (although you can format the rest of the Web page that contains the chat applet).

Contracting with a Chat Service

You can hire a service to host your chats for a monthly fee:

Cybersites (shown in Figure 11-6)
  http://www.cybersites.com/
iChat (owned by KOZ.com)
  http://www.ichat.com/
KOZ
  http://about.koz.com/

ParaChat Professional (use XOOM.com for free ParaChat-based chat rooms, as shown in Figure 11-12)
  http://www.parachat.com/parachat.htm
PeopleLink

http://www.peoplelink.com/
SureSite Java Chat
http://www.suresite.com/accounts/chat.html

Talk City
http://www.talkcity.com/business_services/home.htm

Advantages of contracting out your chat rooms are shown in this list:

- The vendor's server runs the chat, limiting the load on your server.
- You don't have to install or maintain any software.

Disadvantages include

- Cost
- Less control over the appearance and features of your chat system, if you want something not part of the vendor's package

Installing Your Own Chat Software

A number of Perl scripts are available that you can install on your Web server and call from your Web pages. Here are a few:

ChatPro (commercial product)
http://www.chatpro.com/
Communique Chat (freeware)
http://www.creativematrix.com/freecgi/communique_chat.html
e_Chat (low-priced program)
http://www.e-scripts.com/echat/
FreeChat (freeware C programs)
http://www.sonic.net/~nbs/unix/www/freechat/
JabberChat (see Figure 11-13)
http://www.prowler-pro.com/jabberchat/
Maze Interactive Media Chat (freeware)
http://www.maze.se/chatchatchat/download.html
Network Dweebs WebConference (commercial product)
http://www.networkdweebs.com/products/webconference/
Ralf's Chat (simple and widely used shareware)
http://ralfchat.de/
WebMaster's ConferenceRoom (commercial product)
http://www.webmaster.com/
WebTalk (commercial product)

Chapter 11: Creating and Managing Your Own Web-based Community   245

Figure 11-13: JabberChat is a Perl script you can install on your Web server and call from Web pages to display chat rooms.

http://www.codeweb.net/products/webtalk/

For other chat programs you can install, see the **CGI Resource Index** (http://cgi.resourceindex.com/); choose Programs and Scripts, Perl, and then Chat).

Creating Chat Rooms

How you create your chat room (or rooms) depends on which chat system you use.

To create a chat room using a free program from a chat Web site (see "Linking to a Chat Web Site," earlier in this chapter), you follow these general steps:

1. Register as a user at the chat Web site.

2. Follow the links to create a chat room. The chat Web site displays the HTML code you need to copy to your own Web page in order to display your own chat room. Figure 11-14 shows the HTML code that XOOM (http://xoom.com/chat/) creates.

3. Copy the HTML code from the page into your own Web page. (If you don't know how to edit a Web page, have your webmaster do this part.) Be sure to save a copy of the HTML code in case you need to refer to it. For example, the HTML that XOOM creates looks like this:

```
<applet
codebase="http://memberchat.xoom.com:8901/pchat/classes/
"
```

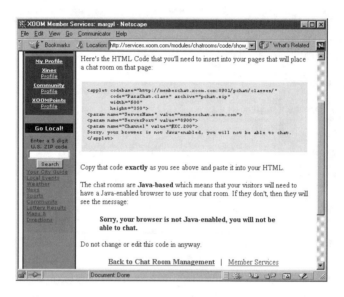

Figure 11-14: XOOM provides HTML code you can use to add a chat room to your own Web page.

```
          code="ParaChat.class" archive="pchat.zip"
          width="600"
          height="350">
<param name="ServerName" value="memberchat.xoom.com">
<param name="ServerPort" value="xxx">
<param name="Channel" value="#XC.xxx">
Sorry, your browser is not Java-enabled, you will not
be able to chat.
</applet>
```

4. Format the rest of your Web page to match the rest of your site, and include instructions for participating in the chat room as well as links to other parts of your community. Figure 11-15 shows the HTML for a sample page that includes a XOOM-based chat room.

5. Test the resulting Web page using several browsers. Be sure to use the latest few versions of Internet Explorer, Netscape Navigator, America Online, and Opera. Figure 11-12 shows the sign-in page of a chat room created by XOOM.

After you've tested out the chat room, it's ready to use!

```
<html>
<head>
   <title>Levine/Young/Arnold Family Chat</title>
</head>

<body>
<h1>Levine/Young/Arnold Family Chat</h1>

Here's a real-time chat room for family members to use
to plan our August get-together. We'll try to meet here
every Tuesday at 9PM EST (6PM PST) -- see you here! If
you have trouble, just write to prboc@gurus.com for
help.
<hr>

<applet
codebase="http://memberchat.xoom.com:8901/pchat/classes/"
        code="ParaChat.class" archive="pchat.zip"
        width="600"
        height="350">
<param name="ServerName" value="memberchat.xoom.com">
<param name="ServerPort" value="8900">
<param name="Channel" value="#XC.2091910">
Sorry, your browser is not Java-enabled, you will not
be able to chat.
</applet>

<hr>
<p><a href="index.html">Return to Family Home Page</a>

<p>Page last updated on April 20, 2001 by Margy Levine
Young
</body>
</html>
```

Figure 11-15: HTML for a Web page with an embedded chat room.

Managing Real-time Chat

Your job as real-time chat manager depends on the capabilities of your chat system. Here are the jobs that many chat systems require of the chat manager:

Let participants know the timing and topic of the chat. If you are running a chat from 7:00 to 8:00 p.m. U.S. Eastern Standard Time to discuss pruning bonsai trees, make sure that people know the schedule and topic. Encourage people to stick to the topic, unless your chat room is purely for socializing.

Discourage bad behavior. If your chat system lets you send private messages to participants, warn people about the consequences of breaking the communities' rules. Then kick people out of the chat room and ban them from returning.

Act as master of ceremonies. Introduce the chat, suggest topics to get the chat going, and remind people when the time's up.

Also see Chapter 13 for ideas for guiding the discussion and dealing with trouble.

Writing Your Welcome Message and FAQ

Message boards and real-time chat rooms should have a brief set of instructions—including rules for participating—on the Web pages that display the message board or chat room. It's a good idea to have an expanded set of rules and instructions on a separate page, too, along with a list of frequently asked questions. Be sure to include these elements:

- The main topic of the message board or chat room
- Topics that are not allowed
- Who should participate
- Who is not allowed to participate (if people must be 18 years old, mention it)
- Rules that postings must follow (see Chapter 13 for ideas)
- Instructions for registering to read or post messages (if applicable), reading messages, posting messages, searching for specific topics, and other message board or chat room functions
- The e-mail address to write to with problems or questions

Part VI

Growing and Managing Your Community

Chapter Twelve
Publicizing Your Community

If you are creating a community for an existing group of people—a committee, for example—you don't have to worry about publicity. You can let the members of your existing group know about the community, help everyone sign up, and you're done. However, if you have a community that is open to anyone who shares a common interest, you may want to have more members than you already have.

What's the Optimum Size for a Community?

The answer depends on what percentage of the members post messages and how much they have to say. For most communities to have interesting and lively discussions, a minimum number of members is 100 to 200, with 10 or 20 people posting messages (about 90 percent of most community members just lurk silently).
If you have too many members, the **traffic** *(the number of messages posted per day) can go through the roof. High traffic can be a hardship for some members. Some people, especially those who use feature-poor e-mail and newsreading programs, like America Online's, have trouble participating in communities in which dozens or hundreds of messages are posted each day. Other people, by using more powerful e-mail and newsreading programs, can sort through hundreds of messages a day to read only those that are of interest. Once a community reaches over 500 members, it frequently needs to be moderated or use some other mechanism to reduce the traffic and make it easier for members to find and read the interesting messages.*

Creating a Home Page for Your Community

If you run a Web-based community, you've already got a Web site. But if you run a mailing list or newsgroup, your community may be invisible to people who search the Web for information on your topic.

Be sure that the Web site includes this information:
- Instructions for joining and leaving the community.
- An address for contacting the community manager.
- A description of the topics the community discusses and what makes this community unique.
- The rules of the community (so that you can refer community members to your Web site if they have questions about the rules).

Your Web site might also include the following:
- A form that people can use to sign up for your community. Be sure to include a page that thanks people for signing up and tells them what happens next. (Do they go to a Web site or sit back and wait for messages to arrive?)
- A searchable archive of the messages on the community.

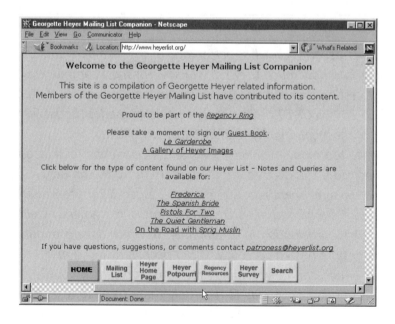

Figure 12-1: Every online community needs a home page so that people can search the Web to get information about the community.

- Links to other Web pages that relate to the topic of the community.
- Pictures and other files that have been shared by members of the community (only if you have permission from the owners of the files to post them on the Web).

For example, the Georgette Heyer mailing list discusses the novels of one of the best Regency romance authors. The list's Web site, **The Georgette Heyer Mailing List Companion** (http://www.heyerlist.org/), is shown in Figure 12-1.

Once your site looks good and the members of your community have seen and critiqued it, submit your site to all the major Web search engines and directories, like **Yahoo** (http://www.yahoo.com/), **Excite** (http://www.excite.com/), and **AltaVista** (http://www.altavista.com/), so that other Internet users will be able to find it. On these sites, try to get your site listed under both the mailing list, newsgroup, or Web-based message-board categories and the topic of your community. For example, if you run a message board for painting contractors, try to get your community's home page listed under both Web-based Communities and Painting Contractors.

To find out how to create a Web site, how to find a Web server on which to post it, how to include keywords on the page so that it is correctly indexed by search engines, and how to submit your Web site to search engines so that people can find it, see *Poor Richard's Web Site*, written by Peter Kent and published by Top Floor Publishing (http://www.poorrichard.com/).

Asking for Links

Once your Web site is up and running and you've submitted it to the general-interest search engines and Web directories—like Yahoo, Excite, and AltaVista—you can also arrange for links to your site from more specialized Web sites. Search the Web for sites that relate to the topic of your community, and write to the webmasters to ask them to include a link to your Web site. Describe why your community would be of interest to visitors to their site, and include the URL of your community's home page. Many webmasters will be more likely to agree if you also offer to include a link from your site to theirs. Better yet, make sure that your Web site already links to their site. Figure 12-2 shows the links page of a Web-based community: The community manager has probably asked all these sites to link back to the community, too.

For more information on getting other Web sites to link to yours, read *Poor Richard's Internet Marketing Promotions,* written by Peter Kent and Tara Calishain and published by Top Floor Publishing (http://www.poorrichard.com/promo/).

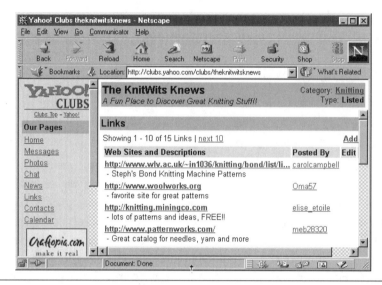

Figure 12-2: Provide links to related Web sites, and ask those sites to link back to you.

Getting Listed in Directories

Many Web sites provide searchable directories of mailing lists. If you'd like your mailing list to show up when users search these sites, visit each site and follow the links to add your community to their database:

DiscussionLists.com: Email Communities That Match Your Unique Interests
http://discussionlists.com/

The List of Lists
http://catalog.com/vivian/interest-group-search.html

ListTool.com (a directory of LISTSERV, ListProc, and Majordomo mailing lists)
http://www.listtool.com/

Liszt: The Mailing List Directory
http://www.liszt.com/

Meta-List
http://www.meta-list.net/

PAML: Publicly Accessible Mailing Lists
http://paml.alastra.com/

The SparkLIST Email Newsletter & Discussion Lists Directory
http://SparkList.net/

TILE.NET/LISTS: The Reference to Internet Discussion and
Information Lists
http://tile.net/lists/

Topica
http://www.topica.com/

WebScout Lists
http://www.webscoutlists.com/

One Web site we know of provides a searchable directory of Web-based message boards. Click its Add URL link to add your Web-based message board to its database:

ForumOne Index (searchable index of Web-based message boards)
http://www.forumone.com/

Two Web sites provide searchable directories of Usenet newsgroups (see Chapter 6):

Deja.com
http://www.deja.com/usenet/

RemarQ
http://www.remarq.com/

These sites automatically include new Usenet newsgroups as they are created. (RemarQ also indexes mailing lists, but we couldn't see a link for adding a new mailing list.)

One site maintains a searchable directory of IRC channels:

Liszt's IRC Chat Directory
http://www.liszt.com/chat/

Posting Announcements

You can post announcements—press releases—about your new community on mailing lists, newsgroups, and Web-based message boards. Getting the word out about your new community is good, but sending spam is not. Keep that in mind as you post announcements on related communities! Here's what to do:

1. Use the directory Web sites listed in the preceding section to find communities that relate to the topic of your community. It's not enough for the people in another community to have the same demographics as your target audience: The topics actually have to have something to do with each other. For example, if you are starting a community about investing, look for other financially related communities—perhaps communities discussing stock tips, mutual funds, or art collecting. Don't include communities that you think would include lots of rich people who must be interested in investing their money.

2. Join these communities and read their messages for a week or two. Check that the communities are actually talking about a subject that relates to your community.

3. Read the FAQ or information file about each community. See whether it mentions the topic of your new community. Check what the rules are about posting announcements: If you think that the rules might forbid announcing your community, you might want to write to the community's managers to ask.

4. Compose a message that describes your community, including the topics it covers, how to join, and how to get more information (ideally, the URL of the community's home page). Be brief, and don't sound like you are selling something.

5. For each community to which you want to post an announcement, edit your announcement message to include an explanation of how your community's topic relates to the topic of that community, and why you think that members might be interested in both communities.

6. Post your messages just once on each community.

You might want to post your announcements on one community at a time, so you can see what the response is from each community.

There are mailing lists specifically for posting announcements about new mailing lists. If you are starting a mailing list, be sure to send an announcement to these lists:

AAnnounce@egroups.com
(announcements of all Internet-based discussion groups)
AAnnounce-subscribe@egroups.com (to subscribe)
http://www.onelist.com/group/Aannounce (home page)
http://www.escribe.com/internet/-aannounce/ (list archives)

ListBuilder
http://egroups.com/community/ListBuilder/
ListBuilder-subscribe@egroups.com (to subscribe)

New-List.com
(a group of announcement mailing lists by topic)
http://New-List.com/

The Scout Report, Net-happenings, and NEW-LIST
(announcement mailing lists about new resources on the Internet: NEW-LIST is shown in Figure 12-3)
http://scout.cs.wisc.edu/scout/

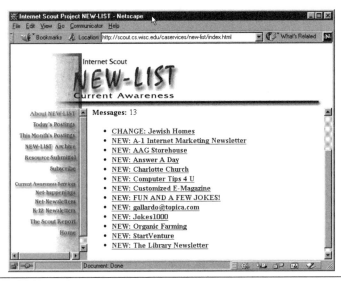

Figure 12-3: The NEW-LIST mailing list is part of the Scout Project.

You can also send information about your mailing list to the **List-a-day** mailing list, which distributes one message per day, reviewing a mailing list. Send your list announcement to submit@listaday.com. To subscribe to the List-a-day mailing list, send a message to join-listaday@listaday.com.

Advertising Your Community

Unless you are planning to make lots of money by running your community, you probably don't want to advertise your online community by taking out full-page ads in newspapers and magazines or even buying banner ads on popular Web portal sites. But advertising might make sense if you choose mailing lists and specialized Web sites that relate directly to the topic of your community. Newsgroups don't accept advertisements—since no one owns them, no one is authorized to make the sale. Don't try paying for advertising until you've already tried asking lists, newsgroups, and Web-based message boards to announce your list for free or have tried free ad swaps and banner exchanges.

Advertising on Mailing Lists

Buying an advertisement on a mailing list is usually fairly cheap, compared to other types of advertising. Mailing list ads usually cost in the range of $2 to $8 CPM (cost per thousand messages sent). You can send out a message to a 10,000-member mailing list for only $20 to $80. Not many discussion mailing lists accept advertisements, but most *e-zines* (e-mail newsletters and magazines) do.

To find mailing lists in which to advertise, search for mailing lists on topics that relate to your community, using the same directories listed in the section "Getting Listed in Directories," earlier in this chapter. Write to the list manager to ask for the advertising policies and rates for that list and how many subscribers the list has. Include information about your own community since the list manager will want to take a look. You might also want to include the ad you'd like to run, while also asking for suggestions about how it could be improved to appeal to the subscribers of that specific list. Be sure to ask for assurances that the mailing list is *confirmed opt-in;* that is, that subscribers have asked to be on the mailing list and have responded to a confirmation message. Otherwise, you will be paying for your ad to be included in spam.

Rather than pay to place an ad in another mailing list, you can propose swapping ads. That is, you will run a free ad on your community for the other mailing list in return for the other mailing list running a free ad about your community. If you want to try swapping ads, several Web sites and mailing lists are devoted to helping mailing lists find each other (Figure 12-4 shows one such site):

The Ad Swap Mailing List
(join the list to post ads for other members to run on their mailing lists while also promising to run their ads on your list)
adswap-subscribe@listbot.com (to subscribe and join the ad swap)
http://adswap.listbot.com/

Advantage Email Coop
http://www.advantageemailcoop.com/

E-zine Swap Mailing List
join-ezine-swap@ezine-swap.com (to subscribe)
http://Ezine-Swap.com/

EzineAdvertising.com: The Search Engine for Ezine Advertisers
http://ezineadvertising.com/

ListCity Ad Exchange Database
http://www.List-City.com/adexdb.html

Some ad-swap services concentrate on e-zines rather than on discussion mailing lists, newsgroups, or Web-based message boards. But you can try asking e-zine publishers to try ads swaps anyway. Lots of advertising agencies also concentrate on selling ads on e-zines, which require you to pay to find out about e-zines in which you might want to advertise.

Chapter 12: Publicizing Your Community 257

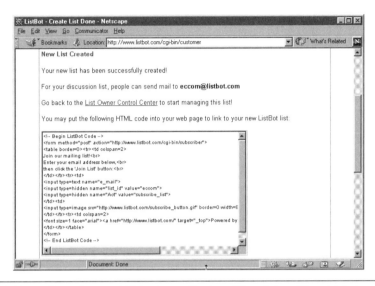

Figure 12-4: Use a list ad-swap Web site to find mailing lists with which to swap ads.

When a mailing list runs an ad (whether paid or part of a swap), the list manager splices the ad into the text of a message sent to the list. The ad may be set off in some way so that it's clearly advertising, using lines of hyphens above and below the ad or indenting the ads with a character like | or >. Ads are usually limited to between four and eight lines of 60 to 65 characters—check with the manager of the list that will run the ad.

Your ad should include the name of the online community, the URL of the community's Web site, a short description of what it's about, brief instructions for joining, and the e-mail address to write to for more information. If the ad works for you, consider repeating it once a month, especially if it's a free swap.

Here's another idea for a place that you can ask for your ad to be run (or that you can run ads yourself): in the welcome message that new community members receive. If you are buying an advertisement in a mailing list, in addition to running the ad in a message that is sent to the list, ask whether you can have your ad included in the text of the welcome message that the list manager sends to new subscribers. (The message is usually sent automatically by the list server program.) Fewer people will see this ad, but people who are receiving a welcome message are people who have just subscribed to one mailing list and may be interesting in trying another!

Instead of placing an ad, you can arrange to swap sponsorship or recommendations so that the other list mentions your list as part of the text of a message from its list manager, rather than in text that looks like an ad. See the article "How To Do Sponsorship Swaps 202," by Christopher Knight, at http://list-tips.com/articles/list-promotion/051099.html (part of the **List-Tips** site).

Placing Banner Ads

Banner ads on Web sites tend to cost more than mailing list ads, in the range of $10 to $20 CPM (cost per thousand Web page views) or more. For more information on placing banner ads, read *Poor Richard's Internet Marketing Promotions*, by Peter Kent and Tara Calishain (http://www.poorrichard.com/promo/).

Rather than pay for banner ads, you can consider reciprocal links from your community's Web site (or other related Web sites you manage). Write to the webmaster or advertising manager at related Web sites and propose an ad swap. One terrific idea came from the **List-Tips** mailing list (http://List-Tips.com/): Swap signup forms with another community's Web site. Ideally, you should put the signup form for the other mailing list on the "thank you" page that your Web site visitors see right after they have signed up for your community. Be sure to join the other community yourself first, to make sure that it's a community you recommend.

Some services help Web sites exchange banner ads with each other for free. Most of these link-exchange services are free. The good ones categorize the Web sites by topic so that you can choose what types of ads to run and what types of sites will run your ads. Here are some link-swapping Web sites that let you specify the types of sites where your ad will appear:

Ad Swap
  http://www.adswap.com/
Exchange-it!
  http://www.exchange-it.com/
Free Banner Exchange MegaList
  http://www.bxmegalist.com/
Link Buddies
  http://www.linkbuddies.com/
SmartClicks
  http://www.smartclicks.com/
Swap-Resources
  http://www.swap-resources.com/

Maintaining Searchable Archives

People are wary of joining an online community unless they know that they will enjoy the content or find it useful. One way to let people "try before they buy" is to let nonmembers search the archives of your community. Web-based message boards already post messages on the Web, although they may not be searchable. Mailing lists and newsgroups can set up Web-based archives: Chapter 5 (for mailing lists) and Chapter 7 (for newsgroups) describe how. IRC channels don't usually keep logs of their chats. Figure 12-5 shows part of the Web page that lets anyone search the archives of the soc.religion.unitarian-univ newsgroup by date, by author, or by topic.

If your community doesn't let nonmembers read community messages, you shouldn't provide publicly accessible archives, but you can post community-related articles on your site; for example:

- Extract useful information from community postings and ask the author for permission to post your extract on the Web.
- Ask community members who write well and provide useful postings to write articles specifically for your community's Web site (and write some yourself!).

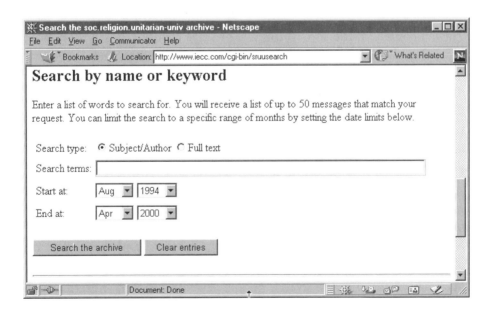

Figure 12-5: A searchable archive for a newsgroup or other online community lets anyone find past postings by author or topic.

Other Ideas

Here are a few other ideas for promoting your community and getting more members:

- For Web-based message boards and newsgroups, send a weekly e-mail newsletter to your community members to draw them back to the site or newsgroup, with the titles of interesting stuff and links to them. Suggest that community members pass these newsletters along to other people who might be interested.

- Include joining information at the bottom of every message distributed to your community or on every page of your Web site (for Web-based communities). Make sure that anyone visiting you, or who receives a forwarded message from your community, knows how to join. (Even if your community forbids forwarding messages to outsiders, it's going to happen.)

- Suggest that community members tell friends about your community—at least, friends who share an interest in the topic of your community. Better than anyone else, your existing members know other people who share their interests.

- Have regular events, like debates, polls, real-time chats, or other things that you can remind people to participate in and bring their friends.

- Have a contest, raffle something off, or stage a publicity stunt of some kind that allows you to send press releases out to magazines, newspapers, and online publications. A mention in an article (as long as the mention includes enough information for people to find you) can draw lots of attention to your community.

- Use *viral marketing*—getting your existing members to help spread the word by giving them some kind of incentive. For an article on viral marketing by Steve Jurvetson and Tim Draper, the people who coined the term, see http://www.drapervc.com/viralmarketing.html. (But be warned that viral marketing often attracts foolish members who will spread the word by spamming, so be sure that they understand up front that spam will get their membership canceled and they'll lose any incentives earned.)

- Start an *affiliate program* so that people get paid for each subscriber they send to your community. **List Partners** (http://www.listpartners.com/) runs a free affiliate marketing program for mailing lists.

- Check the **List-Resources.com** directory of list promotion information (http://List-Resources.com/s/Promotion/) for other ideas.
- Join one of the **Get High (Traffic) Forums** at http://gethighforums.com/bin/Ultimate.cgi—they discuss using community building as a means to build traffic to your Web site, but some of the community-building advice is worthwhile.
- Go to **List-Promotion.com,** a site that promises to start posting articles about promoting e-mail mailing lists real soon now, at http://List-Promotion.com/.

Chapter Thirteen

Encouraging, Sharing, and Responding to Dissension

Whether your community is a mailing list, Usenet newsgroup, Web-based message board, IRC channel, or Web-based real-time chat, your job as community manager involves setting rules, encouraging sharing, and avoiding needless arguments. The manager sets the tone for the entire community, and your management style can determine the community's success. As manager, you can help your community succeed by setting goals for the community, making rules that will further those goals, and then enforcing those rules within the community. This chapter also includes some techniques for dealing with problems that may arise.

Community Goals

To make your community work, the members of the community should share goals. Once you know the goals of your community, you can use them in making and applying rules, guiding the discussion, and dealing with arguments.

The goals of almost every online community include
- Helping members learn from each other
- Providing information to each other
- Supporting each other
- Getting to know each other

For example, the goal of the UU-Parenting mailing list (http://www.uua.org/lists) is for Unitarian Universalist parents to learn from each other how to be the best parents they can be and to support each other while doing so.

But the emphasis may differ from community to community. A message board about home repair might have more emphasis on sharing specific information and have little emphasis on getting to know each other or supporting each other. A closed mailing list for the parents of children with terminal cancer might concentrate primarily on support and sharing experiences while downplaying the sharing of specific information (to avoid people trying to diagnose each other's children, because subscribers aren't doctors). An IRC channel for online auction enthusiasts might emphasize informal chatting about auctions as they happen, with little information-gathering and community-building for the long term.

Some communities have additional goals:
- Provide income for the community manager (for example, if the manager sells advertisements in community messages or gets sales or consulting work through exposure to community members)
- Provide a positive public image for an organization (for example, if an organization provides a message board or Web-based real-time chat as a means for customers to get answers quickly)
- Get something specific done (for example, the community may be the online meeting place for a committee, club, or other organization that has goals for doing something in the real world)

If community members share goals, the community will run more smoothly. When one member has a different goal (like convincing everyone that a particular idea is right), problems are inevitable.

Role of the Community Manager

Every community needs a manager, to keep the place running. Here are some roles a community manager takes on:

Host of the party. Invites new people to come in, makes people feel comfortable, and asks troublemakers to leave

> **Finding Capable People through Communities**
>
> *One nonprofit organization uses a public mailing list to help Internet-savvy members talk about "tech" topics. A secondary goal of the list is to allow the organization to find knowledgable people who want to get involved. When someone consistently posts useful answers to questions posted on the public list, she may be asked to join a private list, which is the meeting place of the people who run Internet-related projects for the organization. The public list provides a place for experts to shine!*

Janitor. Deletes unrelated posts (on Web-based message boards) or prevents unrelated posts from getting distributed (on moderated mailing lists and newsgroups), as well as cleans up the list of members' addresses when addresses bounce

Researcher. Collects news and links that relate to the topic of the community and posts them as messages or adds them to community Web pages

Negotiator. Steps in when dissent breaks out among members

Facilitator. Encourages members to speak up when they have something substantive to say but not to hog the mike

Teacher. Helps members use the community system and the Internet in general

Writer. Composes FAQs, welcome messages, and Web pages about the community; in some communities, writes a weekly newsletter or posts news briefs to the community Web site

Administrator. Deals with error messages, bounced messages, and broken software of all types

Police officer. Informs those who break the rules how to behave and evicts those who persist in disrupting the community

The WELL, one of the oldest online community venues, describes the roles of the community manager as falling into three categories: taking care of technical items, stimulating participation, and dealing with people (including new people, confused people, and troublemakers).

Who chooses the manager? Many communities are managed by the person who created them: The manager hosts the community, and, if the members don't like the manager's style and rules, the members always have the option of starting another community. Other communities are started by existing groups and choose the manager themselves. Traditionally, community managers are unpaid volunteers who spend an amazing amount of time keeping their groups running out of love for the topic or the participants. Online services like America Online and CompuServe sometimes give their community managers free accounts or perks to compensate them for their unpaid work. **About.com** (formerly The Mining Company, now at http://www.about.com) chooses community managers based on their expertise in the topic of the community and pays them based on the amount of traffic they draw to their communities.

Who Owns a Community?

As far as we know, no legal precedent yet exists for determining the ownership of the various types of online communities. The assets of an online community consist of the community's members and the collection of messages and other information they have shared online. Each participant owns the copyright to the messages she has posted, but the community may own the compilation of the messages.

In our opinions (keeping in mind that neither of the authors is a lawyer), a mailing list is probably owned by the managers or creators of the list. If a mailing list is sponsored by an organization, that organization may own the list. (For example, if you manage a list about church fundraising on behalf of a religious denomination, using the list server of that denomination, the denomination probably owns the list.)

Newsgroups aren't owned by anyone—because newsgroups aren't stored or disseminated from a central location (Usenet is a worldwide, Internet-based distribution system), there's no server or newsgroup manager to claim ownership. For moderated newsgroups, the moderators might claim ownership, but who knows whether this claim would hold up in court.

IRC channels aren't owned by anyone, either. Some IRC networks let individuals register channel names, but no one knows what, if any, legal rights that gives channel "owners."

Web-based communities are almost certainly owned by the owner of the Web site on which they appear. For example, if you start a community on eGroups, the eGroups company probably owns the assets of your community. Check the privacy and ownership policies of a Web site before starting a community there!

Making Community Rules

Every community has rules, whether they are created consciously or not. A community with no explicit rules has implicit rules that allow ads, chain letters, personal attacks, copyright violations, grandstanding, and other problematic behavior. Most people don't stick around in online communities in which most of the messages contain junk mail and attacks, so if you want your community to succeed, think about the types of rules you want to enforce.

Another reason to have rules is to protect the community and its managers against liability lawsuits. Chapter 13 describes the types of legal issues that can arise from online communities and what types of rules you might need to make to protect yourself as manager.

Who makes the rules usually depends on who feels that they "own" the community (legally or emotionally). There are (at least) two groups who can create the rules for a community:

The managers. Some communities think of themselves as parties hosted by the community's manager. If the manager is the host and has invited participants into his online space, he gets to make the rules. For example, if you create a mailing list, newsgroup, or Web-based bulletin board to discuss a topic, you own the community—you created it, you chose the name and the venue, and you set the rules.

The community. Other communities form as existing groups of people who want to communicate online, with ownership of the community held by the community itself. Communities of this type usually want to make their own rules—no manager has the authority to impose rules on the group.

Ideally, a community creates its rules at the beginning so that all the participants know the rules for participation right from the start. However, this method isn't always possible. Sometimes, communities don't feel that they need any rules and change their minds only after a single-minded zealot posts 20 messages a day about a single topic or a member posts personal information about another member without permission. A community may also want to establish its own style—freewheeling or formal—before setting rules into stone.

Areas in Which Communities Need Rules

Regardless of who makes the rules, there are general areas in which most communities need rules. Different types of communities need different rules, to respond to both the venue (the different needs of mailing lists, Usenet newsgroups, IRC channels, and Web-based message boards) and the audience (the style that works for the community and the manager). The topics that follow are suggestions for the areas in which you should consider making rules for your community, but we can't suggest the exact rules that would work for all communities.

Topics to Be Discussed

Most online communities have a subject—it can be hard to have a good discussion if it can be about absolutely anything. But how narrowly is the subject defined? For example, if you run a message board about Vermont downhill skiing, do you allow messages about cross-country skiing, or skiing in the Adirondacks, or skating? Do messages have to relate specifically to skiing in Vermont, or can people talk about how to dress for skiing, or how to teach little kids to ski, which could happen anywhere? (Well, maybe not in Florida.)

When you set the topic for your community, think about how narrowly you want to define it. Some communities prefer to stay very focused, to reduce the traffic and keep the signal-to-noise ratio (the ratio of useful information to useless information) high. Other communities like to include general conversations among members as a method of forming friendships and building a community feeling.

Most communities ban forwarded messages, such as chain letters, virus warnings, and lists of jokes that are making the rounds. People who are part of several communities hate receiving these messages because they usually receive them many times and the information they contain is invariably out of date or just plain untrue.

When writing the rules about topics for your community, think about listing both topics that are encouraged and topics that are forbidden (if any). Be sure to mention whether postings should be factual (for a technical list) or anecdotal (for a personal support group list), and how narrowly these guidelines should be applied.

Sharing Files

Most information exchanged in online communities is in the form of text—plain, unformatted text. However, some communities encourage members to exchange other types of information, including

- **Graphics files** with pictures of members or of examples of the subject under discussion. A model railroading community might include pictures of layouts or items for sale.
- **Programs or snippets of programs**; a Visual Basic community might share a library of useful routines.
- **Audio files** for a composer's or performer's community.
- **Word processing files** containing forms and reports that a committee created online.

How files are shared depends on whether the community meets on a mailing list, on Usenet newsgroups, or on a Web-based bulletin board. Here are recommendations for rules that determine how members should share files.

Mailing Lists

Most e-mail programs can send files as attachments to e-mail messages, but this isn't the best way to share files. Some people's e-mail programs can't handle attachments, and some people may not want to receive large messages (which attachments produce) by e-mail. Instead, members can post a message to the list saying where the file is available: either on a Web page (at the Web site for the mailing list, the member's own site, or another site) or by request (members who want the file can write to the person privately to ask for the file to be sent as an attachment by return private e-mail). Ideally, files of interest to community members should be stored at or linked to from the community's Web site so that members who need the file later can find it.

The rules for many mailing lists forbid attaching files to list postings and include directions for sharing files over the Web or by private e-mail. If your list does allow files to be attached to list postings, you may want to include limits on file sizes, and you may want to require files to be compressed (usually as ZIP files, using a program like WinZip or ZipMagic).

Newsgroups

Many newsreader programs can also send files as attachments, but the same problems apply to newsgroup attachments as to mailing list attachments. Some newsgroups are specifically designed for sharing files—take a look at the hundreds of groups in the alt.binaries.* hierarchy of newsgroups. (Try alt.binaries.pictures.fractals if you want material suitable for family viewing.) Usenet newsgroups use a standard method of attaching files called *uuencoding*, and some newsreaders can decode them automatically. Figure 13-1 shows Netscape Newsgroups displaying a picture that was posted to a newsgroup.

However, most newsgroups are not intended for exchanging files. These newsgroups may institute rules against posting files, although unless the newsgroup is moderated, there's little way to enforce them.

IRC Channels

IRC participants can send each other files using DCC (and the `/dcc` send command). Cautious IRCers accept files only from people they know. There's no easy way to send a file to everyone on a channel. A preferred method is to post the file on a Web site and send a message containing the file's URL.

Web-based Message Boards

Most Web-based message boards don't allow files to be posted as part of a message. Instead, many message boards (especially online "clubs") provide

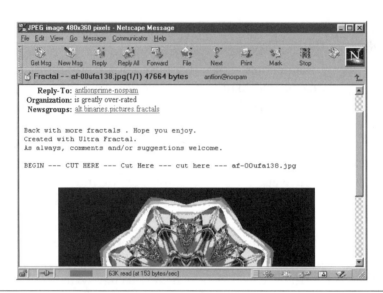

Figure 13-1: Newsgroup subscribers can post files to a newsgroup.

a separate Web page to which community members can upload files to share. There is usually a limit to the total size of all the files available on the files page.

Your Web-based community might want to have rules about what types of files can be uploaded to the shared file pages, and maximum file sizes.

Protection of Copyright

Whenever anyone writes anything (even e-mail), he automatically owns the copyright. (One exception to this rule is that if you are working for someone, your employer may own the copyright to material you write on the job.) See the section "No Copyrighted Material Without Permission" in Chapter 2 for the details of what text is copyrighted; see the "Copyright Issues" section in Chapter 15 for more information about copyright issues.

Your community should have a rule against posting copyrighted material without permission, or you may be liable for damages if a copyright-holder decides to sue. For example, your community might have the following rule:

> *Do not post copyrighted material, including e-mail from others, without the explicit permission of the copyright holder. An exception is made for quotes that are a small percentage of the whole; whose existence for free on the Internet wouldn't hurt the original work's sales; and that are posted in a context—that is, with preceding or following text by the poster that explains how the quote pertains to his/her thoughts on a subject.*

Commercial Announcements

In the early days of the Internet, commercial messages were forbidden because it was run by the U.S. military and various colleges and universities, all of which had no-commerce rules. But those days are long over, and the Internet—especially the Web—seems to have been taken over by companies running advertisements. Worse, the pricing structure of the Internet, in which sending a message to zillions of people is almost free, has given many advertisers the idea of posting unsolicited commercial messages (or *spam*) to mailing lists, newsgroups, and Web-based message boards. (We're sure that chat rooms will be next.) These ads are usually completely unrelated to the topic of the community and are frequently fraudulent ("MAKE MONEY FAST!").

Are any advertisements acceptable in an online community? The answer depends on the goals and style of the community. Some communities have firm rules against posting any kind of commercial announcement. Others allow single postings about a product that directly relates to the topic of the community. For example, a mailing list for computer book authors might allow a posting about voice-recognition systems that authors could use when writing books. When ads are allowed, they usually must be informational, with no hype ("THE BEST EVER!")

Personal Attacks, Rude Words, and Ethnic Slurs

It's hard to develop an open, trusting community if people are in danger of attack. And some mysterious force causes otherwise reasonable people to act like complete jerks online, posting messages with much harsher criticisms, jumping to much quicker conclusions, and making far more assumptions then they would in a face-to-face conversation.

As a result, most communities have rules about what people can say to and about other community members. For example, the UU-Community list at uua.org (an online "coffee hour" mailing list for Unitarian Universalists) has the following rules (see http://www.uua.org/lists/uu-community.html for the list's complete rules):

> *Members respond to ideas with ideas, not with personal denigration or insults. Comments on another member's personality or psychological state are only appropriate when the member being discussed is likely to welcome such comments. Discussions are free and open, friendly and fair. Arguments shall be tempered with compassion. A win-at-all-costs debating style is not appropriate.*

Communities may also have rules about what people can say about nonmembers. This rule has two purposes: to prevent ethnic slurs and other generally negative comments and to protect the community manager from accusations of libel for attacks on specific people. These rules are usually pretty loose—clearly, it's acceptable for someone to say something negative about a public figure ("Jesse Helms is a right-wing fanatic"), but you might want to prevent specific attacks on or accusations about private individuals ("I'm sure that Joe Blow is the one who burglarized the church last week").

Communities may also make rules against criticizing whole groups of people. For example, a community might have a rule like this:

Members may not post messages containing sexual implications, racial slurs, or any comment that offensively addresses someone's age, sexual orientation, religious or political beliefs, national origin, or disability.

Privacy

What can members do with the messages from the community? What can members post about themselves or about each other? Chapter 15 explores privacy issues in depth.

Deliberate Disruptions

The **Jargon File** (http://www.jargon.org/html/) defines Godwin's Law as follows:

"As a Usenet discussion grows longer, the probability of a comparison involving Nazis or Hitler approaches one." There is a tradition in many groups that, once this occurs, that thread is over, and whoever mentioned the Nazis has automatically lost whatever argument was in progress. Godwin's Law thus practically guarantees the existence of an upper bound on thread length in those groups. (http://www.jargon.org/html/entry/Godwin's-Law.html)

Unfortunately, as with any group of people, an online community can be disrupted by only one person. Certain behaviors (such as likening someone to a Nazi) are almost guaranteed to cause trouble. Here are some ways that people may disrupt your community and some ways you can respond.

Types of Disruptive Messages

There are at least six categories of deliberately disruptive messages: flooding, repetition, hijacking, backseat driving, trolling, and attacking the management.

Flooding

Flooding is posting lots of messages, to drown out other voices. The term comes from IRC, where one participant sends so many lines of text that everyone else's messages scroll up off the screen before you have time to read them. The messages may all be the same, or may differ—it's the sheer quantity that defines flooding.

Some communities have limits on the number of messages that members can post. List servers can limit the total number of postings per day on a mailing list or the number of postings from each member. For example, a list might be limited to 50 messages a day, with no more than 3 from each subscriber. (Most members don't post anything most days, so these limits work even for lists with over 100 members.) Usenet newsgroups don't have a mechanism for limiting postings, unless the newsgroup is moderated: The moderators can limit postings by choosing what to approve. Many IRC channels define flooding as sending a specified number of messages in a specified number of seconds (for example, more than five messages in five seconds). Some IRC channels have *bots* (programs) that automatically kick out participants who violate the flooding limit for the channel. Web-based message boards don't (as far as we know) have a limit on how many messages can be posted to the message board in total or by each member, but if flooding turns out to be a problem on message boards, we're sure that the capability will be added. Message board managers can usually delete postings, so they can eliminate messages that they feel constitute flooding.

Repetition

Sometimes community members bring up the same information over and over or raise the same objections over and over. It's not the same as flooding, in which you post dozens or hundreds of messages a day. A community member is guilty of repetition when she keeps bringing up the same information or opinion many times, and it can be over the course of weeks or months.

Repetition can be hard to define because the person who posts the repetitious messages always claims to be responding to questions or explaining the point in a different way. And it's hard to make a rule against it because people rarely post *exactly* the same message over and over.

Hijacking

Hijacking, or *hijacking a thread,* is changing the subject or introducing your pet topic into a series of messages that are about something else. The result is that people get sidetracked and that messages don't have anything to do with their subject lines.

For example, if you have a Pomeranian dog and are a member of a newsgroup about dogs, you would be guilty of hijacking if you posted questions about Pomeranians in response to messages about something else. If you respond to a message with the subject "Reactions to a new puppy" by asking about Pomeranian puppies, the thread would veer off into a discussion of Pomeranians while retaining the "Re: Reactions to a new puppy" subject line.

Done occasionally, changing the subject is a natural part of conversation, online or offline, but when a community member consistently changes the subject to her favorite subject, she is hijacking. Although there's no good way to make a rule against it, some communities ask posters to be careful to change the subject line of the message if they are changing the subject—for example, "Pomeranian puppies (was Re: Reactions to a new puppy)".

Backseat Driving

A member is *backseat driving* when she sends messages that try to correct the behavior of other community members. The manager is responsible for setting people straight, and if other people do so, too, then the community can see a flood of "Don't do that!" messages, which are usually slightly contradictory. It's better for the manager to send a *private* message to the person (see the section "Warning People," later in this chapter). For example, if someone posts an off-topic message, five responses of "That's off-topic!" just waste more of everyone's time.

Some communities have a rule about backseat driving, like this:

> *Leave management to the managers. Don't post messages that correct the behavior of other members. Instead, assume that the managers will send a*

You Made Your Point Already!

In one mailing list that frequently discusses social issues, one subscriber named Marvin persisted in bringing up his objection to civil rights for gays. "I'm not homophobic, but..." was the beginning of countless messages. After many months, the rest of the subscribers got tired of Marvin making the same points over and over. The list managers decided not to remove Marvin because it felt too much like censoring one point of view, but the subscribers to the list stopped reading his messages. Eventually, Marvin gave up and left the list.

private message to the perpetrator of the message, letting him know what he did wrong. If you don't think that the managers are on the job, send them a (friendly) private message about it.

Trolling

Trolling is posting provocative messages designed to start a flame war. Most communities develop certain subjects that people are tired of hearing about or about which they have agreed to disagree. (Gun control and abortion rights are two widespread subjects that many communities are tired of talking about, because people rarely change their minds about their stances on these topics.) A member is posting a *troll* if he brings up one of these subjects again or if he posts a message that is antithetical to the purpose and theme of the group (for example, posting to a midwives' community a message which said that only obstetricians should be allowed to attend births).

Some communities have rules that ban certain subjects or that require members to stick to certain subjects, as a way to cut down on trolling.

Attacking the Management

Every community should be open to discussion of its rules and management, but the managers or moderators are unlikely to continue working on behalf of the community if they are attacked for their work, especially if they are unpaid volunteers. Drawing the line between useful criticism

---

One-track Postings

In one community, a one-issue fanatic named Bert persisted in posting messages about the rights of children and bringing children's rights into every other discussion. A series of flame wars resulted, as people complained that Bert had hijacked their threads. Bert was punished (prevented from posting messages for a while), and everything settled down. Then a new member joined and innocently posted a message about children's rights. The community (including the managers) immediately assumed that the new person was Bert in disguise and reacted with suspicion and downright hostility to the unknowing new member. Many apologies from the community and its members probably never erased the initial impression that the new member got of the community!

and personal attack of the managers or moderators can be hard, but may be necessary.

A community has a rule that gives the managers or moderators the right to stop unnecessary criticism, like this:

> *Don't abuse, libel, defame, or malign the managers [or moderators] in public about the way they manage the community. Don't misrepresent the actions of the managers in public. Don't be abusive to the community managers in private e-mail to them. Any of these actions is cause for expulsion from the community, either summarily or after an initial warning, at the discretion of the managers.*

If the community is sponsored by an organization (for example, it's a support message board for a software program, and it's hosted by the software company), the managers are responsible to the organization for how the community is run. The rules should include a way for community members to ask the organization to review what the managers are doing.

"Cat: The Other White Meat"

The classic case of trolling occurred years ago on the Usenet newsgroup rec.pets.cats. A few people started posting messages about how to cook cats, which resulted in firestorms of messages from upset cat lovers in response, drowning out the normal traffic on the newsgroup. It took months for the group to recover.

Options for Dealing with Trouble

You can't make a rule against every disruptive message. Even if you could, unless your community is moderated (as described in the section "Running Moderated Communities," later in this chapter), people would post problematic messages anyway. You have several options when people cause problems in a community, including asking them privately to stop, posting messages in the community asking people to stop, preventing people from posting, and banning people.

How Problems Develop

One disgruntled, troubled, or immature member of a community can cause havoc, unless the community has a mechanism that lets the managers screen out disruptive messages (through list or newsgroup moderation or the deletion of messages from message boards). The usual sequence is this:

1. One person posts a disruptive message—an attack on another community member, an off-topic message, an advertisement, or some other type of message that is not allowed in the community.
2. Several other people post messages complaining about the original message.
3. Even more people post messages complaining about the complaints, citing (nonexistent) freedom-of-speech rights.
4. Several people post "Get me out of here!" messages, and other people complain that they should have known how to leave the community without posting a public message about it.
5. The community manager suggests that the responses to the disruptive message are even more disruptive than the original message and would everyone please just drop it.
6. The furor eventually dies down, but not before several people have left the community in disgust, usually not including the person who posted the original message.

If the same person keeps posting disruptive messages, you get the following additional steps:

1. The next time the original person posts, everyone's hackles are already up, and responses are more hostile than they would have been if someone else had said the same things.
2. Newcomers don't understand why everyone is so hostile to the original poster and leap to his defense. Some leave because they see the community as a hostile place.
3. Some old-timers post messages to let everyone know that they plan to delete all postings from the original person without reading them.
4. Other old-timers explain the history of the situation to the new folks, which helps the newcomers understand what's going on, but stirs up the issues again for everyone else.
5. Yet other old-timers get sick of the same thing happening again and again and leave.

Warning People

The first time someone breaks a rule (unless it's a flagrant, highly disruptive message), he may have done it out of ignorance. (A sage once said, "Before you suspect a plot, consider stupidity.") Consider these steps when responding to problems in your online community:

1. **Post a message to the community with a general explanation of the rule** that was broken, without mentioning the specific person or message that just broke the rule. Include a warning that people who persist in breaking rules will be asked to leave or will be prevented from posting to the list (mention the penalty your community uses).

2. **Send a private message to the person who posted the problem message**, with copies to the other community managers, if any. Tell the person what rule he broke, quoting the relevant message, and ask him to stop. You can include, if possible, a suggestion for fixing the problem. For a dispute between two people, you might direct them to continue it via private e-mail rather than in the community. For a message with abusive phrasing, require milder phrasing in the future. Ask the person to reply to the community manager(s) privately with questions or concerns, to avoid cluttering the community's messages.

3. **If the person persists in breaking the rule, follow through** with the penalty you mentioned in Step 1.

4. **Post a message to the community to announce when you have instituted a penalty.** This may be embarrassing for the rule breaker, but if you don't, she and other members may accuse you of being secretive. Be sure to quote the appropriate sections of the community rules so that people will understand why you took action.

Time-Outs

One penalty you can use if people persist in breaking community rules is to prevent them from posting messages for a specified period. For mailing lists, you can usually set the person to NOPOST, IGNORE, or some other setting that prevents her from posting (see Chapter 5 to find out how). For moderated mailing lists, newsgroups, and message boards, the moderators can reject postings from that person. IRC channels don't usually have a way for someone to be able to read messages on a channel while being prevented from sending messages. For unmoderated message boards, there is usually a way for the manager to delete a posting: This method requires vigilance because the person can post messages as fast as you can delete them. For unmoderated newsgroups, there's no way to prevent postings (except by writing a *cancelbot,* a program that cancels newsgroup postings automatically).

You might want to use time-outs of increasing lengths for people who keep breaking the rules. For example, you might enforce a one-week timeout for the first infraction, a one-month time-out the second time, and a six-month time-out for the third infraction. Some communities don't count infractions that occurred more than a year ago.

Banning People

If someone persists in breaking the rules and disrupting the community, the time may come to throw her out. Evicting someone from an online community, with the intention of keeping the person out for a specified period (or forever) is called *banning*.

If there's nothing to stop the person from rejoining the community, this penalty isn't very effective. For closed communities, the managers have to approve all new members, so the banned individual can't reenter directly. For open mailing lists, there may be a way to prevent someone from resubscribing (see Chapter 5 to find out how to tell ListProc to ignore requests from a specific address). The channel operators of an IRC channel can kick people off or ban them (so that they can't rejoin the channel). There's no way to prevent someone from reading a Usenet newsgroup, so banning someone from a Usenet newsgroup is meaningless. (Newsgroups that are run on private new servers, rather than as part of the worldwide Usenet system, can require passwords.) Message boards may have commands to prevent someone from joining.

Even if you prevent a person from rejoining using the same address, it's easy for him to get a free Hotmail or Mail.com address and rejoin using the new address and a fake name (unless your community requires more identification than just a name and e-mail address). The fake address is sometimes called a *sock puppet* and can be hard to detect—until the person starts posting. If a new member starts posting the same kind of problematic messages that a recently banned ex-member used to post, you might be suspicious. Of course, if the sock puppet *doesn't* post disruptive messages, it doesn't matter whether the banned member has rejoined your community—she's not causing trouble.

Moderating the Community During a Crisis

If a flame war or other bad situation breaks out in your community, the messages may fly thick and fast, compounding the problem as people share their understanding (or misunderstanding) of what's going on. In this case, you may want to turn on moderation so that each message has to be reviewed by a *moderator* (manager) before it is distributed to the community. See Chapters 5, 7, and 9 to find out how to configure a mailing list, newsgroup, or Web-based message board to be moderated, and then see the section "Running Moderated Communities," later in this chapter, for how best to approve and reject messages.

If you want to switch your community from unmoderated to moderated, be sure to post a message to say that you are doing so, so that no one feels that you are being sneaky. Mention who will be reviewing the messages (usually the community managers), why you have switched to moderation, how long you think it will last, and that you plan to switch the community back to an unmoderated community as soon as possible. Also mention that messages will appear on the community with some delays, depending on when the moderators check their messages.

Preventing Frequent Posters from Taking Over

Some members of online communities have lots to say, and post lots of messages. Some members respond to every question and make a comment about every post. These members may have lots of useful information to add to the community, or they may just have too much time on their hands. If quieter members see that a few people are sending most of the messages, they may be reluctant to post.

There are two approaches to someone who posts lots of messages:
- Assume that everyone has a Delete or down-arrow key on their keyboard and that members can skip messages that don't interest them.
- Reduce the number of messages from the most frequent posters, unless they are truly useful.

The approach you take depends on the nature of the community. If community members prefer a low-traffic list, you need to use the second method. You can send a private message to each member who posts way too many messages, asking him to give other members a chance to respond. If necessary, you may be able to institute a limit on the number of messages each member can post each day.

Encouraging Participation

This section contains tips for getting people to participate. However, don't expect to hear from every member. Most communities get active participation from no more than 10 percent of their members. But *lurking* (joining and not saying anything) isn't a bad thing—lurkers are listening and learning from the more experienced (or more vociferous) members.

Posting Introductions

If you get notified when new members join, send each person a private message telling her that you'd like to introduce her to the rest of the community and asking questions about her. For example, you might send a message like this:

I would like to personally welcome you to the Microsoft Access Programmers Community! I will introduce you to the rest of the community members, unless you'd prefer me not to. Can you provide me information that I can share with others:

Full name:
Job title:
Employer:
City and state/province:
Access project you're most proud of:
Access project you're working on now:
Anything else you think the community should know:

If you have questions about our community, please read the FAQ at <URL>, or feel free to write to me at <address>. Thanks and welcome,

Margy Levine Young, The Microsoft Access Programming Community Manager

When she replies with information, copy the information into a message to post to the community, with a friendly welcome at the beginning. Save these welcome messages, too, so that you can create affinity groups or referrals later.

Starting Threads
If the conversation lags or gets off-topic, it's no help to post messages complaining about the low traffic or irrelevant posts. Instead, post a message with a relevant topic that you think might spark a good discussion. You might want to post a message about a recent event relating to the community, asking for reactions.

Noticing Whether Someone Stops Posting
If a regular poster stops posting, consider writing to her to ask what's up. Make sure that she knows that you appreciate reading her messages.

Running Polls
Some Web-based clubs let the manager set up polls, to which community members are asked to respond when they visit the community's Web site. If you run a mailing list or newsgroup or your Web-based message board doesn't

include a way to create polls, you can run a poll yourself by posting the question in a message, asking a question, suggesting a limited number of responses, and asking people to reply to you *privately* by a specific date. Discourage (or delete) responses to the community if the responses contain just the person's response to the poll—otherwise, you'll get lots of messages containing only one-word answers to the poll questions. Of course, members are welcome to post comments, and extensive responses to the poll are welcome—and may spark interesting discussions. On the ending date of the poll, post the summary of the responses, and ask for comments.

Guiding And Encouraging Discussion

The most important way to encourage people to participate in an online community is to assure them that their ideas will be received thoughtfully, without harsh criticism, and with appreciation. Follow these tips for encouraging people to participate:

- Model the type of participation you'd like others to emulate. As the list manager, people will pay more attention to your messages than to others.
- Assume that members have good intentions when they post. Of course, there's the possibility that someone is up to no good, but this is rare. Instead, assume that you misunderstood and ask for clarification.
- If someone asks a question, make sure that it gets answered. If no one answers, you might want to post a follow-up that asks for more information about the question.
- Post a message with the goals and rules of the community regularly— once every one, three, or six months. Or post a message with the URL of the Web page containing the goals and rules.
- Be very clear when you post. Write as though the reader is not a native speaker of English and has just joined the community—you may well have a reader who fits that description!
- Encourage people to use descriptive subject lines, and to change the subject line when the subject of a post wanders from the subject of the message to which it is responding. For message boards, fix subject lines and move messages to the appropriate message board when needed.
- Use private e-mail to resolve problems rather than bring up conflicts within the community. It's usually easier to work out a conflict without an audience, and community members won't chime in.

- Discourage point-by-point refutation. Because of the way that e-mail programs and newsreaders let you quote the message to which you are responding, some people feel compelled to respond to each point in the original message, interleaving parts of the original message and the response. This method of responding tends to create messages that nitpick about the details of the original message rather than respond to the general idea of the original message. Conversation quickly centers on the areas of disagreement—which are frequently minor—while ignoring the parts of the original message on which people agree. As manager, you can post a message that summarizes the points made, especially the important points of agreement that got lost.

- Ask your community members to let you know what's working well and what's not working within the community. Use this feedback to adjust your style of management or the way the community is structured.

Running Moderated Communities

The ideal community would have an all-knowing, all-seeing, ever-patient moderator who would review each message within seconds of its posting, day or night, weekdays and weekends, and reject those that break the rules of the community, with an explanation to the sender about how to fix the problem. However, this solution can be hard to arrange. This section contains some more realistic ideas for moderating a community.

The specific instructions for how moderation works depend on the type of community and the system that runs it (see Chapters 5, 7, 9, and 11 for instructions). In moderated mailing lists and newsgroups, messages usually go by e-mail to one or more moderators, who send e-mail messages to approve (go ahead and distribute the message) or discard (throw away) the message. On a moderated IRC channel, participants can send private messages to the channel operator, who chooses which messages to send to the moderated channel. Web-based communities usually aren't moderated, but the managers can delete messages that have been posted.

If you moderate a community, be sure to do the following:
- Check your incoming messages often so that messages aren't held up for too long. Otherwise, people may post them again, and things get confusing. Or members may conclude that you are deliberately holding up their posts and get annoyed.
- Approve messages in the order in which they arrive, if possible. Members get justifiably upset if some people's messages appear faster

than others. However, this situation is inevitable if you moderate some members and not others, as described in the next section.

- When you reject a message, forward it back to the member with an explanation of what rules were broken and how the message could be fixed. For example, you might say, "This message consists of a story from *101 Inspirational Stories,* but you aren't the author of that book. Our newsgroup has a rule against posting copyrighted material without the permission of the author. If you want to post the story, you need to get permission from the author. Or you can post a reference to it—if it's on the Web, post a message containing the URL."

- If someone keeps breaking the same rule, be sure to let him know what the penalty will be if he doesn't stop.

Moderating Individual Members

Some communities have a facility for *individual moderation*—messages from specific members are directed to a moderator for approval, although messages from everyone else are distributed directly. Here are ways that individual moderation can be useful:

- When people join the community, you can moderate their messages for the first week or month, to make sure that they understand the rules of the community. Then remove them from the list of moderated members so that their messages are distributed directly.

- When people persist in breaking the rules, you can moderate their messages until they stop or for a set period.

- If a heated argument breaks out, you can moderate the participants to stop the argument from escalating into a flame war (see "Moderating the Community During a Crisis," earlier in this chapter).

In all cases, you've got to tell the people whom you are moderating. Community managers sometimes switch people to individual moderation without telling them, hoping to avoid an argument, but this strategy usually backfires in the end, when the manager ends up looking underhanded and sneaky.

Multiple Moderators

For an active community with lots of messages, moderation can be a time-consuming job. Unless members are willing to put up with silent periods over weekends and vacations, you need to check your messages at least daily, no matter where you are. For many people, these requirements prevent them from volunteering to moderate a community by themselves.

However, you can split the job of moderation among several people. If two or three people share the job of moderator, be sure to work out the following details so that all the moderators can apply the community's rules consistently:

- Make sure that you all understand the community rules. If you notice any gray areas, make some decisions among yourselves. If necessary, propose changes to the rules.
- Agree on a procedure for approving and rejecting messages. For example, you might agree to send copies of all approval and rejection messages to the other moderators.
- Write some boilerplate rejection messages to use for common rules infractions (one for use of abusive language, one for copyright violations, etc.). If all moderators use the same boilerplate messages, you'll be more consistent with the members.
- If known troublemakers are in your group, decide how you plan to deal with them. If one or more of the moderators has a rancorous history with a particular individual, that moderator might want to bow out of decisions about messages from that member.
- Agree to let each other know when you will be away or too busy to review messages so that the other moderators can fill in.

There are several methods by which multiple moderators can split up the job of moderating a community. One way is by day or week: Moderator 1 reviews messages posted on even days and Moderator 2 reviews those posted on odd days. Or Moderator 1 takes Monday to Wednesday noon, Moderator 2 takes Wednesday noon to Friday night, and Moderator 3 takes the weekend.

However, another way allows any moderator with a moment to spare to look at whatever messages are waiting to be reviewed. Here's how it works:

1. Create one e-mail address for use by all the moderators. You can create a **Hotmail** (http://www.hotmail.com/), **Yahoo Mail** (http://mail.yahoo.com/), or **Mail.com** (http://www.mail.com/) mailbox, which you have to check by using the Web. Better yet, see whether you can get your ISP to give you a POP mailbox—many ISPs will provide multiple e-mail mailboxes with each Internet account. The advantage of a POP mailbox is that you may be able to check it using your regular e-mail program. (Check your e-mail program's manual to find out how to configure it to check multiple POP mailboxes.)
2. Give the address and password of this mailbox to each moderator so that all the moderators can read messages sent to the moderator mailbox.

3. Configure your community so that messages to be reviewed are sent to the moderator mailbox, not to individual moderators.

4. When a member posts a message, the next moderator to check the moderator mailbox reads the message, decides whether to approve or reject the message, sends the appropriate messages to approve or reject, and deletes the message.

This method lets any number of moderators share the job of moderation, without worrying about schedules. Messages wait for approval until any moderator decides to check the messages.

Robo-moderation

Robo-moderation is moderation using a program rather than having human moderators review each post. The first auto-moderated Usenet newsgroup was soc.religion.unitarian-univ, a general discussion group for Unitarian Universalists. The "robo-moderator" received all messages posted to the group, checked each message against a list of known spams and chain letters, and approved all other messages.

Most communities don't have the option of robo-moderation. No mailing-list packages we know of have robo-moderation features built in, and Usenet moderation software has always been either home brewed or informally passed around in the small community of Usenet moderators. (The total number of moderated groups is only in the hundreds.)

If a server is available and you have some programming skill, it's not hard to write simple robo-moderation software; one of the authors of this book wrote the original version of the soc.religion.unitarian-univ robot in under a day. As the Internet continues to grow and mailing lists become ever more popular in nontechnical circles, we expect to see more robo-moderation features appear in popular list-management packages.

Chapter Fourteen
Making Money with Your Community

No one that we know of makes money directly off their online communities—no one charges people to participate in communities. This situation may change as the Internet matures and the everything-for-free expectation that people have of the Internet wanes.

Instead, there are a few ways you can make money indirectly:

- Sell banner ads on Web pages.
- Sell advertisements on mailing list messages.
- Sell your membership list.
- Sell other information.
- Sell things via affiliate programs.

Of course, online communities have lots of indirect benefits, which is why most people and organizations choose to run them. These nonmonetary benefits include

- Attracting people to your Web site and inducing them to return regularly (which increases the hit count, and ad revenues, for your whole site)
- Providing information to your customers (so that they are more likely to buy from you)
- Demonstrating an interest in and concern for your customers or other constituency (which provides good public relations)
- Finding out more about what your customers want (so that you can design your products more effectively)
- Providing a group on which to test-market messages and product designs (for example, offering community members new products for

free or for a discount in return for valuable feedback)

If your community is hosted at eGroups, Topica, Yahoo Clubs, or another commercial online community site, the host site gets to make money off your community, too. These sites display ads on the Web pages for your community (see Figure 14-1) and may append ads to e-mail messages sent to community members. Some of these sites also send advertising messages to all registered members of their site, including your community members. If you don't want another organization to make money off your community, don't host it at one of these sites.

This chapter explores direct and indirect ways of profiting from your online community.

Selling Banner Advertising

Banner ads are advertisements that appear on Web sites. When someone clicks the ad, he goes

> **Drawbacks of Making Money from Your Community**
>
> *If community members perceive that the purpose of the community is to make money for its managers, they are less likely to participate wholeheartedly and are unlikely to volunteer their time or information. Be sure that any moneymaking you do online doesn't detract from the atmosphere of the community.*

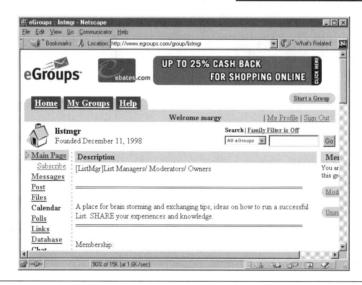

Figure 14-1: eGroups and other "club" sites display their own ads on your community's Web site.

to the advertisers' Web site. Many Web sites display banner ads, usually at the top of the Web page. If your community's Web site gets lots of hits, you may be able to sell the space at the top of the community's Web pages to advertisers. Standard-size banner ads are 468 pixels wide and 60 pixels high. You can sell a banner ad at the top of your community's home page or on each page of your Web site.

Advertisers need to know how many hits your pages get. Your Web hosting company should be able to provide you with Web logs that list the hits (usually in far more detail than you want to know). With any luck, your hosting company will be able to do the data reduction to extract the interesting numbers from the raw data, like visits per page and number of unique visitors.

Prices for ads are quoted in *CPM* (*cost per m*, where *m* is the old-fashioned abbreviation for 1,000), or the cost for each thousand *impressions*, or page views. Ad prices run from a CPM of $5 to more than $100. The more targeted the people visiting the page, the more you can charge. Some Web sites charge advertisers only when someone actually clicks on the ad—a *clickthrough*. Advertisers may pay from 12 to 25 cents per clickthrough. These rates are much higher because, for many banner ads, as few as 1 percent of ad viewers click the ad.

Don't expect to make vast amounts of money unless your Web site has vast numbers of hits. For example, if you decide to charge $30 CPM and your community's home page gets 10,000 hits per month, you'll make $30 x 10 = $300 per month. You can also charge a one-time setup fee for putting the ad on your site.

To sell banner ads on your site, contact an ad agency that specializes in banner ads. Some agencies help sell your ad space by bundling your Web site with other, similar sites so that even if your site gets a relatively small number of hits, advertisers may still be interested. Here are a few banner ad agencies:

247 Media
   http://www.247media.com/
Ad-Up
   http://www.ad-up.com/
AdCentral (searchable database of Web sites that accept ads; requires at least 1,000 hits per day)
   http://www.adcentral.com/
BurstMedia (focuses on specialty Web sites)
   http://www.burstmedia.com/

DoubleClick (the largest banner ad agency; beware that it may track and sell the Web site viewing habits of visitors to your site)
http://www.doubleclick.com/

Flycast Communications (requires at least 20,000 hits per month)
http://www.flycast.com/

ValueClick (charges only for clickthroughs)
http://valueclick.com/

You can find more agencies by starting at **Yahoo** (http://www.yahoo.com/) and choosing Business and Economy, Business to Business, Marketing and Advertising, Internet, and Advertising.

Selling Mailing List Ads

If you run a mailing list or e-mail a newsletter to your community's members, you can sell ads to appear in the e-mail messages. Including ads in messages posted to a discussion mailing list is rarely done because the ads may look as though they come from the original poster rather than from the mailing list, and annoy participants. But ads are frequently placed in newsletter-type messages sent to your community's members or your mailing list's subscribers.

Because your list consists of people who have chosen to subscribe, it is an *opt-in* list (people opt to join). Mailing list ads for opt-in lists usually cost in the range of $2 CPM to $8 CPM (cost per thousand messages sent). You accept an ad in the form of about eight lines of text (you can set the size limit for your list) and insert it into the message you are e-mailing to your members. Some lists accept one ad to appear near the beginning of the list and another to appear at the end (for a lower cost).

Be sure that your members can tell the ads from the content of your message—many newsletters put a row of dashes or asterisks before and after each ad, to separate them from the newsletter content.

To sell ads in a newsletter to your community's members, get listed at one of these sites:

EzineAdvertising.com (a searchable database of newsletters that accept advertising; requires at least 1,000 subscribers; shown in Figure 14-2)
http://ezineadvertising.com/

ListCity Ad Exchange Database
http://www.List-City.com/adexdb.html
You can get more information about selling ads in e-mail newsletters at List-Advertising.com (http://List-Advertising.com/).

Figure 14-2: A few Web sites help advertisers find e-mail mailing lists on specific topics.

Selling Your Membership List

Giving your membership list to outsiders in any form is probably a bad idea. After another person or organization has the list of your community's members, you have little or no control over what he will do with it. The outsider may spam your members or otherwise bombard them with ads. Or he may form a competing online community, contacting your members directly to offer them reasons to switch from your community to his. Release community members' names and addresses only if your agreement with your members allows it—otherwise, your members will be justifiably angry. Some countries have privacy policies that require you to inform members that you are selling their names, so if you have members from outside the United States, you need to check into international privacy laws to protect yourself.

If you do let an outside group get access to your membership list, be sure that you *salt* it—that is, include a few fake names and addresses that go to you. Choose names and addresses that look like regular members so that if the outside group decides to conceal its contact with the community from you by removing your name from the list, these fake names will remain on the list. You can create Hotmail or Yahoo Mail accounts for this purpose (just remember to check them from time to time).

Selling Other Information

You may be able to make money off your community in other, less intrusive ways. One method is to offer the use of your community for market research. For example, if you have a community of parents, you could offer to run polls on specific products or services and report the results back to the company commissioning the poll. The advantage of this type of sale is that you don't bombard your members with ads and you don't compromise their privacy: The only information you sell is aggregated for all your members.

Selling Things via Affiliate Programs

Many Web-based stores have *affiliate programs*, which provide you with a small commission if people buy their merchandise as a result of clicking a link from your Web site. You include specially coded links on your site so that the affiliate program site can tell that the visitors came from your site. The best-known Web-based affiliate program is **Amazon.com** (http://www.amazon.com/), which offers from 5 percent to 15 percent of its revenue from books, videos, and other products that Amazon.com offers. Some ad-based Web sites, including many search engines, pay a small commission to affiliates for anyone who clicks through. Joining an affiliate program is usually free (we wouldn't join any that aren't), and you can do it by filling out a form on the Web.

To use an affiliate program, follow these steps:

1. Choose a type of product your members are likely to be interested in. For example, if you run a community for accountants, your members would probably be interested in books, accounting software, and accounting supplies.

2. Find a Web-based store that sells these materials and that offers an affiliate program.

3. Sign up as an affiliate and find out how to create coded links to the store.

4. Add the links to your community's Web site. You might want to set up a Web page that lists items that would be of interest to your members, with reviews and recommendations from you or other members.

Here are a few Web-based stores that have affiliate programs:

Amazon.com (books, videos, and other items)
   http://www.amazon.com/
Barnes & Noble (books)
   http://www.bn.com/

Carprices.com (new and used cars)
   http://www.carprices.com/
Google (search engine)
   http://www.google.com/
Hooked on Phonics (learn-to-read materials for children)
   http://www.hop.com/
Priceline (discount groceries, travel, and other products)
   http://www.priceline.com/

For more information about affiliate programs, and more sites that offer them, try these Web sites, which contain searchable databases or directories of affiliate programs:

CashPile
   http://www.cashpile.com/
ClicksLink.com
   http://www.clickslink.com/
WebmasterCash.Net
   http://wmcash.bizland.com/frames.html
Webmaster-Programs Affiliate Programs Guide for Webmasters
   http://www.webmaster-programs.com/

Chapter Fifteen
Privacy, Spam, and Other Legal and Practical Issues

As the Internet has grown from an academic and research network into part of mainstream life, it's evolved from a club of reasonably well-mannered nerds into a set of people not very different from the ones you meet in day-to-day life. In this chapter, we deal with some issues that come up where the Internet meets real life.

THE LARGE-PRINT DISCLAIMER: Much of this chapter discusses legal issues. Although we have studied the laws that relate to online issues, we are not lawyers (perish forbid), and this chapter does not constitute legal advice. Consult a knowledgeable lawyer if you need legal advice. When consulting your lawyer, keep in mind that few lawyers have much experience with online issues, many laws that relate to online issues are new and unfamiliar, and few legal decisions have been made, which means that there is little case law to elucidate ambiguous situations. (If this makes the Internet sound like the Wild West of the legal world, you understood this paragraph.)

Preserving Privacy and Creating a Privacy Policy

One of the less pleasant aspects of the Internet is that it is the most effective technology ever invented for vacuuming up personal information and compiling profiles or dossiers about people. As a community manager, you have two related concerns: Ensure that the information you collect is collected in a responsible way, and minimize the chance that others can deliberately or inadvertently collect information about your members.

Your Community's Privacy Policy

Every Web site needs a privacy policy, and it's not a bad idea for mailing lists to have them, too. (Public newsgroups and IRC channels don't have subscriptions, so a privacy policy isn't needed.) The privacy policy needn't be long or complex, but should describe what information you collect and what you do with it. If you run a mailing list, you have the e-mail address of each of your subscribers and probably also their names. If you keep an archive of messages, you have in effect a dossier of each person's contributions to the list. If your list is hosted at a Web site like eGroups, the hosting site probably collects user information of its own. Web sites collect a certain amount of information automatically, notably the IP address from which each request is made and the kind of browser in use. (Contrary to rumor, Web sites do *not* collect the e-mail addresses of their visitors.)

None of this information collection is inherently sinister, although people are often surprised at how complete a picture of themselves can be gleaned from their online messages. (The authors have typed their names into the **Google** search engine, at http://www.google.com/, and quickly found messages they sent to mailing lists ten years ago.) It's useful, however, to make clear to your community members what is going to happen to the information they provide.

A typical privacy policy for a noncommercial list might say:

> **Personal Information That Communities Often Collect**
>
> Name
> E-mail address
> IP address (numeric address by which the member connects to the Internet)
> Browser used
> Nickname or handle
> Street address
> Phone number
> Messages posted by the member
> Files posted by the member

- E-mail addresses are collected only for the purpose of redistributing messages to the list and will not be given or sold to third parties.

- Messages to the list are sent to its subscribers, who may or may not forward them to third parties.

- If you archive the list, note who can get access to the archive.

Protecting Your Members' Information

Different communities need different degrees of privacy. At one extreme, the comp.compilers newsgroup is totally public—it's listed in many directories, anyone can subscribe, anyone can contribute messages that are subject to the moderation rules, and anyone can do anything with the messages, including put them in permanent public archives. At the other end is a mailing list for people teaching classes using a teen sexuality curriculum, where the list isn't advertised anywhere except to the teachers involved, one has to apply to the list manager to be admitted, members are expected to keep all messages private and not to forward them to third parties, and the list isn't archived anywhere. Most online communities fall somewhere between these two extremes, but it's important to think ahead of time just how private you want your community to be.

For mailing lists, Web-based message boards, Web-based chat, newsgroups on private news servers, and closed IRC channels, you can control who can send and receive messages. You should therefore consider ways to protect the privacy of your members. For public newsgroups, anyone on the Internet can read and post messages, so your options are limited.

The first question to ask on a mailing list (or Web-based community or closed IRC channel) is who can subscribe. Most lists are open to the public, with anyone permitted to subscribe, although many require application to and manual approval by the list owner. There are plenty of reasons to restrict a list this way: The list owner might want to have a private conversation among members of an organization, or a list about a particular medical condition might want to limit membership to people with that condition or members of their immediate families.

Another question is how private the correspondence on the mailing list is. On a typical public list, there's little reason to discourage members from forwarding messages from the list to their friends because the friends could have subscribed themselves if they wanted. On a private list, the best policy usually is to allow no forwarding outside the list without the permission of the author of the message. This policy may seem needlessly draconian, but any other rule means that each member has to interpret the forwarding policy, with predictably unfortunate results when two interpretations don't agree. In practice, when it's appropriate to forward messages to someone, that someone often can be invited onto the list.

Many communities of all types have archives of the messages that were posted to the community, and you need a policy for archive access. At one extreme, the archives for the comp.compilers newsgroup are available to anyone and are organized so that search engines can index every message. At the other extreme, we keep archives for some private lists on Web pages known only to list members and with no links to the outside. (We could go so far as to protect them with passwords, but that hasn't been necessary.) The archives for the soc.religion.unitarian-univ newsgroup are in between, with the archive's home pages visible to the public and in search engines but individual messages not in search engines and visible only by searching from the archive's home page. (The URLs for individual messages contain a question mark, which keeps out search engines.) This system makes archives available to the public, but doesn't expose individual messages out of context in search engines.

Depending on how sensitive the messages posted to a community are, you may deliberately want not to archive them. Members may not feel comfortable sharing personal information or sending controversial messages if they know that messages will be stored for years to come. If that's the case, you also need a policy about individual members keeping copies of messages, although such policies are hard to enforce because mail programs generally keep all messages unless the recipient specifically deletes them.

Anonymous Members

Ascertaining the identity of the members of any online community is often hard and frequently unreliable, for many reasons. Even under the best of circumstances, one's e-mail address often bears no resemblance to one's name, particularly on AOL, where all the good addresses were taken five years ago. People can sign up for free e-mail accounts at a moment's notice at Hotmail and its competitors, and many ISPs let you add and delete mailbox names on demand. A few sites offer anonymizing mail servers that make it possible to send mail with little chance of its origin being discovered. Some such systems offer a back channel, which makes it possible to send responses back to the originator of the message.

Web-based systems generally make no attempt to validate any information that members provide, so there's no real information about their identities at all other than the IP address of their Web browsers. Unless a Web-based system ties registrations to a confirmed e-mail address, it's essentially an anonymous system.

Even when people keep the same e-mail address for a long time, sometimes they create a virtual persona that is separate from their real-world names. For example, the head of the abuse department at RCN, a large ISP, is universally known online as Afterburner.

An online community should have some policy about anonymous postings. The most common policy on mailing lists is to require that people have a working e-mail address (confirmed by sending to that address a sign-up acknowledgment to which the member must respond) and using that address on all their messages. In some communities, notably Usenet newsgroups, it's possible to use a completely fake address and many people do, to either prevent getting their addresses collected by spammers or avoid accountability for what they say. In others, the community owners can make more or less diligent efforts to confirm the identity of members, by calling them on the phone, sending paper letters, or even meeting them in person. (This last method can be practical for lists where the membership is supposed to be in a single geographic place, anyway.)

In communities that don't generally permit anonymous messages, sometimes an unusual circumstance merits anonymity. We draw a distinction between *anonymous* and *anonymized* messages. In the former case, nobody knows who the author is; in the latter case, the community manager or other intermediary knows but strips off identifying information before passing along the message. In most cases, we believe that anonymized messages are more appropriate than anonymous ones. Anonymous speech on the Internet provokes a great deal of heated debate, with frequent references to the Federalist Papers or the Pentagon Papers; anonymized speech, however, seems to us closest to what those two documents describe; pure anonymous speech is more akin to scribbling on the wall of a public restroom.

The "Ephemeral Message" Issue

Some people believe that messages to mailing lists, Usenet newsgroups, IRC channels, and Web-based message boards are ephemeral—that is, they will or at least should disappear within a few days, never to be seen again. That's not the case and never has been. Usenet newsgroups have been archived since its earliest days. UUNET, an ISP that originated as a hub for distributing Usenet messages, provided Usenet feeds on magnetic tape to many organizations, some because it was then cheaper to mail a tape than to make international phone calls and some (including the FBI) because they didn't want dial-up phone connections to their internal systems. Those magnetic tapes are presumably still around.

Unless the members of an online community of any type have all specifically agreed to delete all messages that arrive from the community after reading them, you should assume that every message may be archived somewhere. Even with this type of agreement, the chances of a messages' being archived accidentally because of system backups or forwarding to a third party are still substantial.

Avoiding and Dealing with Spam

Any collection of Internet users has the potential to attract spammers. Online community owners have two related issues: Dealing with spam that comes into the community and keeping the list of members from being stolen for use as a spammer's prospect list.

Communities that require subscription (like mailing lists and many Web-based message boards) before accepting messages are largely immune to spam because most spammers are too lazy to join a community before spamming it. Also, communities that use confirmation require a working e-mail address, and most spam is sent with faked identifying info, including a fake return address, making confirmation impossible. The mailing lists we run get their share of spam, but the spam is diverted to the list manager as a nonmember message, where the manager can send off a complaint or discard the message and the subscribers never see it.

A more annoying but less common problem is the spammer who joins a community. Spammers fall into two categories. One is the cynical spammer who's figured out that only members can send messages to the community, so he joins and sends spam to it. This type is relatively rare. Assuming that your community re-quires confirmation, the address from which the spammer joined is known to be his real address, making it easy to identify his ISP and get his access canceled (see the **Network Abuse Clearinghouse**, at http://www.abuse.net/, for instructions). The other category is the spammer who doesn't think that she's a spammer, sure that whatever she's hawking is something the list's members all need. This type most commonly consists of religious spammers, either proselytizers who believe that anyone anywhere is a candidate for conversion or else who don't understand that there are lots of different religions and that, for example, a group of Buddhists isn't likely to be interested in Bibles. This second category can be more disruptive because the spammer generally doesn't understand why she's unwelcome, which can lead to arguments about whether to eject her. Well-written community rules can be very helpful here because persistent off-topic messages are generally grounds for ejection in any community.

If you do have to eject a spammer, it's generally useful to post a short note saying what you did and why and inviting comments in personal e-mail, not on the list. (See Chapter 13 for how to write and enforce rules for your community.)

Spammers are always looking for new target addresses, and the member lists of legitimate communities are particularly tempting because the addresses of members are all known to be valid addresses of people who read their e-mail. Most mailing-list-management software has commands like who to mail back the list of members to anyone who requests it. In the mid-1990s, spammers started systematically harvesting mailing list subscription lists, at which point most list system administrators disabled those commands or at least restricted them so that only the list owner could use them. In practice, the main use for the who command is to help people unsubscribe from a list when they have forgotten what address they used to subscribe. That situation is rare enough that it's reasonable for the list owner to intervene, so we recommend that only the list owner can see who's on the list.

A really nasty spammer could subscribe to a list, send nothing, and then harvest the addresses of everyone who posts to the list as the mail goes by. Not much can be done about that situation other than manual verification of people who want to join, as just mentioned, a process that is quite labor intensive.

Copyright Issues

The copyright status of material contributed to online forums is ambiguous and potentially troublesome. Under the Berne Convention, an international treaty that the United States and nearly every other country in the developed world have ratified, all written material is "born copyrighted" by its author. Copyright lasts for a long time; in the United States, everything written since 1923 is with few exceptions still in copyright. Furthermore, in forums where an editor or moderator manually chooses the material to include, the editor can claim a "compilation copyright" on the collected work in addition to authors' copyrights on individual items.

Copyright gives the owner the right to control who can make copies of protected material and under what terms. Despite lots of wishful thinking to the contrary, material on the Internet is subject to the same copyright rules as material in any other medium. When a member sends in a message to a mailing list or other type of online community, she has pretty clearly granted a license to make copies of the message to send out to members of the community, but it's not at all clear what other rights that implicit license has granted. Can community members send copies to third parties? Can the message be saved in the community manager's archive or in other archives? Can someone quote the message in a magazine or book? Can someone collect a bunch of messages and turn them into a book? The only honest answer to these questions is "nobody knows" because copyright law doesn't address them directly and there have been almost no court cases about online material, so there are few legal precedents to follow. Some people put notices on their messages saying "permission granted to copy not for profit" or "permission granted to make copies of this message except by Microsoft" (or whoever else they're mad at). Are such notices enforceable? Again, nobody knows because there's no case law yet.

In practice, unless the copyright owner has registered the material in the U.S. Copyright Office (or the equivalent in other countries), the only legal relief available is to tell people making infringing copies to stop and to sue for actual economic damages, which are likely to be insignificant for most messages to online communities.

Using Material from Third Parties

One area that can definitely cause problems is the unauthorized use of material by third parties, such as posting articles from newspapers and magazines. The copyright owners feel quite reasonably that their material is valuable (if it weren't, nobody would buy their newspapers and magazines) and they have to be vigilant in policing unauthorized copying. As a result, we recommend that online communities should have a policy forbidding the reposting of third parties' material without permission. In most cases, permission is surprisingly easy to get. If you want to repost an e-mail message, just ask the author of the message. For material to other media, often a phone call to a newspaper or magazine is all you need to get permission to repost an article to your community.

Music, pictures, and video are all copyrighted, and the owners generally enforce their copyrights very fiercely. The copyrights are quite comprehensive. With music, for example, the words and music to songs are copyrighted, and performances of those songs are copyrighted as well. Every picture and piece of clip art you'll find on the Web is copyrighted as well. A discussion of the laws and conventions for multimedia copyright is way beyond the scope of this book, other than to remind you not to reuse them without permission.

Fair Use

One of the most misunderstood aspects of copyright is that of fair use. The law has always carved out a fair use exception to copyright protection, but the definition of fair use is deliberately vague and it is left up to courts to decide in individual cases what is fair use and what isn't. The copyright law directs courts to weigh four factors in deciding what is fair use:

(1) the purpose and character of the use, including whether such use is of a commercial nature or is for nonprofit educational purposes;

(2) the nature of the copyrighted work;

(3) the amount and substantiality of the portion used in relation to the copyrighted work as a whole; and

(4) the effect of the use upon the potential market for or value of the copyrighted work.

None of the four factors is by itself a guarantee that a particular use is fair use. For example, quoting a single sentence from a book would usually seem to be fair use, but there is a case where a court found that it wasn't, where a sentence from a medical text was quoted without permission in a tobacco advertisement.

We're not going to go so far as to say never quote anything, although we do suggest that you be conservative in what you quote and don't believe anyone who says, "My list is nonprofit, so anything we quote is fair use"—because it's not.

Provider Liability

If you operate a Web server, you should be familiar with the part of the Digital Millennium Copyright Act related to "Limitations on liability relating to material online," section 512 of Title 17 of the U.S. Code. (Because of a numbering error, two sections are numbered 512; this is the first one.) The act provides a good-faith escape for server operators whose users put on the server any material that infringes a third party's copyright. The Web server operator has to file contact information with the copyright office that copyright owners can notify them if they believe that they find infringing material on the server. (For details, see the **U.S. Library of Congress Site**, at http://www.loc.gov/. Click Copyright Office. The form is one page, and the fee is nominal.) The infringement notice has to provide specific information, including a clear description of what material is being infringed and where on the Web site the infringing copy is located. If the server owner promptly removes the material, the operator is immune to infringement suits. If the person who put the material on the server disagrees that it was infringing, there are rules for whether it can be put back and who sues whom, but in practice Web server operators always remove the material when they receive an infringement notice with the necessary items, and that's that.

Making a Copyright Policy for a Forum

Every forum should have a specific copyright policy appropriate to the forum. It should state at least what rights the forum owner requires contributors to grant, what restrictions are acceptable, and what rights the forum owner claims. The policy for the comp.compilers newsgroup is at one end of the spectrum. It requires that contributors permit unlimited reproduction of their material in any form and disclaims any compilation copyright on the collected material. (Now and then a message shows up with a restrictive copyright notice, and the moderator sends it back asking whether the author will remove the restrictions. If not, it doesn't get posted.) At the other end, some edited forums consider themselves to be newsletters, with the owner claiming a copyright on the material and not permitting reproduction beyond copies sent to members. Either of these or anything in between is reasonable, but it's important to know up front what the rules are to avoid uncomfortable and potentially expensive arguments later.

Libel, Harassment, and Responsibility for Online Material

Online discourse on the Internet has always been rough and tumble, but sometimes it gets to the point where one of the parties involved takes legal action for libel. (*Libel* is written defamation, and *slander* is oral defamation, so material on the Internet generally would lead to libel rather than slander charges.) With one major exception we discuss later in this section, the rules about libel online are no different from what they are anywhere else. In the United States, true statements are not libelous no matter how unflattering they are, but untrue and disparaging statements can be libelous regardless of where and how they're written.

Online fights also occasionally spill over into the real world and lead to stalking and harassment. One of the most extreme and best known cases involved aspiring writer Jayne Hitchcock and the phony Woodside Literary Agency, which claimed that it would help get manuscripts published if writers would pay "reading fees" and the like. Woodside sent out lots of spam to the Usenet misc.writing newsgroup. Hitchcock contacted the agency, found its claims dubious, started asking other people on Usenet newsgroups about it, and generally exposed the scheme. In retaliation, Woodside's owner mail-bombed her, sent out fake porn spam with Hitchcock's home phone number, and made telephone death threats. Hitchcock sued, at great expense, to get the agency to stop harassing her. The New York Attorney General shut Woodside down, and, the last we heard, Woodside's owners were in jail awaiting trial for mail fraud. See the **Abuse of Usenet: Cyberstalked** site, at http://members.tripod.com/~cyberstalked/, for info on the Hitchcock case and the **Women Hating Online Abuse (WHOA)** site, at http://www.haltabuse.org/, for info on the organization that Hitchcock founded to fight cyberstalking.

Other cases have involved less clear but still troubling material, such as a person who published sexually explicit stories using the names of real people with whom he was acquainted. There's nothing special about the fact that it was on the Internet except perhaps the speed with which material can be distributed.

Making a Community Policy about Libelous or Harassing Speech

There's no easy way to draw a line about what's appropriate for an online forum versus what's libelous, harassing, or otherwise actionable. We see threats to sue all the time. Somewhat over 99 percent of the threats never lead to anything, so they don't count, but the few that do materialize can be messy and expensive.

Some basic rules of politeness can go a long way to avoiding legal problems. In the communities we manage, we invariably have a rule against personal attacks. Disagreeing with someone's viewpoint or someone's statements is fine, but calling someone names isn't. Good-natured flames may or may not be appropriate, depending on how formal the structure of the forum is and how well the participants know each other.

Forum Owner Responsibility

One way that online communities are different from those in other places is that a specific U.S. federal law appears to make the forum owner or operator immune to suits for material written by others. Two lawsuits in the 1990s set the background for community owner liability: *Cubby v. CompuServe* in 1991 and *Stratton Oakmont v. Prodigy Services Co.* in 1995. In both cases, a subscriber to the service posted negative remarks about the plaintiff in the case, who then sued the service for libel, claiming that the service was responsible for the contents of its forums. In the CompuServe case, the court found for CompuServe because it made little attempt to monitor its forums. In the Prodigy case, however, the court found against Prodigy because it touted its monitored forums in which every message was screened.

This perverse result, that it's safer for the community manager to let people say anything than to try to enforce standards, led the Congress to add to the Communication Decency Act of 1996 (CDA) a sentence saying:

> ***Treatment of publisher or speaker:*** *No provider or user of an interactive computer service shall be treated as the publisher or speaker of any information provided by another information content provider.*

This paragraph appears in title 47, section 230 of the U.S. Code. It goes on to say that providers also aren't liable for good-faith attempts to block porn and other offensive material but that this doesn't affect copyright liability. (Part of the CDA was found unconstitutional, but not this part.) This section was specifically added to reverse the Stratton Oakmont decision and encourage providers to create monitored or filtered forums. The section that contains it is generally about porn blocking, although the language applies equally to any kind of material.

Although this law hasn't yet been tested in court, it is presumably valid and offers some defense against being sued for what someone else said in your community, albeit not against the cost of defending such a suit, even if you win.

Children's Issues

The Children's Online Privacy Protection Act of 1998 (COPPA) has specific and somewhat onerous requirements for any forums that knowingly collect information from children under 13. Although the act is quite new, having only gone into effect in April 2000, joining a mailing list and registering for a Web-based club are both covered. If your community does not appeal to children and you don't ask for the age of people who join (or other information that would reveal children's ages), it's probably not covered by the act, but it's worth being aware of COPPA anyway. Some important provisions are summarized here. The act was written with Web sites primarily in mind, so the summary refers to sites, even though other kinds of online forums are also covered:

Privacy policy. The site must have its privacy policy prominently posted. (This is a good idea anyway, of course.)

Verifiable parental consent. Before a child can join, you must have verifiable consent from the child's parent. The exact definition of verifiable is still up in the air, but would include mailing a letter to the parent or calling the parent on the phone. From 2000 to 2002, a "sliding scale" rule permits e-mail verification if the site doesn't collect much information and doesn't disclose it to third parties.

Third Party Opt-Out. If the site discloses information to third parties, a parent can opt out (choose not to include) his child.

The **Federal Trade Commission** enforces COPPA and has an online press release, at http://www.ftc.gov/opa/1999/9910/childfinal.htm, with links to its full rules and other resources.

Chapter Sixteen
Managing Groups of Communities

If you are part of an organization—a company, club, church, nonprofit, or other type of organization—you may need to run not just one online community but rather a group of them. This chapter discusses the concerns of the *site manager*, the person in charge of a group of communities hosted by an organization.

How Organizations Can Use Online Communities

Many types of organizations find online communities to be a valuable and cost-effective way of communicating:

Companies can set up communities for prospective customers (managed by the marketing department and offering product information), existing customers (managed by the technical support department and offering answers to technical questions), distributors (managed by the sales department and offering information about discounts, sales incentives, and co-op advertising), and sales representatives (managed by the sales department and offering information about upcoming sales meetings, product availability, and successful sales techniques).

Nonprofit organizations can set up communities for donors (managed by the fundraising department and offering information about the good works the nonprofit performs), staff (managed by staffers and offering administrative announcements and online committee meetings), and volunteers (managed by the volunteer coordinator and offering information about volunteer opportunities).

Educational and research institutions can set up an online community for each class, allowing discussion among class members and teachers to continue between meetings. Research groups can use communities to distribute preliminary research results, reminders of meetings and deadlines, and other information.

Churches, synagogues, and temples can set up communities for members (for general conversation and announcements and a calendar of events) and for each major committee (offering ongoing discussion of the work of the committee, along with shared files and searchable archives of minutes). Chapter 21 describes how the Unitarian Universalist Association, a religious denomination, hosts more than 150 mailing lists, including public lists about specific topics and private lists for committees.

Organizations can use both open (public) and closed (private) communities:

Open communities to attract newcomers, like new customers, new members, or new sales reps. These communities should have Web sites and be publicized so that visitors can find them.

Closed communities for boards, committees, departments, and other existing groups that need to work privately.

An organization may want to use more than one type of online community:

Mailing lists for newsletters to and discussions among the organization's members, customers, staff, or other group. Mailing lists are also useful for closed discussions of specific products or programs.

Web-based message boards for questions from customers and answers from the organization's staff.

Newsgroups, hosted on a password-protected private news server, for closed discussions of specific products or programs.

Web-based chat or IRC for news conferences, committee meetings, and other real-time communications needs, replacing expensive conference calls.

Roles of the Site Manager

The *site manager* is the person who runs and supports the software needed to host the organization's online communities. The site manager's duties include

Install, maintain, and upgrade community server programs. Mailing list server, news server, Web-based message board package or scripts, IRC server, and other software.

Run the Internet server itself (usually a UNIX, Linux, Windows NT, or Windows 2000 system). The system may be supported by the organization's computer department. Some organizations have two site managers: a technical manager to run the software and a content manager to support the communities.

- **Create new communities** when the organization wants them, based on specifications set by the part of the organization that will manage the community.

- **Configure communities** when needs change. For example, if discussions on a community become contentious, the site manager might switch the community to be moderated.

- **Delete communities** when they are no longer needed. Some organizations require a minimum amount of traffic on a community, or it is deleted. A community may also need to be closed down because the need for the community is ended (for example, the prerelease product the community was discussing has been released) or because the organization can't continue to manage the community (it's better to close a community than to allow it to continue unmanaged).

- **Manage e-mail addresses** for communities. Each online community usually needs a manager address, and some also need subscription and unsubscription addresses. The site manager usually sets up the necessary e-mail addresses so that administrative messages go to the right people.

- **Restart community server programs** as needed (especially on Windows servers).

- **Train and support community managers.** All community managers have to learn the commands necessary to manage the community, the rules the site imposes on all communities hosted there, and netiquette that helps lists to run. The site manager can help each community manager learn these things by providing documentation (usually in the form of Web pages) and online help (usually by e-mail).

- **Respond to problems** that individual community managers can't handle. Some error messages go to the site manager rather than to community managers, for example.

- **Choose, install, and maintain security systems** for the online communities. This may include antispam filters, antiflooding bots, and other systems that prevent malicious users from ruining the communities.

- **Set site-wide policy** for the communities. For example, although individual communities may have rules about acceptable behavior, the organization needs to set some rules that apply to all communities to protect itself from liability (see the section "Policy Issues," later in this chapter).

- **Manages communities.** For a small site, the site manager may also manage, or co-manage, some or all of the communities. For large sites (with more than a few dozen communities), the site manager won't be able to keep up with messages. However, the site manager may still be called on to manage communities that are in trouble, whose managers have left, or that are starting up.

Creating and Maintaining Site-wide Information

It's important for a site manager to know the configuration of all online communities at his site and the names and addresses of the managers of each community. Unfortunately, list servers, mail servers, and Web-based message board packages don't make it easy to track this information. For example, a site manager might be asked for a list of all moderated newsgroups the organization runs, or which mailing lists are managed by a departing employee.

One answer is for the site manager to create a database of this information. Figure 16-1 shows a window from a Microsoft Access database of the mailing lists hosted by an organization. Using this database, the site manager can easily find communities that have potential problems—low traffic, very high traffic, no manager, and configuration open to spam, for example.

We have found few tools for site managers of online communities—no programs that would allow site managers to get a good overview of the performance and management of all communities on the site. The database shown in Figure 16-1 was created using Microsoft Access; the database imports

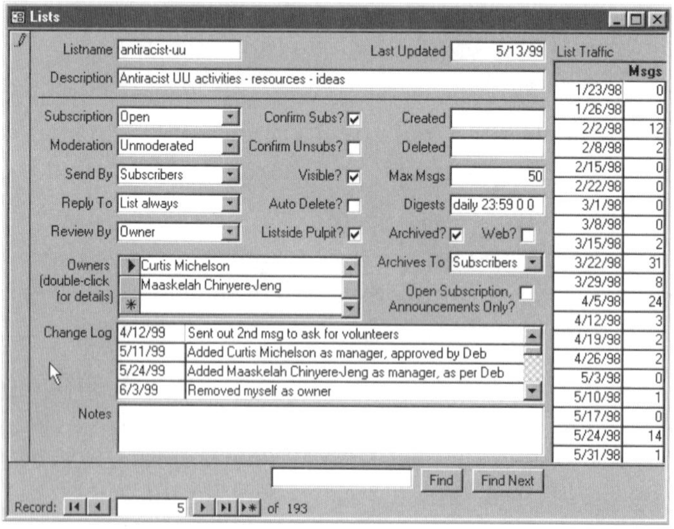

Figure 16-1: The site manager may want to create a database of the organization's online communities.

information about all lists managed at a ListProc list server site by sending configuration queries by e-mail and importing the resulting configuration messages. Some site managers create a spreadsheet listing the communities and information about them. We hope that new versions of list servers, Web message board scripts, and other community software will include more site-management features.

Site managers should be on the lookout for these types of situations:

Communities without managers. Sometimes a community manager becomes incommunicado—she switches Internet accounts or mailbox names or just stops reading her e-mail. Community managers may not bother to let you know when they decide to stop managing the community! If you have a closed mailing list for your community managers, you'll know when mail to a manager bounces.

Communities with no traffic. If a community has no messages on it for a week, something is up. Although some communities have quiet periods (and some are seasonal), it's rare for traffic in a healthy community to dry up for days at a time. Contact the community manager to find out what's going on. Occasionally, there's a good reason—like that the community members are all meeting face-to-face at a conference!

Communities with too much traffic. If traffic on a community goes way up, there is usually a problem—a flamewar, mailbombing, mail loop (programs autoresponding endlessly), or prolific spammer. Join the community yourself to find out what's up, and write to the manager privately.

Lists with configuration problems. Your site should impose configuration standards on all communities hosted at your site. For example, place a limit on the number of messages distributed per day, to stop mail loops or other problems from creating a flood of messages. If managers can change the configuration of their communities, you need to prevent them from violating your standards.

Unfortunately, there's no easy way to know whether there's an unpleasant argument, posting of copyrighted material without permission, or other problem without being a member of every community at your site. Instead, you need to rely on well-trained and well-supported community managers.

Choosing, Training, and Supporting Community Managers

Each community needs one or more managers—it's not a bad idea to require at least two managers for each community. Requiring two managers means that if one manager quits or disappears, the other manager can continue managing the community while you find a replacement. Also, managers can cover for each other when one is unavailable to manage the community and can consult with each other about hard issues. See the section "Role of the Community Manager," in Chapter 13, for details about the tasks that fall to each manager.

Finding Community Managers

A community manager needs these following traits and skills:

Familiarity with the community management software (list server commands, moderation system, Web board software, or IRC channel operator commands). You can provide training if a good candidate doesn't already know how to manage a community.

Expertise in the topic of the community. The manager commands more respect among community members if he has a good command of the subject area and can answer many questions himself. If the manager is weak on the topic of the community, he can't make good decisions about what postings are off topic and which threads are relevant to the community. A good community manager *needs* the community and has a vested interest in running it well.

Good people skills and teaching skills. When someone breaks the rules of the community, a good manager can explain the problem and get resolution quietly and without causing emotions to run high. Because the Internet and online communities are so new, managers usually have to do lots of explaining and need to do so with kindness and tact. The quicker community members learn the ropes, the more effective the community.

Good writing skills. The manager is usually responsible for writing and maintaining the community's FAQ, home page, and other documents and may also write a weekly newsletter or articles for the community's Web site.

Time. Managing a community takes time. The exact amount depends on the volume of messages posted to the community, the number of members, and how much writing the manager is expected to do. Multiple managers can help managers who don't have quite enough time to manage a community themselves.

A thick skin. It's a rare community manager who has never come in for attack. When community members have a problem with the community rules, with another member, or even with the software that runs the community, they frequently blame the manager. An effective manager can just delete obnoxious messages without sending an angry reply, or she can wait to reply until she is calm. Usually, if you respond with a friendly message that assumes the very best about the person who is complaining, you receive an apologetic, happy reply—and you've made a friend, rather than an enemy, for the whole community.

If you are starting a new community, find one or two promising managers first. Work with them to develop the description, goals, topics, and rules for the community. If a community manager leaves and you need a replacement, look among the active participants of the community. Community members usually prefer for the manager to come from among the membership so that she is familiar with the members, topics, inside jokes, taboo topics, and general history of the community. It can be hard for an outsider to come in as manager and command respect.

We suggest that the site manager approve all community managers. You may want to ask for references of some kind or ask some members of an existing community via private e-mail whether they think that the person would make a good manager. Sometimes a known troublemaker on one community volunteers to be the manager of another community—you as site manager can prevent people who have caused trouble in the past, or people with overly excitable temperaments from becoming managers.

Training Community Managers

New managers need to learn about the software used to run the community and about the rules that apply to communities at your site. Write documentation and post it on the Web. Be sure to include the following:

- **List of general responsibilities.** For example, responsibilities might include helping people subscribe and unsubscribe, managing the discussion, deleting spam, and enforcing rules.
- **Rules for community managers.** Managers need to follow rules when dealing with community members (see the section "Policy Issues," later in this chapter). For example, managers must deal fairly with members and not add people without their explicit request.
- **Checklist for setting up a new community.** For example, your checklist might include writing the FAQ, creating a home page, writing the welcome message, checking configuration settings, sending a test message, and publicizing the community.
- **Sample FAQ.** Write a generic FAQ and welcome message that include the standard rules and commands for your site, links to help pages on your

Web site, and other material that you'd like everyone in every community to know. See the section "Looking at a Sample Welcome Message," in Chapter 5, for ideas for your generic FAQ.

Instructions for using management commands. Include how to add someone, delete someone, change someone's configuration settings, deal with bounced mail, see membership lists, update the FAQ or welcome message, and run a moderated community.

Guidelines for keeping the peace in a community. For example, you could suggest how to deal with member complaints, with personal attacks among members, and with copyright infringement.

Replacing community managers. Explain what a community manager should do if she needs to quit, what community members should do if the manager isn't doing a good job, and how new managers are appointed.

Encourage new managers to ask you questions while they are getting started—it's better to get pestered with extra questions up front than to end up with unpleasantness on a community because of a confused manager. One site manager we know gives each new manager "homework," consisting of adding and deleting members and getting a list of members. Some list managers add themselves as co-manager to all their communities so that they can see the error messages and administrative messages that community managers receive.

Providing Ongoing Support: The Community Managers' Community

One of the best ways to provide support for your community managers is to require them to subscribe to a special closed mailing list (or message board or newsgroup) about managing communities on your site. A useful side effect of requiring managers to subscribe to a mailing list is that you can tell right away whether a manager disappears from the Internet, when list messages to that person bounce.

These items should be posted to the community managers' community:

- The creation of new communities
- The closing of communities
- Software updates that affect the communities, along with changes to the commands and procedures that managers use
- Changes to the rules that govern all communities on the site
- Communities that need new managers

- Plans for scheduled maintenance or other down-times
- Viruses or other threats to the communities, and how managers should handle them
- Problems on specific communities: If one community throws a member out, it's good for the other community managers to know about it, so that they can watch that person's behavior in other communities.
- Other news about your community site to all your managers
- Questions and problems from managers about their communities

It's also a good idea to keep a list of community managers' addresses in your own e-mail address book: If the community software goes down, you may not be able to use your community managers' community to let them know what's going on! You can fall back on e-mail to communicate with them.

Making a Web Site for Your Organization's Communities

If your community site doesn't already have a Web site, you may want to create one that includes information about all the communities you host (or at least the communities that are open to the public). Web-based community sites usually have a home page from which members can get to individual communities hosted at the site. But mailing list servers and news servers may not have a Web site.

If not, create a Web site that includes site-wide information. For example, the Unitarian Universalist Association created a site for its 150 mailing lists (see the **UUA Email Lists** site, at http://www.uua.org/lists/, as shown in Figure 16-2).

The site can include

An alphabetical or subject-oriented list of the communities you host, along with information about the topics they cover and who may join

A subscription form that people can use to join a community

The rules that govern all the communities hosted at the site

Instructions for how to subscribe, unsubscribe, and change your configuration settings

A feedback form or e-mail address that people can use to reach the site manager with problems

Web-based searchable archives for communities that maintain public messages archives

You can also include links to pages of instructions for community managers.

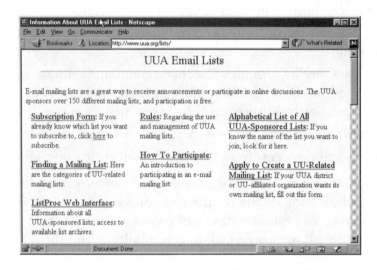

Figure 16-2: The Web site for an organization that hosts more than 150 mailing lists.

Policy Issues

Here are some of the types of site-wide policies you should consider enforcing for all the communities hosted by your site:

Requirements for community size and duration. Creating a community of any type can take hours of a site manager's time. For small groups, or for groups that exist for only a short time, people should use their e-mail programs' address books to maintain informal mailing lists rather than use a list server or other community system. You may also want to require that communities have a connection with your organization.

Limits on number of messages. Most list servers and message boards can enforce a limit on the number of messages distributed per day by the community. Occasionally, someone's vacation program (or other autoresponder) posts vacation notices each time it receives a message from the community—including responding to its own vacation notices. If the community doesn't have a daily message limit, e-mail messages can spiral endlessly, leaving members with hundreds of vacation notices in their inboxes. The best message limit for a community depends on its normal daily volume. Communities set limits at from 50 to 200 messages a day. (Real-time chat communities don't usually need message limits—instead, they have flooding limits—a limit on how many messages may be posted in a five-second period. A real-time chat might prohibit posting more than three messages within five seconds.)

Confirmation of addresses. To prevent people from being added to mailing lists (or any communities that send e-mail to members) against their will, your communities should require members to confirm their membership via e-mail. Most list servers and many Web-based message board registration programs automatically send confirmation messages, to which the person must respond before being added as a member.

Copyright enforcement. To protect your organization from liability, you need a policy against the posting of copyrighted material without the permission of the copyright holder (see Chapter 15 for the details). You may also want to include in your policies the statement that by posting a message, a member grants the community manager and sponsoring organization permission to use the posting in various ways, such as posting it on other parts of your Web site.

Advertising. Some community sites allow advertising by their members, as long as the ads pertain to the topic of the discussion, contain specific information about the product or service without hype, and are not repeated often. Other organizations ban all commercial announcements from their communities.

Preventing nonmembers from posting. If you allow nonmembers to post messages to your mailing list or Web-based message board, you are inviting spam. (Unmoderated newsgroups can't prevent anyone from posting, so different spam-fighting methods are used: See the section "Cancels and Spam," in Chapter 6.) Consider making a policy that allows only members to post messages to your communities.

Anonymous postings. Some communities let people post anonymously, some don't, and some allow people to *anonymize* their messages by asking the community manager to post them without identifying information. See the section "Anonymous Users," in Chapter 15.

Criticism of sponsoring organization. If your organization hosts a group of communities, is it acceptable for members of those communities to criticize the policies, products, or services of the organization? It is perfectly legal for the sponsoring organization to discard messages it doesn't like—U.S. censorship laws apply only to what the U.S. government can do, not to what private organizations can do within forums they own. Some organizations delete all negative postings without a whisper (one large computer hardware company deleted all criticisms of its software from its message archives for years). However, this policy makes the organization appear to be afraid of criticism, and you can quickly lose the trust and respect of your community members. A more reasonable position is to delete *flames*—criticisms with no content, only emotion—and leave critical messages that bring up valid points. Your organization can learn a great deal from your community members if you let them speak honestly.

Criticism of individuals. What about criticisms of individuals, including staff members of the sponsoring organization, other community members, or people outside the community? Personal attacks can lead to claims of libel (see the section "Libel, Harassment, and Responsibility for Online Material," in Chapter 15). Make a policy for your communities that calls for criticism of ideas, actions, and things, but not of people.

Collecting and using information about children. The Children's Online Privacy Protection Act of 1998 (COPPA) sets stringent rules for online communities that include children. See the section "Children's Issues," in Chapter 15.

Communities need managers. If a community can't provide people willing to take on the job of managing the community (and if you can't find managers from outside the community), it's better to shut down the community than to let it run without at least one manager. Consider making a policy that communities without active managers may be closed.

Complaint process. If a member doesn't like the actions or postings of another member or community manager, you need a complaint process the member can follow. A typical process would require the member to take up the issue first with the community manager and then to bring it to the site manager. Someone with a complaint should save all relevant messages so that the site manager can review what happened.

Boilerplate legalese. You may also want to add that members participate at their own risk and that messages posted on the community do not necessarily represent the views of the sponsoring organization or of the community manager. You may also want to say that your communities may not be used for creating offensive or disruptive messages, including those containing sexual implications, racial slurs, or any comment that offensively addresses someone's age, sexual orientation, religious or political beliefs, national origin, or disability.

Post your rules on the Web, including them in the FAQs and welcome messages of each community, and let everyone in all your communities know when the rules change.

If problems arise, support your community managers and let them try to work out problems in their communities. They know the history of the particular community and are familiar with its members. Step in only if the manager appears to be acting in ways that are detrimental to the community or to your community site.

Technical Issues

The most important technical issue in running groups of communities is to realize that you need better tools for running a hundred lists than you do for running just a few and that you need to automate as many tasks as possible. Removing bouncing addresses by hand is tolerable if you have only one or two lists, but is impossible if you have dozens or more.

Mailing List Software

Your choice of tools depends on a combination of how much technical skill you have and how much money. One of the authors of this book hosts a hundred mailing lists on a UNIX system using a combination of freeware, the Majordomo mailing list manager, and the qmail mail system, but it took a couple of days of fiddling and configuring to make all the pieces fit and the bounce handling reliable. For most people with lots of lists, it makes sense to pay for a mailing list manager like LISTSERV, ListProc, or Lyris that provides support unless someone who can provide support is on hand.

Here are some issues a site with many mailing lists needs to have automated:

When the Manager Goes AWOL

An unmanaged community is a disaster waiting to happen. One organization with dozens of mailing lists ran a mailing list about social issues. Unbeknownst to the site manager, the manager for that list had unsubscribed, and no one was managing the community. A flamewar started over the appropriateness of the postings of one individual, and by the time the site manager found out, tempers were running high.

When the site manager joined the list, the members of the list didn't know her and felt that the sponsoring organization was planning to come in with a heavy hand to shut down the conversation. The site manager had the challenge of stopping the flamewar, preserving the goodwill of list members who were not participating in the argument, and determining whether any flamemongers needed to be thrown off the list, while gaining the trust of the list members—a tall order!

MIME and HTML filtering. Most lists have policies that limit or forbid HTML-formatted messages and MIME attachments. Because some people will send them anyway deliberately or by accident, the administrator's life will be much easier if the list software catches it automatically.

Spam filtering. Mailing lists are a very attractive target for spammers because one spam sent to a list will be forwarded to all the list's members with no extra effort by the spammer. Setting lists so that only members can post deters most spam, but other measures are implemented by some list managers to prevent spam even from people who've joined the lists. LISTSERV in particular checks for many similar messages arriving for the same or different lists and traps them all on the assumption that they're spam.

Duplicate filtering. A useful feature related to spam filtering is *duplicate filtering*, or checking for multiple identical or nearly identical messages to a single list and rejecting the duplicates.

Bounce pruning. This is the most important feature for managers of multiple lists. If you have lots of lists with lots of members, a few addresses will go bad on each list every day. Automated bounce handling removes addresses that bounce consistently, so the list administrator doesn't have to.

List creation. The process of creating a mailing list involves creating the file or database to store the list, the descriptive information about the list, the list's options (whether it's moderated or open or closed, for example), any Web pages used to control or access the list, and the various e-mail addresses used to control the list. This process can be completely automated after the site manager enters the information about the list—the more automated, the less work for the site manager.

A perhaps surprising piece of advice is not to update the list management software very often. The basic structure of Internet e-mail hasn't changed in more than a decade, and there's not much new in list management software. In our experience, other than bug fixes, most changes from one version of list software to the next are of only minor interest, so it's often not worth the hassle and possible disruption of upgrading. If a new version has something really useful to you, use it, but don't upgrade just to upgrade.

Web Message-Board Software

The trade-offs in Web board software are similar to those in mailing list software: freeware that needs local support versus more polished commercial offerings. The simplest message boards can use something as simple as the Web board feature in Microsoft Front Page. Automated features to look for in higher-end software include board creation and deletion, aging old messages off the board, and community manager facilities to remove inappropriate messages and ban unruly members. See the section "Installing Your Own Message Board Software," in Chapter 11 for a list of message board programs.

Newsgroup Software

Newsgroup software is all quite automated—if it weren't, the vast traffic in public Usenet groups would be impossible to handle. Creating a new local newsgroup requires no more effort than sending an appropriate newgroup command to the news server. If a FAQ needs to be posted on a regular basis, the site manager needs to set up a job to be run by cron (the UNIX or Linux utility that runs programs on a set schedule), but it need only be a couple of lines of shell script to run the inews program that posts newsgroup messages.

Part VII

True-Life Stories

Chapter Seventeen
The Computer Book Publishing List: One Company Expands Its Visibility

Name of community: Computer Book Publishing List (a.k.a. The Studio B List).

Date formed: April 1996.

Venue: Mailing list (and Web-based archive).

URL of Web site: Computer Book Café at http://www.studiob.com/ (as shown in Figure 17-1).

Average number of members: About 880 and still growing.

Average traffic: Twenty per day.

Manager: David Rogelberg.

Sponsor: Studio B agency and advertiser supported.

Topic: Computer book publishing.

Moderated? First five posts of new members are moderated; managers declare off-topic threads to be closed.

Open, closed, or manager controlled: Open.

Privacy: Only members can post and read messages, although anyone can read the archive at the Web site.

The Origins of the Computer Book Publishing List

David Rogelberg, the community manager, is also the founder of the Studio B literary agency, which specializes in books about computer hardware and software. Rogelberg writes:

The initial idea for the list came from a difficult situation that one of my

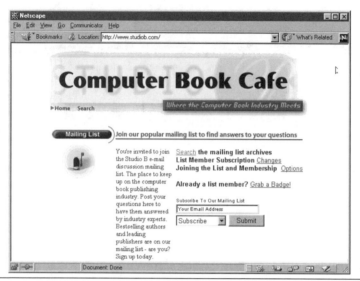

Figure 17-1: The Computer Book Café, the home page for the Computer Book Publishing mailing list.

clients had with a publisher. I felt the publisher wasn't acting in a legal and ethical manner. Unfortunately, there wasn't an industry newsletter or forum where I felt this kind of issue could be addressed. I decided to create a forum of authors and publishers so that public opinion could encourage publishers to act reasonably.

I also formed the community because there was a real need for it. Writers don't have the opportunity to interact with other writers very often, and this mailing list gave them a chance to talk and share information both on list and off. Publishers and authors had no other place to go online to learn about their professions and each other. The list created a forum where people could share information that wasn't really available before—it became a virtual water cooler.

Rogelberg first tried using a Web-based message board for the community, but it just didn't work. Authors and publishers rely on e-mail in their day-to-day business and wouldn't take the time to visit a Web site. When he switched to a mailing list in 1996, the community took off and grew in size and prestige quickly.

Life on the List

The Computer Book Publishing list provides a way for usually solitary writers to chat with a group of colleagues. Topics range from the business of book publishing (royalty rates, advances, and contracts) to the mechanics of writing (keyboards, word processing programs, grammar, editing, and deadlines) to the subject matter of the books (computer hardware and software). Perennial topics include whether authors need agents, whether authors need the permission of Web site owners to use screen shots of Web sites, how badly Microsoft software stinks, whether the ...*For Dummies* series is brilliant or horrible, and whether electronic books spell the end of printed books.

List subscribers are a mix of authors, aspiring authors, editors, acquisitions editors (publishers' staffers who sign up authors to write books), literary agents, and at least one lawyer who specializes in publishing law. Rogelberg says: "I think the list is extremely valuable to its members. The member retention has been incredible, and people usually come back even if they leave the list when they go on vacation."

Tara Calashain, who works for Studio B, posts the *Studio B Buzz* newsletter to the mailing list a few times a week. The *Buzz* contains links to articles and ads on the Studio B Web site along with links to other publishing-related articles on the Web.

Problems and Solutions

Rogelberg says:

People generally get along, and there is a level of trust, but flare-ups happen. There's a lot of noise on the list, but the noise tends to help the list keep its informal tone. The noise also helps bring up new and interesting topics, so I try to moderate with a light hand. People have been thrown out for not following the rules, but it's been a rare occurrence. Topics haven't been banned, but we do try to make sure that there is computer publishing relevance to the topics. And yes, people do meet offline, and they even identify themselves with an orange dot on their name badge at the industry's trade show.

Value of the List to Its Sponsor

The mailing list has increased the visibility of its sponsor within the computer book publishing industry. Rogelberg writes:

I was very pleasantly surprised that it also turned out to be an excellent marketing vehicle for Studio B, my literary agency. It gave authors and publishers a chance to get to know Studio B before they chose to work with us. In short, we developed strong relationships on the list by offering valuable information, and then used the relationships to leverage our business. It also became an excellent way to educate our market about the merits of working with an agency.

I was visiting a publisher when we first started the agency, and the publisher was introducing me to several editors. As I was being introduced to one editor, another editor popped up out of his cubicle and screamed, "Wow! You're the guy with the list!" The entire room went silent, and everyone looked at me. I kind of felt like a rock star for a fleeting moment. It's amazing how a list can make you a celebrity within a very small group of people.

The mailing list lets the Studio B agency stay in touch with its clients, both publishers and authors, and has helped establish the agency as a well-known player in the computer book market. Studio B also makes a small amount of money by charging for placements in a weekly ad posting to the list.

Summary
The Computer Book Publishing mailing list and its Web-based archive have been successful for both its members and its sponsor, the Studio B literary agency. As Rogelberg says, "The mailing list is truly unique in that it's for an entire market. Everyone, at some level, is competing with everyone else on the list, but people still share valuable information."

Chapter Eighteen

Knitting.About.com: Craftspeople Sharing Information on the Web

Name of community: Knitting.About.com.

Date formed: Originally went live in March 1997; in its present incarnation, with new software, since May 1999.

Venue: Web club, including message board, real-time chat, and other features. Part of About.com (formerly The Mining Company), which hires an expert in each field to host his site about the field. About.com has its own custom Web server.

URL of Web site: http://knitting.about.com/ (shown in Figure 18-1).

Average number of members: More than 3,000 as of mid-2000 and growing every week.

Average traffic: About 800 messages a week.

Manager: Barbara Breiter.

Sponsor: About.com.

Topic: Primarily knitters, although the occasional stray spinner or crocheter wanders in.

Moderated? No.

Open, closed, or manager controlled: Open.

Privacy: Messages, including those archived, can be read by members or guests. You must register in order to post.

Figure 18-1: The Knitting.About.com home page.

The About.com Web Site

About.com (at http://www.about.com/) forms Web-based clubs on topics it thinks can attract significant numbers of visitors. Founded by Scott P. Kurnit as **The Mining Company** (at http://www.miningco.com/), the site adds human experts to create and organize information about a wide variety of topics. For each topic, About.com hires an expert guide (community manager) to run the topic site, answer questions, write newsletters, organize files, and keep the community on track and lively. As About.com states, "When they're not posting informative weekly features or combing the Net for fresh links to other useful online resources, About.com guides are hosting live chats, managing forum discussions, recommending books, keeping abreast of relevant news, updating links, publishing newsletters, and responding to e-mail."

Each guide is responsible for running one site, with the URL http://*topic*.about.com (*topic* is replaced by the topic of the club). Each of the more than 700 About.com sites includes

- A home page with news and links to the rest of the site
- A weekly newsletter
- Message boards (hosted by Delphi.com)
- Articles about the topic of the site
- Live chats, usually weekly at scheduled times
- Libraries of files, organized by the guide

Guides get paid a percentage of the advertising revenue that About.com generates from traffic to the site. Running a site for About.com is a way to get paid for organizing and managing an online community about a topic you love and know lots about.

Life in Knitting.About.com

Barbara Breiter is the *guide* (community manager) for Knitting.About.com. She says, "People come for knitting help and often have their questions answered within an hour—by more than one person! They also visit to look for special patterns and are frequently pointed in the right direction by members. They also come just to talk about their latest projects and get inspiration." Knitters love to compare techniques, get free patterns, boast about difficult projects, and get help with problems. Members can post questions and answers to the message board, upload knitting patterns to the patterns pages, upload pictures of finished projects, or suggest links to their own knitting sites.

One popular thread was about ways that members would finish this sentence: "You know you're addicted to knitting when. . . ." Answers included the following:

You know you are addicted to knitting when your child asks you for something and, before you can reply, he holds his hand up and says, "I know, Mum, you gotta finish that row first." And he sits down with a big sigh.

You know you are addicted to knitting when you suddenly hear hushed voices around you, which is your family saying, "Shh, she's counting. . . ." Or you pass a store that sells yarn and your husband stops in front of it and asks, "Well, aren't you going to go in?" Or you always keep in the car a spare pair of scissors, markers, stitch holders, and measuring tape just in case you need them. (I took my hubby's car to swim lessons, and I had to cut the yarn with my key!)

Knitting.About.com carries many articles, organized by subject headings that include adult clothing, afghans and pillows, dolls and toys, holiday patterns, machine knitting, vintage knitting, knitting for charity, clip art, software, and stitches and designs. You can also read or post on the message boards (shown in Figure 18-2) or participate in a real-time chat. (About.com automatically downloads the Parachat Java applet to allow your browser to display the chat.)

Figure 18-2: Knitters pose and answer specific questions about knitting techniques and materials.

Breiter runs frequent contests to encourage members to participate, with prizes that usually consist of yarn or knitting patterns.

The community manager posts an e-mail message to members of the Knitting.About.com club each week, with the names and URLs of new patterns, contests, and other new items on the Web site. This newsletter reminds members to return to the site and alerts them to new material.

Problems and Solutions

Here are the main problems Breiter faces:

- **Off-topic postings on message boards.** The community manager has set up a separate topic specifically for gabbing, where she encourages off-topic chatting to occur. Members can get to know each other better without interfering with topical threads on the message boards. She also posts frequent reminders to stay on topic within threads.

- **Spam.** The community manager bans spammers and deletes spam messages from the message boards. It's easy for spammers to come back by using new e-mail addresses, but their messages never hang around for long. She says, "I don't allow online yarn shops to post about sales, visiting their sites, et cetera. It would turn into one huge free advertisement, and I want to keep us talking about knitting. Posts such as those are deleted."

- **Flame wars.** They have been rare, and invariably about a sore point among knitters and those who design knitting patterns: copyright protection of patterns. Pattern designers have traditionally sold individual patterns in yarn stores and books of patterns in yarn stores and bookstores. Although the Internet provides a great way for knitters to get lots of patterns for free, posting a pattern is legal only if the author of the pattern has given her permission (see Chapter 15 to find out about copyright issues).

Summary

Barbara Breiter sums it up when she says, "There are many people who visit daily, and I love the fact that they have found somewhere to talk about knitting and share something of their lives in a place that they feel is 'theirs.' These same folks continually welcome new people with open arms and help those who may be shy about joining in. A community is only as good as its members, and I have some wonderful people in mine!"

Chapter Nineteen

Comp.compilers: Programmers Sharing Technical Information

Name of community: comp.compilers

Date formed: January 1986.

Venue: Usenet newsgroup, in one of the Big Eight hierarchies; also available as mailing list.

URL of Web site: http://www.iecc.com/compilers/ (as shown in Figure 19-1).

Average number of members: Two hundred subscribers are on the mailing list; probably at least 100,000 people read the newsgroup. More than 900 different people posted in 1999.

Average traffic: Varies; 30 to 70 per week.

Manager: John Levine.

Sponsor: Nobody. The manager hosts moderation software on his own system.

Topic: Compilers (programs that translate one computer language to another) and related program-development software and tools. Readers include practitioners, students, and faculty.

Moderated? Yes.

Open, closed, or manager controlled: Open.

Privacy: Totally public. All messages are available worldwide on Usenet and are available in public archives.

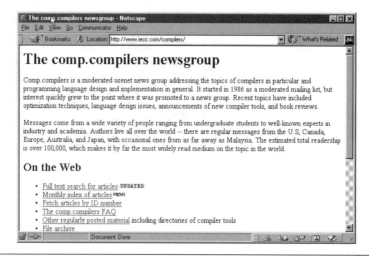

Figure 19-1: The comp.compilers home page.

The Origins of comp.compilers

comp.compilers (as shown in Figure 19-2) is one of the older moderated Big Eight Usenet newsgroups and one of the few early newsgroups still run by the original moderator. In late 1985, a couple of compiler enthusiasts started a moderated mailing list about compilers. When it reached 80 members, which seemed like a great deal at the time, its managers contacted some of the people who were in practice in charge of Usenet at the time—managers of well-connected Usenet "backbone" sites—who quickly agreed to create a moderated

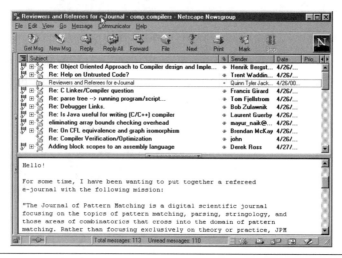

Figure 19-2: Messages in the comp.compilers newsgroup.

Usenet newsgroup. At the time, Usenet was small and informal and newsgroups were created after brief consultation by the backbone managers with no formal proposal, which is why the newsgroup has no formal charter.

In its early years, comp.compilers was hosted by Interactive Systems, an early UNIX vendor that was the moderator's employer. Later, after the moderator (John Levine) left Interactive, he got his own system on Usenet (and later the Internet) and moved the moderation software there.

One could arguably call comp.compilers the most widely read compilers newsletter in the world. Its closest competitor is *ACM SIGPLAN Notices*, a monthly paper put out by the Special Interest Group on Programming Languages of the ACM (the professional society of computer scientists), with about 25,000 subscribers. Although nobody knows how many people read Usenet newsgroups because Usenet makes it impossible to count, statistical estimates put it in the hundreds of thousands.

Value of This Community to Its Members

Compilers are one of the fundamental technologies in computing. Every program written in a high-level programming language like Fortran or C has to be translated by a compiler before it can run. The overall quality of software therefore depends on the quality of the compilers the programmers use. It also turns out that the techniques and tools developed for compilers are useful in other areas. For example, text-searching techniques originally used to recognize keywords in programs are equally useful for other kinds of text searching.

Many participants in comp.compilers are in the business of writing compilers and related tools or are university faculty members specializing in compilers. A larger number are students learning about compilers, either formally in compiler classes or informally working through a textbook. Many others are practitioners in other fields who are using compiler tools and methods in other areas and who exchange questions and advice.

Life in comp.compilers

Because comp.compilers is a moderated newsgroup, all messages to it are funneled through a mailbox on the moderator's computer. An automatic program responds to each message to say that it's been received. Every day or so, the moderator goes through the mailbox to handle waiting messages.

About half the incoming messages are posted; half not. The half that aren't posted fall into a few categories:

Questions answered in the FAQ. comp.compilers has an 800-line FAQ message posted every month that answers lots of basic questions. Nonetheless, some people ask those questions anyway. The moderator has a set of canned messages he can quickly send back in response. (Canned messages are often better than personal messages for this purpose because the canned message can be complete and polite, whereas when you've just gotten four dumb questions in a row, the urge to write a snide response to the fourth can be hard to resist.) Here's the "read the FAQ" message:

```
You have re-asked a frequently asked question that is
answered in the monthly comp.compilers automatic
posting sent out on the first of every month. Please
read the monthly message. If your system doesn't have
the FAQ message, here's how to get it:
* visit the compilers web site at
http://www.iecc.com/compilers
* send "send FAQ" to compilers-server@iecc.com
* FTP it from ftp://ftp.iecc.com/pub/file/FAQ Regards,
John Levine, comp.compilers moderator
compilers-request@iecc.com
```

Messages sent to the wrong group. Although comp.compilers is about writing compilers, some people send in messages about using compilers for specific programming languages or for specific computers, which are outside the newsgroup's purview. There are canned messages for that subject, too, suggesting more newsgroups.

Questions about compiler tools. People use two widely used programming tools to write compilers. The tools are named *lex* and *yacc*, about which the moderator happens to have written the only available book. Sometimes when people write in with lex or yacc questions, the moderator just answers them.

Misdirected personal mail. Some messages are obviously responses that were supposed to be sent to the author of an earlier article. The moderator discards them, on the hard-hearted theory that if it wasn't important enough for the author to send them to the right place, it's not important enough for him to do so either.

Homework. Particularly toward the end of the academic year, people with .edu addresses send in questions that are clearly homework assignments. (The really clueless ones say "I really need the answer by tomorrow morning.") Asking people on the Internet to do your homework has always been considered poor form, and the moderator writes back encouraging people to do their own homework, sometimes suggesting a book or other resource to consult.

Third-party messages. Sometimes people send along messages received in e-mail or other Usenet newsgroups. comp.compilers has always had a policy of first-party–only messages (no forwarded messages), so the moderator sends them back and suggests that the senders ask the authors of the messages to send them directly to comp.compilers, which about half the time they do.

Messages with more quoted than new material. An informal Usenet convention says that a new article should have at least as much new material as quoted, and you should edit down the quoted part of an article to which you're responding. The automatic moderation response program counts the lines to estimate when there's too much quoted material and warns the sender that messages with excess quoting may not be posted. If the count was wrong (the program that counts isn't very sophisticated) or it's easy to edit the quote, the moderator does so and posts the message; otherwise, he discards it.

Anonymous messages. comp.compilers has always required that each message have a real From address to which readers can respond. If the real sender of a message with a munged (spam-proofed) address can easily be discerned from the message, the moderator fixes the address; otherwise, he discards it. Addresses at Hotmail or Deja.com are fine, as long as they're somewhere that the sender can check the mail now and then. The moderator has a standing offer to post anonymized messages with his own name if the sender offers a plausible reason to do so, but in 15 years nobody's asked.

Vapid press releases. comp.compilers has always permitted commercially oriented messages, as long as they're relevant to the newsgroup. Press releases are fine as long as they have enough technical content that people can get some idea of what they're describing. The moderator has an informal hype-o-meter that runs from 0 (pure tech) to 100 (pure hot air), and press releases that score above 30 are sent back.

Personal arguments. Now and then, people get into arguments that turn personal. The moderator tells them to thrash it out in e-mail and, if need be, write back and say who won.

Spam. Lots of spam shows up in the moderator's mailbox, either posted to Usenet or mailed to compilers@iecc.com, the moderation mailbox. Needless to say, it doesn't get posted.

For messages that do get posted, the moderator cleans up the message headers, deleting extraneous ones and fixing the References header if it's a response to a previous article, adds or edits a Keywords line, fixes spelling errors, and posts the messages.

Help-wanted ads are handled specially. Some people who read the newsgroup find them interesting; others find them annoying. After polling the group, the moderator came up with a compromise in which each week's help-wanted messages are collected into a digest with a fixed Subject line. This technique makes it easy for people who hate them to filter them out and those who like them to read them. Jobs in help-wanted ads must be real positions, related to compiler writing, and a single open position can be posted no more than once a month. This compromise works well, and employers have commented that the leads they get from comp.compilers are good ones.

The moderator has the complete set of messages posted to comp.compilers, and several searchable archives are on the Web. Messages from years past remain useful, both because the same tools remain still popular (lex and yacc date from the 1970s) and ideas are constantly rediscovered and reinvented, both good ones and bad ones, and it's often enlightening to see what people said the last time an idea came around.

Problems and Solutions

Fortunately, the compiler community is a pretty friendly one, and heated arguments are rare. Every year or two, someone is outraged that his message wasn't posted, but the comp.compilers moderator is well-enough respected in the online community that attempts to stir up a revolution don't get much support.

Some people have been posting for many years, and a feeling of camaraderie certainly exists among long-timers. Although formal attempts to get together have never been made, people who post often run into each other at technical conferences, and now and then when people find that they're in the same town, they get together for lunch.

Summary

comp.compilers is a successful technical community. Through a combination of a tight technical focus and a consistent and well-respected moderator, it has remained the primary online compiler community for more than a decade.

Chapter Twenty
Soc.religion.unitarian-univ: A Freewheeling Religious Newsgroup

Name of community: soc.religion.unitarian-univ (s.r.u-u, for short).

Date formed: August 1994.

Venue: Big Eight newsgroup..

URL of Web site: http://sruu.iecc.com/ (as shown in Figure 20-1).

Average number of members: Unknown, probably tens of thousands of readers. More than 500 different people posted in 1999.

Average traffic: Varies; average of 236 messages per week in 1999.

Manager: John Levine runs the moderation software as "robot wrangler"; a board of four moderators sets policy.

Sponsor: None; robot wrangler hosts software on his system.

Topic: Unitarian Universalism religion and other topics related thereto. Members and friends of UU societies and anyone else interested in UUism.

Moderated? Robomoderated (first Big Eight robomoderated newsgroup).

Open, closed, or manager controlled: Open.

Privacy: Totally public; all messages are available worldwide on Usenet and are available in public Web-based archives.

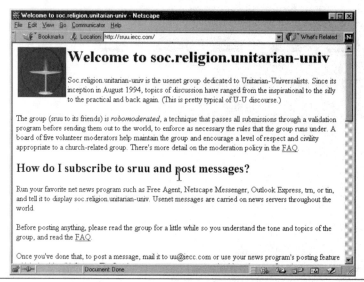

Figure 20-1: The home page for the soc.religion.unitarian-univ newsgroup.

The Origins of soc.religion.unitarian-univ

As discussed in Chapter 7, in the sidebar "Creating soc.religion.unitarian-univ," the soc.religion.unitarian-univ newsgroup (henceforth s.r.u-u) is a Big Eight Usenet newsgroup created in 1994 as part of the existing soc.religion hierarchy. As the oldest robomoderated newsgroup, s.r.u-u has gone through a wide variety

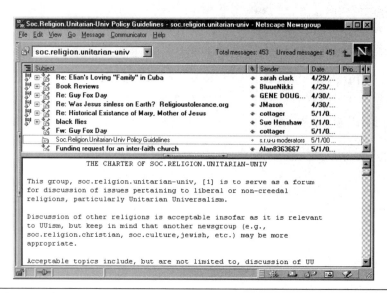

Figure 20-2: Typical messages from the soc.religion.unitarian-univ newsgroup.

of robomoderation techniques, designed to allow unfettered discussion while eliminating spam.

Unitarian Universalists (UUs) are a notoriously chatty bunch, and the ones in s.r.u-u are no exception. Topics range from theological discussions to the nuts and bolts of church services to political arguments to silly jokes (see Figure 20-2). The majority of participants are members of UU congregations, although a regular stream of messages comes from new people who drop by and want to know what UUism is all about as well as the occasional message from someone in a conservative Christian church who can't understand how UUism could call itself a church.

The newsgroup definitely feels like a community, with regular contributors who have very definite personalities. New members get a friendly welcome, and regular members report "joys and concerns" in their lives, with plenty of feedback.

Day-to-Day Management

The s.r.u-u *modbot* (moderation robot, the program that handles messages to the newsgroup) is designed to run unattended, and, for the most part, it does. New messages arrive by mail, and the modbot processes them (as described in the next section) and automatically posts to the newsgroup the ones that match the group's criteria. Occasionally the modbot fails to handle a message, typically because a subscriber is using a new e-mail or newsreading program that formats a message in a hitherto unseen nonstandard way, in which case the human robot wrangler fiddles with the code.

The moderators attempt to read every message in the newsgroup. Because the group has four moderators, every message is seen by at least one moderator. On the relatively rare occasions that they see a fight breaking out or other trouble in the newsgroup, they have to intervene manually, but that happens only about once a month.

The s.r.u-u Modbot

The s.r.u-u modbot program has gone through many revisions since the group started in 1994.

The original modbot was adapted from the one used for the regional ne.general.selected newsgroup. The modbot was quite simple—it just looked for a relatively small set of patterns from common spam messages (including e-mail addresses and subject lines commonly found in spam) and posted everything that didn't match one of the patterns. This worked quite well for the newsgroup's first three years. All the participants were well-enough behaved that the moderators' only job was to send the occasional gentle admonishment when someone was rude and to ratify changes to the spam filters.

In mid-1997, the amount of spam had increased to the point where it became impractical for the moderators to manage the spam filters by hand. Because essentially all spam has a forged From address, a new modbot used a register-once scheme to validate legitimate participants. (Because newsgroups don't have subscriber lists against which postings can be compared, this registration process created a list of registered posters to the newsgroup.) The first time a message arrives from a hitherto unseen address, the modbot files the message and sends a confirmation message to that address with instructions to send a response containing yes on the first line if the original message was real. When the yes message arrives, the original message is posted and the address marked valid in a database. Subsequent messages from the same address are posted immediately. Because most spam has a fake From address to which the registration message gets sent, the modbot never receives a yes message and discards the spam. This scheme has been extremely effective in keeping out spam and forgeries while placing only a modest burden on participants. About once a year, a benighted spammer sends mail from his real address and responds yes. When this happens, the robot wrangler and moderators mark the spammer's address as banned and complain to the spammer's ISP.

In mid-1998, s.r.u-u had participants who for the first time posted disruptive messages and didn't respond to informal requests from the moderators to stop. After considerable debate among the moderators, they tried a new scheme in November 1998 in which troublemakers were subject to hand moderation. Messages from hand-moderated participants were forwarded to the moderators, each of whom could approve or deny messages. If any one moderator approved a message, it was posted immediately. If two moderators denied a message and nobody approved it, it was sent back to the author with the moderators' comments. Even though no more than four people were ever hand moderated, the scheme was a disaster. Predictable cries of censorship arose, and each time a message was returned, the authors argued and wanted to challenge the decision. This technique was a huge drain on the moderators' time and did nothing to resolve the issues that led to hand moderation in the first place.

After two months of hand moderation, it was clear that the scheme would never work, so the moderators came up with a simpler, time-out scheme. Whenever a moderator feels that a participant is misbehaving, the moderator can send a denouncement to a special e-mail address. If two denouncements arrive within three days of each other, the participant is temporarily blocked from posting anything. A participant's first time-out is three days, the next is a week and then two weeks and four weeks, doubling each time. After a year without time-outs, the time resets to three days. This scheme works quite well. A few people were blocked for three days, learned their lesson, and now participate constructively. A few others were blocked multiple times, to the point where they had multimonth timeouts, so in practice they're blocked permanently because they forgot when their time-out ended.

For the first month, though, the time-out system didn't work well because the original set of moderators was extremely reluctant to use it. One newsgroup participant in particular made a practice of viciously attacking anyone with whom he disagreed and refused all advice that he moderate his tone. People started leaving the group en masse, and in desperation the robot wrangler (who, by the charter, is supposed to ratify the moderators' decisions) unilaterally banned him from the group in February 1999. A week or two of furor ensued, and two moderators resigned, as much because they hadn't actually been reading the newsgroup as because they disagreed with the banning. The remaining moderators recruited new moderators to fill the gap, and the newsgroup has since then been running reasonably smoothly, with occasional private admonishments from the moderators and very rare time-outs maintaining a civil tone in the newsgroup.

Two other results of the February 1999 crisis were that some participants created an unmoderated alt.religion.unitarian-univ newsgroup for people who want an uncensored forum, and the moderators made a separate sruu-policy mailing list for people who want to discuss or argue about s.r.u-u's moderation policy. The discussion in alt.religion.unitarian-univ is not all that different from the one in s.r.u-u, and the sruu-policy list rarely has any traffic because nobody's been able to articulate a proposal for a better moderation policy.

Summary

Unitarian Universalists have a longstanding commitment to free speech, and the experience in s.r.u-u points out the difficulty on the Internet in balancing free discussion with the civil tone appropriate for a community at least nominally related to religion. The key to success is a set of moderators willing to take action as needed to keep the newsgroup in order. Because an unmoderated newsgroup also exists, no one can complain that she is being totally censored.

Chapter Twenty-One
The uua.org Mailing Lists: Hosting Dozens of Communities

Name of organization: The Unitarian Universalist Association (UUA).

URL of organization's Web site: http://www.uua.org/ (as shown in Figure 21-1).

Number of communities hosted: About 175.

Venue: Mailing lists, using the ListProc list server.

URL of community Web site: http://www.uua.org/lists/ (as shown in Figure 21-2).

Web-based archives: http://www.uua.org:8080 (maintained by the ListProc Web interface).

Members in largest communities: About 2,100 on the announcement-only newsletter mailing list (UUA-L), more than 800 on the social action information list (uuawo-l), about 400 on the religious education (Sunday school) list (REACH-L).

Average traffic: Active lists average 200 to 300 messages a week; other lists have only occasional messages or seasonal traffic or go dormant.

Managers: Deborah Weiner, director of electronic communication; Kasey Melski, Web designer/developer; Lance Brown, volunteer technical ListProc site manager; Margaret Levine Young, volunteer list management support staff.

Topics: Anything related and of significant interest to Unitarian Universalism, including UU congregations, social issues, committee business, and general discussion.

Moderated? Only a few lists are moderated; most are not.

Figure 21-1: The UUA home page.

Open, closed, or manager controlled: Most lists are open to anyone interested in joining. Some closed lists are for committees, one general discussion list is open only to UUs (UU-Community), and one list is open only to those who are new to UUism (Newcomers).

Privacy: Almost all lists allow posting only by subscribers (to reduce spam) and don't allow nonsubscribers to see the subscriber list (to make it harder for

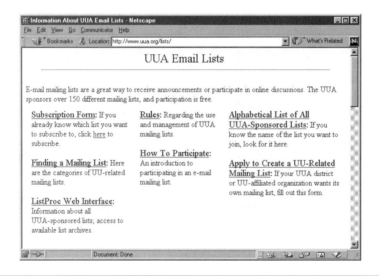

Figure 21-2: The home page for UUA mailing lists.

spammers to harvest subscriber lists). The Web-based archives of most lists are open only to subscribers, except for announcement-only newsletters.

The Origins of the UUA Mailing Lists

The Unitarian Universalist Association of Congregations is an association of about 1,000 congregations in North America that support the principles of Unitarian Universalism, a liberal faith with its roots in the Judeo-Christian tradition. Because Unitarian Universalism is a relatively small denomination, communication among churches and between churches, district offices, and the UUA's main office in Boston, Massachusetts, is crucial.

In the spring of 1994, the UUA board of trustees appointed a committee to investigate the use of electronic communications in support of the association's work. Although fax-on-demand and other technologies were examined, the committee quickly identified the Internet (which was just emerging in the national consciousness) as the key communications medium and installed an Internet host computer, uua.org. Even before setting up a Web site (in 1994, the Web had few sites—neither Netscape nor Internet Explorer existed), the committee installed a list server. It chose ListProcessor, an early version of ListProc.

One of the first lists created was ECC-L, the Electronic Communications Committee's open list for discussion how the UUA should use the uua.org server. This list discussed new mailing lists as well as the design of the UUA Web site.

One impetus for installing a list server so quickly was to set up an announcement-only newsletter list, UUA-L, to "serve as a major communications link between the UUA, districts, and congregations and their members." Managed by the UUA Office of Public Relations, Marketing and Information, which was run by Deborah Weiner, the UUA-L was designed to provide a quick, cheap way to get news from the UUA to UUs and their congregations. Within a few years, the list had more than 2,100 subscribers.

The UUA didn't set up a general discussion list right away. Two online UU communities already existed: the UUS-L mailing list hosted by an individual (Lance Brown), and the soc.religion.unitarian-univ newsgroup (described in Chapter 20). Instead, the UUA concentrated on creating mailing lists about specific topics. The lists and the UUA Web site grew so rapidly that in late 1998 the UUA created an Office of Electronic Communications, headed by Deborah Weiner.

Over the first six years of operation, UU-related groups (including UUA departments, UU-related organizations, and individual UUs interested in specific topics) applied for and received mailing lists on a wide variety of topics. In mid-2000, the UUA ListProc site hosted more than 175 lists.

Types of UUA Mailing Lists
The UUA mailing lists fall into several categories, including

Announcement lists. In addition to the UUA-L list, some lists carry announcements about specific programs, like the activities of the denomination's Washington office.

Committee and commission news and discussion. These closed lists allow various committees, boards, commissions, and task forces to conduct their work without needing to meet face to face as often.

Districts. The UUA congregations are divided into 25 geographical districts, and each district is entitled to as many as ten mailing lists. Many districts use their lists for closed board discussions, announcements, youth groups, and other district-wide groups.

Ministry and worship. The UU Ministers Association runs several lists to which only ministers can subscribe, and an open list lets lay people discuss how their churches run Sunday services.

Running congregations. Some open lists talk about attracting and keeping church members, fundraising, church finances, religious education (including Sunday school), lay leadership, church newsletters, youth groups, and young-adult ministry. Lists also discuss how to run small congregations, large congregations, rural congregations, urban congregations, and new congregations.

Social justice. Unitarian Universalists and the UUA are active in many social issues, and lists discuss many of them, including anti-racism; gay, lesbian; bisexual; and transgender rights; freedom of religion; and economic justice.

Youth. When children leave home, they frequently stop going to church, and many UUs don't return to church until they have kids of their own. The UUA hopes to maintain a connection with college-age youth and young adults via online communities.

Topics of Interest to UUs. UUs tend to connect to particular issues, and lists have been developed to support these interests, including a list about home schooling and another about indigenous affairs.

Most lists are open to UUs and non-UUs, ministers, and lay people. Some lists are sponsored by a specific group—for example, the UUA Youth Office, a UUA district, or an affiliated organization (like a UU summer camp).

Life on the UUA Lists

Traffic on all lists combined runs at about 1,500 messages a week. Many lists are silent many weeks because they are just getting started, because they have gone dormant and no one has yet noticed and closed the list, because the work of the list is seasonal, or because there's a lull in the conversation. Only about ten of the lists are high traffic, with more than 50 postings a week.

To create a new list, an individual or UU-related group can fill out an online application form, which asks for this information:

Name of the list

Description (both a one-line description and a more detailed explanation)

UU-related sponsoring organization if any (if the list is sponsored, the form asks for the name, address, and contact name e-mail at the sponsoring organization)

Name, street address, UU affiliation, and e-mail address of two proposed list managers

Open or closed (if closed, what criteria will be used to accept subscriptions)

Moderation (if moderated, the names and contact information of two moderators)

Other configuration (whether the list name will be visible, whether nonsubscribers can post, whether the subscriber list will be public, and whether, the list will be archived)

Text of the initial welcome message

Text of the FAQ

Name and e-mail address of at least ten people who want to subscribe

Ending date, if the list is for a limited period

Publicity plan for letting the prospective audience for the list know about how to subscribe

Seasonality, if the list will be more active at certain times of the year

Before the list is created, the UUA's Director of Electronic Communications must approve both the list and its managers. If the list is sponsored by an organization, the organization must approve it, too. The technical site manager creates the list, and the support site manager sends instructions for list management to the new managers.

Lists can be deleted for several reasons:

At the request of the managers, usually because the purpose of the list has changed or has ended. For example, a list was created for public discussion of the work of a task force. When the task force completed its work, the list closed, too.

When no managers are available to manage the list (after asking subscribers for volunteers to become managers).

At the request of the sponsoring organization. For example, the organization might replace a general-purpose list with an announcement list, a closed list for its board, and two open lists on specific topics.

When traffic drops to zero. When this happens, the site manager gets on the list and posts a message asking whether the list still has a purpose.

The UUA has written rules that list subscribers must follow. The rules are posted on the Web site and include the ones in this list (paraphrased):

- No commercial announcements.
- No attachments.
- Messages do not represent the views of the UUA or its member congregations, and subscribers participate at their own risk.
- No "offensive or disruptive messages, including those containing sexual implications, racial slurs, or any comment that offensively addresses someone's age, sexual orientation, religious or political beliefs, national origin, or disability."
- No harassing or mistreating list managers and moderators.

People can find out about the lists by reading the UUA mailing list Web site, as shown in Figure 21-2. To join, they can send a command to ListProc by e-mail or use the UUA mailing list subscription form, as shown in Figure 21-3.

List Management

More than 250 managers, almost all volunteers, run the UUA mailing lists. A small number are UUA staffers running lists that relate to the work of their departments or districts. UUA list managers have to follow rules, too, including

- Every list needs at least one manager, and managers must be approved by the UUA. If a manager quits, the remaining manager (or the site managers) looks for a volunteer replacement from among the

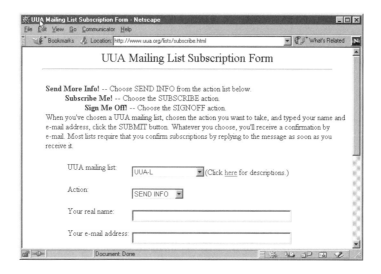

Figure 21-3: Rather than have to send commands to the list server, people can use a Web form.

subscribers. Some lists are allowed to continue with one manager, as long as they try to find a co-manager.
- The criteria for admission to closed (private) lists must be applied fairly.
- All lists must have a FAQ that is posted to the list regularly.
- List managers must subscribe to the uua-list-owners list (and can't set their configurations to `nomail` or `postpone` to avoid getting messages).
- List managers cannot switch their lists from open to closed or from unmoderated to moderated without permission from the UUA.

If a subscriber feels that a list manager is not doing a good job, is not running a list fairly, or has broken one of the list-management rules, she can contact the UUA's Office of Electronic Communications, which may intervene.

The uua-list-owners mailing list (a closed list managed by the site managers) is where site managers can post announcements about ListProc features, uua.org problems, impending virus attacks, and UU events that might affect the mailing lists. (For example, in preparation for the two-year process of electing a new UUA president, rules were posted for how postings about candidates and election issues should be dealt with.) List managers can ask questions about using ListProc, supporting subscribers, and dealing with problems on their lists. One Web page has instructions for list managers, including ListProc commands and advice for handling subscribers.

Site Management

Three people manage the ListProc site on a day-to-day basis:

The technical site manager (Lance Brown) is a volunteer who installs ListProc updates, creates and deletes lists, restarts ListProc when it hangs or crashes, and handles any other jobs that require UNIX software experience.

An Office of Electronic Communications staffer (Kasey Melski) answers e-mail sent to listmgr@uua.org, including address changes and questions from list managers and subscribers.

Another manager (one of the authors of this book) manages the uua-list-owners list, maintains a database of active lists, proposes policy, and deals with problems that erupt.

These three people spend a total of 5 to 10 hours a week running the ListProc site.

The site managers have set some site-wide standards for list configuration. Almost all lists require subscribers to confirm their subscription requests (to prevent lists from being used for mailbombing), have message limits (to prevent flooding on a list), and don't let nonsubscribers post.

The technical site manager wrote a script that extracts message counts from ListProc's log files and sends a weekly "traffic report" to the site managers. Another site manager imports the traffic reports into a Microsoft Access database (as shown in Chapter 16, in Figure 16-1). She also imports configuration messages from ListProc so that the database reflects up-to-date configuration settings for each list. Using this database, site managers can see reports of lists that have problems. Figure 21-4 shows the Access database displaying its main menu and a listing of mailing lists with low traffic.

Problems and Solutions

Individual UUA mailing lists have seen many of the same problems (and solutions) that appear on most lists: flamewars, single-issue fanatics, nitpickers who can't leave an argument unanswered, threads that wander off topic, and new folks who ask basic questions before reading the welcome messages they receive. In addition, some problems arise when an organization tries to run a large number of online communities:

Knowing when something is amiss. When problems arise on a list, the UUA may not know about it until the situation has gotten unpleasant. UUA staffers don't have time to be on all 150 lists. Instead, they rely on list managers or list subscribers to flag a problem or to call for help when needed.

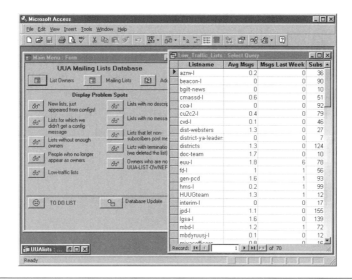

Figure 21-4: A database of mailing lists can provide reports to the site managers—in this case, mailing lists with little or no traffic.

Dormant lists. Using the database of mailing lists and the weekly traffic reports, site managers can identify lists with little or no traffic. If a list appears dormant, its site managers contact the list managers to find out what happened to the list and whether it should be deleted.

Misconfigured lists. Except in unusual cases, the UUA requires lists to allow postings only from subscribers (SEND-BY-SUBSCRIBERS), to allow only subscribers to be able to see the archives (ARCHIVES-TO-SUBSCRIBERS), and to have a message limit to prevent out-of-control mail loops (MESSAGE-LIMIT). The database of mailing lists can show which lists don't follow these guidelines.

Unapproved list managers. The UUA must approve list managers so that it can choose who represents it in managing its lists and so that list managers can be trained and supported. However, a list manager can add other managers to the list or delete other managers. The database of mailing lists can identify lists whose managers have changed without approval.

So far, one list manager has had to be removed (because of a change in professional status, which disqualified him from managing the list in question), and only two subscribers have been kicked off the lists. The training and support must be working!

Summary

More than 9,000 subscribers use the UUA mailing lists to communicate with each other and with the UUA. This number is almost three times the number of UUs who attend the organization's annual meeting! The mailing lists provide a new way in which UUs can work and chat all year at little cost to the organization. The lists have enabled news to get out to congregations quickly, working groups to meet cheaply and effectively, and those with shared interests to support each other on topic-specific lists.

Appendix
Resources for Online Community Managers

If you manage an online community, you can take advantage of the many Web sites and communities dedicated to community managers! It makes sense that community managers would use the Internet—and online community in particular—for information and support.

For a list of Web sites and mailing lists to use in publicizing a new online community, see Chapter 12. For a list of Web sites about selling ads on your community, see Chapter 14.

The authors of this book maintain a Web site with new resources, at http://net.gurus.com/prboc/. Check it for updates!

Resources for All Types of Online Community Managers

This section lists Web sites, mailing lists, newsgroups, and books that are useful for online community managers—regardless of how and where your community is hosted.

Web Sites about Creating and Managing Online Communities

Big Bang Workshops: Virtual Communities—Getting Together on the Net
http://www.bigbangworkshops.com/html/research.html

Children's Online Privacy Protection Act of 1998 (COPPA)
http://www.ftc.gov/opa/1999/9910/childfinal.htm

Facilitips: Quick Tips for Online Facilitation
http://www.fullcirc.com/community/facilitips.htm

Full Circle Associates (links and articles)
http://www.fullcirc.com/

The Jargon File (for definitions of online terms)
http://www.jargon.org/html/The-Jargon-Lexicon-framed.html

The Mailing List Gurus (introduction to mailing lists and list management, by the authors of this book)
http://lists.gurus.com/

Membership Agreements
http://www.ivanhoffman.com/membership.html

The Natural Life Cycle of Mailing Lists, by Kat Nagel
http://www.catalog.com/vivian/lifecycle.html

Netiquette Guidelines (RFC 1855)
http://sunsite.cnlab-switch.ch/ftp/doc/standard/rfc/18xx/1855

Next Generation Research Group: Web Resources on On-Line Communities
http://www.ngrg.com/olclinks.html

Online Community Report (a bimonthly newsletter)
http://onlinecommunityreport.com/

Online Community Toolkit (articles about creating and maintaining communities)
http://www.fullcirc.com/community/communitymanual.htm

The Virtual Community: Homesteading on the Electronic Frontier (the complete text of Howard Rheingold's classic book)
http://www.rheingold.com/vc/book/

The WELL's Host's Manual
http://www.well.com/confteam/hostmanual/section2.html

Online Community Directories

Deja.com's Usenet Discussion Service (search engine for Usenet newsgroups)
http://www.deja.com/usenet/

DoList.net (searchable database of mailing lists and newsgroups, in either English or French)
http://www.dolist.net/annuaire_en.asp

ForumOne Index (searchable index of Web-based message boards)
http://www.forumone.com/

The List of Lists (searchable index of mailing lists)
http://catalog.com/vivian/interest-group-search.html

ListTool.com (directory of LISTSERV, ListProc, and Majordomo mailing lists)
http://www.listtool.com/

Liszt: The Mailing List Directory (searchable index of mailing lists and newsgroups)
http://www.liszt.com/

Liszt's IRC Chat Directory
http://www.liszt.com/chat/

Meta-List
http://www.meta-list.net/

PAML (Publicly Accessible Mailing Lists)
http://paml.alastra.com/

RemarQ (searchable directory of mailing list and newsgroup messages)
http://www.remarq.com/

The SparkLIST Email Newsletter & Discussion Lists Directory
http://sparklist.net/

TILE.NET/LISTS: The Reference to Internet Discussion and Information Lists (newsgroups, too)
http://tile.net/lists/

Topica (mailing list host and search engine)
http://www.topica.com/

WebScout Lists
http://www.webscoutlists.com/

Mailing Lists for Community Managers

Group Facilitation (GRP-FACL) (about facilitation of all types of groups, not just online)
Send "subscribe GRP-FACL *yourname*" to listserv@listserv.albany.edu

Online Facilitation
Send blank message to Onlinefacilitation-subscribe@egroups.com
http://www.egroups.com/list/onlinefacilitation/info.html

Books for Community Managers

Community Building on the Web: Secret Strategies for Successful Online Communities, by Amy Jo Kim, published by Peachpit Press early in 2000. Planning and management ideas for managing communities. ISBN 0-201-87484-9.

Cyberville: Clicks, Culture, and the Creation of an Online Town, by Stacy Horn, published by Warner Books in 1998. The story of one online community. ISBN 0-446-51909-X.

Hosting Web Communities: Building Relationships, Increasing Customer Loyalty and Maintaining a Competitive Edge, by Cliff Figallo, published by Wiley Computer Publishing in 1998. Creating and running communities on the Web. ISBN 0-471-28293-6.

My Tiny Life: Crime and Passion in a Virtual World, by Julian Dibbell, published by Owl Books in 1998. A journalist's accounts of his adventures in a MOO. ISBN 0-8050-3626-1.

The Virtual Community: Homesteading on the Electronic Frontier, by Howard Rheingold, published by HarperPerennial in 1994. A history of The WELL, one of the first online communities, as well as early MUDs and other multiuser communities. Out of print, but new edition to be published by MIT Press in late 2000. ISBN 0-06-0976411 (1994 ed.); 0-262-681218 (new ed.).

Resources for Mailing List Managers

The authors of this book maintain a Web site with articles about mailing list management and links to other mailing list management resources—the Mailing List Gurus page, at http://lists.gurus.com/. We know of one good book about managing lists: *Managing Mailing Lists*, by Alan Schwartz, published by O'Reilly & Associates in 1998 (ISBN 1-56592-259-X).

Hosts for Mailing Lists

Brian Edmond's Internet Mailing List Providers List
http://www.gweep.bc.ca/~edmonds/usenet/ml-providers.html

eGroups (includes ONElist; hosts Web-based clubs that can mail messages to members)
http://www.egroups.com/

List-Business.com's List-Hosting Service Providers
http://list-business.com/list-service-providers/

ListBot (owned by Microsoft)
http://www.listbot.com/

Theglobe.com
http://www.theglobe.com/

Topica
http://www.topica.com/

Vivian Neou's Internet Mailing List Providers List
http://www.catalog.com/vivian/mailing-list-providers.html

Web Sites That Archive Mailing Lists

eScribe (also provides Web page hosting and chat rooms for mailing lists)
http://www.escribe.com/

Geocrawler
http://www.geocrawler.com/

List-Business.com List Archivers Directory
http://list-business.com/list-archivers/

ListQuest
http://www.listquest.com/

The Mail Archive (anyone can add a list, without permission of the list manager, and subscribers' e-mail addresses are displayed)
http://www.mail-archive.com/

RemarQ (adds lists without permission from list owners and makes lists look like they are run by RemarQ itself)
http://www.remarq.com/

Web Sites about List Server Programs

LetterRip Pro
http://www.fogcity.com/letterrip.html

ListProc
http://www.cren.net/
http://www.cren.net/listproc/docs/ (the list manager manual)

LISTSERV
http://www.lsoft.com/
http://www.lsoft.com/manuals/1.8d/owner/owner.html (the list manager manual)

Lyris
http://www.lyris.com/
http://www.lyris.com/help/ListAdministrator.html (the list manager manual)

The Mailing List Gurus page: Mailing List Management Programs
http://lists.gurus.com/mlms.html

Majordomo
http://www.greatcircle.com/majordomo/
http://www.visi.com/~barr/majordomo-faq.html (a FAQ)
http://www-uclink.berkeley.edu/major/major.admin.html (an excellent manual)

Sympa
http://listes.cru.fr/sympa/

Web Sites about Mailing Lists

ListManagers FAQ (mainly about eGroups)
http://pages.ivillage.com/cp/listmanager/faq.html (FAQ)

List-Universe.com (more about e-zines than discussion lists)
   http://List-Universe.com/

Online Communities for Mailing List Managers

Cren-listproc (for ListProc managers)
   Send "subscribe cren-listproc" to listproc@list.cren.net

Egroups-discuss-managers (discussion for eGroups mailing list managers)
   Send blank message to egroups-discuss-managers-subscribe@egroups.com
   http://www.egroups.com/group/egroups-discuss-managers

List-Advertising.com (discussion about how to advertise your mailing list)
   Send blank message to join-list-advertising@list-advertising.com
   http://list-advertising.com/

Listhelp (general tips for running a mailing-list-based e-zine)
   Send blank message to listhelp-subscribe@egroups.com
   http://www.egroups.com/group/ListHelp

List-Moderators (discussion of list management on all list servers)
   Send blank message to join-list-moderators@list-moderators.com or (for the digest) to join-list-moderators-digest@list-moderators.com
   http://list-moderators.com/

List-Tips (general tips for running e-zines)
   Send blank message to join-list-tips@sparklist.com
   http://list-tips.com/

LSTOWN-L (for LISTSERV managers)
   Send "subscribe lstown-L yourname" to listserv@peach.ease.lsoft.com

Lyris-announce and lyris-discuss (for Lyris managers)
   http://www.lyris.com/lists.html

Majordomo-users (for Majordomo managers, despite its name)
   Send "subscribe Majordomo-Users" to majordomo@GreatCircle.com

Resources for Newsgroup Moderators and News Administrators

Many FAQs about creating and managing newsgroups are available on the Web. This section lists Web sites, mailing lists, and newsgroups of use to newsgroup moderators and news administrators.

Web Sites about Creating Big Eight Newsgroups

The Big Eight Newsgroup Creation Process
   http://www.eyrie.org/~eagle/faqs/big-eight.html

Guidelines on Usenet Newsgroup Names
   http://www.faqs.org/faqs/usenet/creating-newsgroups/naming/part1/

Guides for Creating Newsgroups
   http://homepages.go.com/~eacalame/create.html
How to Create a New Usenet Newsgroup: Guidelines for Usenet News Creation
   http://www.faqs.org/faqs/usenet/creating-newsgroups/part1/
How to Create Newsgroups: How to Format and Submit a New Group Proposal
   http://web.presby.edu/~jtbell/usenet/newgroup/how-submit.faq
How to Write a Good Newsgroup Proposal
   http://web.presby.edu/~jtbell/usenet/newgroup/good-proposal.faq
Usenet Newsgroup Creation Companion (may be outdated)
   http://web.presby.edu/~jtbell/usenet/newgroup/creation-companion.faq
User's Guide to the Changing Usenet
   http://cil-www.oce.orst.edu:8080/users.guide.html

Web Sites about alt Newsgroups

The Beginners Guide to Creating New alt.* Groups
   http://usenet.cjb.net/
Guide for Writing an Alt Newsgroup Proposal
   http://homepages.go.com/~eacalame/proposal.html
How to Create an Alt Newsgroup
   http://nylon.net/alt/newgroup.htm
How to Justify a New Newsgroup
   http://www.faqs.org/usenet/alt/justify.html
How to Name a Newsgroup
   http://www.faqs.org/usenet/alt/naming.html
How to Write a Good Newgroup Message
   http://www.gweep.bc.ca/~edmonds/usenet/good-newgroup.html
Index of FAQs about Starting an Alt Newsgroup
   http://www.faqs.org/usenet/alt/
So You Want to Create an Alt Newsgroup
   http://www.faqs.org/faqs/alt-creation-guide/
   http://www.visi.com/~barr/alt-creation-guide.html

Web Sites about Other Newsgroup Hierarchies

aus: aus.* Newsgroup Administration
   http://aus.news-admin.org/
be: Hoe een BE-nieuwsgroep oprichten? (How to set up a BE newsgroup; in Dutch)
   http://users.pandora.be/tdv/be/

biz: Biz.* Frequently Asked Questions (FAQ)
   ftp://ftp.xenitec.on.ca/pub/news/faqs/biz.faq
ch: The ch.* (Swiss newsgroups)
   http://www.faqs.org/faqs/usenet/ch-general/intro-french/ (in French)
   http://www.faqs.org/faqs/usenet/ch-general/intro-german/ (in German)
   http://www.faqs.org/faqs/usenet/ch-general/intro-italian/ (in Italian)
de: Regeln für die Einrichtung und Entfernung von Usenet-Gruppen (Rules for the establishment and removal of Usenet groups; in German)
   http://www.kirchwitz.de/~amk/dai/einrichtung
es: Moderación de la Jerarquía es.* (Moderation of the es.* hierarchy; in Spanish)
   http://www.rediris.es/netnews/moderacion/docs/
fr: Les Groupes USENET fr.* (The fr.* Usenet newsgroups; in French)
   http://www.fr.net/news-fr/
it: I gruppi Usenet it.* - istruzioni per l'uso (The it.* Usenet groups: instructions for use; in Italian)
   http://www.faqs.org/faqs/usenet/Italia-news-faq/
nl: Richtlijnen voor het aanmaken van een newsgroup in de nl-hierarchie (guidelines for the creation of a newsgroup in the nl hierarchy; in Dutch)
   http://www.xs4all.nl/~js/usenet/richtlijnen.html
nz: The nz.* Usenet Hierarchy
   http://www.faqs.org/faqs/usenet/nz-news-hierarchy/
pl: How to Add pl.* Hierarchy to a News Server (FAQ)
   http://www.faqs.org/faqs/usenet/pl-news-hierarchy/
sfnet: Sfnet-ryhmät (Sfnet rules; in Finnish)
   http://www.cs.tut.fi/sfnet/
uk: UK Usenet Homepages
   http://www.usenet.org.uk/
us: Newsgroup Creation in the us.* Hierarchy
   http://www.panix.com/~kingdon/us-create.html

Web Sites about Newsreaders and News Servers

DNews (news server for Windows NT)
   http://netwinsite.com/dnews.htm
Forté, Inc. (Free Agent)
   http://www.forteinc.com/
Frequently Asked Questions about the INN (InterNetNews) NNTP Server
   http://blank.org/innfaq/

INN 2.X FAQ
http://www.eyrie.org/~eagle/faqs/inn.html

INN home page (at the Internet Software Consortium)
http://www.isc.org/products/INN/

Internet Explorer home page (Outlook Express newsreader, which comes with Internet Explorer)
http://www.microsoft.com/windows/ie/

Netscape Netcenter (Netscape Communication, which includes the Netscape Newsgroup newsreader)
http://home.netscape.com/computing/download/

TUCOWS (other newsreaders)
http://www.tucows.com/ (choose your geographical location and your operating system, and then choose News Readers)

Web Sites That Display Newsgroup Messages

Deja.com's Usenet Discussion Service
http://www.deja.com/usenet/

HotBot Usenet
http://hotbot.lycos.com/usenet/

Newsguy
http://www.newsguy.com/

RemarQ
http://www.remarq.com/

Other Web Sites about Usenet Newsgroups

*.Answers Submission Guidelines
ftp://rtfm.mit.edu:/pub/faqs/news-answers/guidelines

Address Munging FAQ: Spam-Blocking Your Email Address
http://members.aol.com/emailfaq/mungfaq.html

B.J.'s Hotlists: Usenet (links to useful pages about newsgroups)
http://www.herbison.com/herbison/bj_usenet.html

Breidbart Index Definition (a system for canceling spam)
http://www.stopspam.org/usenet/mmf/breidbart.html

Finding and Writing FAQs
http://www.ii.com/internet/faqs/

Glimpse (a full text-search program usable for newsgroup archives)
http://webglimpse.org/

Hypermail (a program that turns mailboxes full of messages into Web pages)
http://www.hypermail.org/

Internet FAQ Consortium (FAQs from newsgroups)
http://www.faqs.org/

Moderated Newsgroups FAQ: Newsgroup Moderation Methods and Concepts
http://www.swcp.com/~dmckeon/mod-faq.html

PGP Moose (a system for authenticating approval messages for moderated newsgroups)
http://people.qualcomm.com/ggr/pgpmoose.html

Tortoise Home Page (Windows NT news server)
http://tortoise.maxwell.syr.edu/

Usenet Newsgroup FAQs by Hierarchy FTP site
ftp://rtfm.mit.edu/pub/usenet-by-hierarchy/

Online Communities for Newsgroup Moderators and News Server Administrators

alt.answers (announcement-only newsgroup with periodic postings of alt newsgroup FAQs)

alt.config (newsgroup for discussing the creation of Alt newsgroups)

INN Mailing Lists (hosted at the Internet Software Consortium)
http://www.isc.org/services/public/lists/inn-lists.html

news.admin.hierarchies (newsgroup about Usenet hierarchy configuration)

news.admin.technical (newsgroup about the technical aspects of maintaining Usenet)

news.announce.newgroups (newsgroup with announcements of newly created Big Eight newsgroups)

news.announce.newusers (announcement-only newsgroup with periodic postings for new Usenet participants)

news.answers (announcement-only newsgroup with periodic postings of most newsgroup FAQs)

news.groups (newsgroup for discussing the creation of new Big Eight newsgroups)

news.newusers.questions (moderated newsgroup for new Usenet user questions and answers)

news.software.nntp (newsgroup about the Usenet news server software)

Resources for IRC Channel Operators

Many IRC networks and channels have Web sites, and many IRC FAQs have advice for channel operators. Here are Web sites about IRC along with online communities for IRC chanops.

Web Sites about IRC and IRC Programs

The alt.irc IFAQ (Inordinately Frequently Asked Questions)
http://www.netway.com/~marci/IFAQ.html

DALnet's ChanServ page
http://www.dal.net/services/chanserv/

DALnet's NickServ page
http://www.dal.net/services/nickserv/

Edge's IRC page
http://www.edge-zone.net/irc/

The Internet Gurus IRC page
http://net.gurus.com/irc/

IRC Operators Guide (for the people who run IRC servers)
http://www.irchelp.org/irchelp/ircd/ircopguide.html

IRChelp.org Internet Relay Chat (IRC) Help Archive
http://www.irchelp.org/

mIRC home page (Windows IRC program)
http://www.mirc.com/

NewIRCusers.com
http://www.newircusers.com/

The Official Ircle home page (Mac IRC program)
http://www.ircle.com/

A Short IRC Primer (long)
http://www.irchelp.org/irchelp/ircprimer.html

Talk City TC Pirch and TC Ircle (programs for accessing Talk City channels)
http://www.talkcity.com/download/

The Undernet Documents Project
http://www.undernet.org/documents/

Web-based Directories of IRC Channels

EFnet Channel List
http://www.irchelp.org/irchelp/chanlist/

IRCnet Channel Search
http://www.ludd.luth.se/irc/list.html

Liszt's IRC Chat Directory
   http://www.liszt.com/chat/
Talk City
   http://www.talkcity.com/
Undernet Channel Service
   http://www.cservice.undernet.org/ (click Search)

Web Sites of IRC Networks
AfterNET
   http://www.afternet.org/
AirNet-IRC
   http://www.airnet-irc.net/
   support@airnet-irc.net (for help)
AlternativeNet
   http://www.alternativenet.org/
   #Help (help channel)
AnotherNet (family safe)
   http://www.another.net/chat/
   help@another.net (for help)
   #thecafe (help channel)
Bear Country Net (family oriented)
   http://www.bearcountry.net/
   #BearDen, #Newbies (help channels)
CastleNet.org
   http://www.castlenet.org/
   #Camelot (operator help channel)
ChatNet
   http://www.chatnet.org/
   #Help (general help channel)
   #Nuthouse (operator help channel)
CyNet
   http://www.cynet.org/
   #IRCops (IRC operators' help channel)
DALnet (another large IRC network)
   http://www.dal.net/
   #DALnetHelp (help channel)
   #help (new user help channel)
   #HelpCenter (Windows/DOS help channel)
   #IRCHelp (help channel)

Damaged.Net
http://www.damaged.net/
DarkerNet (for the gothic, pagan, vampire, and role-playing communities)
http://www.darker.net/
DifferentNET
http://www.different.net/
DS2
http://www.ds2.net/irc.htm
help@ds2.net
Efnet (the original IRC network, Eris Free Network)
http://www.efnet.net/
#irchelp (help channel)
#Twilight_Zone (operators' channel)
Esprit.Net (family oriented)
http://www.esprit.net/
#newbies, #services (help channels)
GalaxyNet
http://www.galaxynet.org/
#IRCHelp (help channel)
#mIRC (help channel for mIRC users)
Infinity IRC
http://www.infinity-irc.org/
#infinity (help channel)
IRC.NET
http://www.irc.net/
support@irc.net
#irchelp (help channel)
#new2irc, #newuser, #newbies, #chatback (new user channels)
#new2mirc, #mirchelp (mIRC help channel)
Kidlink (kids up to age 15 only)
http://www.kidlink.org/
KidsWorld (for kids only)
http://www.kidsworld.org/
KnightNet (medieval theme)
http://www.knightnet.net/
NewNet
http://www.newnet.net/
#NewNetHelp, #Services (help channels)
#ChanOp (help for channel operators)

Phishy Net
   http://www.phishy.net/
   #PhishPharm (help channel)
ShadowFire
   http://www.shadowfire.org/
   #shadowfire (help channel)
SorceryNet
   http://www.sorcery.net/
   #SorceryNet, #help, #irchelp (help channels)
StarChat
   http://www.starchat.net/
   #StarChat (help channel)
StarLink
   http://www.starlink.org/
   #oasis (help channel)
   #channels (help channel for registering channels)
SysopNet
   http://www.sysopnet.org/
Undernet (the first spinoff network)
   http://www.undernet.org/
   #help (help channel)
   #new2irc (help channel)
   #newbies (help channel)
   #wasteland (help channel)
X World
   http://www.xworld.org/
   #xworld (help channel)
Xnet
   http://www.xnet.org/
   #xnet-help (help channel)
ZUH!
   http://www.zuh.net/
   #help (help channel)

Online Communities for IRC Channel Operators

Each IRC network has one or more channels where channel operators meet to talk. Here are other places to find fellow IRC participants and chanops:
   alt.irc (newsgroup for IRC users and channel operators)
   alt.irc.dalnet (newsgroup for DALnet users)

alt.irc.undernet (newsgroup for Undernet users)

AnotherNet Mailing List (for AnotherNet users)
Send "subscribe anothernet" to majordomo@another.org

Chatting Online (for users of IRC and other types of chat)
http://chatting.about.com/internet/chatting/

DALnet Mailing Lists
http://www.dal.net/admin/lists.html

General IRC Mailing List
Send "subscribe user-com" to majordomo@undernet.org

Undernet Help Mailing List (for Undernet users)
Send "subscribe help" to majordomo@undernet.org

Undernet Server and Routing mailing list (for Undernet channel operators)
Send "subscribe wastelanders" to majordomo@undernet.org

Resources for Web-based Community Managers

Web-based clubs include message boards, real-time chat, and other ways to share information on Web pages. This section lists sites that host clubs, message boards, and real-time chat. If you start an open Web-based community, be sure to list it at **Forum One**, at http://www.forumone.com/, a searchable index of more than 300,000 Web message boards and Web-based chats.

For sources of message board software you can install on your own Web server, see the section "Installing Your Own Message Board Software," in Chapter 11. For sources of real-time chat software to install, see the section "Installing Your Own Chat Software" in the same chapter.

Hosts for Web-based Clubs

Most of these Web sites require participants to register with their site before joining your club, and the sites display ads to pay for the free service:

About.com (clubs are hosted by paid About.com contractors)
http://www.about.com/
http://beaguide.about.com/ (how to become the guide of a new About.com site)

AltaVista Communities
http://live.altavista.com/ (click Community)

Delphi Forums
http://www.delphi.com/

eCircles.com
http://www.ecircles.com/

eGroups
    http://www.egroups.com/
EShare Expressions
    http://www.eshare.com/products/internet/expressions/
Excite Communities
    http://www.excite.com/communities/directory/
FriendFactory
    http://www.friendfactory.com/
    http://www.friendfactory.co.uk/
JointPlanning.com
    http://www.jointplanning.com/
Lycos Clubs
    http://clubs.lycos.com/
MSN Web Communities
    http://communities.msn.com/home/
MyFamily.com
    http://www.myfamily.com/
Snap Clubs
    http://clubdirectory.snap.com/
Talk City's eFriends (hosts clubs that include message boards and real-time chat for as many as 50 people)
    http://www.talkcity.com/
Yahoo Clubs
    http://clubs.yahoo.com/

Hosts for Message Boards to Add to Your Community

Except where noted, these Web sites let you create a free message board that can appear to be part of your Web site; most of them display ads to pay for their service:

BeSeen
    http://www.beseen.com/board/
BoardHost
    http://www.boardhost.com/
Casual Forums
    http://www.casualforums.com/
EZBoard
    http://www.ezboard.com/
Novogate (formerly ForumsGalore)
    http://forumsgalore.com/
Theglobe.com (message board is on the site)
    http://www.theglobe.com/

Hosts for Real-time Chat to Add to Your Community

These Web sites let you create a free, Java-based, real-time chat page on your own Web site; they display ads to pay for the service:

BeSeen
    http://www.beseen.com/chat/
MultiChat
    http://www.tectonicdesigns.com/chat/
QuickChat (uses a private IRC server)
    http://www.planetz.net/quickchat/
    http://www.quickchat.org/
Roger Wilco (free voice walkie-talkie program)
    http://www.resounding.com/
XOOM.com (uses ParaChat software)
    http://xoom.com/chat/

Commercial Message Board and Real-time Chat Hosts

These companies provide full-service message boards, real-time chat, and other community services to companies and other large organizations:

Caucus Systems
    http://www.caucus.com/
HearMe (hosts live voice chat)
    http://www.hearme.com/lobbies/
Ichat (part of KOZ.com)
    http://www.ichat.com/
iKimbo (requires all community members to install proprietary, free, virally spread software)
    http://www.ikimbo.com/
KOZ
    http://about.koz.com/
ParaChat Professional
    http://www.parachat.com/parachat.htm
Participate.com
    http://www.participate.com/
PeopleLink
    http://www.peoplelink.com/
Prospero Technologies (formerly WellEngaged, used by The WELL)
    http://www.prosperotechnologies.com/
RemarQ
    http://www.remarq.com/corporate/partners.html

SureSite Java Chat
http://www.suresite.com/accounts/chat.html
Talk City
http://www.talkcity.com/business_services/home.htm
VCIX Community Management Service (CMS)
http://www.vcix.com/solutions/

Hosts for Web-based 3D Visual Communities

Blaxxun Contact (browser plug-in)
http://www.blaxxun.com/
Palace Visual Chat (Palace client and Palace server programs)
http://www.thepalace.com/
http://www.itsnet.com/home/lminer/palace/ (tutorial)

Online Communities for Web-based Community Managers

Clubs Foundation Room (for managers of Yahoo clubs)
http://clubs.yahoo.com/clubs/clubsfoundationroom
Delphi Hosts' Forum (for managers of Delphi forums)
http://www.delphi.com/ (go to Hosts' Forum)
Egroups-discuss-managers (discussion for eGroups managers)
Send blank message to egroups-discuss-managers-subscribe@egroups.com
http://www.egroups.com/group/egroups-discuss-managers
Excite Community Admins Corner (for managers of Excite communities)
http://clubs.excite.com/welcome/main?cid=72704
The WELL Hosts Conference (for managers of The WELL conferences)
http://engaged.well.com/engaged/engaged.cgi?c=hosts

Index

Numbers

247 Media Web site, 289
3D visual communities, 216, 372

A

AAII (American Association of Individual Investors) Web site, 222
abbreviations, 33—34
About.com Web site, 217, 265, 327—331, 369. *See also* Knitting.About.com
Abuse of Usenet: Cyberstalked Web site, 304
Access (Microsoft), 3, 310, 352
Ad Swap Web site, 256, 258
AdCentral Web site, 289
Add Alias command, 48
Add button, 128
ADD command, 91
Add E-Mail Aliases command, 48
Add to Favorites command, 46
Address Munging FAQ, 147
administrative (list) addresses, 42—43, 59, 62, 70—71, 96
Ad-Up Web site, 289
Advantage Email Coop Web site, 256
advertisements. *See also* banner ads
  bans on, 25—26
  community sites and, 317
  mailing lists and, 39, 68, 113, 255—256, 290—291
  newsgroups and, 156
  selling, 287, 288—291
  swap services for, 256—258
  for Web-based communities, 255—258
Advertising on Usenet: How to Do It, How Not to Do it page, 156
affiliate programs, 260, 287, 292—293
Afterburner, 298
AfterNet Web site, 366

agreements, membership, 356
AIRNet-IRC Web site, 366
aliases, 48
alt newsgroups, 119, 166—167, 269, 361. *See also* newsgroups
AltaVista Web site
  basic description of, 217—218
  Communities, 369
  registering home pages with, 251
  Web-based communities and, 211
Amazon.com Web site, 292
announcements area, 23
anonymous access, 298—299, 337
AnotherNet Web site, 196, 201, 206, 366, 369
AnswerPoint Web site, 222
AOL (America Online)
  chat, 11, 180, 246
  community managers and, 265
  e-mail addresses, 146—147
  Instant Messenger, 11
  mailing lists and, 50
  MIME digests and, 74
  privacy policy and, 298
  quoted text and, 64
archives
  basic description of, 15, 85
  commercial services for, 86
  configuring, 86, 95, 104, 110
  controlling who can access, 100
  mailing list, 48—49, 54, 57, 59, 61, 63, 85—86, 100, 104, 110
  maintaining searchable, 259
  managing, 86—87
  reading, 48—49, 54, 59, 61, 63
  Web-based communities and, 259
ArsDigita Community System, 235—236
ASIRC (AnotherNet Secure IRC), 196, 201, 206

Ask Me Each Time option, 64
asynchronous communication, 6
attachments, 24, 113, 269
attacks
  against management, 275—276
  personal, 271—272
audience, thinking about your, 150—151
audio files, sharing, 268
Auto Reject option, 88
AutoOps (AutoOperators), 204—205
Avatar Software, 12
/away command, 189

B

backseat driving, 274
backup systems, 69, 237
banner ads, 258—259, 287, 288—290. *See also* advertisements
banning users, 85, 192, 200—201, 279
Barnes & Noble Web site, 292
Barr, David, 166
BBSs (bulletin board systems), 10
bCandid Web site, 236
Berne Convention, 153, 301
BeSeen Web site, 232, 242, 370, 371
Big Bang Workshops Web site, 355
Big Eight Newsgroup Creation Process page, 160, 360—361
binary files, decoding, 141—142
Blaxxun Web site, 216, 372
Boardhost Web site, 232, 238, 240, 241, 370
bookmarks, 46
BootsnAll.com Web site, 222
bounced messages, 84—85, 91, 108—109, 320
Breidbart, Seth, 148
Breidbart Index Definition page, 148, 363

373

Breiter, Barbara, 217, 327, 329—331
Brian Edmond's Internet Mailing List Providers List, 69, 358
Brown, Lance, 345, 352
BurstMedia Web site, 289

C

cable modems, 168
Calishain, Tara, 5, 251, 258
Calendar pages, 228
cancel wars, 147—148
cancelbot, 278
cancelled messages, 147—148, 175
capitalization, 30, 55, 191
Carprices.com Web site, 293
CashPile Web site, 293
CastleNet Web site, 366
Casual Forums Web site, 232, 370
Caucus Systems Web site, 371
CBS MarketWatch Wealth Club, 222
CBS MarketWatch Web site, 222
CBS Sportsline Web site, 222
censorship, 27
CFV (Call For Votes), 160, 162, 165
CGI (Common Gateway Interface), 231—232, 236, 238, 242, 245
CGI Resources Index Web site, 232, 236, 242, 245
chain letters, 24—25, 113
channel(s). See also chanops (channel operators)
   banning people from, 192, 200—201
   basic description of, 179
   configuring, 197—200, 205
   connecting to, 196
   creating, 195—211
   displaying lists of 185—186
   finding, 189—191
   inviting people to join, 200
   joining, 183—185
   leaving, 186
   managing, 195—211
   moderated, 199—200
   modes, locking, 205—206
   names, 195, 201—208
   participants, finding out more about, 186—187
   private, 195—196, 198—199, 206
   registering, 195, 196, 197, 203—204
   rules for, 207
   secret, 198—199
   seeing who's on, 198
   sending messages to, 186
   setting the maximum number of participants for, 200
   setting topics for, 198
   testing, 196
chanops (channel operators). See also channels
   appointing additional, 200
   basic description of, 19, 179, 197—198
   resources for, 197, 365, 368—369
   useful commands for, 208—210
ChanServ, 195—197, 201, 205—208
   DALnet resources for, 208
   locking channel modes with, 205
   reserving channel names with, 203—204
/chanserv command, 203—205, 208
chat, 3—4. See also IRC (Internet Relay Chat); real-time (Web-based) chat
   3D chat, 216
   with AOL, 11, 180, 246
   basic description of, 6—7
   free, 21
   HTML and, 219, 231, 242—243, 245—247
   real-time character of, 6
   software, installing, 244—245
   voice, 215—216
   Web-based communities and, 213—214, 316
ChatNet Web site, 366
ChatPro Web site, 244
Chatting Online Web site, 369
children, issues related to, 33, 305—306, 318, 355. See also safety issues
Children's Online Privacy Protection Act (COPPA), 305—306, 318, 355
citations, 154
ClicksLink.com Web site, 293
clickthroughs, 289
clubs
   basic description of, 214—216
   Yahoo! Clubs, 68, 212, 216, 221—222, 288, 370
commands
   Add Alias command, 48
   ADD command, 91
   Add E-Mail Aliases command, 48
   Add to Favorites command, 46
   /away command, 189
   /chanserv command, 203—205, 208
   config listname password command, 96, 97
   Create Filter command, 65
   finger command, 187
   GET command, 89
   get listname archivename command, 57
   get_access command, 107—108
   help command, 45, 51
   /ignore command, 192
   index listname command, 57
   index_access command, 107—108
   info listname command, 45, 55, 57, 62, 74, 79, 97
   /join command, 197
   /list command, 186
   Make Filter command, 65
   /me command, 187
   /mode command, 195, 199—201, 209
   /msg command, 188, 199
   /nickserv command, 201—202, 209

Index

PUT command, 89
PW ADD password command, 88
/quit command, 186
recipients listname command, 58
review listname command, 58, 56, 96
set listname address password new-address command, 59
set listname digest command, 56
set listname mail ack command, 58, 59
set listname mail command, 56
set listname mail digest command, 59
set listname mail digest-nomime command, 59
set listname mail postpone command, 58
set listname nodigest command, 56
set listname nomail command, 56
signoff listname command, 56, 58
subscribe command, 56, 58, 60
subscribe listname address command, 60
subscribe listname command, 60
subscribe listname yourname command, 58, 62
Subscribe to Newsgroups command, 125
unsubscribe listname address command, 61
unsubscribe listname command, 56, 58, 60, 62
unsubscribe listname old-address command, 61
User Info command, 48
which_access command, 107—108
who listname command, 61
who_access command, 107—108
/who command, 186—187

/whois command, 192, 201
commercial announcements, 271
Communications Decency Act, 305
Communique Chat Web site, 244
Community Building on the Web, (Amy Jo Kim), *357*
community managers, 18—20, 23, 31
   attacks against, 275—276
   basic description of, 263—286
   community goals and, 263—264
   community rules and, 266—267
   finding, 311, 312—312
   that go AWOL, 319
   of moderated communities, 279—280, 283—286
   need for, 318
   online communities for, 372
   options for, for dealing with trouble, 276—280
   resources for, 355—372
   role of, 264—265
   selection of, 265
   supporting, 309, 311, 314—315
   training, 309, 311, 313—314
   traits/skill of, 312—313
comp newsgroups, 118, 161, 333—338. See also newsgroups
Comp.compilers newsgroup, 333—338
   origins of, 334—335
   value of, to its members, 335
complaint process, 318
Composition window, 126
CompuServe
   chat and, 180
   community managers and, 265
   forums, 11
   lawsuits and, 305
Computer Book Publishing List, 323—326
   origins of, 323—324

   value of, to its sponsor, 325—326
Conferencing Software for the Web, 236
config listname password command, 96, 97
confirmation messages, 73, 98, 103, 112, 317
Congress, 27, 305
Constitution, 27
contests, 260
control characters, 154
control messages, 164
Copyright Office Web site, 25, 301, 303
copyrights, 14, 25, 301—303. *See also* legal issues
   community rules and, 270
   enforcement of, 317
   mailing lists and, 113
   newsgroups and, 153—154
CPM (cost per thousand messages sent), 255, 258, 289, 290
Create Filter command, 65
Cren-listproc Web site, 360
crises, moderating communities during, 279—280
criticism
   of individuals, 318
   of sponsoring organizations, 317—318
Cubby v. CompuServe, 305
CyberSites Web site, 235, 243
Cybertown Palace Web site, 216
Cyberville, (Stacy Horn), *357*
CyNet Web site, 366

D

Da Silva, Stephanie, 44
Daily-Threshold settings, 93
DALnet Web site, 178, 197, 203, 366, 369
   ChanServ page, 208, 365
   NickServ page, 208, 365
Damaged.Net Web site, 367
DarkerNet Web site, 367
DCC (Direct Client Connections), 189

Deja.com Web site, 21, 32, 173
  basic description of, 215
  finding newsgroups at, 143
  guide to participating in newsgroups, 148
  Official Usenet Primer page, 157
  registering Web-based communities with, 253
  searching for missing messages at, 121
  Usenet Discussion Service, 142, 356, 363
  Usenet FAQ, 157
deleting
  extra quoted text, 63—64
  filters, 65
  mailing list subscribers, 83—84, 91, 94, 99, 102, 109
  newsgroup messages, 136
  online communities, 309
Delphi Web site, 218, 232, 369, 372
Dibbell, Julian, 358
DifferentNET Web site, 367
digest(s)
  AOL and, 50, 74
  basic description of, 49—50
  options, 80—81, 91, 100, 107
  receiving, 49—50, 56, 59, 61, 63
  text, 49—50, 81
Digital Millennium Copyright Act, 303
Digital Subscriber Line (DSL), 168
DiscussionLists Web site, 252
DiscusWare Web site, 236
disruptions, dealing with, 26—27, 272—280
DoList.net Web site, 44, 356
DoubleClick Web site, 290
downloading
  IRC software, 180
  Netscape Navigator, 123
  newsgroup messages, 126, 134
  Outlook Express, 127
Draper, Tim, 260
DS2 Web site, 367
DSL (Digital Subscriber Line), 168

duplicate filtering, 320

E

E! Online Web site, 223
eCircles.com Web site, 222, 369
EdGateway Web site, 223
Edmond, Brian, 69, 358
educational organizations, 307
EEC-L (Electronic Communications Committee mailing list), 347
EfNet Web site, 178, 189, 365, 367
eGroups, 40, 43—44, 358, 360, 370
  advertising and, 288
  basic description of, 218
  home pages listed on, 75
  posting announcements at, 254
  resources for community managers, 372
  using aliases with, 48
  viewing subscription information with, 53
e-mail. See also e-mail addresses
  formatted, 24, 47, 55, 64, 113
  replying to message authors with, 122, 126, 131, 133, 139
  separating mailing list messages from the rest of your, 64—65
  sending private remarks by, importance of, 30
  signatures, 34, 55, 92, 154—155
e-mail addresses. See also e-mail
  aliases, 48
  for the authors of this book, 2
  changing, 50, 56, 58—59, 61, 63
  forging, 146—147
  mailing lists and, 44, 48, 50, 56, 58—59, 61, 63
  managing, 309
  munged, 147
  necessity of, for joining mailing lists, 44
  subdomain names added to, 48

  using different, 34
Emily Postnews Answers Your Questions on Netiquette page, 156
encryption, 152, 174. See also security
"ephemeral message" issue, 299
ERnet, 197
error messages, 84, 179
eScribe Web site, 86, 359
EShare Expressions, 370
ESPN Web site, 223
Esprit.Net Web site, 367
ethnic slurs, 26, 271—272
Eudora Light, 64, 65
Eudora Pro, 64, 65
Exchange-it! Web site, 258
Excite Web site, 219, 251, 370, 372
exit polls, 113
expiration, of newsgroup articles, 121, 171
EZBoard Web site, 232, 233, 370
EzineAdvertising Web site, 256, 290
e-zines, 255, 256

F

Facilitation
  Group Facilitation, 357
  Online Facilitation, 355, 357
fair-use policy, 25, 302—303
Family Education Network Web site, 223
FAQs (Frequently Asked Questions)
  basic description of, 27—28, 171—172
  community managers and, 314
  disadvantages of, 28
  importance of reading, 30
  mailing lists and, 75, 79, 90—91, 97, 106, 112, 115
  newsgroups and, 143—44, 145, 147, 156, 164, 171—172
  regarding fake e-mail addresses, 147
  typical contents of, 171—172
  URLs for, including, in

Index

footers, 112
  viewing/updating, 79, 90—91, 97, 106, 115
  Web-based communities and, 239, 248
  writing, 75, 171—172, 239, 248, 313—314
FAQs Web site, 28, 156, 164, 360—361, 364
farewell messages, 79, 90—91
Favorites menu, 46
FBI (Federal Bureau of Investigation), 299
Federal Trade Commission Web site, 306
Figallo, Cliff, 358
files, sharing, 268—270
Filter Rules dialog Box, 65
filtering, 7, 64—66, 320
Finding and Writing FAQs page, 172
FindLaw Internet Legal Resources Web site, 27
finger command, 187
First Amendment, 27
flamewar, 15, 26, 275, 330. *See also* flaming
flaming, 15, 20, 26—27, 31—32. *See also* flamewar
flooding, 26, 120, 191, 207, 273
Flycast Communications Web site, 290
folder(s)
  lists, 128—129
  newsgroups and, 134—136
  sorting messages into, 65—66
follow-ups, in newsgroups, 152—153
fonts, 24
footers, of messages, 47, 112
forgery
  of approved moderated articles, 174
  of e-mail addresses, 146—147
form letters, 112–113
Forté Web site, 131
forum(s)
  basic description of, 10
  CompuServe, 11
  owner responsibility, 305

Forum One Web site, 224, 253, 356, 369
Franklin, Benjamin, 1
Free Agent, 121, 131—134
Free Banner Exchange MegaList Web site, 258
free e-mail, 44
free Internet access, 21
FreeChat, 244
FriendFactory Web site, 219, 370
FrontPage (Microsoft), 321
FTP (File Transfer Protocol) sites, 172
Full Circle Associates Web site, 355

G

GalaxyNet Web site, 367
Gamespot Forums Web site, 223
Geocities Web site, 157
Geocrawler Web site, 86, 359
Georgette Heye Mailing List Companion Web site, 251—252
GET command, 89
get listname archivename command, 57
Get New Messages in Subscribed Groups button, 132, 134
get_access command, 107
Glimpse Web site, 173, 363
GO Network Communicate Web site, 219
goals, for online communities, 16, 263—264
Godwin's Law, 272
Google Web site, 293, 296
graphics, 141—142, 214, 268
  3D chat and, 216
  in newsgroup messages, 122

H

harassment, 304—306
headers, 126, 130, 153
HearMe Web site, 215—216, 371
help, 40, 41, 45, 50—51, 228
help command, 45, 51
hijacking, 273—274

Hints on Writing Style for Usenet page, 156
history pages, 228
Hitchcock, Jayne, 304
Homeforums Web site, 230
homework assignments, 155
Horn, Stacy, 357
Hooked on Phonics Web site, 293
Hosting Web Communities (Figallo), 358
HotBot, 142, 215, 363
Hotmail, 21, 32, 85, 279, 285, 298
How to Create an ALT Newsgroup page, 167
How to Find the Right Place to Post FAQ page, 156
How to Format and Submit a New Group Proposal page, 164
How to Write a Good Newsgroup Message page, 167
How to Write a Good Newsgroup Proposal page, 164
HTML (HyperText Markup Language)
  chat and, 219, 231, 242—243, 245—247
  embedded, 242—243
  filtering, 320
  formatting, 24, 64
  mailing list pages and, 72
  newsgroups and, 130
  Web-based communities and, 219, 231, 242—243, 245—247
humanities newsgroups, 118, 161. *See also* newsgroups
humor, 151—152
Hypermail Web site, 173, 363

I

iChat Web site, 243, 371
ICQ, 11
/ignore command, 192
iKimbo Web site, 371
images, 141—142, 214, 268
  3D chat and, 216
  in newsgroup messages, 122
IMDB (The Internet Movie Database) Message Boards

Web site, 223
index listname command, 57
Index of FAQs about Starting an alt Newsgroup page, 167
index_access command, 107—108
individual moderation, 284
Infinity IRC Web site, 367
info listname command, 45, 55, 57, 62, 74, 79, 97
INN news server, 168, 169, 170. *See also* news servers
INN Web site, 363
installing
    chat software, 244—245
    list servers, 69—70
    message board software, 235—237
Instant Messenger (AOL), 11
Interactive Systems, 335
Internet Accounts window, 127
Internet Connection Wizard, 128
Internet Explorer browser (Microsoft), 10, 246
    Favorites menu, 46
    home page, 127, 363
Internet FAQ Consortium Web site, 143, 364
Internet Gurus Web site, 12, 170
Internet Software Consortium, 159, 364
IP (Internet Protocol), 168—169
IRC (Internet Relay Chat), 229, 308. *See also* channels; chat
    basic description of, 7, 9, 177—194
    commands, 180, 206—207
    community goals and, 264
    community rules and, 269
    disruptions and, 278, 279
    etiquette, 191—192
    flooding and, 273
    getting more information about, 193—194
    how it works, 177—180
    networks, 177—178, 196—197, 366
    operators (IRCOps), 178
    participating in, 180—189

    real-time character of, 6, 9
    resources for, 365—369
    sending private messages with, 188—189
    servers, 177—182, 206—207
    software, 180
IRC.NET Web site, 367
IRChelp.org Web site, 193, 194, 208
ircII, 9, 177
Ircle, 177, 180
IRCnet Channel Search page, 189, 365
IRCOps (IRC operators), 178
ISPs (Internet Service Providers), 68, 69, 285, 300
    newsgroups and, 120, 123, 169
    privacy policy and, 298, 299
    reporting problems to, 33
iVillage Web site, 223

J

JabberChat, 244, 245
Jargon File Web site, 34, 272, 356
Java, 219, 231, 242—243
/join command, 197
JointPlanning.com Web site, 222, 370
Jurvetson, Steve, 260

K

Kent, Peter, 5, 251, 258
Kidlink Web site, 367
KidsWorld Web site, 367
kill files, 140—141, 149
Kim, Amy Jo, 357
K-lining, 192
KnightNet Web site, 367
Knitting.About.com, 10, 217, 327—331
KOZ Web site, 243, 371
Kurnit, Scott P., 328

L

lags, 191

languages, using multiple, 25
Lawrence, David, 159—160, 165
legal issues. *See also* copyrights; liability
    basic description of, 295—306
    community rules and, 266—267
    fair-use policy, 25, 302—303
    harassment, 304—306
    libel, 304—306
    licenses, 153—154
    privacy policy, 295—301, 306
    provider liability, 303
    related to spam, 299—301
    responsibility for online material, 304—306
LeGuin, Ursula K., 21
LetterRip Pro Web site, 359
Levine, John, 333
Levine Young, Margaret, 345
liability, 14, 267. *See also* legal issues
libel, 304—306
Library of Congress Web site, 303
licenses, 153—154
Link Buddies Web site, 258
Links pages, 214, 228, 251—252
Linux, 69, 70, 180
    message board software for, 237
    newsgroups and, 121, 168, 169, 172, 173
/list command, 186
list headers, getting, 89—90
list managers, 51, 72, 83, 94, 102, 109
List of Lists Web site, 252, 356
List Partners Web site, 260
list server(s)
    basic description of, 7, 38—42
    installing, 69—70
    message distributors in, 38
    moderation options and, 82—83
    moving your list to a different, 114—115
    restrictions on names, 70

run by ISPs, 68
sending commands to, 55
subscriber databases in, 38
Web sites about, 359
Web sites that act as, 39—42
List-Advertising.com Web site, 360
ListBot Web site, 40—41, 43, 52, 70, 258
  HTML provided by, 72
  home pages listed on, 75
  using aliases with, 48
ListBuilder Web site, 254
List-Business.com Web site, 69, 258, 359
ListCity Web site, 256, 290
Listhelp Web site, 360
ListManagers FAQ, 359
List-Moderators Web site, 360
ListProc, 69, 85
  basic description of, 38—39
  directories, 356
  information on list servers, 359
  instructions for using, 57—59, 111
  lists, managing, 95—104
  options, 95—104
List-Promotion Web site, 261
ListQuest Web site, 87, 359
List-Resources Web site, 261
LISTSERV, 69, 85, 359
  administrative addresses, 42—43, 54
  basic description of, 38, 88—95
  descriptions, changing, 90
  directories, 356
  instructions for using, 54—57
  Lite, 70
  options, 89—92
List-Tips Web site, 258, 360
ListTool Web site, 252, 356
List-Universe.com Web site, 360
Liszt Web site, 44, 190, 252—253, 366
local newsgroups, managing, 170—171
login, 123

lurking, 14, 23, 46
  basic description of, 15
  benefits of, 280
  netiquette and, 29—30
Lycos Web site, 215, 219—220, 370
Lyris, 62—63, 110—111, 359—360

M

Mac Orchard Web site, 50
McAffee Web site, 25
Macintosh, 69
Mail Archive, 359
Mail.com Web site, 285
mailbombing, 45, 80, 83
MailCity, 44
mailing list(s). *See also* list servers; mailing-list subscriptions
  additional resources for, 111
  advertisements and, 255—256, 290—291
  banning users from, 85
  basic description of, 7—8, 37—66
  choosing a name for, 70
  choosing a site for, 68
  closed (private), 80—81, 91, 98
  community rules and, 269
  concealing your participation in, 50, 54, 56, 59, 61, 63, 100
  configuration of, 74
  creating/managing, 67—116, 320
  descriptions, 74—75, 97, 105
  disruptions and, 274—275
  distribution of messages by, 37—38
  dormant, 353
  finding, 44—45, 52
  finding knowledgeable people through, 264
  holding/stopping mail from, 49, 54, 56, 58, 61, 63
  home pages, 43—44
  hosts for, 358—359
  managers, 80, 91, 98, 360

message limits, 93
misconfigured, 353
moderated, 23, 93—94, 101—102, 108—109
open (public), 80, 91, 98
options, 80—83, 92, 99—100, 107—108
posting messages to, 47, 48
resources for, 358—360
software, 319—320
testing, 74—75
tricks, 63—66
use of, by organizations, 308
Web-based, 51—54, 71—72, 87—88
Web sites for, 39—42, 68, 215—216, 359—360
Mailing List Gurus Web site, 38, 40, 69, 356
mailing-list subscriptions, 40, 43—62, 73—74
  adding, 83, 94—95, 102—103, 109
  confirmation messages for, 91
  deleting, 83—84, 94—95, 99, 102—103, 109
  lists of, 48, 56, 58, 61, 63, 100, 103
  managing, 83—85, 99
  notifications for, 99
  options for, 80, 85, 91—92, 98—99, 106
  preventing, 95, 104, 109
Majordomo, 42—43, 359, 360
  directories, 356
  basic description of, 38, 59—61, 104—111
Make Filter command, 65
Make Filter dialog box, 65
manager addresses, 43, 71
Managing Mailing Lists (Schwartz), 358
mass acknowledgements, 163
Maze Interactive Media Chat, 244
Maze Web site, 244
/me command, 187
Melski, Kasey, 345
member(s). *See also* membership

banning, 85, 192, 200—201, 279
profiles pages, 227—228
use of the term, 15
membership. *See also* members
agreements, 356
lists, selling, 287, 291
MemoServ, 197
message board(s)
basic description of, 9—11, 212—213
community rules and, 269—270
creating, 238—239
hosts for, 370—371
managing, 240—241
names for, 238
options, 232—237
organizing, 227
setting up, 232—248
software, 235—237, 320—321
testing, 239
types of, 228—229
unthreaded (linear), 229
use of, by organizations, 308
Web sites, linking to, 232—234
Meta-List Web site, 252
MetaLab Web site, 157
Microsoft Access, 3, 310, 352
Microsoft Chat, 9, 177, 180
Microsoft Internet Explorer browser, 10, 246
Favorites menu, 46
home page, 127, 363
Microsoft NetMeeting, 9
Microsoft Outlook Express, 8, 34, 64—66, 137, 147
basic description of, 127—134
downloading, 127
newsreader, 121—122
Microsoft Web site, 127, 363
Microsoft Windows, 69, 180, 236, 237
chat software for, 190
newsreaders, 121
Mijenix Software, 50
MIME (Multipurpose Internet Mail Extensions), 24, 50, 59, 64, 81, 320
Mining Company, 217, 265. *See also* About.com Web site
mIRC, 9, 177, 180—185, 189, 365
mIRC Web site, 365
misc newsgroups, 119, 161. *See also* newsgroups
/mode command, 195, 199—201, 209
modelocks, 205
modems, 168
moderated communities
basic description of, 283—286
crises and, 279—280
moderated by multiple moderators, 284—286
MOOs (MUDs Object Oriented), 6—7, 11—12
Moraes, Mark, 148
MOTD (message of the day), 182, 207
Motley Fool Web site, 223
Move It To The Specified Folder option, 66
/msg command, 188, 199
MSN (Microsoft Network), 44, 84
handling of e-mail addresses by, 48
Messenger, 11
MoneyCentral Web site, 223
Web Communities, 220, 370
MUDS (Multi-User Dimensions), 6—7, 11—12
MultiChat Web site, 242, 371
munged addresses, 147
My Tiny Life: Crime and Passion in a Virtual World (Dibbell), 358
MyFamily Web site, 5, 12, 222, 370

N

Nagel, Kat, 14, 356
Natural Life Cycle of Mailing Lists page, 14, 356
Neou, Vivian, 69, 358
netiquette, 29—31, 356
NetMeeting (Microsoft), 9
Netscape Collabra, 123. *See also* Netscape Newsgroups
Netscape Navigator browser, 10, 46
chat and, 246
downloading, 123
Netscape Communicator, 121—122, 124—126. *See also* Netscape Messenger; Netscape Newsgroups
Netscape Messenger, 64, 65
Netscape NetCenter, 123
Netscape Newsgroups, 8, 64, 123—127, 269
netsplits, 191
Network Abuse Clearinghouse Web site, 300
Network Dweebs Web Conference, 244
Network54 Web site, 220
New Mail Rule dialog box, 65—66
New Post option, 130
New York Times, The, 27
NewIRCusers.com Web site, 194
New-List Web site, 254
NewNet Web site, 367
news newsgroups, 118, 161. *See also* newsgroups
news server(s), 119—121, 127, 167—171, 364
configuring, 124
names, 123
Pine and, 134—135
newsfeed mode, 168
newsgroup(s)
asking questions about, 144
auto-moderated, 286
basic description of, 3—4, 7—9, 117—158
"Big Eight," 118, 160—165, 360—361
canceling messages in, 147—148
community rules and, 269
creating, 159—175
etiquette, 150
finding, 143
hierarchies, 8, 117—119, 125, 159—160

how they work, 117—158
managing, 119, 159—175
moderated, 20, 23, 145—146, 171, 172—175, 364
names, 117—119, 165—166, 170, 360
private, 167—171
proposals, 160—167
public, 171—173
reading, 127—142
resources for, 156, 360—364
robomoderated, 145, 172—173, 286
software, 321
trolls and, 31
use of, by organizations, 308
Web sites, 215—216, 360—361
Newsguy Web site, 142, 363
newsreaders, 8, 34, 121—123, 168—169, 362—363
nicknames, 179—183, 196, 201—208
NickServ, 183, 196—197, 201—203, 208
/nickserv command, 201—202, 209
Nico Mak Software, 50
NNTP (Network News Transport Protocol), 168, 169
"No Authorization" message, 179
NOLOCK option, 90
nonprofit organizations, 307
Novogate Web site, 232, 370

O

off-topic messages, 24
Official Usenet Primer page, 157
ONElist, 40—41, 218
Online Community Report Web site, 356
Online Community Toolkit Web site, 356
Opera, 246
opt-in subscriptions, 73
Options dialog box, 64
Outlook Express (Microsoft), 8, 34, 64—66, 137, 147

basic description of, 127—134
downloading, 127
newsreader, 121—122
ownership, of communities, 266

P

Palace Visual Chat, 216, 372
PAML (Publically Accessible Mailing Lists) Web site, 44, 252
ParaChat Professional Web site, 243, 371
parental consent, 306
ParentsPlace Web site, 223
Participate Web site, 371
participation, encouraging, 280—282
passwords. See also security
changing, 105, 206
chat and, 182, 202—204, 206
mailing lists and, 58, 71, 88, 96—100, 105
newsgroups and, 123
protecting, 32, 33
paths, for newsgroup messages, 120
PeopleLink Web site, 243, 371
Perl, 235—237, 245
personal attacks, 26
personal information, protecting, 32—33, 296—301. See also passwords
personalities, creating separate, 34
PGP (Pretty Good Encryption), 174—175, 364
PGP Moose system, 174—175, 364
Phishy Net Web site, 368
Pine, 121, 134—136
plus sign (+), 199, 205
polls, running, 281—282
Poor Richard's Almanac (Franklin), 1
Poor Richard's Internet Marketing Promotions (Kent and Calishain), 5, 251, 258
Poor Richard's Web Site (Kent), 251
POP (Post Office Protocol), 173, 285

posting(s)
announcements, 253—255
anonymous, 317
basic description of, 122
care in writing, 150
cross-, 144, 146, 173—174
disruptive, 280
distribution of, by news servers, 120—121
fine points of, 143—148
with Free Agent, 133
guidelines, 23—24, 35
introductions, 280—281
limiting the line length for, 154
mailing list messages, 47—48, 92—93, 101, 104, 109, 112
to moderated newsgroups, 134—146
to multiple newsgroups, 152, 156
with Netscape Newsgroups, 126
news servers and, 120
one-track, 275
options for, 22—27, 92, 101
with Outlook Express, 130
with Pine, 136
preventing, 95, 103, 109, 317
problems with, 48, 112, 280
rules for, 23—27
test messages, 144
with trn, 139
use of the term, 15
to Web-based message boards, 240—241
pound sign (+), 179, 198
Preferences dialog box, 124
press releases, 337
Priceline Web site, 293
printing messages, 21
privacy policy, 228, 295—301, 306
Prospero Technologies Web site, 371
provider liability, 303
pseudo-accounts, 85
public libraries, 21
publicity
for mailing lists, 73—75

for Web-based communities, 249—261
for Web-based message boards, 239
PUT command, 90
PW ADD password command, 88

Q

QuickChat Web site, 242, 371
/quit command, 186
quoting, excessive, 113

R

Ralf's Chat Web site, 244
reader mode, 168
real life (RL), use of the term, 15
real-time chat, 213—214, 227. *See also* chat; real-time communication
   basic description of, 229—231, 241—248
   hosts for, 243—244, 371
   rooms, creating, 245—246
   software, installing, 244—245
real-time communication, 6, 9. *See also* real-time chat
rec newsgroups, 118, 161. *See also* newsgroups
recipients listname command, 58
RemarQ Web site, 21, 87, 142, 173, 215, 253, 359
Reply-to line, 47, 81, 92, 108
Reply to Sender and Newsgroup option, 126
Reply to Sender Only option, 126
reporting problems, 32—33, 40, 41
research institutions, 307
Resounding Web site, 216
responsibility, for online material, 304—306. *See also* legal issues
retromoderation, 175
review listname command, 58, 56, 96
RFD (Request For Discussing), 160, 162, 166
Rheingold, Howard, 356

robo-moderation, 145, 172—173, 286
Rogelberg, David, 323, 325, 326
Roger Wilco Web site, 216, 371
Rowling, J. K., 3
rules, community, 17, 23—27, 228
   basic description of, 266—272
   censorship and, distinction between, 27
   enforcing, 277—280
   importance of, 29
   about libelous or harassing speech, 304—305
   making, 266—267
   posting, 318—319
   for sharing files, 268—270
   topics for, 267—268

S

safety issues, 32—33, 193, 207
sarcasm, 151—152
schedules, of events, 215
Schwartz, Alan, 358
sci newsgroups, 118, 161. *See also* newsgroups
Search tab, 125
security. *See also* passwords
   encryption, 152, 174
   news servers and, 168—169
   systems, managing, 309
Send button, 126, 130
Send Now button, 133
Send Plain Text Only option, 64
SeniorNet RoundTables Web site, 224
Senior-site Web site, 224
servers. *See also* list servers
   installing, 69—70
   IRC, 177—182, 206—207
   news, 119—121, 123—124, 127, 134—135, 167—171, 364
   running, 308
   site managers and, 308
set listname address password new-address command, 59
set listname digest command, 56

set listname mail ack command, 58, 59
set listname mail command, 56
set listname mail digest command, 59
set listname mail digest-nomime command, 59
set listname mail postpone command, 58
set listname nodigest command, 56
set listname nomail command, 56
Set Up a Newsgroup Account option, 127
ShadowFire Web site, 368
SheClicks Web site, 224
shopping pages, 228
Short IRC Primer page, 194
shouting, 30
signal-to-noise ratio, 268
signatures, 34, 55, 92, 154—155
signoff listname command, 56, 58
site managers, 308—311, 319
slander, 304
Slashdot Web site, 224
slrn newsreader, 121
SmartClicks Web site, 258
smileys, 33—34, 151—152
SMTP (Simple Mail Transfer Protocol), 131
Snap Clubs Web site, 220, 370
soc newsgroups, 119, 161, 165, 339—343. *See also* newsgroups
soc.religion.unitarian-univ. newsgroup, 339—343
sock puppets, 85, 279
Sonic Web site, 244
SorceryNet Web site, 368
spam, 70, 320, 330
   avoiding, 148, 175, 299—301, 363
   basic description of, 15
   community rules and, 271
   newsgroups and, 144—148, 156, 175, 338, 342
SparkLIST Web site, 252
spelling flame, 154
spelling errors, 150, 154

spoilers, 154
s.r.u-u modbot, 341—342
Star Island Corporation Web site, 71
StarChat Web site, 368
StarLink Web site, 368
Status window, 183, 184
StopSpam Web site, 148, 363
Stratton Oakmont v. Prodigy Services Co., 305
Student Center Teen Forums Web site, 224
STUMP, 173
subscribe command, 56, 58, 60
subscribe listname address command, 60
subscribe listname command, 60
subscribe listname yourname command, 58, 62
Subscribe to Newsgroups command, 125
summarization, in newsgroup postings, 152—153
SuperOps (SuperOperators), 204—205
SureSite Web site, 243, 372
Swap-Resources Web site, 258
swearing, 207
Symantec Web site, 25
SysopNet Web site, 368
system administrators, 149, 154

T

taboo_body option, 109—110
taboo_header option, 109—110
talk newsgroups, 119, 161
Talk City Web site, 190, 220—221, 242—243, 370, 372
TeenMovies Web site, 230
telnet, 12
testing
　channels, 196
　mailing lists, 74—75
The WELL, 265, 356, 358, 372
Theglobe.com Web site, 221, 358, 370
Thomas, Eric, 38
threads
　basic description of, 15, 122, 129
　choosing, 139—140
　hijacking, 273—274
　ignoring, 129—130
　off-topic, 15
　selecting/watching, 129—130
　starting, 281
　Web-based communities and, 212
Tile.net Web site, 45, 253
time zones, 241, 248
Time.com Web site, 224
time-outs, 278—279
titles, for newsgroup articles, 150
Topica Web site, 40—43, 45, 48, 50, 288, 358
　home pages listed on, 75
　registering Web-based communities with, 253
　viewing subscriptions with, 53
TopicLock feature, 205
Tortoise Web site, 168, 364
Travel Experiences Community for Backpackers page, 229
trn newsreader, 121, 137—142
trolling, 31, 275, 276
TUCOWS Web site, 180, 363
Twister Discussion Server, 236
Typhoon, 168

U

Ultimate Bulletin Board Web site, 236
Ultimate TV.com Web site, 224
UltraBoard 2000, 236
Undernet Web site, 178, 190, 196—197, 365—366, 368—369
Unitarian Universalism, 165, 339—354. *See also* UUA Web site
UNIX, 121, 152, 168—169, 172—173, 187
　mailing lists and, 69, 70
　message board software for, 237
unsubscribe listname address command, 61
unsubscribe listname command, 56, 58, 60, 62
unsubscribe listname old-address command, 61
USA Today Web site, 221
U.S. Constitution, 27
U.S. Copyright Office Web site, 25, 301, 303
Usenet FAQ, 157
Usenet newsgroup(s)
　asking questions about, 144
　auto-moderated, 286
　basic description of, 3—4, 7—9, 117—158
　"Big Eight," 118, 160—165, 360—361
　canceling messages in, 147—148
　community rules and, 269
　creating, 159—175
　etiquette, 150
　finding, 143
　hierarchies, 8, 117—119, 125, 159—160
　how they work, 117—158
　managing, 119, 159—175
　moderated, 20, 23, 145—146, 171, 172—175, 364
　names, 117—119, 165—166, 170, 360
　private, 167—171
　proposals, 160—167
　public, 171—173
　reading, 127—142
　resources for, 156, 360—364
　robomoderated, 145, 172—173, 286
　software, 321
　trolls and, 31
　use of, by organizations, 308
　Web sites, 215—216, 360
Usenet Volunteer Votetakers (UVV), 162—163
User Info command, 48
U.S. Library of Congress Web site, 303
UUA Web site, 19—20, 55, 216, 263, 271, 315, 345—354
uuencoding, 269

V

ValueClick Web site, 290
VCIX Community Management Service (CMS), 372
Vine Networks, 235
viral marketing, 260
virtual worlds, 6—7, 11—12
Virtual Community: Homesteading on the Electronic Frontier Web site, 356, 258
VirtualTourist Web site, 224
Virus Information Library, 25
virus warnings, 24—25, 113
Vivian Neou's Internet Mailing List Providers Lists Web site, 69, 358
voice chat, 215—216.
See also chat
voting, on newsgroup proposals, 160, 162—163

W

warnings, 277—278
Web sites (listed by name). See also Yahoo! Web site
247 Media Web site, 289
AAII (American Association of Individual Investors) Web site, 222
About.com Web site, 217, 265, 327—331, 369
Abuse of Usenet: Cyberstalked Web site, 304
Ad Swap Web site, 256, 258
AdCentral Web site, 289
Ad-Up Web site, 289
Advantage Email Coop Web site, 256
AfterNet Web site, 366
AltaVista Web site, 211, 217—218, 251, 369
AIRNet-IRC Web site, 366
Amazon.com Web site, 292
AnotherNet Web site, 196, 201, 206, 366, 369
AnswerPoint Web site, 222
Barnes & Noble Web site, 292
bCandid Web site, 236
BeSeen Web site, 232, 242, 370, 371
Big Bang Workshops Web site, 355
Blaxxun Web site, 216, 372
Boardhost Web site, 232, 238, 240, 241, 370
BootsnAll.com Web site, 222
BurstMedia Web site, 289
Carprices.com Web site, 293
CashPile Web site, 293
CastleNet Web site, 366
Casual Forums Web site, 232, 370
Caucus Systems Web site, 371
CBS MarketWatch Web site, 222
CBS Sportsline Web site, 222
CGI Resources Index Web site, 232, 236, 242, 245
ChatNet Web site, 366
ChatPro Web site, 244
Chatting Online Web site, 369
ClicksLink.com Web site, 293
Communique Chat Web site, 244
Cren-listproc Web site, 360
CyberSites Web site, 235, 243
Cybertown Palace Web site, 216
CyNet Web site, 366
DALnet Web site, 178, 197, 203, 208, 365, 366, 369
Damaged.Net Web site, 367
DarkerNet Web site, 367
Deja.com Web site, 21, 32, 121, 142—143, 148, 157, 173, 215, 253, 356, 363
Delphi Web site, 218, 232, 369, 372
DifferentNET Web site, 367
DiscussionLists Web site, 252
DiscusWare Web site, 236
DoList.net Web site, 44, 356
DoubleClick Web site, 290
DS2 Web site, 367
E! Online Web site, 223
eCircles.com Web site, 222, 369
EdGateway Web site, 223
EfNet Web site, 178, 189, 365, 367
eScribe Web site, 86, 359
ESPN Web site, 223
Esprit.Net Web site, 367
Exchange-it! Web site, 258
Excite Web site, 219, 251, 370, 372
EZBoard Web site, 232, 233, 370
EzineAdvertising Web site, 256, 290
Family Education Network Web site, 223
FAQs Web site, 28, 156, 164, 360—361, 364
Federal Trade Commission Web site, 306
FindLaw Internet Legal Resources Web site, 27
Flycast Communications Web site, 290
Forum One Web site, 224, 253, 356, 369
Free Banner Exchange MegaList Web site, 258
FriendFactory Web site, 219, 370
Full Circle Associates Web site, 355
GalaxyNet Web site, 367
Gamespot Forums Web site, 223
Geocities Web site, 157
Geocrawler Web site, 86, 359
Georgette Heye Mailing List Companion Web site, 251—252
Glimpse Web site, 173, 363
GO Network Communicate Web site, 219
Google Web site, 293, 296
HearMe Web site, 215—216, 371
Homeforums Web site, 230
Hooked on Phonics Web site, 293
Hypermail Web site, 173, 363
iChat Web site, 243, 371

Index

iKimbo Web site, 371
IMDB (The Internet Movie Database) Message Boards Web site, 223
Infinity IRC Web site, 367
INN Web site, 363
Internet FAQ Consortium Web site, 143, 364
Internet Gurus Web site, 12, 170
IRC.NET Web site, 367
IRChelp.org Web site, 193, 194, 208
iVillage Web site, 223
Jargon File Web site, 34, 272, 356
JointPlanning.com Web site, 222, 370
Kidlink Web site, 367
KidsWorld Web site, 367
KnightNet Web site, 367
Knitting.About.com, 10, 217, 327—331
KOZ Web site, 243, 371
LetterRip Pro Web site, 359
Link Buddies Web site, 258
List of Lists Web site, 252, 356
List Partners Web site, 260
List-Advertising.com Web site, 360
ListBot Web site, 40—41, 43, 48, 52, 70, 72, 75, 258
ListBuilder Web site, 254
List-Business.com Web site, 69, 258, 359
ListCity Web site, 256, 290
Listhelp Web site, 360
List-Moderators Web site, 360
List-Promotion Web site, 261
List-Resources Web site, 261
List-Tips Web site, 258, 360
ListQuest Web site, 86, 359
ListTool Web site, 252, 356
List-Universe.com Web site, 360
Liszt Web site, 44, 190, 252—253, 357, 366
Lycos Web site, 215, 219—220, 370
Mac Orchard Web site, 50
McAffee Web site, 25
Mail.com Web site, 285

Mailing List Gurus Web site, 38, 40, 69, 356
Maze Web site, 244
Meta-List Web site, 252, 357
MetaLab Web site, 157
Microsoft Web site, 127, 363
mIRC Web site, 365
Motley Fool Web site, 223
MSN MoneyCentral Web site, 223
MultiChat Web site, 242, 371
MyFamily Web site, 5, 12, 222, 370
Network Abuse Clearinghouse Web site, 300
Network54 Web site, 220
NewIRCusers.com Web site, 194
New-List Web site, 254
NewNet Web site, 367
Newsguy Web site, 142, 363
Novogate Web site, 232, 370
Online Community Report Web site, 356
Online Community Toolkit Web site, 356
PAML (Publically Accessible Mailing Lists) Web site, 44, 252, 357
ParaChat Professional Web site, 243, 371
ParentsPlace Web site, 223
Participate Web site, 371
PeopleLink Web site, 243, 371
Phishy Net Web site, 368
Priceline Web site, 293
Prospero Technologies Web site, 371
QuickChat Web site, 242, 371
Ralf's Chat Web site, 244
RemarQ Web site, 21, 86, 142, 173, 215, 253, 357, 359
Resounding Web site, 216
Roger Wilco Web site, 216, 371
SeniorNet RoundTables Web site, 224
Senior-site Web site, 224
ShadowFire Web site, 368
SheClicks Web site, 224
Slashdot Web site, 224
SmartClicks Web site, 258

Snap Clubs Web site, 220, 370
Sonic Web site, 244
SorceryNet Web site, 368
SparkLIST Web site, 252, 357
Star Island Corporation Web site, 71
StarChat Web site, 368
StarLink Web site, 368
StopSpam Web site, 148, 363
Student Center Teen Forums Web site, 224
SureSite Web site, 243, 372
Swap-Resources Web site, 258
SWCP Web site, 157
Symantec Web site, 25
SysopNet Web site, 368
Talk City Web site, 190, 220—221, 242—243, 370, 372
TeenMovies Web site, 230
Theglobe.com Web site, 221, 358, 370
Tile.net Web site, 45, 253, 357
Time.com Web site, 224
Topica Web site, 40—43, 45, 48, 50, 75, 253, 288, 357—358
Tortoise Web site, 168, 364
TUCOWS Web site, 180, 363
Ultimate Bulletin Board Web site, 236
Ultimate TV.com Web site, 224
Undernet Web site, 178, 190, 196, 197, 365—366, 368—369
USA Today Web site, 221
U.S. Copyright Office Web site, 25, 301, 303
U.S. Library of Congress Web site, 303
UUA Web site, 263, 271, 315, 345—354
ValueClick Web site, 290
Virtual Community: Homesteading on the Electronic Frontier Web site, 356, 258
VirtualTourist Web site, 224
Vivian Neou's Internet Mailing List Providers Lists Web site, 69, 358
WebCrossing Web site, 236
WebmasterCash.Net Web

site, 293
Webmaster-Programs Affiliate Programs Guide for Webmasters Web site, 293
WebScout Lists Web site, 253, 357
WinZIP Web site, 50
Women Hating Online Abuse (WHOA) Web site, 304
WorldWideMart Web site, 236
WWWThreads Web site, 236, 237
Xnet Web site, 368
XOOM Web site, 242, 243, 245—246, 371
XWorld Web site, 368
ZDNet Web site, 224
ZUH! Web site, 368
Web Talk, 244
Web-based chat, 213—214, 227. *See also* chat
   basic description of, 229—231, 241—248
   hosts for, 243—244, 371
   rooms, creating, 245—246
   software, installing, 244—245
Web-based communities
   adding, to Web site directories, 252—253
   basic description of, 211—226
   creating a home page for, 250—251
   designing, 227—231
   directories for, 224—225
   finding, 224—225
   finding a Web site to host, 225
   how they work, 212—216
   optimum size for, 249
   organizing, 227—228
   private, 216, 222
   public, 217—222
   topic-oriented, 216, 222—224
   types of, 216
Web-based message board(s)
   basic description of, 9—11, 212—213
   community rules and, 269—270

creating, 238—239
hosts for, 370—371
managing, 240—241
names for, 238
options, 232—237
organizing, 227
setting up, 232—248
software, 235—237, 320—321
testing, 239
types of, 228—229
unthreaded (linear), 229
use of, by organizations, 308
Web sites, linking to, 232—234
WebCrossing Web site, 236
WebmasterCash.Net Web site, 293
Webmaster-Programs Affiliate Programs Guide for Webmasters Web site, 293
WebScout Lists Web site, 253
WebTV, 21
Weiner, Deborah, 347
welcome messages, 46—47, 75—79, 90—91, 97, 106, 112, 115, 248
WELL, 265, 356, 358, 372
What Is Usenet? page, 156
which_access command, 107
who listname command, 61
who_access command, 107
/who command, 186—187
/whois command, 192, 201
windows, sizing, 131
Windows (Microsoft), 69, 180, 236, 237
   chat software for, 190
   newsreaders, 121
WinZIP Web site, 50
Women Hating Online Abuse (WHOA) Web site, 304
Woodside Literary Agency, 304
WorldWideMart Web site, 236
WWWBoard, 236
WWWThreads Web site, 236, 237

Xnet Web site, 368

XOOM Web site, 242, 243, 245—246, 371
XWorld Web site, 368

Y

Yahoo! Web site
   Chat, 190, 231
   Clubs, 68, 212, 216, 221—222, 288, 370
   Mail, 32, 44, 85, 285
   Messenger, 11
   registering home pages with, 251
   Web-based communities and, 211
"You have been K-lined" message, 179

Z

ZDNet Web site, 224
ZIP files, 50
ZipMagic, 50
ZUH! Web site, 368

Other Titles in the Poor Richard Series

NEW! *Poor Richard's Internet Recruiting*
Easy, Low-Cost Ways to Find Great Employees Online
Here's how to use the Internet to find employees fast—using industry sites, professional organizations, state and city job banks, search engines, mailing lists, and much more.

NEW! *Poor Richard's Creating Electronic Books*
How Authors, Publishers, and Corporations Can Get Into Digital Print
Why publish electronically? How should content be formatted and marketed, sold, and protected? These are just a few of the questions this book answers.
Available January 2001

NEW! *Poor Richard's Home and Small Office Networking*
Room-to-Room or Around the World
Today's businesses have multiple offices, mobile workers, telecommuters, and virtual offices. How do they all keep in touch, share information, and collaborate? Here's an easy-to-understand explanation of the technology available for connecting employees.
Available February 2001

Poor Richard's Web Site, 2nd Edition
Geek-Free, Commonsense Advice on Building a Low-Cost Web Site
How to build a Web site without spending lots of time or money and without having to learn a complicated programming language.

Poor Richard's E-mail Publishing
Newsletters, Bulletins, Discussion Groups & Other Powerful Communications Tools
All of the information and tools needed to start and maintain an e-mail newsletter.

Poor Richard's Internet Marketing and Promotions
How to Promote Yourself, Your Business, Your Ideas Online
Hundreds of proven techniques for getting attention online.

To Order Visit	Or Call
http://TopFloor.com/	1-877-693-4676

(Continued from the back cover)...

There are lots of reasons to set up an online community. Maybe you want to discuss your favorite topic, but no one in town shares your interest. Or perhaps you want to find a way for an existing community to communicate more efficiently. The case study of the Unitarian Universalist Association in Chapter 21 is a perfect example of this. Communities can also be used to market a product or service. But be careful.

Many companies and organizations are very interested in creating an online community as a way of driving traffic to their Web sites. Often these "communities" are not communities in the true sense of the word. They don't provide information that people can use. They don't create a sense of belonging and trust. And guess what? They don't have active, loyal members.

Once you have defined your reasons and your goals for creating an online community, *Poor Richard's Building Online Communities* describes the types of systems you can use.

- Mailing lists
- Usenet newsgroups
- Web-based message boards
- Web-based "all in one" community sites
- Internet Relay Chat (IRC)
- Instant-messaging systems
- Virtual worlds
- MUDs and MOOs

You'll learn the advantages and disadvantages of each system as well as how to create and manage each type of community. But before you create your own community, you'll want to join other communities. The authors explain how.

Successful online communities work for the same reasons traditional communities work—because the relationships members form, the information they gather, and the entertainment they view all provide immediate value and comfort. And they fall apart for the same reasons traditional communities fall part—poor management, needless arguments, personal attacks, and other bad